Frommer's

Caribbean Ports of Call

6th Edition

by Tamar Schreibman & Christina Colón

Here's what the critics say about Frommer's:

"Amazingly easy to use. Very portable, very complete."

—*Booklist*

"Detailed, accurate, and easy-to-read information for all price ranges."
—*Glamour Magazine*

"Hotel information is close to encyclopedic."
—*Des Moines Sunday Register*

"Frommer's Guides have a way of giving you a real feel for a place."
—*Knight Ridder Newspapers*

WILEY

Wiley Publishing, Inc.

Published by:

Wiley Publishing, Inc.

111 River St.
Hoboken, NJ 07030-5774

ISBN-13: 978-0-471-94490-4
ISBN-10: 0-471-94490-4

Editor: Leslie Shen
Production Editor: Heather Wilcox
Cartographer: Tim Lohnes
Photo Editor: Richard Fox
Production by Wiley Indianapolis Composition Services

Front cover photo: Cozumel, Mexico: Couple snorkeling in clear shallow water, cruise ship in distance.
Back cover photo: Grand Cayman Islands, Grand Cayman, Rum Point: Colorful beach hut beneath palm trees.

For information on our other products and services or to obtain technical support, please contact our Customer Care Department within the U.S. at 800/762-2974, outside the U.S. at 317/572-3993 or fax 317/572-4002.

Wiley also publishes its books in a variety of electronic formats. Some content that appears in print may not be available in electronic formats.

Manufactured in the United States of America

5 4 3 2 1

Contents

List of Maps

About the Authors

Tamar Schreibman has traveled to Sedona, Las Vegas, Longboat Key, Scottsdale, the Arizona wine country, Charleston, Montego Bay, and Budapest to research travel stories for *Time Out New York, Modern Bride, Elle, New Woman,* and *Mode.* Her other articles have appeared in various publications including *Self, Fitness, Marie Claire, Seventeen, Men's Fitness, Cosmopolitan, Working Mother, New York Daily News, Star,* and *Working Woman.* This is her third nonfiction book. She also writes fiction.

Christina Colón has two great passions in life: nature and travel. She has been everywhere from Borneo (where she lived for 2 years tracking wild animals) to Belize (where she did her master's thesis in a jaguar preserve). With a Ph.D. in ecology, a master's in environmental education, and adjunct positions at several universities, she is a scientist and an educator, as well as an author. When she is not exploring a tropical rainforest or an exotic island, she can be found in the Bronx, where she loves to seek the wilder side of the borough. In addition to scientific and academic texts, she has contributed to numerous travel guides, including *Frommer's Portable Aruba* and *The New York Times Guide to New York City.*

An Invitation to the Reader

In researching this book, we discovered many wonderful places—hotels, restaurants, shops, and more. We're sure you'll find others. Please tell us about them, so we can share the information with your fellow travelers in upcoming editions. If you were disappointed with a recommendation, we'd love to know that, too. Please write to:

Frommer's Caribbean Ports of Call, 6th Edition
Wiley Publishing, Inc. • 111 River St. • Hoboken, NJ 07030-5774

An Additional Note

Please be advised that travel information is subject to change at any time—and this is especially true of prices. We therefore suggest that you write or call ahead for confirmation when making your travel plans. The authors, editors, and publisher cannot be held responsible for the experiences of readers while traveling. Your safety is important to us, however, so we encourage you to stay alert and be aware of your surroundings. Keep a close eye on cameras, purses, and wallets, all favorite targets of thieves and pickpockets.

Other Great Guides for Your Trip:

Frommer's Caribbean Cruises & Ports of Call

Frommer's Caribbean

Cruise Vacations For Dummies

Caribbean For Dummies

The Unofficial Guide to Cruises

Frommer's Florida

Frommer's South Florida

Frommer's Jamaica

Frommer's Puerto Rico

Frommer's Virgin Islands

Frommer's Star Ratings, Icons & Abbreviations

Every hotel, restaurant, and attraction listing in this guide has been ranked for quality, value, service, amenities, and special features using a **star-rating system.** In country, state, and regional guides, we also rate towns and regions to help you narrow down your choices and budget your time accordingly. Hotels and restaurants are rated on a scale of zero (recommended) to three stars (exceptional). Attractions, shopping, nightlife, towns, and regions are rated according to the following scale: zero stars (recommended), one star (highly recommended), two stars (very highly recommended), and three stars (must-see).

In addition to the star-rating system, we also use **seven feature icons** that point you to the great deals, in-the-know advice, and unique experiences that separate travelers from tourists. Throughout the book, look for:

Finds	Special finds—those places only insiders know about
Fun Fact	Fun facts—details that make travelers more informed and their trips more fun
Kids	Best bets for kids and advice for the whole family
Moments	Special moments—those experiences that memories are made of
Overrated	Places or experiences not worth your time or money
Tips	Insider tips—great ways to save time and money
Value	Great values—where to get the best deals

The following **abbreviations** are used for credit cards:

AE	American Express	DISC	Discover	V	Visa
DC	Diners Club	MC	MasterCard		

Frommers.com

Now that you have the guidebook to a great trip, visit our website at **www.frommers.com** for travel information on more than 3,000 destinations. With features updated regularly, we give you instant access to the most current trip-planning information available. At Frommers.com, you'll also find the best prices on airfares, accommodations, and car rentals—and you can even book travel online through our travel booking partners. At Frommers.com, you'll also find the following:

- Online updates to our most popular guidebooks
- Vacation sweepstakes and contest giveaways
- Newsletter highlighting the hottest travel trends
- Online travel message boards with featured travel discussions

Introduction: Cruising to the Ports of Call

Though today's cruise ships are sailing to more and more places, the Caribbean is still number one, the destination most of us imagine when we think "cruise." Picture pulling up in your big white ship to a patch of sand-and-palm-tree paradise, a steel band playing as you stroll down the gangway in shorts and flip-flops. Throughout the region you're guaranteed nearly constant sunshine, plenty of beaches, and relaxation, but you're also likely to find rich culture and (depending on the island) Mayan ruins, European colonial architecture, lush rainforests, winding mountain roads, beautiful tropical flowers and marine life, and opportunities to be as active or laid-back as you want to be. And it's all so easy: Between the major Florida home ports (Miami, Fort Lauderdale, Cape Canaveral, and Tampa), the big new "alternative" home ports (New York, Galveston, and Charleston), and a handful of others (Jacksonville, Mobile, and a resurgent, post-Katrina New Orleans), anyone in the northeastern and southeastern U.S. can easily drive to their ship, if they want to. Once there, it's all smooth sailing.

1 Choosing the Itinerary & Shore Excursions That Are Best for You

If you count every rocky little outcropping and sandbar, there are hundreds of islands in the Caribbean, but of the 40 or 50 that make it onto the map, cruise ships regularly visit only about 25 of them. Most Caribbean cruises are 7 nights long and visit anywhere from three to six different ports, with the 2,000-passenger-plus megaships tending toward the lower number and spending the rest of their time on leisurely (and more profitable) days at sea. There are also 3- and 4-night cruises out of Florida visiting the Bahamas or Mexico's Yucatán Peninsula; 4- and 5-night cruises out of Tampa, Miami, New Orleans, and Galveston doing western Caribbean itineraries; and 10- to 14-night Caribbean cruises that transit the Panama Canal, sailing either round-trip from Florida or one-way between Florida and Mexico's west coast, visiting three to seven ports.

Though they're all appealing in some way, the Caribbean islands are not all created equal. Some are better for shopping, others for beaches or scenic drives. Some are quite built up, whereas others are hardly developed at all. Some have piers that can accommodate several megaships at one time; others require that ships anchor up to a mile offshore and shuttle passengers back and forth in small, motorized launches called "tenders." Big ships tend to visit the more commercialized, developed islands, while small ships are able to access the less-developed, off-the-beaten-path islands.

The Gulf of Mexico & the Caribbean

ATLANTIC OCEAN

BAHAMAS
Freeport/
Lucaya
Nassau

Andros Is.

Turks & Caicos
Islands

Great
Inagua

CUBA
Camagüey

DOMINICAN
REPUBLIC

HAITI

Port-au-Prince

Santo
Domingo

San Juan

Puerto
Rico

VIRGIN
ISLANDS

St. Martin/
Sint Maarten
Barbuda
Antigua
Montserrat
St. Kitts
& Nevis
Guadeloupe
Dominica
Martinique

See Eastern Caribbean map
on following page

St. Lucia

Barbados
St. Vincent

GREATER ANTILLES

Kingston

JAMAICA

Grenada
Tobago

LESSER ANTILLES

Trinidad

Caribbean Sea

Aruba
Curaçao
Bonaire

Caracas

Barranquilla

Maracaibo

Orinoco

Caroni

PANAMA
Colón
Panama
City

Gulf of
Panama

Medellín

San Cristóbal

VENEZUELA

COLOMBIA

Apure

Cauca

Magdalena

Meta

Bogotá

Uraricuera

BRAZIL

Days at Sea vs. Days in Port

When evaluating an itinerary, take a look at its day-by-day schedule. A few ships will visit a different port every day, but it's much more typical for them to have at least 1 or 2 **days at sea**—either because they have to sail a long way between ports or so they can just give passengers a chance to rest (and spend some money on board, while they're at it). Many cruises these days—especially ones that sail from more northerly home ports to Caribbean destinations—are spending up to 3 days at sea on 7-night itineraries, and 4 on 8-night itineraries. That's not a bad thing if your main vacation goal is to decompress, but if your goal is to see a lot of different ports, this is not an ideal situation. Ditto if you think you'll get "are we there yet?" antsy between ports.

Typically, cruise lines divide Caribbean itineraries into eastern, western, and southern routings, but as ships become faster and able to sail greater distances between ports, more and more of those lines are blurring.

MEGASHIP ITINERARIES

EASTERN CARIBBEAN   Eastern Caribbean itineraries typically sail out of Florida and from the alternate home ports up the Eastern Seaboard, and may include visits to San Juan (Puerto Rico), the U.S. Virgin Islands (particularly St. Thomas), St. Martin, and Nassau or Freeport in the Bahamas—all very popular and busy ports of call, especially St. Thomas, Nassau, and San Juan. Grand Turk, located just east of the Bahamas, is also showing up on some of these sailings.

WESTERN CARIBBEAN   Western Caribbean itineraries depart from Miami, Fort Lauderdale, Tampa, New Orleans, and Galveston, and usually visit Grand Cayman, Jamaica, and Cozumel or one of the other ports on Mexico's Yucatán Peninsula. This is a popular itinerary for many lines, so you'll see throngs of other cruise passengers in each port—often three or four (or more) ships will be visiting at a time. Belize City and the Bay Islands of Honduras are also popping up more frequently on western Caribbean itineraries, as is the new port at Grand Turk in the Turks & Caicos Islands.

SOUTHERN CARIBBEAN   Southern itineraries typically sail round-trip out of San Juan or sometimes out of Aruba or Barbados. They often overlap with eastern Caribbean itineraries and may visit St. Thomas, St. Martin, St. Lucia, Martinique, Antigua, and maybe Dominica, Guadeloupe, Aruba, and Grenada or one of the other islands in the Grenadines.

SMALL-SHIP ITINERARIES

Most small ships cruise in the eastern and southern Caribbean, where distances between islands are shorter. Instead of Florida, they may sail out of Barbados, Grenada, St. Kitts, or San Juan and visit more remote islands.

EASTERN CARIBBEAN   These itineraries may include visits to St. Barts, the British Virgin Islands, and the U.S. Virgin Islands (lush St. John as well as more touristy St. Thomas).

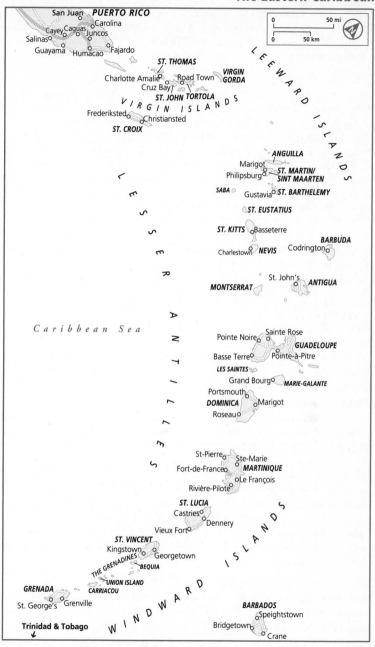

SOUTHERN CARIBBEAN   Southern Caribbean cruises may visit Guadeloupe, Dominica, Les Saintes, St. Kitts, Nevis, Martinique, St. Lucia, St. Vincent, Grenada, and Bequia, and maybe the truly unspoiled and remote Palm, Canouan, Mayreau, and Carriacou islands.

SHORTER ITINERARIES

Short and affordable **2- and 3-night cruises** offer a more action-packed, nonstop party ambience than longer 7-night Caribbean itineraries. It's obvious why: These are weekend cruises, departing on Thursday or Friday afternoon, so people are ready to squeeze in as much fun, relaxation, drinking, gambling, dancing, and eating as possible before going back to work on Monday. Though you'll definitely find more 20- and 30-somethings on these shorties than on any other type of cruise, you'll still see a wide range of ages. Aside from the fun factor, short cruises are a great way for first-time cruisers to test the waters (so to speak) before committing to a full week. They're also a good idea if you're short on time or moola.

The ships that offer these minicruises tend to be the oldest in their fleets and are a bit beat-up compared to the newest megaships. We've also noticed that service tends to not be as good on the short party cruises. Then again, most passengers don't notice the difference—they're too busy having fun.

Because they typically depart on Sunday or Monday afternoon and sail through the workweek, **4- and 5-night cruises** represent the opposite end of the liveliness spectrum, tending to attract an older and less party-oriented crowd.

MATCHING YOUR HABITS TO YOUR ITINERARY

Some ports are better for certain things than others. Here's a short rundown; see p. 79 for a comparison chart that rates shore excursions, activities, beaches, shopping, and dining for all the Caribbean ports. The island reviews in chapter 5, "Ports of Call," provide detailed information.

PORTS FOR SHOPPERS
Eastern Caribbean: St. Thomas, San Juan, Nassau, St. Martin. **Western Caribbean:** Grand Cayman, Cozumel, Playa del Carmen. **Southern Caribbean:** Aruba, Barbados.

PORTS FOR BEACH LOVERS
Eastern Caribbean: Antigua, British Virgin Islands, St. John, St. Martin, St. Barts. **Western Caribbean:** Grand Cayman, Jamaica, Grand Turk. **Southern Caribbean:** Aruba, Grenada, Bequia, Barbados, Nevis, Martinique.

PORTS FOR SCUBA DIVERS & SNORKELERS
Eastern Caribbean: St. Croix, St. John, St. Thomas. **Western Caribbean:** Grand Cayman, Belize, Cozumel, Grand Turk. **Southern Caribbean:** Bonaire, Curaçao, Dominica.

PORTS FOR HISTORY & ARCHAEOLOGY ENTHUSIASTS
Eastern Caribbean: San Juan. **Western Caribbean:** Cozumel and the other Yucatán ports. **Southern Caribbean:** Barbados, Curaçao.

PORTS FOR NATURE BUFFS
Eastern Caribbean: St. John, San Juan. **Southern Caribbean:** Aruba, Bonaire Dominica, St. Kitts, Grenada, Trinidad.

PORTS FOR FRANCOPHILES

Eastern Caribbean: Guadeloupe, Les Saintes, St. Martin, St. Barts, Martinique.

SHORE EXCURSIONS: THE WHAT, WHY & HOW

Sometimes a port's real attractions may be miles (occasionally, a lot of miles) from where your ship is docked. In such cases, touring on your own could be an inefficient use of your time, entailing lots of hassles and planning, and possibly costing more. This is when the **shore excursions** offered by the cruise lines are a good way to go.

Shore excursions run the gamut, from snoresville bus tours and catamaran booze cruises to more stimulating options like snorkeling and rainforest walks. For those who like a little sweat in their port visit, there are more physically challenging options than ever, such as kayaking, horseback riding, mountain biking, zip lining, and river rafting. Most islands offer at least 10 to 20 different excursions, all of them operated not by the cruise line, but by land-based tour companies with which the cruise lines contract. When you receive your cruise documents and/or confirmation numbers (or, at the latest, when you board ship), you'll get a listing of the excursions offered for your itinerary. To get a jump on things, you can also glance at the shore-excursion lists on most cruise lines' websites, many of which also allow you to prebook or prereserve excursions. It's a good option if you have your heart set on a particular one, since some popular choices fill up fast.

In chapter 5, "Ports of Call," we discuss shore excursions in more depth, providing information on the best excursions and noting when you may want to skip the excursions entirely and set out on your own.

2 When to Go

The greatest number of ships sail the Caribbean from late November to mid-April, though many ships take advantage of the year-round good weather and just stay here full-time. The only trouble in paradise is **hurricane season,** which officially runs June 1 to November 30 but rarely causes cruisers any problems bigger than a few days of rain and a bit of rocking and rolling. We've taken many cruises in the Caribbean during this period and have only occasionally run into stormy weather; it's rare, but it's a risk you take. The big hurricanes of 2005, which did so much damage to New Orleans, Cozumel, and others areas, made several affected ships merely reroute around the storms; others had to alter their post-storm itineraries while islands rebuilt their infrastructure. The chance of actually getting caught in the perfect storm is next to nil, as modern communications (and generally speedy vessels) allow captains to change course and pilot their ships out of danger as soon as they get word of a storm.

Defining seasons as "low" and "high" is hardly a science, but it's generally accepted that **high season** in the Caribbean is mid-December to mid-April. During this time, weather will most likely be perfect, the islands and ships will be packed, and the prices will be higher. The **holiday weeks** of Christmas, New Year's, Presidents' Day, and Easter are the absolute busiest and most expensive periods, especially on the family-oriented megaships—these are often the few times in the year when the cruise lines' brochure rates are not discounted.

Despite it being hurricane season, the **summer months** of June, July, and August are the next busiest times; in fact, many lines consider these months high season along with December through April because families traditionally vacation during the summer and because many ships migrate to Alaska and Europe for the season, leaving fewer vessels in the Caribbean. Temperatures may be a bit hotter in summer, but the islands' colorful flowering trees are also at their most lush.

September, October, and early November are considered **low season** (often referred to as "value season") and are the times when you'll encounter the fewest crowds onshore and on board, as well as some of the lowest rates. Sometimes there will be a lull during the first 2 weeks of January, just after the rush of the holidays, and sometimes in late April and May, so look for good prices then as well.

The **Panama Canal cruise season** generally parallels the Caribbean high season, with most cruises departing between November and April. Some ships offer only two Panama Canal cruises annually, when repositioning between their summer season in Alaska and their fall/winter season in the Caribbean. These days, many cruise lines are including **partial canal crossings** as part of extended western Caribbean itineraries from Florida, sailing through the canal's locks westbound to Gatun Lake, docking for a day of excursions, and then sailing back out in the evening.

2

The Cruise Lines in Brief

People feel very strongly about ships. For centuries, mariners have imbued their vessels with human attributes, and even though cruise passengers are typically aboard for only a week at a time, they really do bond with their vessels. They find themselves in the gift shop, buying T-shirts with the ship's name emblazoned on the front. They get to port and the first question they ask other cruisers they meet is "Which ship are you sailing on?"—and after engaging in a friendly comparison, they walk away knowing in their hearts that their ship is the best. We know people who have sailed the same ship a dozen times or more, and feel as warmly about it as though it were their own summer cottage.

Following is a quick primer on the cruise lines operating in the Caribbean. If you're an experienced cruiser, you may already have a favorite, but if not,

this will give you a little background to help you make your choice. The important thing is to find a cruise line and a ship that says "you." To make your selection easier (and to make sure you're not comparing apples and oranges), we've divided the cruise lines into three distinct categories based on the type of experiences they offer: mainstream, ultraluxury, and small-ship/adventure cruises (which includes both motorized and sailing vessels). If you want more info, with in-depth discussions of the different aspects of each line's onboard experience, detailed reviews of the different ships, and itinerary schedules, pick up a copy of *Frommer's Cruises & Ports of Call 2006,* which covers all cruises sailing from U.S. and Canadian home ports to the Caribbean, Alaska, Hawaii, the Mexican Riviera, New England/Eastern Canada, Bermuda, and U.S. coasts and rivers.

1 The Mainstream Lines

Part theme park, part shopping mall, part ocean-view high-rise hotel, these cruise ships will blow you away with their sheer grandeur and size. Gigantic 12-story-plus tributes to fun, food, and drink, today's megaships are all about dazzling passengers with gimmicks and trendy pursuits, from surfing machines to bowling alleys. With their often-wacky decor and endless options in dining and entertainment, these ships are bold, bustling, busting-at-the-scenes hubs of vacation ecstasy for anyone searching for a Vegas-style floating resort . . . and for lots of other people sharing the experience with you—nowadays, as many as 4,370 of them, plus 1,000 or 2,000 crewmembers. The action is just outside your cabin door, though if you crave some downtime, there's always your private balcony or perhaps some quiet lounge that's deserted while everybody else is at the pool.

Since the mainstream category is, well, mainstream (meaning the most popular), it's the one that's seen the most growth, innovation, and investment in recent years, so the ships, as a general rule, are remarkably new—and also remarkably big. This is the category where the **megaships** reside, those hulking 2,000- to 4,000-passenger floating resorts that offer the widest variety of activities and entertainment. Most of the lines in this segment (but particularly the "Big Four"—Carnival, Royal Caribbean, Princess, and Norwegian) have been pumping billions into building newer, bigger, and fancier ships, offering an extensive variety of cabin sizes and layouts, a mix of formal and informal dining options, a wide array of entertainment (heavy on the Vegas style), sports facilities, bars, Internet cafes, giant spas, and more activities than you can possibly squeeze into a day.

The intense competition among cruise lines means they're constantly trying to outdo one another with cool stuff you'd never expect to find on a ship, from rock-climbing walls and ice-skating rinks to pottery studios, planetariums, and multimillion-dollar art collections. You can choose from a dizzying number of things to do, from dancing lessons, bingo, and game-show contests to lectures on finance and nutrition, wine tastings, and classes on photography and website design. Mixers allow singles to mingle and grandmothers to pull out the grandkid pictures, while nutty contests by the pool encourage passengers to toss away all restraint as they try to stuff the most Ping-Pong balls down their bathing suits or swim across the pool with a bagel in their mouths. Overall, the atmosphere is very social. Steer clear, of course, if you suffer from agoraphobia.

The more elegant and refined of the lines are commonly referred to as **premium,** a notch up in the sophistication department from others that are described as **mass-market.** In terms of quality, for the most part they're all on equal footing and are more alike than different, especially with regard to dining and entertainment. Ditto for lines like Oceania and MSC, whose fleets of midsize ships are almost throwbacks to the days before supersizing. For even more of a throwback, there's Imperial Majesty, with its one midsize antique ocean liner. Though these lines have little in common with the Carnivals and Royal Caribbeans of the world, they're in this section because they offer well-rounded cruises for a fairly diverse mix of passengers.

CARNIVAL CRUISE LINES

3655 NW 87th Ave., Miami, FL 33178-2428. (C) **800/227-6482** or 305/599-2200. Fax 305/405-4855. www.carnival.com.

THE LINE IN A NUTSHELL   The everyman cruise, Carnival's got the most recognized name in the biz and serves up a very casual, down-to-earth, middle-American Caribbean vacation aboard colorful, jumbo-size resort ships. If you like the flash of Vegas mixed with a big dose of beach party, you'll love Carnival's brand of flamboyant fun.

THE EXPERIENCE   Like the frat boy who graduated to a button-down shirt and an office job, Carnival has definitely moved up and on to some extent from its riotous, party-boat beginnings. But like that reformed frat boy who stills meets his old pals for happy hour once a week, the line hasn't lost touch with its past. Sure, the ships' decor, like the clientele, has mellowed to some degree since the line's raucous beginnings, but each vessel is still an exciting, bordering-on-nutty collage of textures, shapes, and images. Where else but on these floating playlands would you find a giant octopus-like chandelier with lights that change color, bar stools designed to look like baseball bats, or real oyster-shell wallpaper? The outrageousness is part of the fun. On many ships in the fleet, you'll find a sushi bar, supper club, wine bar, coffee bar, and great amenities for children. Food and service are pretty decent, considering the huge numbers served, and Carnival gets points for trying to offer a higher-quality vacation than in years past. Enhancements include partnering with Michelin three-star chef Georges Blanc to create a series of signature dishes for the dining rooms, switching from plastic to china in the buffet restaurants, and stocking cabins with thicker towels, duvets, and more TV channels.

PASSENGER PROFILE   A Carnival cruise is a huge melting pot—couples, singles, and families; young, old, and lots in between. We've met doctors as well as truck drivers on Carnival cruises. And no matter what their profession, you'll see people wearing everything from Ralph Lauren shirts and Gucci glasses to Harley-Davidson T-shirts and tattoos. Carnival estimates about 30% of its passengers are under age 35, another 40% are between 35 and 55, and 30% are over 55. At least half of all passengers are first-time cruisers. While it's one of the best lines to choose if you're single, Carnival's ships certainly aren't overrun by singles—families and couples are definitely in the majority. The line's 3-, 4-, and 5-night cruises tend to attract the most families with kids and the highest number of 20- and 30-something single friends traveling together in groups.

Regardless of their age, passengers tend to be young at heart, ready to party, and keyed up for nonstop fun and games. Many have visited the casinos of Las Vegas and Atlantic City, and the resorts of Cancún and Jamaica, and are thus no strangers to soaking in sardine-can hot tubs, sunbathing, hitting the piña coladas and beer before lunch, and dancing late into the night.

CELEBRITY CRUISES

1050 Caribbean Way, Miami, FL 33132. ℰ **800/437-3111** or 305/539-6000. Fax 800/722-5329. www.celebrity.com.

THE LINE IN A NUTSHELL   You can have it all with Celebrity: If you like elegance without stuffiness, fun without bad taste, and pampering without a high price, Celebrity delivers—and then some.

THE EXPERIENCE   Celebrity has the goods in a lot of categories: Its spas are among the most attractive at sea, its decor the most original and art collections the most compelling, its onboard activities and entertainment among the most varied, and the alternative restaurants on its Millennium-class ships the best in the mainstream category for both quality of food and gorgeous decor. The line's megaships are the most elegant in the industry, each one of them spacious, glamorous, and comfortable, mixing sleekly modern and Art Deco styles. An exceedingly polite and professional staff contributes greatly to the mood.

Like all the big-ship lines, Celebrity offers lots for its passengers to do, but its focus on mellower pursuits and innovative programming sets it apart. Niceties such as roving a cappella groups lend a warmly personal touch, while seminars on topics like astronomy, photography, and history offer a little more cerebral meat than the usual.

PASSENGER PROFILE   Celebrity tries to focus on middle- to upper-middle-income cruisers, and even wealthy patrons who want the best megaship experience out there (while happily nestled in one of the line's amazing Penthouse Suites). But since its rates are more or less comparable to those of Carnival and Royal Caribbean, you'll find a very wide range of folks aboard—those who appreciate the elegance of its ships as well as those who could care less. Clients who choose their cruise based on more than just price like Celebrity because it's not Carnival and because it offers a well-balanced cruise, with lots of activities and a glamorous, exciting atmosphere that's both refined and fun.

Many passengers are couples in their 40s and 50s, though you'll see people of all ages, with a decent number of honeymooners and couples celebrating anniversaries, as well as families with children in summer and during the holidays.

COSTA CRUISES

200 S. Park Rd., Suite 200, Hollywood, FL 33021-8541. ℂ **800/462-6782** or 954/266-5600. Fax 954/266-2100. www.costacruises.com.

THE LINE IN A NUTSHELL Imagine a Carnival megaship hijacked by an Italian circus troupe: That's Costa. The words of the day are *fun, festive,* and *international,* with big, bright new megaships providing the venue. Expect a really good time, but don't set your sights too high for cuisine.

THE EXPERIENCE For years, Costa has played up its Italian heritage as the main factor that distinguishes it from Carnival, Royal Caribbean, and the rest—even though the line is part of the Carnival Corporation empire, and many members of the service staff are as Italian as Chico Marx. Still, there's an Italianate essence here, with more pasta dishes on the menu than on any other line; more classical Italian music among the entertainment offerings; Italian-flavored activities facilitated by a young, mostly Italian, and ridiculously attractive "animation staff"; and a huge number of Italian Americans among the passengers. The interiors of the line's huge new ships are by Carnival's designer-in-chief Joe Farcus, who took inspiration from Italy's traditions of painting and architecture but still stuck close to his signature "more is more" style—think Venice a la Vegas.

PASSENGER PROFILE Costa attracts passengers of all ages who want lots of fun and action—and who like the idea of "Cruising Italian Style," as the line's slogan goes. Italian Americans are heavily represented aboard every Caribbean cruise, and, in general, Costa passengers are big on participation—the goofier, the better: Witness, for instance, the number of passengers wearing togas on Roman Bacchanal Toga Night. And we've never seen as many guests crowding the dance floor, participating in contests, or having a go at bocce ball or mask painting as aboard Costa's ships.

Most of Costa's ships sail in Europe, where the passengers are 80% to 85% Europeans. In the Caribbean, though, about 90% to 95% of passengers are from North America, with the remainder mostly from Europe and South America. Costa's Caribbean cruises appeal to retirees and young couples alike, although there are more passengers over 50 than under. Typically, you won't see more than 40 or 50 kids on any one cruise except during holidays such as Christmas and spring break, when there may be as many as 500 children on board. Because of the international mix, public announcements, lifeboat drills, and some entertainment are given in both English and Italian. For Caribbean sailings, the cruise director is often American or British, but many of the activities staff members are multilingual Italians.

DISNEY CRUISE LINE

P.O. Box 10210, Lake Buena Vista, FL 32830. ℂ **800/951-3532** or 888/325-2500. Fax 407/566-3541. www.disneycruise.com.

THE LINE IN A NUTSHELL   Disney is king of the hill when it comes to family fun. Though Royal Caribbean, Carnival, Celebrity, NCL, and Princess all devote significant attention to children, it took Disney to create vessels where both kids and adults are really catered to equally, and with style and elegance. If you love Disney, you'll adore its two floating theme parks.

THE EXPERIENCE   Both classic and ultramodern, the line's two ships are like no others in the industry, designed to evoke the grand transatlantic liners but also boasting a handful of truly innovative features, including extra-large cabins for families, several restaurants through which passengers rotate on every cruise, fantastic Disney-inspired entertainment, separate adult pools and lounges, and the biggest kids' facilities at sea. In many ways, the experience is more Disney than it is cruise (for instance, there's no casino), but, on the other hand, the ships are surprisingly elegant and well laid out, with the Disneyisms sprinkled around subtly, like fairy dust, amid the Art Deco and Art Nouveau design motifs. Head to toe, inside and out, they're a class act.

Disney is nothing if not organized, so its 3- and 4-night cruises aboard *Disney Wonder* are designed to be combined seamlessly with a Disney theme park and hotel package to create a weeklong land/sea vacation. You can also book shorter cruises (as well as *Disney Magic*'s weeklong cruises) separately.

PASSENGER PROFILE   Disney's ships attract a wide mix of passengers, from honeymooners to seniors, but naturally a large percentage is made up of young American families with children (with a smallish number of foreign passengers as well). Because of this, the overall demographic tends to be younger than that aboard many of the other mainstream ships, with many passengers in their 30s and early to mid-40s. The bulk of the line's passengers are first-time cruisers, and since the line attracts so many families (sometimes large ones), more than half of its bookings are for multiple cabins.

HOLLAND AMERICA LINE

300 Elliott Ave. W., Seattle, WA 98119. (© **877/724-5425** or 206/281-3535. Fax 800/628-4855. www.hollandamerica.com.

THE LINE IN A NUTSHELL   Holland America, in business since 1873, has managed to hang on to more of its seafaring history and tradition than any line today except Cunard. It offers a moderately priced, classic, and casual yet refined cruise experience.

THE EXPERIENCE   Holland America is a classy operation, offering all-around appealing cruises with a touch of old-world elegance and cushy amenities like plush bedding and flat-panel TVs with DVD players in all cabins. Though the line has been retooling itself to attract younger passengers and families, it still caters mostly to older folks and so generally offers a more sedate and stately experience than other mainstream lines (plus excellent service for the money). Its fleet, which until a few years ago consisted of midsize, classically styled ships, is in the process of being supersized, and the new Vista-class megaships are a mite bolder in their color palate. New or old, the vessels are all well maintained and have excellent (and remarkably similar) layouts that ease passenger movement. In the ships' public areas, you'll see flowers that testify to Holland's place in the floral trade, Indonesian fabrics and woodcarvings that evoke the country's relationship with its former colony, and seafaring memorabilia that often harks back to Holland America's own history.

PASSENGER PROFILE   For years, HAL was known for catering to an almost exclusively older crowd, with most passengers in their 70s on up. Today, following intense efforts to attract younger passengers, about 40% of the line's guests are under 55 (with the average age being 57), with a few young families peppering the mix, especially in summers and during holiday weeks. While the average age skews a bit lower on the newer Vista-class ships, HAL just isn't Carnival or Disney, and its older ships especially were designed with older folks in mind—a few even have fold-down seats in the elevators.

Passengers tend to be amiable, low key, better educated than their equivalents aboard sister line Carnival, and much more amenable to dressing up—you'll spot lots of tuxedos and evening gowns on formal nights. Though you'll see some people walking laps on the Promenade Deck, others taking advantage of the ships' large gyms, and some taking athletic or semiadventurous shore excursions, these aren't terribly active cruises, and passengers overall tend to be sedentary. HAL has a very high repeat-passenger rate, so many of the people you'll see aboard will have sailed with the line before.

IMPERIAL MAJESTY CRUISES

4161 NW Fifth St., Suite 200, Plantation, FL 33317. © **800/394-3865** or 954/453-4625. Fax 954/453-4626. www.imperialmajesty.com.

THE LINE IN A NUTSHELL   Imperial Majesty operates nothing but 2-night round-trips between Fort Lauderdale and Nassau, year-round. The one big reason to sail? The line's ship, the 1953-vintage *Regal Empress,* is probably the last chance you'll ever get to sail on a real, old-fashioned ocean liner. They don't make 'em like this anymore.

THE EXPERIENCE   If you want to get a glimpse of what ocean travel was like in the 1950s, plunk down a couple hundred bucks and take a quick ride aboard *Regal Empress.* Today, the 54-year-old vessel is more over-the-hill vaudeville trouper than glamorous star, but she's one of the very few ships left with the kind of woody interiors and chunky steelwork that characterized the great old liners. She's a real *ship* ship, totally unlike today's hotel-like megaships. Former owner Regal Cruises kept her in good shape, initiating several well-planned refurbishments that ripped out bad, glitzy '80s additions and reemphasized the classic elements of the decor. Let's not be dishonest, though: The *Empress* shows her age, and for every classic element there's a worn one to balance it, like scuffed cabin walls, stained or sagging ceiling tiles, and a "been at sea too long" smell in some areas. Quirks and all, though, the *Regal Empress* is an absolute classic—and with international maritime regulations practically guaranteeing retirement for vessels like this by 2010, time is running out.

PASSENGER PROFILE   At any given time, about 50% of passengers are aboard the ship as part of land/sea package deals, often sold via telemarketers. The other 50% are generally South Florida locals and vacationers looking to add a quick Bahamas hop to their Florida itinerary. A fair number are first-timers sampling the cruise experience before committing to a longer voyage, while a few are ocean-liner buffs looking for a dose of the real thing.

MSC ITALIAN CRUISES

420 Fifth Ave., New York, NY 10018. © **800/666-9333** or 212/764-4800. Fax 212/764-1486. www.msccruises.com.

THE LINE IN A NUTSHELL   MSC is a line in transition, its sugar-daddy European owners ordering up new ships at an amazing rate and its high-profile U.S. management team busy with the goal of turning MSC into a premium line on par with Holland America and Celebrity.

THE EXPERIENCE   Based in Italy, where it was born as an adjunct of Mediterranean Shipping Company (the world's second-largest container-shipping operation), MSC is all about "Italian style." You're probably thinking, "What, another Costa?" Not exactly. Where Costa goes for a flashy megaship vibe, MSC is deliberately low-key in the decor and whoopee department. Its U.S.-based ship, the midsize *Lirica,* was launched in 2003 and is almost a throwback to an earlier era of cruising, carrying "only" 1,590 passengers and with almost none of the pop-culture themes and flashiness of most modern ships. Ditto for the onboard ambience, which has been retuned by the U.S. management team. New head honcho Rick Sasso, formerly president of Celebrity Cruises, has his eye on re-creating what he sees as cruising's glory days. "The '70s were my favorite era in cruising," he told us. "It was all about the experience then: the personality of the brand and the way passengers interacted with each other." The idea—and the reality—is a line that doesn't rely on gadgets and gimmicks, but where the staff helps the passengers have a great time simply interacting with one another.

PASSENGER PROFILE   MSC's typical age range in the Caribbean is mid-40s and up, and while its Mediterranean itineraries tend to carry 85% Europeans and 15% "other" (including North Americans), Caribbean itineraries are exactly the opposite, with Americans dominating. Also, while European itineraries tend to carry a lot of kids, those in the Caribbean don't—except at holidays. Announcements in the Caribbean are usually made in only two languages, English and Italian (in that order).

NORWEGIAN CRUISE LINE

7665 Corporate Center Dr., Miami, FL 33126. ℭ **800/327-7030** or 305/436-4000. Fax 305/436-4126. www.ncl.com.

THE LINE IN A NUTSHELL   NCL may be the most mainstream of the mainstream lines these days—and we mean that in a good way. At a time when even Carnival is pushing some "luxury" elements of its onboard program, NCL hews to the center, with always-casual dining (and lots of it), bright and cheerful decor, and fun innovations like gourmet-beer bars and onboard bowling alleys. Its newest ships are standouts, giving Royal Caribbean and Princess a run for their money. Nutshell? NCL's the kind of cruise line you want to sit down and have a beer with.

THE EXPERIENCE   Back in the '90s, NCL operated a mixed-bag fleet of older ships whose onboard vibe was only a couple steps above budget. What a difference a few years makes. Today, NCL is one of the top players in the industry, with innovative itineraries, a fleet of mostly new megaships, a casual onboard atmosphere, quality entertainment, and a staggering number of dining choices. The line was the first to dump the old system of formal/informal/casual nights, going totally casual in 2000 and starting a trend across the industry. The new program also did away with fixed dining times and seating assignments, leaving passengers free to choose when and where they want to dine among a variety of venues. Traditional tipping also went away, replaced by a system where gratuities are added directly to passenger accounts.

PASSENGER PROFILE Passengers in general are younger, more price conscious, and more active than those aboard lines such as HAL, Celebrity, and Princess. Typical NCL passengers are couples between 25 and 60, including a fair number of honeymooners and families with kids during summers and holidays. Kids under 2 travel free. The atmosphere aboard all NCL vessels is informal and well suited to casual types, party-makers, and first-time cruisers.

OCEANIA CRUISES

8300 NW 33rd St., Suite 308, Miami, FL 33122. ✆ **800/531-5658** or 305/514-2300. www.oceaniacruises.com.

THE LINE IN A NUTSHELL Oceania is the phoenix that rose from the ashes of Renaissance Cruises, which went belly-up in September 2001. Headed by former Renaissance and Crystal Cruises executives, the line operates three of Renaissance's ships and mimics some attributes of much pricier lines, with excellent service and cuisine along with a quiet, refined onboard feel.

THE EXPERIENCE Oceania is positioned as an "upper premium" line intended to fill the gap between big-ship premium lines such as Celebrity and real luxe lines such as Regent, in terms of both ship size and level of luxury. It's going for a kind of floating country-club feel, with a low-key ambience; few organized activities; low-key entertainment; a casual, sporty dress code; an emphasis on cabin comfort; and long itineraries that favor smaller, less-visited ports such as St. Kitts and St. Barts. Despite such luxe-travel touches, the line's prices are competitive with—and often even lower than—those of the other premium lines.

PASSENGER PROFILE Due partially to the length of these cruises (mostly 10, 12, and 14 days) and partially to the low-key onboard atmosphere, Oceania tends to attract older passengers who prefer to entertain themselves, reading in the library and enjoying the destination-heavy itineraries. Most are Americans, with many from the West Coast and many "returning," having sailed previously with Oceania (or with Renaissance back in the old days). A sprinkling of younger couples usually find themselves on board as well, though children are rare enough to be surprising. Whatever their age, passengers tend to be drawn by the line's 100%-casual dress code and ambience.

Because of Oceania's stringent no-smoking rules, most passengers are nonsmokers. Aside from one corner of the pool deck and one corner of the Horizons nightclub, smoking is not permitted anywhere on board—even in your cabin or private balcony.

PRINCESS CRUISES

24305 Town Center Dr., Santa Clarita, CA 91355. ✆ **800/PRINCESS** or 661/753-0000. Fax 661/259-3108. www.princess.com.

THE LINE IN A NUTSHELL With a fleet of mostly large and extra-large megaships, L.A.-based Princess offers a quality mainstream cruise experience with a nice balance of tradition and innovation, relaxation and excitement, casualness and glamour.

THE EXPERIENCE If you were to put Royal Caribbean, NCL, and Holland America in a blender and mix them together, then add a pinch of British maritime tradition and California style, you'd come up with Princess. Dining, entertainment, and activities are geared to a wide cross-section of cruisers: The more traditional-minded can spend time in the library, join a bridge tournament, enjoy a meal in a grand dining room, and then take in a show. Those seeking something different can spin a pottery wheel or work toward their PADI scuba certification, grab a bite in an intimate Italian restaurant, and take in a jazz set. The line's largest vessels are some of the biggest at sea, yet still manage to offer intimate spaces for quiet time, as well as lots to do.

PASSENGER PROFILE   The majority of Princess's passengers are in their 50s, 60s, and older, though more and more 30- and 40-somethings (and their families) are sailing these days, particularly during summer school holidays. Overall, Princess passengers are less boisterous than those aboard Carnival and not quite as staid as those aboard Holland America. Its ships all have extensive kids' facilities and activities, making them suitable for families, while their balance of formal and informal makes them a good bet for a romantic vacation, too, with opportunities for doing your own thing mixed in among more traditional cruise experiences. For serious *Love Boat*–style romance, Princess has things covered, offering secret proposal packages and onboard weddings in which the captain officiates.

ROYAL CARIBBEAN INTERNATIONAL

1050 Caribbean Way, Miami, FL 33132. ℭ **800/327-6700** or 305/539-6000. Fax 800/722-5329. www.royalcaribbean.com.

THE LINE IN A NUTSHELL   Good-looking, activity-packed floating resorts, Royal Caribbean's ships are all-around winners. It's among the most innovative lines in the cruise biz, offering not only the biggest ships, but also the most fun. Onboard surfing, rock climbing, ice-skating, boxing . . . what's next?

THE EXPERIENCE   Royal Caribbean prides itself on being ultrainnovative and cutting edge, pushing the envelope with each new class of ship it builds. If there's something that's never been done at sea before, Royal Caribbean will figure out how to offer it. The latest ship, *Freedom of the Seas,* has not only the rock-climbing walls and ice-skating rink inherited from the Voyager class before her, but also a slew of even more eye-popping features, from a surfing simulator to a full-size, bona-fide boxing ring and the industry's first onboard water park for kids. Cruises on these fun, active, and glamorous (but not too over-the-top-glitzy) megaships offer a great experience for a wide range of people, whether your idea of a good time is riding a wave or relaxing in the Solarium pool. There are huge children's centers, and entertainment for adults is varied and sometimes even novel, like the comedians and jugglers who parade through the Royal Promenade on the Voyager ships. Decor-wise, these ships are a shade or two toned down from the Carnival brood: Rather than trying to overwhelm the senses, many of their public areas are understated and classy. The Radiance-class vessels are the line's most elegant to date, with a sophistication that's up near the level of Royal Caribbean's sister line, Celebrity Cruises.

PASSENGER PROFILE   You'll find all walks of life on a Royal Caribbean cruise: passengers in their 20s to 60s and older, mostly couples (including a good number of honeymooners), some singles traveling with friends, and also lots of families. While the majority of passengers come from somewhere in North America, the huge Voyager- and Freedom-class ships, in particular, attract a lot of foreigners, including many Asians and Latin Americans. There are books in the library in French, Spanish, and Dutch; in-cabin documents (such as room-service menus) are in five languages, including Italian and Portuguese.

Over the past several years, the line has been making a push for younger, hipper, more active passengers with its "Get Out There" ad campaign, which portrays the ships as a combination of hyperactive urban health club, chic restaurant district, and adventure-travel magic potion—which, of course, is a bit of a stretch. They're active, yes, but don't expect the Shackleton expedition. Overall, passengers are energetic, social, and looking for a good time, no matter what their age. And they want a less glitzy, theme-parkish, and party-on experience than they'll get with RCI's main competitor, Carnival. RCI's shorter 3- and 4-night cruises do tend to attract more of the partying crowd, however, as is the case with most short cruises.

2 The Ultraluxury Lines

On these top-shelf cruises, guests don't line up for a look at an ice sculpture or a slice of pepperoni pizza en route to St. Thomas or Nassau. Instead, they sip a '98 Bordeaux with their filet de boeuf in truffle sauce while sailing to St. Barts. They order jumbo shrimp from the room-service menu, and take indulgent baths in ritzy marble bathrooms. There are no midnight buffets, dancing waiters, belly-flop contests, or many of the other typical cruise ship trappings, but instead doting service, spacious suites with walk-in closets, and an overall feeling of calmness and elegance. Delicious French, Italian, and Asian cuisine often rivals that of respected shoreside restaurants, and even if it's not quite what you find at a three-star Michelin restaurant, it's pretty darn good and absolutely the best you'll find at sea, served in high style by gracious waiters who know their jobs. A full dinner can even be served to you in your cabin, if you like.

Ships in the luxury class come in three basic flavors: the enormous 2,620-passenger *Queen Mary 2* and Crystal's pair of 1,000-passenger vessels; the midsize vessels of Regent Seven Seas (formerly Radisson Seven Seas) and Silversea, which carry between 300 and 700 guests; and the small boutique ships of Seabourn and SeaDream, which serve only 110 to 208 passengers at a time. Whatever their size, they all cater to discerning travelers who don't blink at paying top dollar to be pampered. Service is very personal, and staff will get to know your likes and dislikes early on. The onboard atmosphere is much like a private club, with guests trading traveling tales and meeting for drinks or dinner.

Entertainment and organized activities are more dignified than on other ships, and are more limited as guests tend to amuse themselves, enjoying cocktails and conversation in a piano bar, or watching small-scale Broadway-inspired song-and-dance revues.

While the high-end lines discount at times, they'll still cost two or three times as much as your typical mainstream cruise. Expect to pay at least $2,000 per person for a week in the Caribbean, and easily more if you opt for a large suite or choose to cruise during the busiest times of the year. Many extras are often included in the cruise rates. For instance, Silversea, Seabourn, and SeaDream include unlimited wine, liquor, and beverages, along with gratuities, a stocked minibar, and one complimentary shore excursion per cruise. Regent's rates include tips, wine with dinner, one-time stocked minibar, and unlimited soda and bottled water. Crystal includes all soft drinks in its rates. Many of these lines also include other free perks the mainstream lines don't, from Godiva chocolates on your pillow at night (Silversea) to cotton logo PJs (SeaDream), a CD of classic jazz (Seabourn), luggage tags and document portfolio (Seabourn offers Tumi versions), personalized stationery (Silversea, Seabourn, and

Regent), and high-end bathroom amenities from names such as Bronnley, Molton Brown, and Acqua di Parma.

Most people attracted to these types of cruises are sophisticated, wealthy, relatively social, and used to the finer things in life. Most are well traveled, though not necessarily adventurous, and tend to stick to five-star experiences. These ships are not geared to children, although aboard lines like Crystal and especially Cunard you might see 100 or more during holidays or school vacation months. Babysitting can often be arranged privately with an off-duty crewmember.

CRYSTAL CRUISES

2049 Century Park E., Suite 1400, Los Angeles, CA 90067. ℂ **888/799-4625** or 310/785-9300. Fax 310/785-0011. www.crystalcruises.com.

THE LINE IN A NUTSHELL   Fine-tuned and fashionable, Crystal offers top-shelf service and cuisine on ships large enough to offer lots of outdoor deck space, generous fitness facilities, tons of activities, multiple restaurants, and more than half a dozen bars and entertainment venues.

THE EXPERIENCE   Aside from Cunard's *Queen Mary 2,* Crystal has the only truly upscale large ships in the industry. Carrying 940 to 1,080 passengers, they aren't huge, but they're big enough to offer much more than their high-end peers. You won't feel hemmed in and you likely won't be twiddling your thumbs from lack of stimulation. Unlike Seabourn's small ships, which tend to be more calm and staid, Crystal's sociable California ethic and large passenger capacity tend to keep things mingly, chatty, and more active. If you want to learn something while you're on vacation, the line's enrichment program is one of the best at sea, and there are also dozens of themed sailings focused on food and wine, art, film, jazz, wellness, and other subjects.

Both service and dining are excellent, with passengers free to choose from four or five different restaurants: a formal dining room, two or three alternative restaurants (including, on *Serenity,* two with cuisine by famed chef Nobu Matsuhisa), plus a poolside grill, an indoor cafe, and a casual restaurant that puts on great theme luncheon buffets. The ships' reservations-only Asian restaurants serve up utterly delicious, authentic, fresh Japanese food, including sushi. At least once per cruise, an Asiantheme buffet lunch offers an awesome spread.

PASSENGER PROFILE   Like other high-end lines, Crystal draws a lot of repeat passengers. On many cruises, more than 50% hail from affluent regions of California, and most are on their second, third, or fourth Crystal cruise. There's commonly a small contingent of passengers (about 15% of the mix) from the United Kingdom, Australia, Japan, Hong Kong, Mexico, Europe, and South America. Most passengers are well-heeled couples over 55. A good number of passengers step up to Crystal from lines such as Princess and Holland America. Many enjoy dressing up for dinner.

Though not a kid-centric line compared to the mainstream options, Crystal is the most accommodating high-end choice for families with kids. Each ship has a dedicated playroom, and supervised activities for children 3 and up are offered when demand warrants it. During holidays and the summer vacation months of July and August, 100 or so kids on board is not that unusual.

CUNARD LINE

24303 Town Center Dr., Suite 200, Valencia, CA 91355-0908. ℂ **800/7-CUNARD** or 661/753-1000. Fax 661/284-4773. www.cunard.com.

THE LINE IN A NUTSHELL   The most venerable line in the cruise industry, Cunard is a classic, offering a link to the golden age of passenger ships.

THE EXPERIENCE   The Cunard of today is not the Cunard of yesterday, but then again, it is. Formed in 1840 by Sir Samuel Cunard, the line provided the first regular steamship service between Europe and North America. It was one of the dominant players during the great years of steamship travel, which lasted roughly from 1905 to the mid-1960s. From the early '70s on, it was the only line offering scheduled transatlantic crossings (aboard the legendary *QE2*), a tradition that continues today with *QE2*'s successor, the massive *Queen Mary 2,* the second-largest passenger ship in the world.

Faster than a speeding bullet, more powerful than a locomotive, *QM2* is literally in a class by herself: a modern reinterpretation of the golden-age luxury liner, bigger than anything that went before her and built to sail hard seas well into the 21st century. She's got oversize grandeur, old-world formality, new-world technology (including the only planetarium at sea), and even a dose of blatant class structure: Some restaurants and outdoor decks are set aside specifically for suite guests only, if you please. She divides her year between transatlantic crossings and cruises, some in the Caribbean.

PASSENGER PROFILE   In general, Cunard attracts a well-traveled crowd of passengers mostly in their 50s and up, many of them repeaters who appreciate the line's old-timey virtues. It's more the 4 o'clock tea crowd than the hot-tub-and-umbrella-drink set. That said, the hoopla surrounding the launch of *QM2* is attracting a much wider demographic.

REGENT SEVEN SEAS CRUISES (FORMERLY RADISSON)

1000 Corporate Dr., Suite 500, Fort Lauderdale, FL 33334. ☎ **800/285-1835.** Fax 402/501-5599. www.rssc.com.

THE LINE IN A NUTSHELL   Operating a fleet of stylish and extremely comfortable midsize vessels, Regent—which changed its name from Radisson Seven Seas in 2006—offers a casually elegant and understated luxury cruise experience. Its service is as good as it gets, and its cuisine is near the top.

THE EXPERIENCE   If you insist on luxury but like to keep it subtle, Regent might be your cruise line of choice. Its ships are spacious and understated, with a relaxed onboard vibe that tends to be less stuffy than Seabourn and Silversea. As aboard all the luxury ships (with the exception of the huge *QM2*), entertainment and activities are relatively low-key, with passengers left to enjoy their vacations at their own pace. Dress tends toward casual, though tuxedos and gowns aren't uncommon on formal evenings. Service is friendly and absolutely spot-on, and cuisine is some of the best at sea, in both the formal dining rooms and the alternative restaurants. Even if what tickles your fancy isn't on the menu, the chef will prepare it for you.

PASSENGER PROFILE   This line appeals primarily to well-traveled and well-heeled passengers in their 50s and 60s, but younger passengers and honeymooners pepper the mix. Many clients are frequent cruisers who have also sailed on Silversea, Seabourn, and Crystal, or are taking a step up from Holland America, Celebrity, or one of the other mainstream lines. The passengers tend to be unpretentiously wealthy; though they have sophisticated tastes (and can do without inane activities such as napkin-folding classes), they also appreciate the line's less formal ambience. When we've sailed, our social circle at dinner has included an Atlantic City nightclub owner, retired recycling and travel executives, a graphic artist, a theatrical casting director, and a woman who owned a string of Taco Bell franchises—all of them aboard to enjoy a quiet, relaxed vacation. On our recent cruises, casual nights in the formal dining room saw some passengers dressed in polo shirts and jackets, and others in nice T-shirts with khakis and sneakers. You're also likely to find some women in full makeup, coiffed hairdos, and coordinated jewelry, shoes, and handbags strolling the pool deck, and many men sporting gold Rolexes. A kids' program on summer sailings and some holiday sailings attracts some families, but the limited number of third berths in cabins tends to keep those numbers down.

SEABOURN CRUISE LINE

6100 Blue Lagoon Dr., Suite 400, Miami, FL 33126. ℂ **800/929-9391** or 305/463-3070. Fax 305/463-3055. www.seabourn.com.

THE LINE IN A NUTSHELL   Genteel and refined, these small megayachts are intimate, quiet, and very comfortable, lavishing guests with plenty of personal attention and very fine cuisine.

THE EXPERIENCE   Strictly upper-crust Seabourn caters to guests who are well mannered and prefer their fellow vacationers to be the same. Generally, they aren't into pool games and deck parties, instead preferring a good book and cocktail chatter, or a taste of the line's special complimentary goodies, such as free mini-massages on deck and soothing eucalyptus-oil baths drawn in suites upon request. Due to the ships' small size (with a capacity for just 208 passengers), everybody mingles easily and enjoys mellow pursuits such as trivia games and presentations by guest lecturers. With 157 crewmembers (a higher staff-to-guest ratio than on almost any other line), service is very personal; staff members greet you by name from the moment you check in, and your wish is their command.

PASSENGER PROFILE   Seabourn's guests are well-traveled mature adults mostly in their 50s, 60s, and 70s, and are used to the five-star treatment. Many have net worths in the millions. You are likely to encounter former CEOs, lawyers, investment bankers, real-estate tycoons, and entrepreneurs. The majority of passengers are couples, but there is always a handful of singles as well, usually widows or widowers. A few British, German, Swiss, and Australian guests might spice up the mix, but no matter what their nationality, these are experienced globe-trotting travelers. While you'll occasionally see families with children during the holidays and summers, it's the exception rather than the rule. These ships do not cater to kids at all, and passengers prefer it that way.

SEADREAM YACHT CLUB

2601 S. Bayshore Dr., Penthouse 1B, Coconut Grove, FL 33133. ℂ **800/707-4911** or 305/631-6100. Fax 305/631-6110. www.seadreamyachtclub.com.

THE LINE IN A NUTSHELL   Intimate cruise-ships-turned-yachting-vessels, SeaDream's two 110-passenger ships deliver an upscale yet casual experience without the regimentation of traditional cruise itineraries and activities.

THE EXPERIENCE   SeaDream was created for independent-minded travelers craving high-end service and food sans formality and rigid schedules. Step aboard one of these yachts, and you're entering a floating club of mostly like-minded travelers who cringe at the thought of sailing en masse to the St. Thomases of the world. It's an intimate group that wants to feel like it's inhabiting an exclusive and remote seaside hamlet on some hard-to-reach, difficult-to-spell island, where the food is good, the spa well equipped, and the drinks flowing. On a SeaDream cruise, everything is included in the fare—and you'll never be pestered to pay for drinks or tip the crew. You won't have art auctions, roving photographers, or "special" restaurants vying for your money, but instead appealing Caribbean ports off the megaship drag, cool adult toys like WaveRunners, and pampering service that includes complimentary orders of jumbo shrimp served to you in the hot tub (or wherever) whenever the desire strikes. The line's flexible itineraries and fluid daily schedules should appeal to landlubbers used to exclusive resort vacations.

PASSENGER PROFILE   Most passengers are in their 40s to 60s, are 70% American (with British, Canadians, and other Europeans making up most of the remainder), and are not veteran cruisers. They're the kind who have refined tastes, want top-notch service and gourmet food, but are secure enough to dispense with a stuffy atmosphere. Many passengers have chartered their own small yachts or actually own one. On a recent sailing aboard the *SeaDream I,* the mix included a fun-loving middle-aged doctor and his wife from Texas, a 30-something couple-next-door from Pennsylvania who ran a successful baking business and liked to swig beer from the bottle, a retired travel executive who was clearly used to the good life, a restaurant owner, and a group of well-dressed, hard-drinking friends celebrating a 40th birthday. Passengers were friendly and mingled easily, and by day 3, alliances had been made and clusters of new friends enjoyed drinks by the pool and dined together in the open-seating restaurants.

SILVERSEA CRUISES

110 E. Broward Blvd., Fort Lauderdale, FL 33301. © **800/722-9955.** Fax 954/522-4499. www.silversea.com.

THE LINE IN A NUTSHELL   It doesn't get better than Silversea if you're looking for a total luxury experience at sea. From exquisite service and cuisine to niceties like free-flowing Pommery Brut Royal champagne and Acqua di Parma products in the marble cabin bathrooms, these gorgeous ships offer the best of everything.

THE EXPERIENCE   Fine-tuned and genteel, a Silversea cruise caters to guests who won't settle for anything but the best. The food and service are the finest at sea, and nothing seems to have been forgotten in the creation of the plush fleet, which features warm and inviting Italian-style decor and tables set with Christofle silver and Schott Zwiesel crystal. Each ship has two alternative venues for dinner, buffets are bountiful, and the room-service menu includes jumbo shrimp and other extravagant snacks. These are dignified vessels for a dignified crowd that likes to dress for dinner. If you want the VIP treatment 24/7, this is your cruise line. **Pros:** Doting, gracious, and ultraprofessional service; truly all-inclusive rates (covering gratuities and unlimited wines and spirits); excellent cuisine that rivals the best restaurants ashore; dimly lit and romantic cigar lounges; large staterooms; and great marble bathrooms. **Cons:** Stuffy crowd. Of course, not every guest fits that bill, but expect a good portion of the passengers to be, shall we say, reserved.

PASSENGER PROFILE   Silversea's typical passenger mix is age 48-plus, but shorter cruises and Caribbean sailings often skew the mix a tad younger, adding at least a handful of 30- and 40-something couples to the pot. Typically, about 70% of passengers are Americans who are well traveled, well heeled, well dressed, and well accessorized. Most guests are couples, though singles and small groups of friends traveling together are usually part of the scene, too. Many have cruised with Silversea before, and they expect the best of everything.

3 Small Ships, Sailing Ships & Adventure Cruises

Aside from the fact that they both sail in the water, mainstream cruise ships and the small ships in this section have hardly anything in common. Where big ships allow you to see a region while immersed in a resortlike onboard atmosphere, small ships allow you to see it from the waterline, without distraction from anything that's not an inherent part of the locale—no glitzy interiors, no big shows or loud music, no casinos, no spas, and no crowds, either, as these little ships carry only 100 to 300 passengers.

Of the lines reviewed here, American Canadian Caribbean operates motorized coastal cruisers that are like hostels at sea, while Star Clippers, Windjammer Barefoot Cruises, and Windstar all operate sailing ships, though the onboard style of each is distinct. Aside from Windstar (whose onboard experience might be called "high premium" if it didn't operate large sailing ships, and thus fit better in this section), these vessels don't provide room service, midnight buffets, lots of activities and entertainment, or overly doting stewards. What you get instead is a chance to visit mostly small, nonmegaship ports and immerse yourself in nature, island culture, and the sea. You're a part of your destination from the minute you wake up to the minute you fall asleep, and for the most part you're left alone to form your own opinions.

AMERICAN CANADIAN CARIBBEAN LINE

461 Water St., Warren, RI 02885. ✆ **800/556-7450** or 401/247-0955. Fax 401/247-2350. www.accl-smallships.com.

THE LINE IN A NUTSHELL   A family-owned New England line, ACCL operates tiny, no-frills ships that travel to offbeat places and attract a well-traveled, extremely casual, and down-to-earth older crowd.

THE EXPERIENCE   ACCL began in 1966 when Rhode Island shipbuilder Luther Blount realized there was a demand for small-ship sailing on the rivers, canals, and coast of New England and Canada. Over the years, his vessels have gone well beyond their regional home and now offer cruises down the Intracoastal Waterway and in the Caribbean and Central America. Blount's extremely informal small ships won't win any awards for decor (they are, in fact, about the most bare-bones vessels you'll find in terms of amenities, service, and meals), but that's not what they're all about. Instead, this is a line that gets passengers close to the real life of the regions it visits, stopping at small islands and sometimes even debarking passengers right from the ship onto the beach, courtesy of the ships' shallow draught and long bow ramp.

PASSENGER PROFILE   This ultracasual line appeals to a sensible, early-to-bed crowd of mostly senior couples in their 60s to 80s, with the average age being 72. While some are physically fit, there are usually a few walking with canes and using hearing aids. Besides senior couples, there may be a few mother-daughter teams. All are attracted by the line's casual atmosphere (windbreakers and wash-and-wear sportswear are about as fancy as these folks get on vacation) and want to visit some unusual, interesting ports while simultaneously avoiding overcrowded ones. Repeat passengers (who make up 65%–70% of the guests on an average cruise) appreciate the line's lack of glitz and gimmicks, as well as "just us folks" features such as a BYOB liquor policy, which can save travelers scads of cash.

These ships won't appeal to the vast majority of young couples, singles, honeymooners, and families. Children under 14 are prohibited, and the line offers no children's facilities or activities, nor any particularly active pursuits such as water-skiing or excursions in inflatable Zodiac boats.

STAR CLIPPERS
4101 Salzedo Ave., Coral Gables, FL 33146. ✆ **800/442-0551** or 305/442-0550. Fax 305/442-1611. www.starclippers.com.

THE LINE IN A NUTSHELL   It doesn't get much better than this if you appreciate tall ships. With the sails and rigging of classic clipper ships and some of the cushy amenities of modern megas, a cruise on this line's 170- to 227-passenger beauties spells adventure and comfort.

THE EXPERIENCE   The more ships we've sailed on, the more Star Clippers' stock goes up. Few other lines offer the best of two worlds in such an appealing package. On the one hand, the ships feature comfortable, almost cushy public rooms and cabins. On the other, they espouse an unstructured, let-your-hair-down, hands-on ethic— you can climb the masts (with a harness), help raise the sails, crawl into the bow netting, or chat with the captain on the open-air bridge. Ducking under booms, stepping over coils of rope, leaning against railings just feet above the sea, and watching sailors work the winches are constant reminders that you're on a real working ship. Furthermore, as you listen to the captain's daily talk about the next port of call, the history of sailing, or some other nautical subject, you'll feel like you're exploring some of the Caribbean's more remote stretches in a ship that really belongs there—an exotic ship for an exotic locale. In a sea of look-alike megaships, *Star Clipper* and newer *Royal Clipper* stand out, recalling a romantic, swashbuckling era of ship travel.

PASSENGER PROFILE   With no more than 227 passengers aboard even the largest ship in the fleet, each Star Clippers cruise seems like a triumph of individuality and intimacy. The line's unusual niche appeals to passengers who might recoil at the lethargy and/or sometimes forced enthusiasm of cruises aboard larger, more typical vessels. Overall, the company reports that a whopping 60% of passengers on average are repeaters back for another Star Clippers cruise.

While you're likely to find a handful of late-20-something honeymoon-type couples and an extended-family group or two, the majority of passengers are well-traveled couples in their 40s to 60s, all active and intellectually curious professionals (such as executives, lawyers, and doctors) who appreciate a casual yet sophisticated ambience and enjoy mixing with fellow passengers. During the day, polo shirts, shorts, and topsiders are standard issue; for dinner, many passengers simply change into cleaner and better-pressed versions of the same, with perhaps a switch from shorts to slacks for most men. However, men in jackets and women in snazzy dresses aren't uncommon on the night of the captain's cocktail party.

With a nearly even mix of North Americans and Europeans (most often from Germany, Austria, Switzerland, France, and the U.K.) on a typical Caribbean cruise, the international onboard flavor is as intriguing as the ship itself. Announcements are made in English, German, and French.

WINDJAMMER BAREFOOT CRUISES

1759 Bay Rd., Miami Beach, FL 33139 (P.O. Box 190-120, Miami Beach, FL 33119).
℃ **800/327-2601** or 305/672-6453. Fax 305/674-1219. www.windjammer.com.

THE LINE IN A NUTSHELL   Ultracasual and delightfully carefree, this eclectic fleet of cozy, rebuilt sailing ships (powered by both sails and engines) lures passengers into a fantasy world of pirates-and-rum-punch adventure.

THE EXPERIENCE   When you see that the captain is wearing shorts and shades and is barefoot like the rest of the laid-back crew, you'll realize Windjammer's vessels aren't your typical cruise ships. Their yards of sails, pointy bowsprits, chunky port-holes, and generous use of wood create a swashbuckling, storybook look, and while passengers don't have to fish for dinner or swab the decks, they are invited to help haul the sails, take a turn at the wheel, sleep out on deck whenever they please, and (with the captain's permission) crawl into the bow net. With few rules and lots of freedom, this is the closest thing you'll get to a real old-fashioned Caribbean adventure, visiting off-the-beaten-track ports of call. The ships are seriously informal, and the hokey yet endearing rituals make the trip feel like summer camp for adults. Add in the line's tremendous number of repeat passengers (and a few of its signature rum swizzle drinks), and you have an experience that's ultracasual, ultrafun, and downright chummy.

PASSENGER PROFILE   Can we say nutty, quirky, nonconformist? That's why Windjammer is so appealing: It's different—a rare concept in today's mostly homogenous megaship cruise world. Unlike some "all things to all people" lines, Windjammer is for a particular kind of informal, fun-loving, down-to-earth passenger, and though some compare the experience to a continuous frat party, we wouldn't go that far. In fact, the passenger and age mix gives lie to that description. From honeymooning couples in their 20s to grandparents in their 70s, the line attracts a broad range of adventurers who like to have fun and don't want anything resembling a highly regimented vacation. Passengers are pretty evenly divided between men and women, and 15% to 20% overall are single. Many love the Windjammer experience so much that they return again and again—often a few times a year, or at least annually.

Young children should probably not go (in fact, the line doesn't accept kids under 6), nor should anyone prone to seasickness (there's quite a bit of that the first days out) or anyone wanting to be pampered (there's none of that during any day out). These ships are not for people with disabilities, either.

WINDSTAR CRUISES

300 Elliott Ave. W., Seattle, WA 98119. ℃ **800/258-7245** or 206/281-3535. Fax 206/281-0627. www.windstarcruises.com.

THE LINE IN A NUTSHELL   Windstar walks a tightrope between luxury line and sailing-ship line, with an always-casual onboard vibe, beyond-the-norm itineraries, and first-class service and cuisine.

THE EXPERIENCE   You say you want a cruise that visits interesting ports; boasts superfriendly yet efficient, on-the-nose service; serves excellent cuisine; offers active options like watersports from a retractable platform in the stern; has sails for a romantic vibe; and still doesn't cost an arm and a leg? You pretty much have only one option: Windstar.

This is no barefoot, rigging-pulling, paper-plates-in-lap, sleep-on-the-deck kind of cruise, but rather a refined yet down-to-earth, yachtlike experience for a sophisticated, well-traveled crowd who wouldn't be comfortable on a big ship with throngs of tourists, or on a more formal high-end ship. Days are loose and languid, with passengers exploring ashore (the itineraries visit a port almost every day) or kicking back and relaxing aboard ship with pretty much zero distraction. At dinner, few small ships can match Windstar for cuisine and ambience, with menus by renowned Los Angeles chef Joachim Splichal served in open-seating restaurants where guests can usually get a table for two. Service by mostly Indonesian and Filipino staff is extremely professional and friendly.

The ships themselves are lovely, full of teak, brass details, and lots of navy-blue fabrics and carpeting that lend a traditional nautical ambience. While the ships' white sails cut a traditional profile, they're also state-of-the-art, controlled by a computer so that they can be furled or unfurled at the touch of a button. Despite the vessels' relatively large size (*Wind Surf* is one of the world's largest sailing ships, if not the largest), they're able to travel at upward of 12 knots under sail power alone, though usually the sails are up as a fuel-saving aid to the diesel engines.

PASSENGER PROFILE   These cruises are for those seeking a romantic escape, who like to visit islands and ports not often touched by regular cruise ships, and who can happily live without a large menu of onboard activities. Most passengers are couples in their late 30s to early 60s, with the average around 51. Overall, an amazing 60% to 70% of passengers are repeaters, back for their annual or semiannual dose of Windstar. There are also usually a handful of honeymoon couples aboard any given sailing—a good choice on their part, as Windstar ranks high on our list of most romantic cruise lines. The line gets very few families with young kids—rarely more than six or seven on any sailing, and those usually in the 10+ age range, and only during school holiday periods.

Things to Know Before You Go

You've bought your ticket and you're getting ready to cruise. Here are a few details you need to consider before you go.

1 Passports & Visas

For decades, U.S.-based cruise ships operated under rules that permitted U.S. citizens to travel to Canada, Mexico, and the Caribbean without need of a passport, but all that's changing. On **December 31, 2006,** the first phase of the **Western Hemisphere Travel Initiative** (part of the Intelligence Reform and Terrorism Prevention Act of 2004) will require U.S. citizens to possess a valid passport for all air or sea travel—including cruise travel—to or from Canada, Mexico, Central and South America, the Caribbean, and Bermuda. On December 31, 2007, the second phase of the initiative will extend the passport requirement to all land border crossings as well.

If you don't currently have a passport or you need to replace an expired one, the **U.S. State Department website** (http://travel.state.gov) provides information. You can also inquire at your local passport-acceptance facility or call the **National Passport Information Center** (© 877/487-2778). Fees for new passports are $97 for adults, $82 for children under 16. Renewals cost $67. If you're leaving within a few weeks, you can pay an additional $60 fee to have your passport expedited for delivery within 2 weeks.

As you would before any trip abroad, make two photocopies of your documents and ID before leaving home. Take one set with you as a backup (keeping it in a different piece of luggage from the one holding your originals) and keep one at home.

After accepting your passport to board the ship at the beginning of your cruise, the cruise line might hang on to it for the duration of your trip, thus allowing it to facilitate clearance procedures quickly at each port. Don't worry; this is normal. Your documents will be returned to you after departing the last foreign port of call, en route back to your home port.

Vaccinations Required?

Travel to the Caribbean does not generally warrant inoculations against tropical diseases. Ditto for the Mexican ports you might be visiting. The Centers for Disease Control (CDC) recommends prescription antimalarial drugs for travelers in certain parts of Central America, including Panama's San Blas Islands, a regular cruise stop. CDC recommendations and warnings can be viewed at **www. cdc.gov/travel/destinat.htm.**

Safety at Sea: More Security, Fewer Germs

For better or worse, we're currently living in a security-obsessed world. People have to show ID to get into office buildings and take off their shoes to go through airport X-rays, so you'd better believe security measures are in place on cruise ships, too.

All the major cruise lines have their own **dedicated onboard security forces** who monitor people coming aboard (passengers, crew, delivery people, and contractors) and keep an eye out during the cruise, and we're not just talking the kind of rent-a-cops you see at your local convenience store. Some lines have even hired ex–Navy SEALs as top-level security consultants and have trained deck officers in how to react to takeover attempts and generally prepare them for security emergencies. Other security measures are also in place, but the cruise lines prefer to keep them under their hats.

Immediately following 9/11, all cruise ships went to MARSEC (Maritime Security) Security Level III, the highest dictated by the Coast Guard. At press time, it was down to MARSEC I. No matter what the current level, there's a heck of a lot more focus on security than ever before. Hand-carried bags are screened (and usually X-rayed), checked bags are screened, sniffer dogs are used, and a security zone around all cruise ships is maintained (varying between 150–300 ft.); it's also common to see concrete barriers, patrol boats, and sometimes Coast Guard escorts at some ports.

Many of these systems were already in place at most cruise lines and ports, so passengers generally don't notice much difference. Other changes have been made in the back office, including a rule that ships must submit a complete list of passengers and crew to the Coast Guard 96 hours before arriving at a U.S. port. Internationally, new regulations issued by the International Maritime Organization (IMO) in 2004 require all ports around the world to operate within a consistent framework to address security issues.

Non-U.S./Canadian citizens departing from and/or returning to the U.S./Canada should check with their travel agent or cruise line to determine the required paperwork. Generally, you'll need a valid passport, alien-registration card as applicable, and any visas required by the ports of call.

2 Customs

All cruises to the Caribbean visit at least one foreign port on their itinerary, meaning you'll have to go through Customs and be subject to duty-free purchase allowances when you return. We've found clearing Customs at U.S. cruise ports usually painless and speedy, with officials rarely asking for anything more than your filled-out declaration form as they nod you through. Better safe than sorry, though. Keep receipts for all purchases you make abroad. And if you're carrying a particularly new-looking camera and expensive jewelry (and are a particularly nervous type), you may want to

On a day-to-day basis, passengers will mostly notice ship security when boarding, both initially and at the ports of call. Most cruise lines photograph passengers digitally at embarkation and then match their pictures to their faces every time they get back on board thereafter. Digital passcards also allow them to tell instantly who's aboard at any given time. Many lines have also hired additional security personnel—in some cases, Gurkhas, the famed Nepalese fighters—to assist officers at the gangway and be on hand as needed.

The other major cruise safety issue that occasionally hits the news is **norovirus** (aka Norwalk-like virus), a stomach bug that causes nausea, vomiting, and diarrhea. An extremely common bug that hits millions of Americans a year (mostly on land), it's also extremely contagious. According to the Centers for Disease Control (CDC), people infected with norovirus can pass the bug on from the moment they begin feeling ill to between 3 days and 2 weeks after they recover—meaning the cruise ship outbreaks reported between 2003 and 2005 were probably the result of contagious passengers bringing the infection aboard rather than of unsanitary practices on the ships themselves. Face it, cruise ships are a lot like kindergarten: When one kid shows up sick, everybody gets sick.

In any case, don't worry too much. It's no fun to have your vacation spoiled by illness, but norovirus causes no long-term health effects for most people. Persons unable to replace liquids quickly enough—generally the very young, the elderly, and those with weakened immune systems—may become dehydrated and require special medical attention, but that's about the worst of it. More good news: Outbreaks have been on the downswing since they were first reported. Cruise lines are keeping a close eye on boarding passengers for signs of illness, and have further stepped up their already vigilant sanitation routines to reduce the chance of transmission.

consider carrying proof that you purchased them before your trip. Similarly, if you use any medication containing controlled substances or requiring injection, carry an original prescription or note from your doctor.

The standard personal duty-free allowance for U.S. citizens is $800, an amount that applies to **Mexico** and most of the **Caribbean islands.** There are also limits on the amount of alcoholic beverages (usually 1 liter), cigarettes (1 carton), cigars (100 total, and no Cubans!), and other tobacco products you may include in your personal duty-free exemption. If returning directly from the **U.S. Virgin Islands,** you may bring in $1,600 worth of merchandise duty-free, including 5 liters of alcohol, of which at least 1 liter should be a product of those islands.

As you may be visiting both foreign and U.S.-territory ports, things get more complicated: If, for instance, your cruise stops in the U.S. Virgin Islands and the Bahamas, your total limit is $1,600, of which no more than $800 can be from the Bahamas. Note that you must declare on your Customs form all gifts received during your cruise.

Joint Customs declarations are possible for family members traveling together. For instance, for a husband and wife with two children, the total duty-free exemption from most destinations would be $3,200.

Note that most meat or meat products, fruits, plants, vegetables, or plant-derived products will be seized by U.S. Customs agents unless they're accompanied by an import license from a U.S. government agency. The same import rules apply even if you are returning from Puerto Rico, Hawaii, or the U.S. Virgin Islands.

For more specifics, visit the **U.S. Customs Service** website at **www.customs.gov**. Canadian citizens should look at the **Canada Border Services Agency** site at www.cbsa.gc.ca, while citizens of the U.K. should visit the **U.K. Customs and Excise** site at www.hmce.gov.uk.

3 Money Matters

Know how they say cruises are all-inclusive vacations? They're lying. True, the bulk of your vacation expenses are covered in your fare, but there are plenty of extras. In this section, we'll examine the way monetary transactions are handled on board and in port.

ONBOARD CHARGE CARDS

Cruise ships operate on a cashless basis. Basically, this means you have a running tab and simply sign for what you buy onboard during your cruise—bar drinks, meals at specialty restaurants, spa treatments, shore excursions, gift-shop purchases, and so on—and then pay up at the end. Very convenient, yes—and also very, very easy to forget your limits and spend more than you intended.

Shortly before or after embarkation, a purser or check-in clerk will take an imprint of your credit card and issue you an **onboard charge card,** which, on most ships, also serves as your room key and as your cruise ID—you swipe it through a scanner every time you leave or return to the ship. Some ships issue separate cards for these functions, or a card and an old-fashioned room key. Some adventure lines that carry 100 or fewer passengers just ask for your cabin number for onboard purchases.

On the last night of your cruise, an **itemized account** of all you've charged will be slipped beneath your cabin door. If you agree with the charges, they'll automatically be billed to your credit card. If you'd rather pay in cash or if you dispute any charge, you'll need to stop by the office of the ship's cashier or purser. There may be a long line, so don't go if you don't have to.

BRINGING CASH ASHORE

The cashless system works just fine on board, but remember, you'll need cash in port. Many people get so used to not carrying their wallets aboard ship that they get off in port and find themselves without any money in their pockets—a minor annoyance if your ship is docked and it just means trudging back aboard for cash, but a major annoyance if it's anchored offshore and you have to spend an hour ferrying back and forth by tender.

Credit cards are accepted at most port shops, but we recommend having some real cash, ideally in small denominations, to cover the cost of taxi rides, tips to tour leaders, or purchases you make from crafts markets and street vendors. Information on local currency is included in the ports chapter of this book, but for the most part you don't have to worry about exchanging money at all. In the Caribbean, the **U.S. dollar** is the legal currency of the U.S. Virgin Islands, Puerto Rico, and (oddly enough) the British

Virgin Islands, but vendors on islands that have their own currency will also usually accept dollars. Even on islands such as Guadeloupe and Les Saintes (both French possessions), where they may prefer euros, we've never had our U.S. dough turned away. Mexican and Central American ports are similarly dollar-friendly.

If you're running low on cash, **ATMs** are easy to find in nearly every cruise port covered in this guide, often right at the cruise terminal. Remember that you'll get local currency from machines where the dollar isn't the legal tender, so don't withdraw more than you need. Many megaships also have ATMs (surprise, surprise: usually near the casino), but you can expect to be charged a hefty fee for using them—up to $5 in addition to what your bank charges you.

Many lines will cash **traveler's checks** at the purser's desk, and sometimes **personal checks** of up to about $200 to $250 (but sometimes only when accompanied by an American Express card, for guarantee). You can also often get a **cash advance** through your Visa, MasterCard, or Discover card.

TIPPING THE CREW

Most cruise lines pay their service staff low base wages with the understanding that the bulk of their income will come from tips. Each line has clear guidelines for gratuities, which are usually printed in its brochures and on its website, on your cruise documents, and in the daily schedule toward the end of your trip. The traditional way of tipping was to simply hand your waiter, assistant waiter, and cabin steward cash in a little envelope, but these days many lines (Carnival, Costa, Holland America, NCL, Oceania, and Princess, to be exact) add an **automatic gratuity** (sometimes called a "service charge") to passengers' onboard account—generally between $8.50 and $11.50 per person, per day total, with the amount adjustable up or down if you request it at the purser's desk before the end of the cruise. Other lines, such as Royal Caribbean and Disney, often give you the option of paying cash directly to staff or adding the gratuities onto your account. Some small-ship lines pool the tips and divide them equitably among all crew. Ultraluxury lines like Silversea, Seabourn, SeaDream, and Regent include tips in the cruise rates. Windstar promotes its "tipping not required" policy, but "required" is the operative word: Tipping really is expected.

Among lines that don't add an automatic charge, **suggested tipping amounts** vary slightly with the line and its degree of luxury, from about $8 to $14 total per passenger, per day, and half that for children. As a rule of thumb, each passenger (not each couple) should expect to tip at least $3.50 per day for the cabin steward, $3.50 for the dining-room waiter, about $2 for the assistant waiter, and sometimes 75¢ for the headwaiter. Some lines suggest you tip the maitre d' about $5 per person for the week and slip another couple bucks to the chief housekeeper, but it's your choice. If you've never even met these people, don't bother. Guests staying in suites with butler service should also send $3.50 per day his or her way. A 15% gratuity is usually included on every **bar bill** to cover gratuities to bartenders and wine stewards. The captain and other professional officers definitely do not get tips. That'd be like tipping your doctor.

On lines that follow traditional person-to-person gratuity policies, tip your waiter and assistant waiter during the cruise's final dinner, and leave your cabin steward his or her tip on the final night or morning, just before you disembark. Tip **spa personnel** immediately after they work on you, but note that on some ships the spa will automatically add a tip to your account unless you indicate otherwise, so inquire before adding one yourself.

4 Keeping in Touch While at Sea

Some people take a cruise to get away from it all, but others are communication addicts. For them, today's mainstream and luxury vessels (and some small ships) offer a spectrum of ways to keep in touch.

CELLPHONES & SATPHONES

Look out, here they come. Over the past couple of years, technology has become available that allows cellphone users to make and receive calls while aboard ship, even when far out at sea. Costa was the first to introduce it, in late 2003 (with service going fleetwide by 2006), and now Celebrity, NCL, Oceania, and Royal Caribbean are all scheduled to have service fleetwide, or nearly so, by the end of 2006. At press time, industry big-gun Carnival hasn't made a firm decision on the cellular issue, though it's still a possibility. Ditto for Carnival sister line Holland America. Among the luxury lines, the Regent Seven Seas fleet and Crystal Cruises' *Crystal Serenity* are the only vessels wired for service at this writing, though Silversea is testing a system and hopes to have its fleet wired before the end of 2006.

Get ready: Your boss will be calling you in the hot tub any minute now.

Wireless Maritime's service is available to most passengers with GSM phones that operate at 900 MHz and 1900 MHz, which are common in the United States. In addition to regular voice and text messaging, the service—which kicks in once a ship sails beyond range of shoreside towers—lets passengers with data-capable GSM/GPRS devices access data services such as e-mail and picture messaging. Passengers are billed by the carrier to which they subscribe at roaming rates set by that carrier, just as if they were roaming on land instead of at sea.

Though each user's carrier sets its own rates, expect charges of roughly $1.70 per minute. That ain't cheap, but it's nowhere near the average $8 or $9 per minute (and sometimes up to $15 a minute) cruise lines typically charge for **in-cabin satellite-phone service.**

In addition to cabin satphones and cell service, each ship has a central phone number, fax number, and e-mail address, which you'll sometimes find in the cruise line's brochure and usually in the documents you'll get with your tickets. Distribute these to family members or friends in case they need to contact you in an emergency. It also can't hurt to leave behind the numbers of the cruise line's headquarters and/or reservations department, both of which will be able to get people in touch with you.

E-MAIL & INTERNET ACCESS AT SEA

Aside from some of the small ships and sailing vessels, pretty much every cruise ship has computers from which passengers can send and receive e-mail and browse the Internet. In many cases, these computer centers are decked out with state-of-the-art flat-screen monitors, plush chairs, coffee bars, and webcams so users can send their vacation pictures to family and friends. They're often open around the clock, and many offer basic classes for computer novices.

E-mail access is usually available through the Web via your Earthlink, AOL, Hotmail, Yahoo!, or other personal account, with charges calculated on a per-minute basis (usually between 50¢ and $1) or in prepurchased blocks (say, $40 for a 3- or 4-night cruise, or $90 for a 7-night cruise). A few ships still offer e-mail through temporary accounts you set up once aboard ship, with rates averaging roughly $1 to $4 per message.

Many ships built over the past several years have been wired with **dataports** in all, most, or some cabins and suites, allowing passengers who travel with laptops to log on in privacy. The cost for these services tends to be higher than access in the Internet centers. **Wireless Internet access (Wi-Fi)** is also offered aboard all the Carnival, Holland America, NCL, Princess, and Regent Seven Seas vessels, and MSC's newest ships, usually in designated areas such as the atrium and

> ### Plugging in Your Gadgets
> All ships reviewed in this book run on 110 AC current (both 110 and 220 on many), so you won't need an adapter.

some public rooms. A few ships—the small luxury ships of Seabourn and the huge *Carnival Valor*—offer wireless access everywhere on board. To take advantage of this service, you must have a wireless card for your laptop or rent a card or a laptop, and then purchase minutes either on an as-used basis or in packages.

KEEPING ON TOP OF THE NEWS

Most ships have CNN and sometimes other news stations as part of their regular TV lineup. Some ships also maintain the old tradition of reprinting headline news stories pulled off the wire and slipping them under passengers' doors each morning.

5 What to Pack

One of the great things about cruising is that even though you'll be visiting several countries (or at least several ports) on a typical weeklong itinerary, you won't be living out of your suitcase: You just check into your cabin on day 1, put your clothes in the closet, and settle in. The destinations come to you. But what exactly do you need to pack? Eveningwear aboard ship is pretty much the same wherever you go, but your destination definitely affects what you'll need during the day.

SHIPBOARD DRESS CODES (OR LACK THEREOF)

Ever since Norwegian Cruise Line started the casual trend back at the turn of the 20th century, cruise lines have been toning down or turning off their dress codes. During the day, no matter what the itinerary, you'll find T-shirts, polo shirts, and shorts or khakis predominating, plus casual dresses for women and sweat shirts or light sweaters to compensate for the air-conditioning. The vibe is about the same on the luxury lines, though those polos and khakis probably sport better labels.

Evenings aboard ship used to be a lot more complicated, requiring passengers to pack for more situations than today's cruises demand. On most lines these days, **formal nights** have either melted away entirely or slid closer to what used to be considered semiformal. When Oceania Cruises started up in 2003, its dress code was set as "country-club casual" every single night, on every voyage. NCL has also pretty much ditched formal nights completely, though its "optional formal" captain's cocktail night accommodates those who choose to dress up. Disney Cruise Line has toned down formality to the point that a sport jacket is considered dressy enough. Most other mainstream lines still have 2 traditional formal nights during any 7-night itinerary—usually the second and second-to-last nights of the cruise, the former for the captain's cocktail party. For these, imagine what you'd wear to a nice wedding: Men are encouraged to don tuxedos or dark suits; women are attired in cocktail dresses, sequined jackets, gowns, or other fancy attire. For those who just hate dressing up, men can get

Tuxedo Rentals

Despite the casual trend, there's usually a contingent of folks on board who like to get all decked out—and why not? After all, how many chances do you get these days to dress like you're in a Fred Astaire/Ginger Rogers movie? If you don't own a tux or don't want to bother lugging one along, you can often arrange a rental through the cruise line or your travel agent for about $75 to $120 (the higher prices are for packages with shirts and both black tux jacket and white dinner jacket). Shoes can be rented for an additional $10 to $12. In some cases, a rental offer arrives with your cruise tickets; if not, a call to your travel agent or the cruise line can facilitate a rental. If you choose this option, your suit will be waiting in your cabin when you arrive.

away with a blue blazer and tie, while women can wear a blouse and skirt or pants—and, of course, jewelry, scarves, and other accessories can doll up an otherwise nondescript outfit. (Most cabins have personal safes where you can keep your good jewelry when you're not wearing it.) **Casual nights** (sometimes called "smart casual" or something similar) make up the rest of the week, though some lines still cling to an old distinction between full casual (decent pants and collared shirts for men, and maybe a sport jacket; dresses, skirts, or pantsuits for women) and informal or semiformal (suits or sport jackets; stylish dresses or pantsuits). Suggested dress for the evening is usually printed in the ship's daily schedule. Cruise lines also usually describe their dress codes in their brochures and on their websites.

Most of the **ultraluxury lines** maintain the same ratio of formal, semiformal, and casual nights, with passengers tending to dress on the high end of all those categories. Tuxedos are very common. That said, even the luxe lines are relaxing their dress standards. Seabourn doesn't even request ties for men anymore, except on formal nights, and Windstar and SeaDream have a casual "no jackets required" policy every single day, though dinners usually see some men in sport jackets and women in nice dresses.

Aboard all the **small-ship lines** covered in this book, it's very rare to see anything dressier than a sport jacket at any time, and those usually appear only for the captain's dinner. Most of these lines are 100% casual, 100% of the time, with passengers sometimes changing into clean shirts, trousers, or dresses at dinner.

DRESSING FOR YOUR DESTINATION

In the **Caribbean,** the temperature stays within a fairly narrow range year-round, averaging between 75°F and 85°F (24°C–29°C), though in summer the combination of sun and humidity can get very intense, especially at mid-afternoon. Trade winds help cool things off on many of the islands, as will rainfall, which differs from island to island—Aruba, for instance, is very dry, while it seems to rain briefly every other time we're in Nassau. Winter is generally the driest season throughout the region, but even then it can be wet in mountainous areas, and afternoon showers often give the shores a good soaking—sometimes just for a few minutes, sometimes for hours. Temperatures on Mexico's **Yucatán Peninsula** and in **Central America** can feel much hotter, especially on shore excursions to the humid interior. Hurricane season lasts officially from June 1 to November 30, traditionally the low cruise season.

Casual daytime wear aboard ship means shorts, T-shirts or polos, sundresses, and bathing suits. The same dress code works in port, too, but in many places it's best to cover the skimpy bikini top if straying from the beach area. If you plan on hitting the gym, don't forget **sneakers** and **workout clothes.** Bring a good pair of **walking shoes** or **sandals** if you intend to do more than lie on the beach; **aqua-socks** might also be a good idea if you plan to snorkel, take inflatable launches to shore, or participate in watersports. They're also very good for shore excursions that traverse wet, rocky terrain, such as Jamaica's Dunn's River Falls trip. They're cheap to buy, but if you forget, many cruise lines rent them for excursions for about $5 a pair. A folding **umbrella** or lightweight **poncho** or raincoat is a good idea for destinations that experience regular tropical showers.

Lastly, remember to pack **sunglasses,** a **hat,** and **sunscreen.** All are available aboard ship and in the ports, but sunscreen, in particular, will be a lot cheaper at your local market than in a gift shop. You might also consider bringing a **plastic water bottle** that you can refill aboard ship, rather than buying overpriced bottled water in port.

SUNDRIES

Except on the small ships, most vessels have a **laundry service** on board and some dry cleaning, too, with generally about a 24-hour turnaround time; a price list will be in your cabin. Cleaning services tend not to be cheap—$1 or $1.50 per pair of socks, $2.50 to $3 for a T-shirt, and $9 to dry-clean a suit—so if you plan to pack light and wear the same outfit several times, consider the self-service laundry rooms aboard some ships (Carnival, Crystal, Princess, and Holland America, among others). The small-ship lines often provide no laundry service at all.

Like hotel rooms, most cabins (especially those aboard the newest and the most high-end ships) come with **toiletries** such as soap, shampoo, conditioner, and lotion, although you may still want to bring your own products—the ones provided often seem watered down. If you forget something, all but a few of the smallest ships in this book have at least one onboard shop, selling razor blades, toothbrushes, sunscreen, film, and other sundries, usually at inflated prices.

Most cabins also have **hair dryers,** but they tend to be weak, so don't expect miracles—if you have a lot of hair, bring your own.

You don't need to pack a **beach towel,** as they're almost always supplied on board (again, except aboard some small-ship lines). If you insist on big and fluffy, however, you might want to pack your own. Bird-watchers will want their **binoculars** and manuals, golfers their **golf clubs** (unless they intend to rent), and snorkelers their **snorkel gear** (which can also be rented, usually through the cruise lines).

If you like to read but don't want to lug hefty novels on board, most ships of all sizes have libraries stocked with books and magazines. Some are more extensive than others. Most ships also stock paperback bestsellers in their shops.

4

The Ports of Embarkation

In this chapter, we describe the major ports of embarkation, tell you how to get to them, and suggest things to see and do there, including shopping and hitting the beach. We also recommend a sampling of restaurants and places to stay.

Hands down, the busiest of the ports of embarkation is **Miami,** followed by **Port Everglades** in Fort Lauderdale; **Port Canaveral** at Cape Canaveral, directly east of Orlando; **Tampa,** on Florida's west coast; and **New Orleans,** which, at press time, is already starting to make a post-Katrina comeback as a port for ships sailing to Mexico and the western Caribbean. We profile all of these ports in detail in this chapter. **San Juan,** Puerto Rico, is both a major port of embarkation in the eastern Caribbean and a major port of call, so we include its review in chapter 5.

These ports of embarkation are tourist destinations themselves, so most cruise lines now offer special deals that allow passengers to extend their vacations with a stay in the port of embarkation either before or after their cruise. These packages, for 2, 3, or 4 days, often offer hotel and car-rental discounts, as well as sightseeing savings. Have your travel agent or cruise specialist check for the best deals.

The big news this year is alternative ports of embarkation, U.S. population centers where the lines are positioning ships to allow passengers to drive rather than fly to their cruise (or, at the least, to allow a wider range of flight options). For the Caribbean, the most significant of these alternative ports are **Galveston,** Texas; **New York City;** and **Charleston,** South Carolina. We've included brief descriptions of each of the cities at the end of this chapter.

Note that the hotel prices listed here are winter rates for standard double rooms unless stated otherwise. Prices in the off season will be lower. In addition to the hotels listed in this chapter, the following motel chains have branches in all the mainland port cities, unless noted otherwise:

- **Best Western,** © 800/780-7234; www.bestwestern.com
- **Clarion,** © 877/424-6423; www.clarioninn.com (no Galveston branch; Houston only)
- **Comfort Inn,** © 800/424-6423; www.comfortinn.com (no New Orleans branch)
- **Comfort Suites,** © 800/424-6423; www.comfortsuites.com
- **Courtyard by Marriott,** © 800/321-2211; www.courtyard.com (no Galveston branch; Houston only)
- **Days Inn,** © 800/329-7466; www.daysinn.com
- **Doubletree,** © 800/222-8733; www.doubletree.com
- **Econo Lodge,** © 800/424-6423; www.econolodge.com
- **Holiday Inn,** © 800/465-4329; www.holiday-inn.com
- **Howard Johnson,** © 800/466-4656; www.hojo.com (no Galveston branch; Houston only)
- **Motel 6,** © 800/466-8356; www.motel6.com (no Miami or New York City branch)

- **Quality,** ℂ 800/424-6423; www. qualityinn.com
- **Red Roof Inn,** ℂ 800/733-7663; www.redroof.com (no Galveston branch; Houston only)

All the ports in this chapter can be reached by train as well as by air and car. **Amtrak** (ℂ **800/872-7245;** www. amtrak.com) has a New York–Miami route that stops in Miami, Fort Lauderdale, and Orlando (for Cape Canaveral); a New York–Tampa route that stops in Tampa; a Los Angeles–Orlando route that stops in Orlando, New Orleans, and Houston (for Galveston); and a route from Chicago to New Orleans.

For more information about each destination, check out *Frommer's Florida, Frommer's South Florida, Frommer's New Orleans, Frommer's Texas, Frommer's New York City, Frommer's Philadelphia & the Amish Country, Frommer's The Carolinas & Georgia,* and *Frommer's Puerto Rico.*

1 Miami

The most Latin city in the U.S. offers a hot-hot-hot club scene, sparkling beaches, crystal-clear waters, and more palm fronds, glittering hotels, and red sports cars than you'd find just about anywhere else, save Monte Carlo and Rio de Janeiro maybe. On top of all that, Miami is the undisputed cruise capital of the world. More cruise ships, especially supersize ones, berth here than anywhere else on earth, and more than three million cruise passengers pass through yearly. Not surprisingly, the city's port facilities are extensive and state of the art, and Miami International Airport is only 8 miles away from the port, about a 15-minute drive.

Industry giants Carnival and Royal Caribbean both have long-term agreements with the port, and to accommodate the influx of new ships over the past few years, Miami has spent $76 million on major improvements to terminals 3, 4, and 5, plus added a 750-space parking facility.

GETTING TO MIAMI & THE PORT

The **Port of Miami** is at 1015 N. America Way, in central Miami. It's on Dodge Island, accessible via a four-lane bridge from the downtown district. For information, call ℂ **305/371-7678** or go to www.miamidade.gov/portofmiami.

BY PLANE   Miami International Airport is about 8 miles west of downtown Miami and the port. If you've arranged air transportation and/or transfers through the cruise line, a cruise line rep will meet you at the airport and direct you to shuttle buses to the port. Taxis are also available; the fare is about $41. Some leading taxi companies include **Central Taxicab Service** (ℂ **305/532-5555**), **Diamond Cab Company** (ℂ **305/545-5555**), and **Metro Taxicab Company** (ℂ **305/888-8888**).

SuperShuttle (ℂ **305/871-2000**) charges about $10 per person, with two pieces of luggage ($2 for each additional piece), for a ride within Dade County, which includes the Port of Miami. Its vans operate 24 hours a day. Call to make a reservation.

BY CAR   The Florida Turnpike (a toll road) and Interstate 95 are the main arteries for those arriving from the north. Continue south on I-95 to I-395 and head east on I-395, exiting at Biscayne Boulevard. Make a right and go south to Port Boulevard. Make a left and go over the Port Bridge. Coming in from the northwest, take Interstate 75 to State Road 826 (Palmetto Expwy.) South to State Road 836 East. Exit at Biscayne Boulevard. Make a right and go south to Port Boulevard. Make a left and go over the Port Bridge. Parking lots right at street level face the cruise terminals. Parking runs $10 per day. Porters can carry your luggage to the terminals.

EXPLORING MIAMI

A sizzling, multicultural mecca, Miami offers cutting-edge restaurants, unusual attractions, entertainment, shopping, beaches, and a whole range of hotels, from luxury to boutique, kitschy to charming. South Beach is a people-watching paradise.

VISITOR INFORMATION   Contact or visit the **Greater Miami Convention & Visitors Bureau,** 701 Brickell Ave., Suite 2700, Miami, FL 33131 (© **888/76-MIAMI** for a free vacation planner, or 305/673-7311 for questions; www.gmcvb.com).

GETTING AROUND   See "Getting to Miami & the Port," above, for taxi contact information. The meter starts at $1.50 and ticks up another $2 for each mile and 30¢ for each additional minute, with standard flat-rate charges for frequently traveled routes. **Metromover** (© **305/770-3131**), a free 4⅓-mile elevated line, circles downtown, stopping near important attractions and the shopping and business districts. It runs daily from about 5am to midnight, offering a fun way to see the sights if you've got time to kill.

HITTING THE BEACH

A 300-foot-wide sand beach (that's really wide for a beach) runs for about 10 miles from the south of Miami Beach to Haulover Beach Park in the north. (For those of you who like to get an all-around tan, Haulover is a known nude beach.) Although most of this stretch is lined with a solid wall of hotels, beach access is plentiful, and you are free to frolic along the entire strip. A wooden boardwalk runs along the hotel side from 21st to 46th streets—about 1½ miles.

You'll find lots of public beach areas along this stretch, wide and well maintained, with lifeguards, toilet facilities, concession stands, and metered parking (bring lots of quarters). There are also public garages on 7th and 13th streets; prices range from $7 to $24. Lifeguard-protected public beaches include 21st Street, at the beginning of the boardwalk; 35th Street, popular with an older crowd; 46th Street, next to the Fontainebleau Hilton; 53rd Street, a narrower, more sedate beach; 64th Street, one of the quietest strips around; and 72nd Street, a local old-timers' spot. At the southern tip of the beach is family-favorite South Pointe Park, where you can watch the cruise ships. Lummus Park, in the center of the Art Deco District, is the best place for people-watching and model-spotting. The beach between 11th and 13th streets is popular with the gay crowd. The beach from 1st to 15th streets is popular with seniors.

In Key Biscayne, **Crandon Park,** 4000 Crandon Blvd. (© **305/361-5421**), is one of metropolitan Miami's finest white-sand beaches, stretching for some 3½ miles. It has lifeguards and rental cabanas with a shower and chairs ($22 per day). The beach can be extremely crowded on Saturday and Sunday. Parking nearby is $5 for cars and $10 for campers and buses.

ATTRACTIONS

Miami's finest attraction is a part of the city itself. Located at the southern end of Miami Beach below 20th Street, **South Beach's Art Deco District** is filled with outrageous and fanciful 1920s and 1930s architecture that shouldn't be missed (oh, and the characters strolling about in teeny-tiny beachwear are pretty interesting, too). This treasure trove, called "the Beach" or "SoBe," features more than 900 pastel, Pez-colored buildings in the Art Deco, Streamline Moderne, and Spanish Mediterranean Revival styles. The district stretches from 6th to 23rd streets, and from the Atlantic Ocean to Lennox Court. Ocean Drive boasts many of the premier Art Deco hotels.

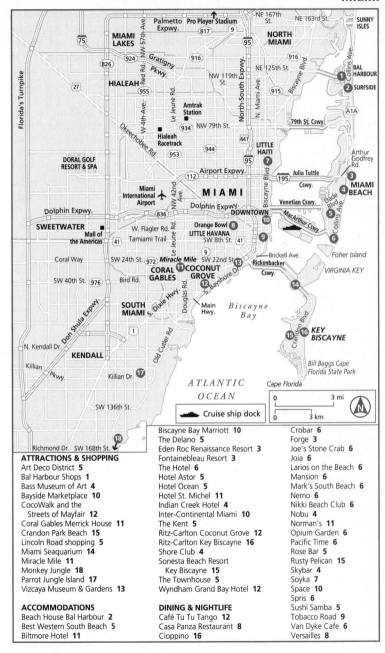

Cruise ship dock

ATTRACTIONS & SHOPPING
Art Deco District **5**
Bal Harbour Shops **1**
Bass Museum of Art **4**
Bayside Marketplace **10**
CocoWalk and the
  Streets of Mayfair **12**
Coral Gables Merrick House **11**
Crandon Park Beach **15**
Lincoln Road shopping **5**
Miami Seaquarium **14**
Miracle Mile **11**
Monkey Jungle **18**
Parrot Jungle Island **17**
Vizcaya Museum & Gardens **13**

ACCOMMODATIONS
Beach House Bal Harbour **2**
Best Western South Beach **5**
Biltmore Hotel **11**
Biscayne Bay Marriott **10**
The Delano **5**
Eden Roc Renaissance Resort **3**
Fontainebleau Resort **3**
The Hotel **6**
Hotel Astor **5**
Hotel Ocean **5**
Hotel St. Michel **11**
Indian Creek Hotel **4**
Inter-Continental Miami **10**
The Kent **5**
Ritz-Carlton Coconut Grove **12**
Ritz-Carlton Key Biscayne **16**
Shore Club **4**
Sonesta Beach Resort
  Key Biscayne **15**
The Townhouse **5**
Wyndham Grand Bay Hotel **12**

DINING & NIGHTLIFE
Café Tu Tu Tango **12**
Casa Panza Restaurant **8**
Cioppino **16**
Crobar **6**
Forge **3**
Joe's Stone Crab **6**
Joia **6**
Larios on the Beach **6**
Mansion **6**
Mark's South Beach **6**
Nemo **6**
Nikki Beach Club **6**
Nobu **4**
Norman's **11**
Opium Garden **6**
Pacific Time **6**
Rose Bar **5**
Rusty Pelican **15**
Skybar **4**
Soyka **7**
Space **10**
Spris **6**
Sushi Samba **5**
Tobacco Road **9**
Van Dyke Cafe **6**
Versailles **8**

Also in South Beach is the **Bass Museum of Art,** 2121 Park Ave. (© **305/673-7530;** www.bassmuseum.org), which has a permanent collection of old masters, along with textiles, period furnishings, objets d'art, ecclesiastical artifacts, and sculpture. Rotating exhibits cover subjects such as pop art, fashion, and photography. A new wing is opening soon. The museum is open Tuesday through Saturday from 10am to 5pm, Sunday from 11am to 5pm. Admission is $8 for adults, $6 for seniors and students.

The adjoining **Coral Gables** and **Coconut Grove** neighborhoods are also fun to visit for their architecture and ambience. In Coral Gables, the Old World meets the new, with curving boulevards, sidewalks, plazas, fountains, and arched entrances evoking Seville. Today, the area is an epicurean's Eden, boasting some of Miami's most renowned eateries as well as the University of Miami and the ½-mile-long Miracle Mile, a 5-block retail mecca (see "Shopping," below). You can even visit the boyhood home of George Merrick, the man who developed Coral Gables. The **Coral Gables Merrick House,** 907 Coral Way (© **305/460-5361**), has been restored to its 1920s look and is filled with Merrick memorabilia. Tours are on Wednesday and Sunday at 1, 2, and 3pm. Admission is $5 for adults, $3 for seniors and students, and $1 for children 6 to 12.

Coconut Grove, South Florida's oldest settlement, remains a village surrounded by the urban sprawl of Miami. It dates back to the early 1800s, when Bahamian seamen first came to salvage treasure from the wrecked vessels stranded along the Great Florida Reef. Mostly people come here to shop, drink, dine, or simply walk around and explore. Don't miss the **Vizcaya Museum & Gardens,** 3251 S. Miami Ave. (© **305/250-9133;** www.vizcayamuseum.org), a spectacular 70-room Italian Renaissance–style villa. It's open every day except Christmas from 9:30am to 5pm. Admission, which is $12 for adults and $5 for children 6 to 12, includes a guided tour.

THE ANIMAL PARKS   Just minutes from the Port of Miami in Key Biscayne, the **Miami Seaquarium,** 4400 Rickenbacker Causeway (© **305/361-5705;** www.miami seaquarium.com), is a delight. Performing dolphins such as Flipper, TV's greatest sea mammal, entertain along with Lolita the Killer Whale. You'll also discover sea lions, a tropical-fish aquarium, and the gruesome shark feeding. The park is open daily from 9:30am to 6pm. Admission is $28 for adults and $22 for children 3 to 9.

At **Monkey Jungle,** 14805 SW 216th St. (© **305/235-1611;** www.monkeyjungle. com), the trick is that the visitors are caged, while nearly 500 monkeys frolic in freedom and make fun of them. The most talented of these free-roaming primates perform shows daily for the amusement of their guests. Monkey Jungle's site contains one of the richest fossil deposits in South Florida, with some 5,000 specimens. The park is open daily from 9:30am to 5pm. Admission is $20 for adults and $14 for children 3 to 9.

Parrot Jungle Island, 1111 Parrot Jungle Trail (© **305/2-JUNGLE;** www.parrot jungle.com), is a botanical garden, wildlife habitat, and bird sanctuary all rolled into one. Children can enjoy a petting zoo and a playground. It's open daily from 10am to 6pm. Admission is $25 for adults and $20 for children 3 to 10.

ORGANIZED TOURS

BY BOAT   From September through May, **Heritage Schooner Cruises** (© **305/442-9697;** www.heritageschooner.com) offers daily 2-hour jaunts at 1:30, 4, and 6:30pm aboard the 85-foot schooner *Heritage of Miami II,* departing from the

Bayside Marketplace. Tickets cost $20 for adults and $10 for children under 12. On Friday, Saturday, and Sunday evenings, 1-hour tours at 8, 9, 10, and 11pm show off the lights of the city ($15 adults, $10 children).

ON FOOT   An **Art Deco District Walking Tour,** sponsored by the Miami Design Preservation League (✆ **305/672-2014;** www.mdpl.org), leaves every Thursday at 6:30pm and every Wednesday, Friday, Saturday, and Sunday at 10:30am from the Art Deco Welcome Center at 1001 Ocean Dr., Miami Beach. The 90-minute tour costs $20.

SHOPPING

Most cruise ship passengers shop right near the Port of Miami at **Bayside Marketplace,** 401 Biscayne Blvd. (✆ **305/577-3344;** www.baysidemarketplace.com), a mall with 150 specialty shops, street performers, live music, and some 30 eateries, including a Hard Rock Cafe and restaurants serving everything from Nicaraguan to Italian food. Many restaurants have outdoor seating right along the bay for picturesque views of the yachts harbored there. Bayside Marketplace can be reached via regular shuttle service from the port or by walking over the Port Bridge.

You can find a Miami version of Rodeo Drive at **Bal Harbour Shops,** 9700 Collins Ave. (✆ **305/866-0311;** www.balharbourshops.com). This complex features big-name stores, from Chanel and Prada to Lacoste and Neiman Marcus (and Florida's largest Saks Fifth Avenue).

In South Beach, **Lincoln Road,** an 8-block pedestrian mall, runs between Washington Avenue and Alton Road, near the northern tier of the Art Deco District. It's filled with popular shops such as Gap and Banana Republic, interior-design stores, art galleries, and even vintage-clothing outlets, as well as coffeehouses, restaurants, and cafes. Despite the recent influx of commercial anchor stores, Lincoln Road manages to maintain its funky, arty flair, attracting an eclectic, colorful crowd.

Coconut Grove, centered on Main Highway and Grand Avenue, is the heart of the city's boutique district and features two open-air shopping and entertainment complexes, **CocoWalk** and the **Streets of Mayfair.**

In Coral Gables, **Miracle Mile,** actually a ½-mile stretch of SW 22nd Street between Douglas and Le Jeune roads (aka 37th and 42nd aves.), features more than 150 shops.

For a change from the fast-paced glitz of South Beach or the serene luxury of Coral Gables, head for Little Havana, where pre-Castro Cubans commingle with the young artists who have begun to set up performance spaces in the area. Little Havana is located just west of downtown Miami on SW 8th Street. In addition to authentic Cuban cuisine, you'll find a lively Cubano cafe culture.

WHERE TO STAY

Thanks to its network of highways, you can stay virtually anywhere in greater Miami and still be within 10 to 20 minutes of your ship.

DOWNTOWN   Two hotels—the 34-story **Inter-Continental Miami,** 100 Chopin Plaza (✆ **800/327-3005** or 305/577-1000; www.intercontinental.com/miami; rates: $199), and the **Biscayne Bay Marriott,** 1633 N. Bayshore Dr. (✆ **800/228-9290** or 305/374-3900; www.marriott.com/miami; rates: $189)—are right across the bay from the cruise ship piers, near Bayside Marketplace, a mecca of shops and restaurants.

SOUTH BEACH   The Art Deco, comfy-chic **Hotel Astor,** 956 Washington Ave. (✆ **800/270-4981** or 305/531-8081; www.hotelastor.com), originally built in 1936, reopened in 1995 after a massive renovation. In December 2002, the hotel launched a new restaurant, Metro Kitchen and Bar (which replaced Astor Place), and also made significant renovations to its guest rooms and public areas. Rates: $125. The Astor is only 2 blocks from the beach, but if that's still too far for you, the upscale **Hotel Ocean,** 1230–1238 Ocean Dr. (© 800/783-1725 or 305/672-2579; www.hotel ocean.com), may be the right choice. Rates: $190. If you're on a budget but want a cozy Deco feel, try the **Best Western South Beach,** which comprises four buildings— the Kenmore, Taft, Belaire, and Davis—right next door to the Astor at 1020–1050 Washington Ave. (© **305/532-1930;** www.bestwestern.com/southbeach). Rates: $85.

The **Delano,** 1685 Collins Ave. (© 800/555-5001 or 305/672-2000; www.delano-hotel.com), is a sleek, postmodern, self-consciously hip celebrity hot spot; it's worth at least a peek. Rates: $475. The **Hotel,** 801 Collins Ave., at 8th Street (© **305/531-5796;** www.thehotelofsouthbeach.com), formerly known as the Tiffany Hotel (until the folks behind the little blue box threatened to sue), is a Deco gem—and the most fashionable hotel on South Beach, thanks to the whimsical interior designed by Todd Oldham. Rates: $225.

The **Townhouse,** 150 20th St. (© **877/534-3800** or 305/534-3800; www.townhousehotel.com), a funky newcomer with exercise bikes in the hallways and CD players and dataports in all rooms, caters to young, trendy movers and shakers. Rates: $140. The **Kent,** 1131 Collins Ave. (© **866/826-5368** or 305/604-5068, www.thekenthotel.com), attracts a less upwardly mobile yet no less chic crowd of young, hip travelers. Rates: $145. Finally, the trendy **Shore Club,** 1901 Collins Ave. (© **877/640-9500** or 305/695-3100; www.shoreclub.com), is where you'll find Miami's very first Nobu, a branch of the Japanese restaurant that took Manhattan by storm some years ago. Rates: $305.

MIAMI BEACH At the **Indian Creek Hotel,** 2727 Indian Creek Dr., at 28th Street (© 800/491-2772 or 305/531-2727; www.indiancreekhotel.com), each room has hardwood floors and modern decor. Rates: $95. The **Beach House Bal Harbour,** 9449 Collins Ave., in Surfside (© **305/535-8600;** www.thebeachhousehotel.com), brings a taste of Nantucket to Miami with soothing hues, comfortable furniture, oceanfront views, and a Ralph Lauren–decorated interior. Rates: $179.

The **Eden Roc Renaissance Resort and Spa,** 4525 Collins Ave. (© 800/327-8337 or 305/531-0000; www.edenrocresort.com; rates: $259), and the **Fontainebleau Resort,** next door at 4441 Collins Ave. (© 800/548-8886 or 305/538-2000; www.fontainebleauresorts.com; rates: $209), are both popular, updated 1950s resorts that evoke the bygone Rat Pack era, with health clubs, outdoor pools, and beach access.

COCONUT GROVE Near Miami's City Hall and the Coconut Grove Marina, the **Wyndham Grand Bay Hotel,** 2669 S. Bayshore Dr. (© **305/858-9600;** www.wyndham.com), overlooks Biscayne Bay. Rates: $179. The **Ritz-Carlton Coconut Grove,** 3300 SW 27th Ave. (© **800/241-3333** or 305/644-4680; www.ritzcarlton.com), the third and smallest of Miami's Ritz-Carlton hotels, is surrounded by 2 acres of tropical gardens and overlooks Biscayne Bay and the Miami skyline. Decorated in an Italian Renaissance style, the hotel's understated luxury is a welcome addition to an area known for its gaudiness. Biscaya is the hotel's extremely elegant restaurant—we're talking footstools for women to put their purses on! Rates: $229.

CORAL GABLES The famous **Biltmore Hotel,** 1200 Anastasia Ave. (© **305/445-1926;** www.biltmorehotel.com), was restored a few years ago, but despite renovations, it exudes an old-world, stately glamour and is rumored to be haunted by ghosts of travel days past. Rates: $279. The **Hotel St. Michel,** 162 Alcazar Ave. (✆ **800/848-HOTEL** or 305/444-1666; www.hotelstmichel.com), is a three-story establishment reminiscent of an inn in provincial France. Rates: $125.

KEY BISCAYNE The **Sonesta Beach Resort Key Biscayne,** 350 Ocean Dr. (✆ **800/SONESTA** or 305/361-2021; www.sonesta.com/keybiscayne), offers relative isolation from the rest of congested Miami. Rates: $169. The **Ritz-Carlton, Key Biscayne,** 455 Grand Bay Dr. (✆ **800/241-3333** or 305/365-4500; www.ritzcarlton. com), offers a to-die-for spa, not to mention stunning ocean views. Rates: $239.

WHERE TO DINE

DOWNTOWN Up Biscayne Boulevard near the burgeoning Miami Design District is **Soyka,** 5556 NE Fourth Court (✆ **305/759-3117**), the hip downtown sibling of South Beach's News and Van Dyke cafes, serving American food. Dinner main courses: $11 to $30.

SOUTH BEACH Join the celebs and models for international cuisine at **Nemo,** 100 Collins Ave. (✆ **305/532-4550**). Dinner main courses: $25 to $36. Take time to stroll down the pedestrian mall on Lincoln Road, which offers art galleries, specialty shops, and several excellent outdoor cafes such as **Spris,** a pizzeria at 731 Lincoln Rd. (✆ **305/673-2020**), and the **Van Dyke Cafe,** 846 Lincoln Rd. (✆ **305/534-3600**). Prices range from $5 to $14 at Spris, $10 to $20 at the Van Dyke.

The standout culinary trendsetter on Lincoln Road is **Pacific Time,** 915 Lincoln Rd. (✆ **305/534-5979**), where you can enjoy a pan-Asian taste of the Pacific Rim with a deliciously modern South Beach twist. Dinner main courses: $29 to $40. The newest haute eateries-cum-lounges imported from New York (or at least inspired by the city's hot spots) include **Sushi Samba,** 600 Lincoln Rd. (✆ **305/673-5337;** dinner main courses: $19–$39), which features a delectable fusion of South American and Japanese cuisine; and **Nobu,** 1901 Collins Ave. (✆ **305/695-3232**), the revered name in nouvelle Japanese cuisine. Dinner main courses: $21 to $80.

At the legendary **Joe's Stone Crab,** 11 Washington Ave., between South Point Drive and First Street (✆ **305/673-0365**), about a ton of stone-crab claws are served daily during stone-crab season from October to May (the joint is usually closed May 15–Oct 15), when people wait for up to 2 hours for a table. Crab prices vary depending on the market rate, but start around $25 per order. If the sky's the limit in the budget department, try **Mark's South Beach** in the Hotel Nash, 1120 Collins Ave. (✆ **305/604-9050**), for fine dishes such as slow-roasted salmon with horseradish. Dinner main courses: $26 to $46. Even if Gloria Estefan weren't co-owner of **Larios on the Beach,** 820 Ocean Dr. (✆ **305/532-9577**), the crowds would flock to this bistro, which serves old-fashioned Cuban dishes such as *masitas de puerco* (fried pork chunks). Dinner main courses: $13 to $19.

COCONUT GROVE If you want to people-watch while you eat, head for **Café Tu Tu Tango,** 3015 Grand Ave., Suite 250 (✆ **305/529-2222**), on the second floor of CocoWalk. Designed to look like a disheveled artist's loft, it has original paintings (some half-finished) on easels or hanging from the walls. The tapas courses range from $5 to $11.

CORAL GABLES **Norman's,** 21 Almeria Ave. (✆ **305/446-6767**), possibly the best restaurant in the entire city of Miami, is run by its namesake, Norman Van Aken, a winner of the James Beard Award and pioneer of new-world and Floribbean cuisine. Dinner main courses: $29 to $40.

KEY BISCAYNE   The surf and turf is routine at the **Rusty Pelican,** 3201 Rickenbacker Causeway (© **305/361-3818**), but it's worth a visit for a drink and the spectacular sunset view. Dinner main courses: $17 to $50. **Cioppino,** at the Ritz-Carlton, 455 Grand Bay Dr. (© **800/241-3333** or 305/365-4500), serves Tuscan fare. Dinner main courses: $23 to $39.

LITTLE HAVANA   Little Havana offers excellent Spanish and Cuban cuisine. **Casa Panza Restaurant,** 1620 SW Eighth St. (© **305/643-5343**), a taste of Old Seville in Little Havana, is a feast for the senses with flamenco dancers, tempting tapas, and a lively atmosphere that reels in crowds nightly. At 11pm on Tuesday and Thursday, everyone, no matter what their religion, is given a candle to pray to La Virgen del Rocio, one of Seville's most revered saints—it's a party with piety! Dinner main courses: $15 to $20. Another place to check out is **Versailles,** 3555 SW Eighth St. (© **305/444-0240**), a palatial, late-night (open Sun–Fri until 2am, Sat until 4am), mirrored diner serving all the Cuban mainstays in large and reasonably priced portions. Dinner main courses: $9 to $23.

MIAMI AFTER DARK

Miami's nightlife is as varied as its population, and the sizzling scene is no stranger to A-list celebrities from Leonardo DiCaprio and Gwyneth Paltrow to Al Pacino, Sylvester Stallone, and Madonna. Look for the klieg lights to direct you to the hot spots of South Beach. While the blocks of Washington Avenue, Collins Avenue, and Ocean Drive are the main nightlife thoroughfares, you're more likely to spot a celebrity in an off-the-beaten-path eatery such as **Barton G. The Restaurant,** 1427 West Ave., Miami Beach (© **305/672-8881;** www.bartong.com), or the **Forge,** 432 41st St., Miami Beach (© **305/538-8533;** www.theforge.com), an ornately decorated rococo-style restaurant boasting one of the finest wine selections around. Dinner main courses: $18 to $62 at Barton G. The Restaurant, and $26 to $60 at the Forge.

Restaurants and bars are open late—usually until 5am. Hotel bars are very popular, particularly the **Rose Bar** at the Delano, 1685 Collins Ave. (© **305/672-2000;** www.delano-hotel.com), and the Shore Club's hot, hauter-than-thou celeb magnet **Skybar,** 1901 Collins Ave. (© **786/276-6772;** www.shoreclub.com). Command central for the chic elite at all hours of the night includes the restaurants-cum-lounges Sushi Samba and Nobu, listed in the "Where to Dine" section, above.

As trends come and go, so do clubs, so before you head out for a decadent night of disco, make sure the place is still in business! At press time, some of the clubs at which to see, be seen, and, of course, dance, include **Crobar,** 1445 Washington Ave. (© **305/531-5027**); **Mansion,** 1235 Washington Ave. (© **305/532-5535**); and **Opium Garden,** 136 Collins Ave. (© **305/531-5535**), an open-air nightclub that's a magnet for the trendoid brass (be sure to check out the hot new V-VIP lounge, called Privé). For a Playboy Mansion–type scene by day, check out the **Nikki Beach Club,** 1 Ocean Dr. © **305/538-1111**), complete with Tiki huts and teepees on the beach.

But South Beach isn't the only place for nightlife in Miami. Not too far from the Miami River is the city's oldest bar, **Tobacco Road,** 626 S. Miami Ave. (© **305/374-1198**), a gritty place that still attracts some of the city's storied, pre–*Miami Vice* natives. **Space,** 142 NE 11th St. (© **305/372-9378;** www.clubspace.com), occupies a very large warehouse in downtown Miami and is vaguely reminiscent of a funky, SoHo-style dance palace. Down in Little Havana is **Hoy Como Ayer,** 2212 SW Eighth St. (© **305/541-2631**), where salsa is not a condiment but a way of life.

Other nocturnal options abound in Coconut Grove and Coral Gables and, slowly but surely, the downtown and Design District areas. Check the *Miami Herald, Miami New Times,* and www.miami.citysearch.com for specific events.

2 Fort Lauderdale

Broward County's Port Everglades is the second-busiest cruise port in the world, drawing more than three million cruise passengers a year. It boasts the deepest harbor on the Eastern Seaboard south of Norfolk, 12 ultramodern cruise ship terminals, and an easy access route to the Fort Lauderdale–Hollywood International Airport, less than a 10-minute drive away.

The port itself is fairly free of congestion, offering covered loading zones, drop-off and pickup staging, and curbside baggage handlers. Terminals are comfortable and safe, with seating areas, snack bars, lots of taxis, clean restrooms, and plenty of pay phones. Parking lots have recently been expanded to offer a total of 4,500 spaces.

GETTING TO FORT LAUDERDALE & THE PORT

Port Everglades is located about 23 miles north of Miami within the city boundaries of Fort Lauderdale, Hollywood, and Dania Beach. I-595 will take you right onto the grounds. For information, contact **Port Everglades** (© **954/523-3404;** www.broward.org/port).

BY PLANE   Small and extremely user friendly, the **Fort Lauderdale–Hollywood International Airport** (© **954/359-6100**) is less than 2 miles from Port Everglades (5 min. by bus or taxi), making this the easiest airport-to-cruise-port trip in Florida. (Port Canaveral, by contrast, is about a 45-min. drive from the Orlando airport.) If you've booked air or transfers through the cruise line, a representative will show you to your shuttle bus after you land at the airport. If not, taking a taxi to the port costs less than $10.

BY CAR   The port has three passenger entrances: Spangler Boulevard, an extension of State Road 84 East; Eisenhower Boulevard, running south from the 17th Street Causeway/A1A; and Eller Drive, connecting directly with Interstate 595. Interstate 595 runs east-west, with connections to the Fort Lauderdale–Hollywood Airport, Interstate 95, State Road 7 (441), Florida's Turnpike, Sawgrass Expressway, and Interstate 75. Parking is available at the port in two large garages. The 2,500-space Northport Parking Garage, next to the Greater Fort Lauderdale/Broward County Convention Center, serves terminals 1, 2, and 4. The 2,000-space Midport Parking Garage serves terminals 18, 19, 21, 22, 24, 25, and 26. Garages are well lit, security-patrolled, and designed to accommodate RVs and buses. The 24-hour parking fee is $12 daily.

EXPLORING FORT LAUDERDALE

Fort Lauderdale Beach, a 5-mile strip along Florida A1A, gained fame in the 1950s as a spring-break playground, popularized by the movie *Where the Boys Are.* But in the 1980s, partying college kids (who brought the city more mayhem than money) began to be less welcome, as Fort Lauderdale sought to attract a more mainstream, affluent crowd, a task at which it has largely been successful.

In addition to miles of beautiful wide beaches, Fort Lauderdale has more than 300 miles of navigable natural waterways, as well as innumerable artificial canals that permit thousands of residents to anchor boats in their backyards (and which has led to the city's nickname: "Venice of the Americas"). You can easily get onto the water by renting a boat or hiring a private, moderately priced water taxi.

VISITOR INFORMATION   The **Greater Fort Lauderdale Convention & Visitors Bureau,** 100 E. Broward Blvd., Fort Lauderdale, FL 33316 (© **954/765-4466;** www.sunny.org), is an excellent resource, distributing a comprehensive guide on accommodations, events, and sightseeing in Broward County.

GETTING AROUND   For a taxi, call **Yellow Cab** (© **954/565-5400**). Rates start at $2.75 for the first mile and $2 for each additional mile. **Broward County Mass Transit** (© **954/357-8400**) runs bus service throughout the county. One-day passes are $2.50. **Water Taxi** (© **954/467-6677;** www.watertaxi.com) offers all-day passes for $5.

HITTING THE BEACH

Backed by an endless row of hotels, and popular with visitors and locals alike, the **Fort Lauderdale Beach Promenade** underwent a $30-million renovation not long ago, and today it looks marvelous. The beach is located along A1A, also known as the Fort Lauderdale Beach Boulevard, between SE 17th Street and Sunrise Boulevard. The fabled strip from *Where the Boys Are* is **Ocean Boulevard,** between Las Olas and Sunrise boulevards. On weekends, parking at the oceanside meters is difficult to find.

Fort Lauderdale Beach at the Howard Johnson is a perennial local favorite. A jetty bounds the beach on the south side, making it rather private, although the water gets a little choppy. High-school and college students share this area with an older crowd. One of the main beach entrances is at 4660 N. Ocean Dr., in Lauderdale-by-the-Sea.

ATTRACTIONS

The **Museum of Discovery & Science,** 401 SW Second St. (© **954/467-6637;** www.mods.org), is an excellent interactive science museum with an IMAX theater. Check out the 52-foot-tall "Great Gravity Clock" in the museum's atrium. Admission is $14 for adults, $12 for children, and $13 for seniors and students. It's open Monday through Saturday from 10am to 5pm, Sunday from noon to 6pm.

The **Museum of Art,** 1 E. Las Olas Blvd. (© **954/763-6464;** www.moafl.org), is a truly terrific small museum whose permanent collection of 20th-century European and American art includes works by Picasso, Calder, Warhol, Mapplethorpe, Dalí, Stella, and William Glackens. African, South Pacific, pre-Columbian, Native American, and Cuban art are also on display. Admission is $7 for adults, $6 for seniors, $5 for students, and free for kids younger than 6. The museum is open Tuesday through Saturday from 10am to 5pm, Sunday from noon to 5pm.

Bonnet House, 900 N. Birch Rd. (© **954/563-5393;** www.bonnethouse.org), a plantation-style home and 35-acre estate, survives in the middle of an otherwise highly developed beachfront condominium area, offering a glimpse into the lives of Fort Lauderdale's pioneers. Guided tours are offered Wednesday through Sunday, from 10am to 4pm December through April and from 10am to 3pm May through November. Admission is $10 for adults, $9 for seniors, $8 for students, and free for children younger than 6.

Fort Lauderdale

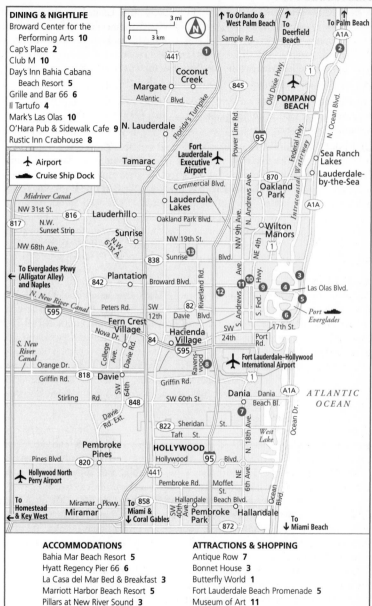

✈ Airport

⛴ Cruise Ship Dock

0   3 mi
0   3 km

↑ To Orlando &
West Palm Beach

↑ To
Deerfield
Beach

↑ To Palm Beach

Sample Rd.

Coconut
Creek

Margate

Atlantic   Blvd.

POMPANO
BEACH

N. Ocean Blvd.

Old Dixie Hwy.

Sea Ranch
Lakes

Lauderdale-
by-the-Sea

N. Lauderdale

Fort
Lauderdale ✈
Executive
Airport

Tamarac

Commercial Blvd.

Oakland
Park

Power Line Rd.

Federal Hwy.

Intracoastal Waterway

N. Andrews Ave.

Midriver Canal

NW 31st St.

Lauderhill

N.W.
Sunset Strip

Sunrise

NW 68th Ave.

Lauderdale
Lakes

Oakland Park Blvd.

NW 19th St.

Sunrise   Blvd.

Wilton
Manors

N. 9th Ave.

NE 4th

To Everglades Pkwy.
← (Alligator Alley)
and Naples

Plantation

Broward Blvd.

Riverland Rd.

S. Andrews Ave.

S. Fed. Hwy.

Las Olas Blvd.

N. New River Canal

Peters Rd.

SW
12th   Davie   Blvd.

Port
Everglades ⛴

*S. New
River
Canal*

Fern Crest
Village

Nova Dr.

Hacienda
Village

SW
24th

Port
Rd.

17th St.

Orange Dr.

College Ave.

Davie Rd.

Ravens-
wood

Fort Lauderdale–Hollywood
International Airport

Griffin Rd.

Davie

Griffin Rd.

Stirling   Rd.

SW 64th

Davie Rd. Ext.

SW 60th St.

Dania   Dania
Beach Bl.

*ATLANTIC
OCEAN*

Sheridan   St.

Taft   St.

*West
Lake*

Ocean Dr.

N. 18th Ave.

Pembroke
Pines

Pines Blvd.

HOLLYWOOD

Hollywood   Blvd.

Hollywood North
✈ Perry Airport

Pembroke Rd.

Moffet
St.

NE
6th Ave.

Ocean
Blvd.

To
← Homestead
& Key West

Miramar   Pkwy.

Miramar

To
Miami &
↓ Coral Gables

Hallandale   Beach Blvd.

SW
40th Ave.

Pembroke
Park

Hallandale

To
↓ Miami Beach

Butterfly World, Tradewinds Park South, 3600 W. Sample Rd., Coconut Creek, west of the Florida Turnpike (② **954/977-4400;** www.butterflyworld.com), is home to more than 150 species. In the park's walk-through, screened-in aviary, visitors can watch newly hatched butterflies emerge from their cocoons and flutter around as they learn to fly. It's open Monday through Saturday from 9am to 5pm, Sunday from 1 to 5pm. Admission is $18 for adults and $13 for kids 4 to 12.

ORGANIZED TOURS

The Mississippi-style riverboat **Jungle Queen,** Bahia Mar Yacht Center, Florida A1A (② **954/462-5596;** www.junglequeen.com), is one of Fort Lauderdale's best-known attractions. Four-hour dinner cruises and 3-hour sightseeing tours take visitors up the New River past Millionaires' Row, Old Fort Lauderdale, the new downtown, and the Port Everglades cruise ship port. Call for prices and departure times.

Water Taxis of Fort Lauderdale, 651 Seabreeze Blvd. (② **954/467-6677;** www. watertaxi.com), operates a fleet of old port boats that offer taxi service on demand around this city of canals, carrying up to 72 passengers each. You can be picked up at your hotel and shuttled to the dozens of restaurants and bars on the route for the rest of the night. The service operates daily from 10am to 11pm. The cost is $4 per person per trip, or $5 for a full day. Opt for the all-day pass—it's worth it.

SHOPPING

Not counting the discount "fashion" stores on Hallandale Beach Boulevard, there are a few places visitors should know about, including **Antique Row,** a strip of U.S. 1 around North Dania Beach Boulevard (in Dania, about 1 mile south of Fort Lauderdale–Hollywood International Airport) that holds about 200 antiques shops. Most shops are closed on Sunday.

The **Swap Shop,** 3291 W. Sunrise Blvd. (② **954/791-SWAP;** www.floridaswap shop.com), is one of the world's largest flea markets. In addition to endless acres of vendors, there's a mini amusement park and a 15-screen drive-in movie theater. It's open daily.

WHERE TO STAY

Fort Lauderdale Beach has a hotel or motel on nearly every block, and the selection ranges from run-down to luxurious. Call the **Greater Fort Lauderdale Convention & Visitors Bureau** (② **954/765-4466;** www.sunny.org) for a copy of *Superior Small Lodgings,* a guide to small accommodations in the area.

Located very close to the port, the **Hyatt Regency Pier 66,** 2301 SE 17th St. (② **800/233-1234** or 954/525-6666; www.pier66.hyatt.com), is a circular landmark with larger rooms than those at some equivalently priced hotels in town. Its famous Piertop Lounge, a revolving bar on the roof, is often filled with cruise ship patrons. Rates: $219 to $259.

Located just south of Fort Lauderdale's strip, the **Marriott Harbor Beach Resort,** 3030 Holiday Dr. (② **800/222-6543** or 954/525-4000; www.marriottharborbeach. com), is set on 16 acres of beachfront property. Most rooms have private balconies overlooking either the ocean or the Intracoastal Waterway. Rates: $349 to $429.

Bahia Mar Beach Resort, 801 Seabreeze Blvd. (② **800/327-8154** or 954/764-2233; www.bahiamarbeachresort.com), is scattered over 42 acres of seacoast. The 4-story and 16-story row of units is adjacent to Florida's largest marina. Rates: $199 to $410.

The **Riverside Hotel,** 620 E. Las Olas Blvd. (© 800/325-3280 or 954/467-0671; www.riversidehotel.com), which opened in 1936, is a local favorite. Try for one of the ground-floor rooms, which have higher ceilings and more space. Rates: $129.

The Spanish Mediterranean–style **La Casa del Mar Bed & Breakfast,** 3003 Granada St. (© 954/467-2037; www.lacasadelmar.com), has 10 individually furnished rooms and is only a block away from Fort Lauderdale Beach. Rates: $110 to $145. The **Pillars at New River Sound,** 111 N. Birch Rd. (© 800/800-7666 or 954/467-9639; www.pillarshotel.com), is a small 23-room hotel, the best of its size in the region. Rates: $169 to $199.

Several area properties associated with **Best Western** (www.bestwestern.com) are reasonably priced and located within 5 miles of the airport and port: Best Western Inn, 1221 W. S.R. 84 (© 800/528-1234 or 954/462-7005; rates: $99–$199); Best Western Marina Inn & Yacht Harbor, 2150 SE 17th St. (© 800/327-1390 or 954/525-3484; rates: $89–$129); and Best Western Oceanside Inn, 1180 Seabreeze Blvd. (© 800/367-1007 or 954/525-8115; rates: $109–$119).

WHERE TO DINE

Cap's Place, 2765 NE 28th Court (© 954/941-0418; www.capsplace.com), is a famous old-time seafood joint, offering good food at reasonable prices. The restaurant is on a peninsula, so you get a ferry ride over (see the website for directions). Dolphin (not the mammal, but a local saltwater fish also known as mahimahi) and snapper are popular and, like the other meat and pasta dishes here, can be prepared any way you want. Dinner main courses: $14 to $33.

Il Tartufo, 2400 E. Las Olas Blvd. (© 954/767-9190), features oven-roasted specialties and Italian standards, plus a selection of fish baked in rock salt. Dinner main courses: $15 to $22. **Mark's Las Olas,** 1032 E. Las Olas Blvd. (© 954/463-1000), is the showcase of Miami restaurant mogul Mark Militello. The gourmet Continental menu changes daily and may include white duck with sweet-potato-and-vanilla-bean purée and a superb sushi-quality tuna. Dinner main courses: $14 to $46.

Garlic crabs are the specialty at the **Rustic Inn Crabhouse,** 4331 Anglers Ave. (© 954/584-1637), located west of the airport. This riverside dining choice has an open deck over the water. Dinner main courses: $12 to $29. **Grille and Bar 66,** 2301 SE 17th St. (© 954/728-3500), serves steak, seafood, and pasta dishes at affordable prices. Dinner main courses: $14 to $48.

The restaurant and patio bar at the **Day's Inn Bahia Cabana Beach Resort,** 3001 Harbor Dr./S.R. A1A (© 954/524-1555; www.bahiacabanaresort.com), are charming and laid-back, serving inexpensive American-style dishes on a covered open-air deck overlooking Fort Lauderdale's largest marina. The Fort Lauderdale water taxi makes a stop here. Dinner main courses: $10 to $17.

FORT LAUDERDALE AFTER DARK

On weekends, pack yourself into **Club M,** 2037 Hollywood Blvd. (© 954/925-8396), one of the area's busiest music bars, featuring live bands playing blues, rock, and jazz.

O'Hara Pub & Sidewalk Cafe, 722 E. Las Olas Blvd. (© 954/524-1764; www. oharasjazzcafe.com), is often crammed with a trendy crowd that comes to listen to live R&B, pop, blues, and jazz. Call the jazz hot line at © 954/524-2801 to hear the lineup.

The **Broward Center for the Performing Arts,** 201 SW Fifth Ave. (© **800/249-ARTS;** www.browardcenter.org), hosts top opera, symphony, dance, and Broadway productions. Call the 24-hour **Arts Entertainment Hotline** (© **954/357-5700**) for schedules and performers, or look for listings in the *Sun-Sentinel* or the *Miami Herald.*

3 Cape Canaveral & Cocoa Beach

Known as the Space Coast because of nearby Kennedy Space Center, the Cape Canaveral/Cocoa Beach area boasts 72 miles of beaches, plus fishing, golfing, surfing, and proximity to Orlando's theme parks, which are only about an hour west—this is exactly why long-underutilized Port Canaveral is now busier than ever before, offering many 3- and 4-night cruise options (often sold as packages with pre- or postcruise visits to the Orlando resorts) as well as weeklong itineraries. This year Port Canaveral has even become a port of call, with NCL's *Norwegian Dawn* visiting on round-trip Florida/Caribbean itineraries from New York.

Outside the port area, Cape Canaveral is . . . well, it's no Miami. Highways, strip malls, chain stores, and tracts of suburban homes predominate from the port area south into Cocoa Beach, where most of the hotels, restaurants, and beaches discussed here are located. The central areas of Cocoa Beach are mildly more interesting, with some great '50s and '60s condo and hotel architecture—but stylish they're not.

GETTING TO CAPE CANAVERAL & THE PORT

Port Canaveral is located at the eastern end of the Bennett Causeway, just off State Road 528 (the Bee Line Expwy.), the direct route from Orlando. From the port, the 528 turns sharply south and becomes State Road A1A, portions of which are known as Astronaut Boulevard and North Atlantic Avenue. For information about the port, contact the **Canaveral Port Authority** (© **888/767-8226** or 321/783-7831; www.portcanaveral.org).

BY PLANE   The nearest airport is **Orlando International Airport** (© **407/825-2001;** www.orlandoairports.net), a 45-mile drive from Port Canaveral via the State Road 528/Bee Line Expressway. Cruise line representatives will meet you at the airport if you've booked air and/or transfers through the line. **Cocoa Beach Shuttle** (© **800/633-0427** or 321/784-3831) offers shuttle service between Orlando's airport and Port Canaveral; the trip costs $30 per person each way.

BY CAR   Port Canaveral and Cocoa Beach are about 45 miles east of Orlando and 186 miles north of Miami. They're accessible from virtually every interstate highway along the East Coast. Most visitors arrive via Route 1, Interstate 95, or State Road 528. At the port, park in the North Lots for north terminals 5 and 10, or the South Lots for terminals 2, 3, and 4. Parking costs $10 a day for vehicles up to 20 feet, $20 a day for vehicles 20 feet and over.

EXPLORING CAPE CANAVERAL & COCOA BEACH

Port Canaveral probably wouldn't be on the cruise industry's radar if it weren't so close to Orlando; most passengers shuttle directly from theme park to pier rather than spending any significant time here. Nevertheless, anyone interested in the space program and its history should plan to arrive a day early (or stay a day after) to check out Kennedy Space Center and the Astronaut Hall of Fame.

Cape Canaveral & Cocoa Beach

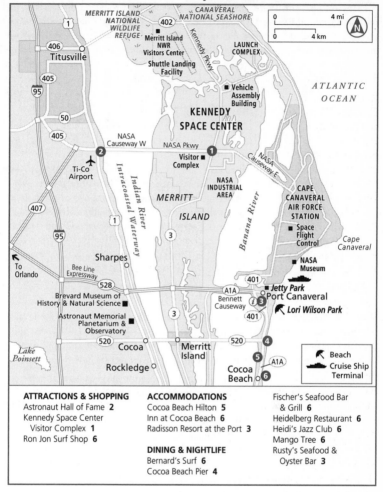

ATTRACTIONS & SHOPPING
Astronaut Hall of Fame **2**
Kennedy Space Center
   Visitor Complex **1**
Ron Jon Surf Shop **6**

ACCOMMODATIONS
Cocoa Beach Hilton **5**
Inn at Cocoa Beach **6**
Radisson Resort at the Port **3**

DINING & NIGHTLIFE
Bernard's Surf **6**
Cocoa Beach Pier **4**

Fischer's Seafood Bar
   & Grill **6**
Heidelberg Restaurant **6**
Heidi's Jazz Club **6**
Mango Tree **6**
Rusty's Seafood &
   Oyster Bar **3**

VISITOR INFORMATION   Contact the **Florida Space Coast Office of Tourism,**
2725 Judge Fran Jamieson Way, Vierra, FL 32940 (② **800/872-1969** or 321/637-5483; www.space-coast.com). Its office is open Monday through Friday from 8am
to 5pm.

GETTING AROUND   For a cab, call **Yellow Top Taxi** (② **321/636-1234**).

THE ORLANDO THEME PARKS

All it took was a sprinkle of pixie dust in the 1970s to begin the almost-magical transformation of Orlando from a large swath of swampland into the most visited tourist destination in the world. Today the city is home to three giants—Walt Disney World, Universal Orlando, and SeaWorld—and to seven of the eight most popular theme parks in the United States.

Many cruises from Port Canaveral are sold as land/sea packages that include park stays; if you decide to visit Orlando before or after your cruise, it's essential to plan ahead. Otherwise, the number of attractions begging for your time and the hypercommercial atmosphere can put a serious dent in your psyche as well as your wallet and stamina. Even if you had 2 weeks, it wouldn't be long enough to hit everything, so don't even try. Stay selective, stay sane. That's our motto.

It would take a significant portion of this book to detail everything to do in Orlando, but we list some basic information on the major theme parks below. If you plan to spend a considerable amount of time here, we suggest picking up a copy of *Frommer's Walt Disney World & Orlando*.

WALT DISNEY WORLD

Walt Disney World is the umbrella covering four theme parks: the Magic Kingdom, Epcot, Disney–MGM Studios, and Animal Kingdom, which combined drew over 37 million guests in 2002 despite a decline in international visitors, according to *Amusement Business* magazine. Besides its theme parks, Disney has an assortment of other attractions, including three water parks, several entertainment venues, and a number of shopping spots.

VISITOR INFORMATION Walt Disney World is located southwest of Orlando off Interstate 4, west of the Florida Turnpike. For information, vacation brochures, and videos, call ✆ **407/934-7639;** for general information, call ✆ 407/824-2222 or visit www.disneyworld.com.

TICKET PRICES At press time, **1-day/1-park tickets,** for admission to the Magic Kingdom, Epcot, Disney–MGM Studios, or Animal Kingdom, were $67 for adults, $56 for children 3 to 9, and free for children under 3. Discounted multiday, multipark passes are available, and many land/sea cruise packages include these passes.

OPERATING HOURS Park hours vary and are influenced by special events and the economy, so call ahead or go to www.disneyworld.com to check. Generally, expect Animal Kingdom to be open from 8 or 9am to 5 or 6pm, Epcot to be open from 10am to 9pm, and Magic Kingdom and Disney–MGM Studios to be open from 9am to 5 or 7pm. All may open or close earlier or later.

The Parks

MAGIC KINGDOM The most popular theme park on the planet offers some 40 attractions, plus restaurants and shops, in a 107-acre package. Its symbol, Cinderella Castle, forms the hub of a wheel whose spokes reach to seven "lands" simulating everything from an Amazonian jungle to colonial America. If you're traveling with little kids, this is the place to go.

EPCOT This 260-acre park (the acronym stands for Experimental Prototype Community of Tomorrow) has two sections. **Future World** is centered on Epcot's icon, a giant geosphere that looks like a big golf ball. Major corporations sponsor the park's 10 themed areas, and the focus is on discovery, scientific achievements, and tomorrow's technologies in areas ranging from energy to undersea exploration. The **World Showcase** is a community of 11 miniaturized nations surrounding a 40-acre lagoon. All of these "countries" have indigenous architecture, landscaping, restaurants, and shops; cultural facets are explored in art exhibits, dance or other live performances, and innovative films. This park definitely appeals more to adults than children. It has few thrill rides, so if that's a requirement, go elsewhere. *Note:* Hiking through this park will often exhaust even the fittest person—some folks say *Epcot* really stands for "Every Person Comes Out Tired"—so we recommend splitting your visit over 2 days, if possible.

DISNEY–MGM STUDIOS   You'll probably spy the Earful Tower—a water tower outfitted with gigantic mouse ears—before you enter this 110-acre park, which Disney bills as "the Hollywood that never was and always will be." You'll find pulse-quickening rides such as the Aerosmith-themed **Rock 'n' Roller Coaster** and the **Twilight Zone Tower of Terror,** plus movie- and TV-themed shows such as Jim Henson's Muppet*Vision 3D, as well as some wonderful street performers. Adults and kids both love it; best of all, it can be done comfortably in a day.

ANIMAL KINGDOM   This 500-acre park opened in 1998, combining animals, elaborate landscapes, and a handful of rides. It's a conservation venue as much as an attraction, so it's easy for most of the animals to escape your eyes here (unlike at Tampa's Busch Gardens, the state's other major animal park). The thrill rides are better at Busch, but Animal Kingdom has much better shows, such as **Tarzan Rocks!** and **Festival of the Lion King.** The park is good for both adults and children, and can be done in a single outing, but if you come on a hot summer day, get here early—or it's unlikely you'll see many of the primo animals, which are smart enough to seek shade.

UNIVERSAL ORLANDO
Universal Orlando is Disney World's number-one competitor in the ongoing Orlando-area "anything you can do we can do better" theme brawl. Although it's a distant second in terms of attendance, it's unquestionably the champion at entertaining teenagers and the older members of the thrill-ride crowd, with two major parks—the original Universal Studios Florida and the newer Islands of Adventure—plus an entertainment district and several resorts.

VISITOR INFORMATION   Located at Universal Boulevard, Orlando, off Interstate 4. For information, call © **800/837-2273** or 407/363-8000, or go to www.universalorlando.com.

TICKET PRICES   A **1-day/1-park** ticket costs $60 (plus 6.5% sales tax!) for adults, $48 for children 3 to 9; a **Universal Orlando Bonus Pass** gets you 5 consecutive days at Universal Studios and Islands of Adventure for $105 (available online only).

OPERATING HOURS   The parks are open 365 days a year, generally from 9am to 6pm, though often later, especially in summer and around holidays, when they're sometimes open until 9pm. Call before you go for exact hours on the days you're visiting.

The Parks
UNIVERSAL STUDIOS FLORIDA   Even with fast-paced, grown-up rides such as **Back to the Future, Terminator,** and **Men in Black Alien Attack,** Universal Studios Florida is fun for kids. It's also a working motion-picture and TV studio, so filming is often going on at Nickelodeon's sound stages or elsewhere in the park. A talented group of actors portraying a range of characters from Universal films usually roam the park. You can do the park in a day, although you'll be a bit breathless when you get to the finish line.

ISLANDS OF ADVENTURE   This 110-acre theme park opened in 1999 and is, bar none, *the* Orlando theme park for thrill-ride junkies. With areas inspired by

Dr. Seuss, Jurassic Park, and Marvel comics, the park successfully combines nostalgia with state-of-the-art technology. Roller coasters roar above pedestrian walkways, while water rides slice through the park. The **Amazing Adventures of Spider-Man** is a 3D track ride that is arguably the best all-around attraction in Orlando, the **Jurassic Park River Adventure** has a 70-foot drop that scared creator Steven Spielberg into jumping ship before going over, and **Dueling Dragons** draws more raves from coaster crazies than any other in Orlando. Unless it's the height of high season, the park can be done in a day. It is not, however, a place for families with young kids: Nine of the park's 14 major rides have height restrictions. If, however, you have teens or are an adrenaline junkie, this is definitely the place for you.

SEAWORLD

A 200-acre marine-life park, SeaWorld explores the deep in a format that combines conservation awareness with entertainment—pretty much what Disney is attempting at Animal Kingdom, but SeaWorld got here first, and its message is subtler and a more integrated part of the experience. The park is fun for everyone from small children to adults (who doesn't like dolphins and whales?) and is easily toured in a single day. The pace is much more laid-back than at Universal or Disney, so it makes for a nice break if you're in the area for several days. SeaWorld has a handful of high-tech water rides such as **Journey to Atlantis** and **Kraken,** but all in all, the park can't compete in this category with Disney and Universal. On the other hand, those parks don't let you discover the crushed-velvet texture of a stingray or the song of a sea lion, not to mention the killer whale **Shamu,** the park's star attraction, and the six other resident orcas.

VISITOR INFORMATION The park entrance is at the intersection of Interstate 4 and State Road 528 (the Bee Line Expwy.), 10 minutes south of downtown Orlando and 15 minutes from Orlando International Airport. For information, call ℂ **800/ 423-8368** or 407/351-3600, or go to www.seaworld.com.

TICKET PRICES A **1-day ticket** costs $62 for ages 10 and over, $48 for children 3 to 9, plus 6% sales tax; kids 2 and under get in free.

OPERATING HOURS The park is usually open daily from 9am to at least 6pm, and later during summer months and holidays, when there are additional shows at night.

KENNEDY SPACE CENTER & THE ASTRONAUT HALL OF FAME

Set amid 150,000 acres of marshy wetlands favored by birds, reptiles, and amphibians, the **Kennedy Space Center** (ℂ **321/449-4444;** www.kennedyspacecenter.com) is where astronauts left for the moon in 1969, where the shuttles have lifted off since 1981, and where America's components of the International Space Station are sent into orbit. Even if you've never really considered yourself a science or space buff, you can't help but be impressed by the achievements this place represents.

Security restrictions mean that most of the center is off-limits, but the **Visitor Complex** is designed to offer a glimpse of the works, with real NASA spacecraft; exhibits; hands-on activities for kids; a daily question-and-answer session with a real astronaut; IMAX 3D movies; a space-shuttle mock-up; a Launch Status Center where presentations are given on current shuttle missions; an outdoor rocket garden displaying now-obsolete Redstone, Atlas, Saturn, and Titan rockets; and more. There's also the obligatory gift shop and several ridiculously pricey stops where you can grab a bite. Plan to eat before or after your visit.

Some people stick to the Visitor Complex, but for a more complete insight into the space age, take the **bus tour** of the larger complex. Buses depart at 15-minute intervals, but the wait to get aboard can easily take an hour or more, so figure this into your planning. Buses stop at three sites—Launch Complex 39, the International Space Station Center, and the Apollo/Saturn V Center—with visitors allowed to spend as much time at each as they like before catching the next bus. You can experience a narrated simulation of the Apollo 8 launch while looking into an actual Mission Control room that was used for the mission. Following the show, you'll enter an enormous hall where an entire Saturn V rocket is on display, held up horizontally by huge metal supports. Numerous exhibits cover various aspects of the Apollo program, and a lunar module hangs from the ceiling above the snack bar.

The **Astronaut Hall of Fame,** located 6 miles west of the Space Center Visitor Complex on State Road 405, near the intersection with U.S. 1, focuses on the heroic human element of the space program and holds the world's largest collection of astronaut memorabilia. Film presentations introduce visitors to the origins of rocketry and to the sheer power of the rockets themselves, while displays of personal memorabilia offer insight into the astronauts' lives. And the displays of NASA memorabilia are just plain awesome: actual Mission Control terminals at which you can sit to access interactive information; Jim Lovell's logbook from Gemini VII; and, most mind-blowing of all, the actual Apollo 14 command module Kitty Hawk, whose plaque bears the inscription "This spacecraft flew to the moon and back January 31–February 9, 1971." 'Nuff said.

But let's get down to brass tacks. The Astronaut Hall of Fame offers one main thing the rest of the KSC Visitors Complex doesn't: the chance to pretend you're an astronaut through various simulations. In the G-force simulator, two wannabe spacemen at a time are strapped tightly into pods at opposite ends of what looks like a giant barbell, which then whirls around on its axis so fast that your cheeks start to flap, just like in the movies. A film projected in the pod simulates a high-speed test flight. Just across the room, the 3D 360 simulator takes a group of passengers on a simulated shuttle flight to the new International Space Station, pitching you backward, forward, sideways, and upside down along the way. At the Walk on the Moon simulator, visitors are strapped into a harness, which is then counterbalanced to their weight so that they can bounce around as if weightless, doing their "one small step for man" imitation. Next door, the Mission to Mars simulator bumps you over the surface of the red planet in a rover. Not bad, but of the group, it's the simulator to skip if you've got limited time. Now the warnings: Simulators are off-limits to folks under 48 inches, which is okay because smaller kids would probably freak out anyway. Also, if you tend to suffer from motion sickness, you'll probably want to avoid everything except the weightlessness simulation. Lastly, on the off-chance you're there on a slow day, be sure to allow at least a few minutes between simulations, even if you've got a cast-iron constitution. Trust us on this one.

Kennedy Space Center is accessible via State Road 405, just off U.S. 1. The Visitor Complex is open daily, except Christmas and certain launch days, from 9am to 5:30pm. The Astronaut Hall of Fame is open daily from 10am to 6:30pm. The last bus tour departs at 2:15pm from the Visitor Complex. Admission to the Visitor Complex is $30 for adults, $20 for children 3 to 11; admission to the Hall of Fame is $18 for adults, $13 for children. Combined tickets are available for $37 for adults, $27 for children. Parking at the Visitor Complex and Hall of Fame is free, but there is no shuttle between the two. Be sure to pick up maps as you enter each branch, and expect to spend most of the day here to get the full experience.

HITTING THE BEACH

Though the Cape Canaveral/Cocoa Beach area doesn't have the spectacular beach culture of Miami, it doesn't lack for pleasant coastline. The following beaches (or "parks," in the local lingo) are located within an easy drive of the port area.

Closest to the cruise ship port and actually part of the larger port complex, the clean, nicely landscaped **Jetty Park,** 400 E. Jetty Rd. (© **321/783-7111**), is the most elaborate and possibly the nicest of the local beaches, perched at a point from which the whole expanse of the Cape Canaveral/Cocoa Beach coastline stretches away to the south. It's some view. A massive stone jetty juts seaward as protection for the mouth of Port Canaveral, and alongside is an elevated platform from which fishermen dangle their lines right into the surf. A snack bar, bathrooms, picnic facilities, a children's playground, and fishing are among the perks here. Parking costs $5 per car. Follow the signs after entering the port area, near where state roads 528 and A1A intersect.

A series of beaches are accessible (and generally signposted) off the A1A heading south from the port. The **Cocoa Beach Pier** area, off the A1A at Meade Avenue, is a great surfing spot with volleyball, an open-air bar, and a party atmosphere. **Lori Wilson Park,** farther south at 1500 N. Atlantic Ave., is another nicely landscaped area on the order of Jetty Park, with bathrooms and showers; a rustic boardwalk with some shaded picnic areas and benches; a nature center; and the Hammock, a .25-mile boardwalk nature trail that winds through ferns, twisted trees, and other *Jurassic Park*–looking foliage, while butterflies flutter by and spiders eye them from their webs. Parking is free.

SHOPPING

Let's be unkind: You could shop here, but why bother? The offerings in Cape Canaveral and Cocoa Beach are mostly the kind of national mall chains that you've probably got at home, so save your energy and dollars for the Caribbean. An exception—as much for the experience as for the goods—is the **Ron Jon Surf Shop,** 4151 N. Atlantic Ave./S.R. A1A (© **321/799-8888**; www.ronjons.com). Inside the blue-and-yellow South Beach–looking Art Deco building is enough au courant beachwear to transform you and a good-size army into surfer dudes. The store also rents beach bikes, body boards, surfboards, kayaks, beach chairs, and other equipment by the hour, day, or week. It's open 24 hours a day, 365 days a year.

WHERE TO STAY

Only a 5-minute drive from the port, **Radisson Resort at the Port,** 8701 Astronaut Blvd./S.R. A1A (© **800/333-3333** or 321/784-0000; www.radisson.com/capecanaveralfl), offers comfortable standard rooms, but families will want to go for the two-room suites that feature a kitchenette with microwave and fridge, a living room with sofa bed and giant TV, and a bedroom with Jacuzzi and second giant TV. The great jungle-motif front courtyard has a large amoeba-shaped pool, while a second courtyard has tennis courts. Cruise passengers who are arriving by car can leave their vehicles in the hotel's lot for free during their cruise and can take advantage of the complimentary Radisson shuttle to and from the port. Rates: $119.

At the other end of the spectrum, the **Inn at Cocoa Beach,** 4300 Ocean Beach Blvd., just off the A1A behind the Ron Jon Surf Shop (© **800/343-5307** or 321/799-3460; www.theinnatcocoabeach.com), is almost entirely couples oriented, presenting itself as more of a personalized inn than a traditional hotel. Almost all of its 50 comfortable rooms face the ocean and include rocking chairs on their balconies, king- or queen-size beds, TVs, and large bathrooms. A bar off the lobby operates on the honor system (just sign for what you take), and two lobby dogs and four tropical birds in cages around the property add to the homey, low-key atmosphere. Rates: $165.

Located near Lori Wilson Park on the A1A (and, for you '60s TV fans, near a street called I Dream of Jeannie Lane), the **Cocoa Beach Hilton,** 1550 N. Atlantic Ave./S.R. A1A (© **800/526-2609** or 321/799-0003; www.cocoabeachhilton.com), is the most upscale of the mainstream beachfront hotels, though it looks like a downtown business hotel that's been transplanted to the seashore. Rooms are spacious but have smallish picture windows only, and none offers a balcony. Rates: $145 to $182.

WHERE TO DINE

In the heart of Cocoa Beach, two of the Fischer Family restaurants, **Bernard's Surf** and **Fischer's Seafood Bar & Grill,** are bunched together at 2 S. Atlantic Ave., at Minuteman Causeway Road (all restaurants at © **321/783-2033;** www.bernardssurf. com). At Bernard's, open since 1948, photos testify to the many astronauts—and Russian cosmonauts, too—who celebrated their safe return to Earth with the restaurant's steak and seafood, the latter provided by the Fischer family's own boats. Fischer's Seafood Bar & Grill is a *Cheers*-like lounge popular with the locals, serving fried combo platters, shrimp, crab-claw meat, and the like. Bernard's main courses: $17 to $25. Fischer's main courses: $14 to $22; sandwiches and salads: $4 to $8. Another casual option is **Rusty's Seafood & Oyster Bar** (on the south side of Port Canaveral harbor at 628 Glen Cheek Dr.), which serves up spicy seafood gumbo, raw or steamed oysters, burgers and sandwiches, pasta, and so on—accompanied by views of the fishing boats and cruise ships heading in and out of the port. Rusty's main courses: $11 to $25; sandwiches and salads: $5 to $9.

The **Mango Tree,** 118 N. Atlantic Ave./S.R. A1A, between North First and North Second streets (© **321/799-0513**), is the most beautiful and sophisticated restaurant in Cocoa Beach, featuring gourmet seafood, pasta, chicken, and Continental dishes in a plantation-home atmosphere. Dinner main courses: $15 to $39.

In downtown Cocoa Beach, the **Heidelberg Restaurant,** 7 N. Orlando Ave./S.R. A1A, at the Minuteman Causeway (© **321/783-6806**), serves German and Continental cuisine such as beef Stroganoff, goulash, roast duck, sauerbraten, and grilled loin pork chops, in a middling-elegant atmosphere. The adjoining Heidi's Jazz Club (see "Port Canaveral After Dark," below) has music Tuesday through Sunday nights. Dinner main courses: $16 to $27.

PORT CANAVERAL AFTER DARK

The **Cocoa Beach Pier,** 401 Meade Ave., off the A1A, a half-mile north of State Road 520 (© **321/783-7549;** www.cocoabeachpier.com), juts out 500 feet over the Atlantic, where it offers a casual beer-and-fruity-drinks atmosphere, an open-air bar with live music most nights, an ice-cream shop, sit-down seafood restaurants, and an arcade, plus beach-equipment rentals and volleyball right next door on the sand.

At the Heidelberg Restaurant (see "Where to Dine," above), **Heidi's Jazz Club,** 7 N. Orlando Ave./S.R. A1A, at the Minuteman Causeway (© **321/783-4559;** www.heidisjazzclub.com), offers live jazz and blues Tuesday through Sunday, with featured performers on selected Friday and Saturday evenings and an open jam session Sunday at 7pm. Check out the website for a schedule of performances. The cover is $3.

4 Tampa & St. Petersburg

Tampa was a sleepy port until Cuban immigrants founded Ybor City's cigar industry in the 1880s. A few years later, Henry B. Plant built a railroad to carry tourists into town and constructed his garish Tampa Bay Hotel (now the Henry B. Plant Museum). During the Spanish-American War, Teddy Roosevelt trained his Rough Riders here and walked the Ybor City streets with Cuban revolutionary José Marti. A land boom in the 1920s gave the city its charming, Victorian-style Hyde Park suburb (now a gentrified area, just across the Hillsborough River from downtown), and the go-go 1980s and 1990s brought skyscrapers, a convention center, a performing-arts center, and lots of shopping and dining options to the downtown area.

On the western shore of Tampa Bay, St. Petersburg is the picturesque and pleasant opposite of busy, industrial, business-filled Tampa. Originally conceived and built primarily for tourists and wintering snowbirds, it's got a nice downtown area, some quality museums, and a few good restaurants.

The Port of Tampa is set amid a complicated network of channels and harbors near historic Ybor City and its deepwater Ybor Channel. Ships sailing from here head primarily to the western Caribbean, the Yucatán, and Central America.

GETTING TO TAMPA & THE PORT

The **Tampa Port Authority** is located at 1101 Channelside Dr. (© **813/905-7678;** www.tampaport.com). The Garrison Seaport Center's Cruise Terminal 2 is located at 651 Channelside Dr.; Terminal 3, 815 Channelside Dr.; Terminal 6, 1333 E. McKay St.; and Terminal 7, 2303 Guy N. Verger Blvd.

BY PLANE **Tampa International Airport** (© **813/870-8700;** www.tampaairport.com) is 5 miles west of downtown Tampa, near the junction of Florida 60 and Memorial Highway. If you haven't arranged for transfers with the cruise line, the port is an easy 30-minute taxi ride away; the fare is about $20 per person via **Yellow Cab** (© **813/253-0121**) or **United Cab** (© **813/253-2424**). You can also take the shared-ride **Bay Shuttle** (© **813/259-9998;** www.tampabayshuttle.com) to the port for $11. **SuperShuttle** (© **800/282-6817** or 727/572-1111; www.supershuttle.com) will take you via town car for $55.

BY CAR Tampa lies 188 miles southwest of Jacksonville, 50 miles north of Sarasota, and 245 miles northwest of Miami. **From I-75 and I-4:** To terminals 2 and 6, take I-4 west to Exit 1 (Ybor City), go south on 21st Street, then turn right on Adamo Drive (Hwy. 60) and then left on Channelside Drive; for Terminal 7, go south on 21st Street (21st St. merges with 22nd St. after crossing Adamo Dr.), turn right on Maritime Boulevard, and then go left on Guy N. Verger to Hooker's Point. **From Tampa International Airport:** To terminals 2 and 6, follow signs to I-275 north, go to I-4 east and then to Exit 1 (Ybor City), go south on 21st Street, turn right on Adamo Drive (Hwy. 60), and then turn left on Channelside Drive; for Terminal 7, use directions from I-75 above. The port has ample parking (at $8 per day), with good security.

EXPLORING TAMPA

Tampa is best explored by car, as only the commercial district can be covered on foot. If you want to go to the beach, you'll have to head to neighboring St. Petersburg.

VISITOR INFORMATION Contact the **Tampa Bay Convention & Visitors Bureau,** 400 N. Tampa St., Suite 2800, Tampa, FL 33602 (© **800/44-TAMPA** or

Tampa

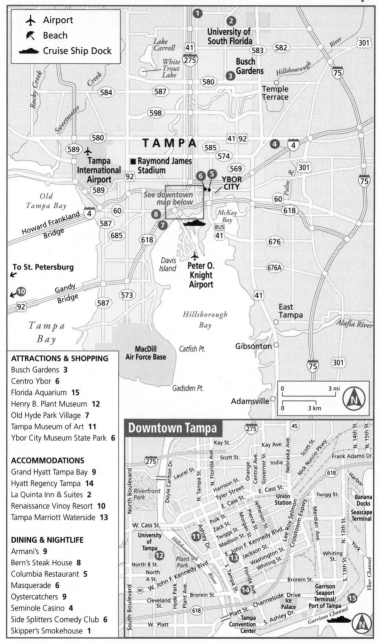

✈ Airport
🏖 Beach
⛴ Cruise Ship Dock

University of South Florida

Busch Gardens

Temple Terrace

Lake Carroll
White Trout Lake

Rocky Creek
Sweetwater Creek

Hillsborough River

T A M P A

Tampa International Airport

Raymond James Stadium

YBOR CITY

See downtown map below

McKay Bay

Old Tampa Bay

Howard Frankland Bridge

To St. Petersburg

Gandy Bridge

Tampa Bay

Davis Island

Peter O. Knight Airport

MacDill Air Force Base

Catfish Pt.

Gadsden Pt.

Gibsonton

East Tampa

Hillsborough Bay

Alafia River

Adamsville

0   3 mi
0   3 km

ATTRACTIONS & SHOPPING
Busch Gardens **3**
Centro Ybor **6**
Florida Aquarium **15**
Henry B. Plant Museum **12**
Old Hyde Park Village **7**
Tampa Museum of Art **11**
Ybor City Museum State Park **6**

ACCOMMODATIONS
Grand Hyatt Tampa Bay **9**
Hyatt Regency Tampa **14**
La Quinta Inn & Suites **2**
Renaissance Vinoy Resort **10**
Tampa Marriott Waterside **13**

DINING & NIGHTLIFE
Armani's **9**
Bern's Steak House **8**
Columbia Restaurant **5**
Masquerade **6**
Oystercatchers **9**
Seminole Casino **4**
Side Splitters Comedy Club **6**
Skipper's Smokehouse **1**

Downtown Tampa

Kay St.
Kay Ave.
Scott St.
Scott St.
Frank Adamo Dr.

North Boulevard
Riverfront Park
Doyle Carlton Dr.
Laurel St.
Harrison St.
N. Florida Ave.
N. Tampa St.
Tyler Street
Orange
Central Ave.
Governor St.
India
Nebraska Ave.
Nick Nuccio Pkwy.
Twiggs St.
Banana Docks
Seascape Terminal

E. Cass St.
Union Station
W. Cass St.
Polk St.
Zack St.
Twiggs St.
Madison St.
Pierce St.
Morgan St.
Jefferson St.
E. John F. Kennedy Blvd.
Jackson St.
Washington St.
Whiting St.
Lee Roy Selmon Crosstown Expwy.
Meridian Ave.
N. 13th St.
N. 14th St.
N. 15th St.
Harbor
York
Whiting St.

University of Tampa
Hillsborough River
Plant Park
John F. Kennedy Blvd.
North B St.
North A St.
Hyde Park Ave.
Plant Ave.
Brorein St.
Cleveland St.
Channelside Drive
Ice Palace
Garrison Seaport Terminal/Port of Tampa
Ybor Channel

South Boulevard
W. Platt
Platt St.
S. Tampa St.
S. Ashley Dr.
S. Florida Ave.
Tampa Convention Center
Garrison Channel

59

813/223-2752; www.visittampabay.com). You can also stop by the **Tampa Bay Visitor Information Center,** 3601 E. Busch Blvd. (© **813/985-3601**), north of downtown, in the Busch Gardens area.

GETTING AROUND Taxis in Tampa do not normally cruise the streets for fares; instead, they line up at public loading places, such as the airport, the cruise terminal, and major hotels. **Yellow Cab** (© **813/253-0121**) and **United Cab** (© **813/253-2424**) charge about $2.25 per mile; the meter starts at $2.

The **Hillsborough Area Regional Transit/HARTline** (© **813/254-HART**) provides regularly scheduled bus service between downtown Tampa and the suburbs. Fares are $1.30 for local service and $2.25 for express routes; exact change is required.

ATTRACTIONS
BUSCH GARDENS

Yes, admission prices are high, but **Busch Gardens,** 3605 E. Bougainvillea Ave. (© **888/800-5447;** www.buschgardens.com), remains Tampa Bay's most popular attraction. The 335-acre family entertainment park features thrill rides, animal habitats, live entertainment, shops, restaurants, and games. The park's safari ranks among the best in the country, with nearly 3,400 animals.

Rhino Rally is the newest addition. It's an off-road adventure in 16-passenger "Ralliers," or Land Rovers, that travel a bumpy course with views of Asian elephants, buffalo, antelope, and more. Hang on to your hat when a flash flood whisks away the bridge—and your vehicle.

Montu, the world's tallest and longest inverted roller coaster, is part of **Egypt,** one of the park's themed areas, which also includes a replica of King Tutankhamen's tomb and a sand-dig area for kids. **Timbuktu** is a replica of the ancient desert trading center, complete with African craftspeople at work. It also features a sandstorm ride, a boat-swing ride, a roller coaster, and a video-game arcade. **Morocco,** a walled area with exotic architecture, has Moroccan crafts demonstrations and a sultan's tent with snake charmers. The **Congo** features white-water raft rides; **Kumba,** the largest steel roller coaster in the southeastern United States; and **Claw Island,** a display of rare white Bengal tigers in a natural setting.

The **Serengeti Plain** is an open area with more than 500 African animals roaming in herds. This 80-acre natural grassy veldt can be viewed from a tram, the **Trans-Veldt Railway,** or the **Skyride,** a sky tram. **Nairobi** is home to a natural habitat for various species of gorillas and chimpanzees, a baby-animal nursery, a petting zoo, reptile displays, and Curiosity Caverns, where visitors can observe animals active at night. **Bird Gardens,** the original core of Busch Gardens, offers rich foliage, lagoons, and a free-flight aviary holding hundreds of exotic birds, including golden and American bald eagles, hawks, owls, and falcons. This area also features **Land of the Dragons,** a children's land and water play area.

The **Crown Colony** area encompasses the **Crown Colony House Restaurant,** overlooking the Serengeti Plain; stables with a team of Clydesdale horses; and the Anheuser-Busch hospitality center. **Akbar's Adventure Tours,** which offers a flight simulator, is located here and offers behind-the-scenes tours.

To get here, take Interstate 275 northeast of downtown to Busch Boulevard (Exit 33) and go east 2 miles to the entrance on 40th Street (McKinley Ave.). Admission is $58 for adults and $48 for kids 3 to 9 (plus 7% tax). Parking is $8. Park hours are at least 10am to 6pm; hours are extended during summer. See the website for exact opening and closing times.

The best fish in Tampa is served at the Grand Hyatt's **Oystercatchers,** 2900 Bayport Dr. (© **813/207-6815;** www.oystercatchersrestaurant.com). Pick your desired fish from a glass-fronted buffet, or enjoy mesquite-grilled steaks, chicken parmigiana, and shellfish. Dinner main courses: $20 to $30.

At **Bern's Steak House,** 1208 S. Howard Ave. (© **813/251-2421**), the steaks are close to perfect. You order according to thickness and weight. Dinner main courses: $21 to $40.

In Ybor City, the nearly 100-year-old **Columbia Restaurant,** 2117 Seventh Ave. E., between 21st and 22nd streets (© **813/248-4961**), occupies an attractive tile-sheathed building that fills an entire city block about a mile from the cruise docks. The aura is pre-Castro Cuba and the food is primarily Cuban. The simpler your dish is, the better it's likely to be. Filet mignon, roasted pork, and black beans, yellow rice, and plantains are flavorful and well prepared. Catch a flamenco show on the dance floor Monday through Saturday. Dinner main courses: $10 to $25.

TAMPA AFTER DARK

Nightfall transforms Ybor City, Tampa's century-old Latin Quarter, into an orgy of music, ethnic food, poetry readings, and after-midnight coffee and dessert. Seventh Avenue, one of Ybor City's main arteries, is closed to all but pedestrian traffic Wednesday through Saturday evenings. The **Masquerade,** 1503 E. Seventh Ave. (© **813/247-3319**), housed in a 1940s movie palace, is just one of the many nightclubs that pepper the streets here. Other options include **Side Splitters Comedy Club,** 12938 N. Dale Mabry Hwy. (© **813/960-1197**), which features stand-up pros. The cover is $10 for general admission and $14 for preferred admission.

In North Tampa, **Skipper's Smokehouse,** 910 Skipper Rd., at Nebraska Avenue (© **813/971-0666;** www.skipperssmokehouse.com), is a favorite evening spot, with an all-purpose restaurant and bar where oysters and fresh shellfish are sold by the dozen and half-dozen. You'll find live music back in the Skipper Dome, a sprawling deck sheltered by a canopy of oak trees.

Northeast of town, at Exit 6 off the I-4, the **Seminole Casino,** 5223 N. Orient Rd., at Hillsborough Avenue (© **813/621-1302;** www.seminolehardrock.com), is open 24 hours every day of the year, offering poker and slots.

For more on Tampa nightlife, the **Tampa/Hillsborough Arts Council** maintains **Artsline** (© **813/229-ARTS**), a 24-hour information service about current and upcoming cultural events.

5 New Orleans

Before Hurricane Katrina, New Orleans was, of course, best known as a world-class party town, but it was also, by some yardsticks, the busiest seaport in the nation, visited by thousands of cargo vessels transporting grain, ore, machinery, and building supplies. In addition, it was one of the fastest-growing cruise ports in the country, with a number of cruise ships bound for ports in the western Caribbean, including Cancún, Playa del Carmen, and Cozumel. While not quite completely back on its feet, at press time officials say the port is back up at 80% of its pre-Katrina traffic, and Norwegian, Royal Caribbean, Carnival, and P & O have all committed to returning to the Crescent City—some as early as September 2006, just a year after the disaster struck.

GETTING TO NEW ORLEANS & THE PORT

The **Julia Street Cruise Terminal Complex** sits at the foot of Julia Street on the Mississippi River, in the Convention Center district, a 10-minute walk or a short streetcar or taxi ride away from the edge of the French Quarter. The **Erato Street Cruise Terminal** (with parking garage) is, at press time, scheduled for completion in September 2006. There are also plans in the works for the new **Poland Avenue Cruise Terminal,** scheduled for completion some time in 2007. For information, call the **Port of New Orleans** at © **504/522-2551** or check out www.portno.com.

BY PLANE   The **Louis Armstrong New Orleans International Airport** (© **504/ 464-0831**) is about 15 miles northwest of the port. Cruise line representatives meet all passengers who have booked transfers through the line. For those who haven't, a taxi to the port costs about $28 and takes about 45 minutes. **Airport Shuttle** (© **866/ 596-2699** or 504/592-0555) runs vans at 10- to 12-minute intervals from outside the airport's baggage claim to the port and other points in town. It costs $13 per passenger each way, free for children under 5.

BY CAR   Take the I-10 downtown. Then take the Tchoupitoulas/St. Peters Street exit, the last one before you cross the Mississippi. Stay to the right, and head toward the New Orleans Convention Center. Turn right onto Convention Center Boulevard, then left onto Henderson Street, which will take you to Port of New Orleans Place. Turn left and continue on to the cruise ship terminal. You can park your car in long-term parking at the port; inquire through your cruise line. You must present a boarding pass or ticket before parking.

EXPLORING NEW ORLEANS

The French Quarter, the most celebrated and oldest part of the city, escaped serious damage from Katrina, and stores and restaurants reopened relatively soon afterward. The Warehouse and Arts District, Faubourg Marigny, Audubon Zoo, Garden District with its impressive homes, Magazine Street, and St. Charles Avenue are also mostly intact. But in outlying areas, away from the popular tourist attractions, community and infrastructure were battered and, at press time, remain in need of serious rebuilding.

VISITOR INFORMATION   Contact or visit the **New Orleans Convention & Visitors Bureau,** 2020 St. Charles Ave., New Orleans, LA 70130 (© **800/672-6124** or 504/566-5011; www.neworleanscvb.com), for brochures, pamphlets, and information.

GETTING AROUND   Taxis are plentiful. If you're not near a taxi stand, call **United Cabs** (© **504/522-9771**) and a car will come in 10 minutes. The meter begins at $2.50, plus $1 for each additional person, and goes to $1.30 per mile thereafter.

At press time, the St. Charles Streetcar is still not in service, but it's expected to be up and running again in November 2006; the other lines are running on a limited schedule and are currently free of charge. You can board the streetcar at the **French Market Riverfront** stop (where Esplanade Ave. meets the river, at the entrance of the French Market). The Riverfront line runs from 7am to 7pm daily. A **Canal Street** route also runs from the Esplanade to the historic former Krauss Building (near Basin St.). It operates from 6:30am to 10pm daily. Visit www.norta.com for updated information.

The city buses are still being phased back into operation at this writing—but those that are running are currently free. For route information, call © **504/248-3900.**

Greater New Orleans

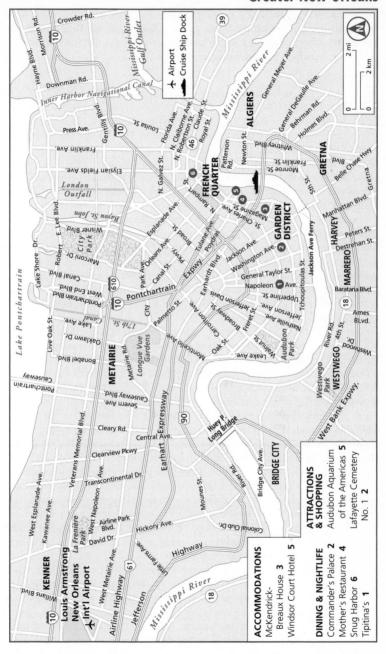

✈ Airport
⚓ Cruise Ship Dock

2 mi

2 km

London Outfall

Bayou St. John

Lake Pontchartrain

FRENCH QUARTER

GARDEN DISTRICT

ALGIERS

GRETNA

HARVEY

MARRERO

METAIRIE

KENNER

WESTWEGO

BRIDGE CITY

Louis Armstrong New Orleans Int'l Airport ✈

Mississippi River Gulf Outlet

Inner Harbor Navigational Canal

Crowder Rd.
Hayne Blvd.
Morrison Rd.
Downman Rd.
Press Ave.
Gentilly Blvd.
Franklin Ave.
Elysian Fields Ave.
Florida Ave.
N. Claiborne Ave.
N. Robertson St.
Claude St.
Royal St.
Louisa St.
N. Galvez St.
N. Rampart
Esplanade Ave.
Broad St.
Tulane Ave.
Canal St.
Orleans Ave.
Park Ave.
City Park Ave.
Pkwy.
Poydras
St. Charles Ave.
Magazine St.
Jackson Ave.
Washington Ave.
General Taylor St.
Napoleon Ave.
Upperline St.
Jefferson Davis Pkwy.
Earhart Blvd.
Broadway St.
Freret St.
Nashville Ave.
Jefferson Ave.
Tchoupitoulas St.
Jackson Ave Ferry
Patterson Rd.
Monroe St.
Franklin St.
Newton St.
Whitney Blvd.
General Meyer Ave.
General DeGaulle Ave.
Behrman Hwy.
Holmes Blvd.
Belle Chase Hwy.
Gretna Blvd.
5th St.
Manhattan Blvd.
Peters St.
Destrehan St.
Barataria Blvd.
Ames Blvd.
Westwood Dr.
4th St.
River Rd.
West Bank Expwy.
Westwego Park
Huey P. Long Bridge
Audubon Park
Walnut St.
Leake Ave.
Oak St.
Carrollton Ave.
Palmetto St.
Monticello Ave.
17th St. Canal
Live Oak St.
Oaklawn Dr.
Bonabel Blvd.
Longue Vue Gardens
Severn Ave.
Metairie Rd.
Causeway Blvd.
Pontchartrain Causeway
Veterans Memorial Blvd.
Clearview Pkwy.
Transcontinental Dr.
Cleary Rd.
Central Ave.
Earhart Expressway
West Esplanade Ave.
Kawanee Ave.
West Napoleon Ave.
West Metairie Ave.
Airline Park Blvd.
La Frontere Park
David Dr.
Hickory Ave.
Airline Highway
Jefferson Highway
Little Farms Ave.
Colonial Club Dr.
Mounes St.
Bridge City Ave.
River Rd.
Williams Blvd.
Wisner Blvd.
E. Lee Blvd.
Robert
Marconi Dr.
Lake Shore Dr.
Canal Blvd.
West End Blvd.
Pontchartrain Blvd.
City

Mississippi River

ACCOMMODATIONS
McKendrick-Breaux House **3**
Windsor Court Hotel **5**

DINING & NIGHTLIFE
Commander's Palace **2**
Mother's Restaurant **4**
Snug Harbor **6**
Tipitina's **1**

ATTRACTIONS & SHOPPING
Audubon Aquarium of the Americas **5**
Lafayette Cemetery No. 1 **2**

65

From Jackson Square (at Decatur St.), you can take a 2¼-mile, 30-minute horse-drawn carriage ride through the French Quarter. **Royal Carriage Tour Co. (© 504/943-8820)** offers private rides for up to four passengers in a Cinderella carriage for $60 a pop, daily from 9am to midnight.

ATTRACTIONS

At press time, the **Audubon Aquarium of the Americas,** 1 Canal St., at the Mississippi River (© **800/774-7394** or 504/581-4629), is closed, but it is scheduled to reopen in the summer of 2006. Visit www.auduboninstitute.org for more information.

Incorporating seven historic buildings connected by a brick courtyard, the **Historic New Orleans Collection,** 533 Royal St., between St. Louis and Toulouse streets (© **504/523-4662;** www.hnoc.org), evokes the New Orleans of 200 years ago. The oldest building in the complex escaped the tragic fire of 1794. The others hold exhibitions on Louisiana's culture and history. All are open Tuesday through Saturday from 10am to 4:30pm. Admission is free.

Founded in 1950, the **New Orleans Pharmacy Museum,** 514 Chartres St., at St. Louis Street (© **504/565-8027**), is just what the name implies. In 1823, the first licensed pharmacist in the United States, Louis J. Dufilho, Jr., opened an apothecary shop here. Today, you'll find old apothecary bottles, voodoo potions, pill tiles, and suppository molds, as well as the old glass cosmetics counter and a jar of leeches, in case you feel the need to be bled. It reopened after Katrina in April 2006 but, at press time, operates only on limited hours. Call ahead to schedule a visit; admission is $5.

Constructed from 1795 through 1799 as the Spanish government seat in New Orleans, the **Cabildo,** 701 Chartres St., at Jackson Square (© **800/568-6968** or 504/568-6968), was the site of the signing of the Louisiana Purchase transfer. The building is now the center of the Louisiana State Museum's facilities in the French Quarter, with a multiroom exhibition that traces the history of Louisiana from exploration through Reconstruction, covering all aspects of life, including antebellum music, mourning and burial customs, immigrants, and the changing roles of women in the South. It's open Tuesday through Sunday from 10am to 4pm; admission is $6 for adults, $5 for students and seniors, and free for children younger than 12.

Also on Jackson Square is the **Presbytère,** 751 Chartres St. (© **800/568-6968** or 504/568-6968), planned as housing for clergy but now serving as a Mardi Gras museum that traces the history of the annual event, with everything from elaborate Mardi Gras Indian costumes to Rex Queen jewelry from the turn of the 20th century on display. A re-creation of a float allows you to pretend you're throwing beads to a crowd on a screen in front of you. The museum is open Tuesday through Sunday from 10am to 4pm; admission is $6 for adults, $5 for seniors and students, and free for children younger than 12. Call ahead before visiting; at press time, the Presbytère hasn't yet reopened, but it is expected to by mid-2006.

The city's **cemeteries** are a bit peculiar: Because New Orleans has always been prone to flooding, bodies have been interred aboveground since the city's earliest days, in sometimes very elaborate tombs that are definitely worth a visit. **St. Louis Cemetery No. 1,** at Basin Street between Conti and St. Louis streets, at the top of the French Quarter, is the oldest extant cemetery (1789) in the area and the most iconic. The acid-dropping scene from *Easy Rider* was shot here, prompting the city to declare that no film would ever, ever, ever be shot again in one of its cemeteries. In the Garden District, **Lafayette Cemetery No. 1,** 1427 Sixth St., right across the street from the Commander's Palace restaurant, is another old cemetery that's been beautifully

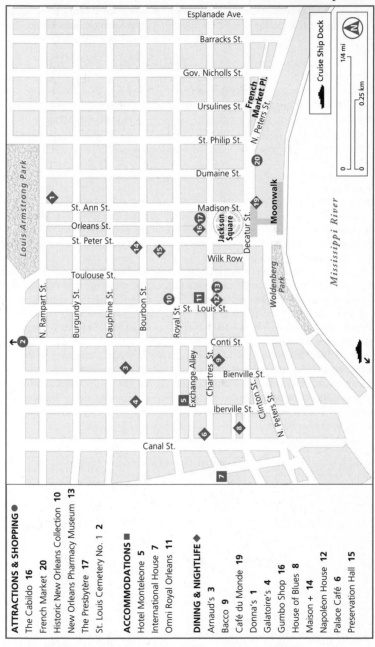

The French Quarter

Esplanade Ave.

Barracks St.

Gov. Nicholls St.

Ursulines St.

St. Philip St.

Dumaine St.

St. Ann St.

Orleans St.

St. Peter St.

Toulouse St.

Madison St.

Jackson Square

Wilk Row

St. Louis St.

Conti St.

Bienville St.

Iberville St.

Canal St.

French Market Pl.

N. Peters St.

Moonwalk

Decatur St.

Mississippi River

Woldenberg Park

Louis Armstrong Park

N. Rampart St.

Burgundy St.

Dauphine St.

Bourbon St.

Royal St.

Exchange Alley

Chartres St.

Clinton St.

N. Peters St.

Cruise Ship Dock

1/4 mi

0.25 km

ATTRACTIONS & SHOPPING ●

The Cabildo **16**
French Market **20**
Historic New Orleans Collection **10**
New Orleans Pharmacy Museum **13**
The Presbytère **17**
St. Louis Cemetery No. 1 **2**

ACCOMMODATIONS ■

Hotel Monteleone **5**
International House **7**
Omni Royal Orleans **11**

DINING & NIGHTLIFE ◆

Arnaud's **3**
Bacco **9**
Café du Monde **19**
Donna's **1**
Galatoire's **4**
Gumbo Shop **16**
House of Blues **8**
Maison + **14**
Napoléon House **12**
Palace Café **6**
Preservation Hall **15**

67

restored. Though both of these cemeteries are usually full of visitors during the day, you should exercise caution when touring, as they've seen some crime over the years.

ORGANIZED TOURS

BY BUS   Gray Line, 1 Toulouse St. (✆ **800/535-7786** or 504/587-0861), offers a 2-hour bus tour that gives a fast overview of the city. The cost is $28 for adults and $13 for children; advance booking is required.

ON FOOT   There are a lot of tours offered in New Orleans, but **Historic Tours** (✆ **504/947-2120;** www.tourneworleans.com) are the ones to take for authenticity. The company offers tours of the French Quarter and the Garden District (including Lafayette Cemetery), plus a cemetery and voodoo tour. Prices are about $12 to $15 per person.

SHOPPING

Despite what you may think while making your first walk down **Bourbon Street,** there's more to New Orleans shopping than tourist traps selling cheap T-shirts, alligator snow globes, and other souvenir items—although there are plenty of those, too (most of them with an absolutely mind-boggling selection of hot sauces). The city's antiques stores are especially good.

On Decatur Street across from Jackson Square, the **French Market** (✆ **504/522-2621;** www.frenchmarket.org) has shops selling candy, cookware, fashion, crafts, candles, toys, and New Orleans memorabilia. There's a lot of kitsch, but some good buys are mixed in, and it's always fun to stroll through and grab a few beignets at **Café du Monde** (see "Snacks & Sweets," below). The French Market is open daily from 10am to 6pm; Café du Monde is open 24 hours.

From Camp Street down to the river on Julia Street, you'll find many of the city's best contemporary **art galleries.** Of course, some of the works are a bit pricey, but there are good deals to be had if you're collecting, and fine art to be seen if you're not.

Magazine Street is the Garden District's premier shopping street, with countless antiques stores, art galleries, boutiques, and crafts shops among the 19th-century brick storefronts and cottages.

WHERE TO STAY

In the Garden District, the **McKendrick-Breaux House,** 1474 Magazine St. (✆ **888/570-1700** or 504/586-1700; www.mckendrick-breaux.com), was built at the end of the Civil War by a wealthy plumber and Scottish immigrant. Today, it's one of the best guesthouses for value. It's been completely restored to its original charming state, and each room furnished with antiques, family collectibles, and fresh flowers. Rates: $145 to $235.

In the Central Business District, just outside the French Quarter and close to the cruise ship terminal, the **International House,** 221 Camp St., just west of Canal Street (✆ **800/633-5770** or 504/553-9550; www.ihhotel.com), is a modern, minimalist hotel housed in an old Beaux Arts bank building. Rooms are simple, with high ceilings, modern bathrooms, ceiling fans, dataports, Wi-Fi, CD players and CDs, and photos and knickknacks that remind you that you're in New Orleans. It's all corridors and dark and chic. Rates: $179 to $229.

Another option in the Central Business District, the **Windsor Court Hotel,** 300 Gravier St. (✆ **800/262-2662** or 504/523-6000; www.windsorcourthotel.com), was named "Best Hotel in North America" by *Condé Nast Traveler,* so feel free to hold it to a high standard. Accommodations are exceptionally spacious and classy, with large bay windows or a private balcony overlooking the river or the city. Downstairs, two corridors display original 17th-, 18th-, and 19th-century art. A plush reading area with international newspapers is on the second floor. Rates: $195 to $450.

About 7 blocks from the cruise ship terminal is the atmospheric **Hotel Monteleone,** 214 Royal St., between Iberville and Bienville streets (© **800/535-9595** or 504/523-3341; www.hotelmonteleone.com), the oldest hotel in the city and also the largest one in the French Quarter (because of its size, you can almost always get a room here, even when other places are booked). Everyone who stays here loves it, probably because its staff is among the most helpful in town. Decor and floor layouts are slightly different in each of the rooms, so ask to see a few different ones, if you care. Rates: $199 to $510.

The **Omni Royal Orleans,** 621 St. Louis St., between Royal and Chartres streets (© **800/843-6664** or 504/529-5333; www.omnihotels.com), is an elegant hotel located smack in the center of the French Quarter. The lobby is a small sea of marble, and the rooms are sizable and elegant, filled with muted tones, plush furniture, and windows that let you gaze out over the Quarter. Service varies but can be exceptional. Rates: $179 to $279.

WHERE TO DINE

New Orleans is essentially one giant restaurant. In 1997, a U.S. survey named it "the fattest city in the country," which makes sense once you've tasted what's being whipped up at 3 or 4 or 8 or 40 of the city's best restaurants. We've profiled many of the best below. Most of them are in the French Quarter.

In business since 1918 and still mighty fine, the legendary **Arnaud's,** 813 Bienville St. (© **504/523-2847;** www.arnauds.com), is set in three interconnected, once-private houses from the 1700s. The restaurant's three Belle Epoque dining rooms are lush with Edwardian embellishments. Especially delicious menu items include snapper or trout topped with crabmeat, filet mignon, oysters stewed in cream, roasted duck in blueberry sauce, and a classic bananas Foster. Dinner main courses: $22 to $38.

Bacco, 310 Chartres St., between Bienville and Conti streets (© **504/522-2426;** www.bacco.com), a great New Orleans bistro, has an elegant setting of pink faux-marble floors and Venetian chandeliers. You can feast on wood-fired pizzas, regional seafood, and such specialties as black-truffle fettuccine and lobster ravioli. Dinner main courses: $16 to $30.

Galatoire's, 209 Bourbon St., at Iberville Street (© **504/525-2021**), feels like a bistro in turn-of-the-20th-century Paris. It's one of the city's most legendary places—and one of the spots that locals head to for a good meal. Menu items include trout (meunière or amandine), rémoulade of shrimp, oysters en brochette, and a savory Creole-style bouillabaisse. Dinner main courses: $18 to $28.

The **Gumbo Shop,** 630 St. Peter St., at Royal Street (© **504/525-1486;** www.gumboshop.com), is a cheap and convenient place to get solid, classic Creole food. The menu reads like a textbook list of traditional local food: red beans and rice, shrimp Creole, crawfish étouffée. The seafood gumbo with okra is a meal in itself, and do try the jambalaya. Dinner main courses: $7 to $19.

Louisiana Heritage Café, in the Bienville House hotel, 320 Decatur St., at Conti Street (© **504/299-8800;** www.bienvillehouse.com), serves contemporary Creole cuisine in a formal setting. Entrees include garlic shrimp and saffron pasta, plus a Gulf fish of the day. Dinner main courses: $10 to $20.

Snacks & Sweets

Café du Monde, 800 Decatur St. ((✆ **504/581-2914**), right on the river, is basically a 24-hour coffee shop that specializes in beignets—square, really yummy French doughnut–type things, served hot and covered in powdered sugar. This is a great spot for people-watching, but if you don't want to wait for a table, you can always get a bag of beignets to go. Grab lots of napkins. Premoistened towelettes would be a good idea, too.

Not far outside the Quarter, **Mother's Restaurant,** 401 Poydras St., at Tchoupitoulas Street ((✆ **504/523-9656;** www.mothersrestaurant.net), has long lines and zero atmosphere, but damn, those po' boys. Customers have been flocking here since 1938 for homemade biscuits and red-bean omelets at breakfast, po' boys at lunch, and softshell crabs and jambalaya at dinner. Everything's between $5 and $21.

Napoleon House, 500 Chartres St., at St. Louis Street ((✆ **504/524-9752;** www.napoleonhouse.com), would have been the home of the lieutenant himself if some locals' wild plan to bring him here to live out his exile had panned out. A landmark 1797 building with an incredible atmosphere, this place is a hangout for drinking and good times, but also serves food. The specialty is Italian muffuletta, with ham, Genoa salami, pastrami, Swiss cheese, and provolone. Dinner main courses: $12 to $24.

Right on the border of the French Quarter, the open kitchen at **Palace Café,** 605 Canal St., between Royal and Chartres streets ((✆ **504/523-1661;** www.palacecafe.com), serves contemporary Creole food with a big emphasis on seafood: catfish pecan meunière, andouille-crusted fish of the day, and lots more. Don't miss the white-chocolate bread pudding. Dinner main courses: $19 to $28.

Outside the Quarter, at the corner of Washington Avenue and Coliseum Street in the Garden District, **Commander's Palace,** 1403 Washington Ave. ((✆ **504/899-8221;** www.commanderspalace.com), still reigns as one of the finest dining choices in not only New Orleans, but the whole United States—the James Beard Foundation voted it the country's best restaurant in 1996. The cuisine is haute Creole. Try anything with shrimp or crawfish, or the Mississippi quail, or . . . oh, just try anything. Dinner main courses: $26 to $38.

NEW ORLEANS AFTER DARK

Life in the "Big Easy" has always been conducive to all manner of nighttime entertainment, usually raucous, and that spirit is still more or less intact. There's a reason why jazz was born in this town.

Most of the places in this section have a cover charge that varies depending on who's performing; some are free.

Do what most people do: Start at one end of **Bourbon Street** (say, around Iberville St.), walk down to the other end, and then turn around and do it again. Along the way, you'll hear R&B, blues, and jazz pouring out of dozens of bars, be beckoned by touts from the numerous strip clubs, and see one tiny little storefront stall after another sporting hand-lettered signs that say OUR BEER IS CHEAPER THAN NEXT DOOR. It's a scene. Bacchanalian? Yes. Will you spend time in purgatory for it? Maybe, but it's loads of fun. Grab yourself a big $2 beer or one of the famous rum-based Hurricanes—preferably in a yard-long green plastic vessel shaped like a Roswell alien—and join the party.

Because of Katrina, at press time, **Preservation Hall,** 726 St. Peter St., just off Bourbon Street (℃ **504/522-2841** during the day, 504/523-8939 after 8pm; www. preservationhall.com), is open only on a limited basis. Check the website for the nightly schedule. If it's open while you're in town, this deliberately shabby little hall, with very few places to sit and no air-conditioning, will inevitably be packed with people there to see the house band, a bunch of mostly older musicians who have been at this for eons. Don't request "When the Saints Go Marching In" 'cause the band won't play it—even classics get to be old smelly hats when you've played them 45,000 times.

Close by, **Maison +,** 641 Bourbon St. (℃ **504/522-8818**), presents authentic and often fantastic Dixieland and traditional jazz. Stepping into the brick-walled room, or even just peering in from the street, takes you away from the mayhem outside. There's a one-drink minimum.

If you're looking to get away from the Bourbon scene and hear some real brass-band jazz, head up to **Donna's,** 800 N. Rampart St., at the top of St. Ann Street (℃ **504/596-6914;** www.donnasbarandgrill.com). There's no better place to hear the authentic sounds that made New Orleans famous. The cover varies but is always reasonable.

Jazz, blues, and Dixieland pour out of the nostalgia-laden bar and concert hall **Tipitina's,** way out in Uptown at 501 Napoleon Ave. (℃ **504/891-8477;** www. tipitinas.com).

House of Blues, 225 Decatur St. (℃ **504/529-2583;** www.hob.com), is one of the city's largest live-music venues. Patrons stand and move among the several bars that pepper the club. There's also a restaurant.

One block beyond Esplanade, on the periphery of the French Quarter, **Snug Harbor,** 626 Frenchman St. (℃ **504/949-0696;** www.snugjazz.com), is a jazz bistro, a classic spot to hear modern jazz in a cozy setting. Sometimes R&B combos and blues are added to the program. There's a full dinner menu in the restaurant, but only appetizers are served in the club.

6 Alternative Home Ports

Whether it's because of convenience or an aversion to flying (that is, the cost of flying or the fear of it), the cruise lines realize that lots of you love the idea of hopping on a cruise within driving distance of your home. That's why you can now cruise to the Caribbean from the big Florida cruise ports or from ports up and down the Eastern seaboard and throughout the Gulf of Mexico. In addition to the primary alternative ports below, ships are sailing from Houston, Tex. (www.portofhouston.com); Norfolk, Va. (www.cruisenorfolk.org); Baltimore, Md. (www.mpa.state.md.us); Jacksonville, Fla. (www.jaxport.com); and Philadelphia, Pa. (www.cruisephilly.com).

GALVESTON, TEXAS

Galveston is an island some 50 miles south of Houston, just off the mainland. It was one of the first big alternative ports developed for Caribbean-bound megaships. Ships departing from Galveston can reach the open sea in about 30 minutes, compared to the several hours of lag time from the Port of Houston—which, like New Orleans, sits inland, on the edge of the Houston Ship Channel, above Galveston Bay. (The Port of Houston does have one advantage: It's closer to the airports. It takes 45–90 min. to travel between the Port of Galveston and the airports, depending on which airport you're using. Currently, Royal Olympia Cruises' *Olympia Voyager* and NCL's *Norwegian Sea* are sailing out of Houston to the western Caribbean.)

Until recently, the Port of Galveston offered just one 132,000-square-foot cruise ship terminal, but in 2002, a warehouse adjacent to Terminal 1 was converted into a second terminal, offering facilities and services for 4-, 5-, 7-, 10-, 11-, and 12-night sailings. Within walking distance of the terminal is the historic Strand District, Galveston's revitalized downtown, with shops, art galleries, museums, and eateries lining its quaint brick streets.

GETTING TO GALVESTON & THE PORT

The **Texas Cruise Ship Terminals on Galveston Island** is at Harborside Drive and 25th Street. It's reached via I-45 south from Houston. For information, call © **409/766-6113** or check out www.portofgalveston.com.

BY PLANE   You'll fly into one of two Houston airports: **William P. Hobby Airport** (south of downtown Houston, and about 31 miles, or a 45-min. drive, from the terminal) or **George Bush Intercontinental Airport** (just north of downtown Houston, and about 54 miles, or an 80-min. drive, from the terminal). Information on both is available at www.houstonairportsystem.org. Bush is the larger airport and is international.

If you've arranged air transportation and/or transfers through the cruise line, a cruise line representative will direct you to shuttle buses that will take you to the port. Taxis are also available. **United Cab** (© **713/699-0000**) charges $85 per carload from Hobby Airport and $143 from George Bush Intercontinental Airport. The following taxi companies provide service from the port to the airports only (not the other way around): **Busy Bee** (© **409/762-6666**), which charges $85 to Hobby Airport and $125 to George Bush (each additional passenger is $5), and **Yellow Cab Company** (© **409/763-3333**), with rates of $85 to Hobby and $135 to Bush. **Galveston Limousine Service** (© **800/640-4826** or 409/744-5466) provides the same service, charging $30 per person to/from Hobby and $35 to/from Bush. Round-trip rates are $50 and $60, respectively. All three companies require reservations.

BY CAR   Interstate 45 is the main artery for those arriving from the north. To get to the terminals, follow I-45 south to Exit 1C (at Harborside Dr./Hwy. 275); it's the first exit after the causeway. Turn left (east) onto Harborside Drive and continue for about 5 miles to the cruise terminals.

Long-term lot parking at the port is $45 for a 4-night cruise, $50 for a 5-night cruise, $70 for a 7-night cruise, $80 for a 10-night cruise, $85 for an 11-night cruise, and $90 for a 12-night cruise. The fee is $10 to $15 more for limited covered parking. The lots are a half-mile from the cruise ship terminals. Shuttle buses transport passengers between the lots and the terminals, where porters are available to carry luggage.

NEW YORK CITY

Up until the 1950s, New York City was one of the biggest ports in the world for both cargo and passenger vessels, its famous skyline and the Statue of Liberty offering a dramatic approach that no other ports could match. So many ships parked their noses against Manhattan's west side that it was dubbed Luxury Liner Row. All the greats were there, from the *Normandie* to *Queen Mary* and *France,* their horns echoing across Midtown. All that ended when the jet plane put the liners out of business, allowing people to cross the Atlantic in half a day rather than a week. Never again would the Port of New York see as much traffic, though today it's reclaiming a bit of its former glory as a cruise home port.

Joining a handful of lines that have long based ships in New York for summer and/or fall cruises to Bermuda, New England, and Canada are several Caribbean-bound ships, including NCL's *Norwegian Dawn* (which offers 7-night round-trip cruises year-round to Florida and the Bahamas).

Like the ports of New Orleans, San Francisco, and Charleston, New York's cruise ship piers are in the heart of town. Passengers are a short stroll away from 42nd Street and Times Square, and a slightly longer one from Fifth Avenue, Central Park, and many other sights. Much of the Big Apple can be explored on foot (Manhattan is only about 2 miles wide by 13 miles long, with most visitors remaining in its bottom half). If you need a break, hail one of the ubiquitous yellow taxis (meters start at $2.50, with a 50¢ surcharge after 8pm, and increase 40¢ every ⅕-mile or 20¢ per 2 min. when stuck in traffic) or hop on the red double-decker tour buses that crisscross the city and are operated by **Gray Line** (© **800/669-0051** or 212/445-0848; www.graylinenew york.com); you can join the tour loop at the Circle Line terminal just a few steps south of the cruise ship piers.

GETTING TO NEW YORK CITY & THE PORT

The historic (if a bit ugly) **New York City Passenger Ship Terminal** (© **212/246-5450;** www.nypst.com) is stretched out along the Hudson River between 46th and 54th streets in Manhattan. It's reached via a vehicle ramp located at 55th Street off the West Side Highway. It's frequently crowded on turnaround days, though the city has begun a multimillion-dollar project to reduce roadway congestion and improve passenger circulation. Parking is available for $24 a day.

Two other pier facilities have come online in New York over the past few years to handle the growing ship traffic. Down in the old blue-collar neighborhood of Red Hook, the **Brooklyn Cruise Terminal** (© **718/858-3450;** www.nycruiseterminal. com/bct_info.cfm) opened for business in April 2006. Located just across New York Harbor from Lower Manhattan and Governors Island (once site of the largest U.S. Coast Guard base in the world), the port is easily accessible to locals driving by car, as well as to visitors flying into Kennedy, LaGuardia, and Newark airports. While Red Hook itself is industrial and gritty (if rapidly gentrifying), it's just minutes from picturesque Colonial-era Brooklyn Heights and the great expanse of the Brooklyn Bridge. The Brooklyn terminal's most high-profile ship is the *Queen Mary 2,* which home-ports here on the western end of her transatlantic crossings. From wherever you're driving, get onto the Brooklyn-Queens Expressway and exit at Hamilton Avenue (Exit 26) onto the service road. Stay to the left and make a left-U-turn at the intersection of Hamilton and Clinton Street/Ninth Street; then continue west along the westbound Hamilton Avenue service road. Take the service road to its end at Van Brunt Street. Turn left, travel 2 blocks, and then turn right onto Bowne Street to enter the terminal. Parking is $18 per day.

Across the river in Bayonne, N.J., **Cape Liberty Cruise Port** (www.bayonnenj.org/ royal.htm) opened in 2004 as a homeport for Royal Caribbean and Celebrity vessels. We know: Sailing from Bayonne doesn't sound as romantic as sailing from Manhattan, but the Cape Liberty Cruise Port, like the Brooklyn terminal, does have the advantage of being less congested—and of offering a great view of the Manhattan skyline and the Statue of Liberty. The 430-acre man-made peninsula was constructed in the late 1930s as a port for international shipping, and was then used by the U.S. Navy from 1942 to 2002. Located just off the New Jersey Turnpike and I-278, and approximately 15 minutes from the Newark airport, it's easily accessible to those coming from New Jersey, Long Island, and the New York City boroughs of Brooklyn and Staten Island. From the New Jersey Turnpike, take Exit 14A and follow signs for Route 440 south. Follow Route 440 to Cape Liberty Terminal Boulevard, which will be on your left. Parking is $12 per day.

BY PLANE   If you're coming in by plane, you'll fly into one of three New York–area airports. **John F. Kennedy International Airport** is east of Manhattan in the borough of Queens, 15 miles from Midtown Manhattan and a 30- to 60-minute drive from the piers, depending on traffic. **LaGuardia Airport** is also in Queens, 8 miles from Midtown and a 20- to 40-minute drive from the piers. **Newark International Airport** is west of Manhattan in New Jersey, about 16 miles from Midtown and a 30- to 60-minute drive from New York. Information on all three is available at www.panynj.gov. Kennedy and Newark are the larger airports and accommodate both domestic and international flights.

If you've arranged air transportation and/or transfers through the cruise line, a cruise line representative will direct you to shuttle buses that take you to whichever port your ship is sailing from. Yellow taxis are usually lined up in great numbers at the airports and can take you to any of the ports or your hotel. From JFK to Manhattan, taxis charge a flat fee of $45 per carload, plus tolls and tip; there is no flat fee from Newark or LaGuardia—you pay the standard metered rate: $2.50 just to get going, then 40¢ for every ⅕ mile (about 4 blocks) thereafter, with additional surcharges for peak hours and after 8pm. Don't forget about tolls and tip—and if you take a yellow cab to Newark, a $15 surcharge is added to the metered fare.

Carmel Car Service (© **800/9-CARMEL** or 212/666-6666; www.carmellimo. com) charges $31 per carload from Manhattan (including the cruise ship piers) to LaGuardia, $46 to JFK, and $45 to Newark; if you're heading into Manhattan from the airport, the rates are $28 from LaGuardia, $40 from JFK, and $42 from Newark. Book a few days in advance to avoid surcharges. Freelance (also known as "gypsy") drivers may solicit you in the airport; to avoid being gouged, it's better to stick with a car service or the official New York yellow cabs.

SuperShuttle (© **212/258-3826;** www.supershuttle.com) shared-ride vans are another way to get between the airports and the piers. Per-person fares are $15 to LaGuardia and $19 to JFK or Newark (so it's no bargain if you're a group of three or more). Twenty-four-hour advance reservations are recommended.

BY CAR   Manhattan's Henry Hudson Parkway/West Side Highway is the main artery into the port. To get to the terminals at 48th, 50th, and 52nd streets, cars should enter via the vehicle ramp at 54th Street, directly off the highway.

Long-term parking at the port is $24 a day if parking for multiple days, or $22 for up to 10 hours. If you want to park for 9 days or more, the monthly rate is $180. The lots are on top of the three terminals, with escalators leading down.

CHARLESTON, SOUTH CAROLINA

One of the most important seaports and cultural centers of America's colonial period, Charleston is one of the best-preserved cities in the U.S., boasting 73 pre–Revolutionary War buildings, 136 structures from the late 18th century, and more than 600 buildings built before the 1840s. Horse-drawn carriages carry visitors through gas-lit cobblestone streets, as the fragrances of jasmine and wisteria fill the air. No small wonder the city was named one of the "Top 10 Most Romantic Ports of Call" by *Porthole Cruise Magazine* in 2006.

Cruise passengers can walk right from the docks to the heart of the city. Highlights include the **Old City Market,** at East Bay and Market streets, a 3-block collection of boutiques and crafts stalls; **Fort Sumter,** in Charleston Harbor, where the first shots of the Civil War were fired; and innumerable antiques-filled colonial homes and manicured gardens.

At press time, Carnival's *Carnival Victory,* NCL's *Norwegian Majesty,* and Clipper's *Nantucket Clipper* offer sailings from Charleston. Other vessels, including Holland America's *Maasdam,* Princess's *Sea Princess,* and Royal Caribbean's *Constellation,* are also using Charleston as a port of call on several coastal itineraries.

GETTING TO CHARLESTON & THE PORT

The Port of Charleston's 18,000-square-foot cruise ship terminal is located in the peninsular city at 196 Concord St., at the foot of Market Street, in the heart of the historic district. For information, visit www.port-of-charleston.com.

BY PLANE   The **Charleston International Airport** (© 843/767-7009; www.chs-airport.com) is located in North Charleston, 12 miles from the cruise ship terminal. If you've made arrangements for transfers through your cruise line, a representative will meet your arriving flight and direct you to shuttle buses. Taxis are available at a rate of approximately $20 for one or two passengers, with each additional person charged an extra $12. Shuttle service is available through the **Airport Limo/Taxi Association** (© 800/750-1311 or 843/607-5456), but because the per-person rate is $12, you may as well get a taxi.

BY CAR   The Port of Charleston is located 2 miles from the terminus of I-26. **From I-95 north or south,** take I-26 east toward Charleston. Exit at East Bay Street/Morrison Drive (Exit 219B) and turn left at the bottom of the ramp. Continue onto Morrison Drive, which becomes East Bay Street. Turn left onto Market Street, then right onto Concord Street. **From U.S. Highway 17 north,** after crossing the Ashley River Bridge bear right onto Lockwood Boulevard. Turn left on Calhoun Street, right on East Bay Street, left on Market Street, and right on Concord Street. **From U.S. Highway 17 south,** take the East Bay Street exit and turn left at the bottom of the ramp, then left onto Market Street and right onto Concord Street. **From Charleston Airport,** exit onto I-526 and connect to I-26 (Charleston). Continue to East Bay Street/Morrison Drive (Exit 219B) and turn left at the bottom of the ramp. Continue onto Morrison Drive, which becomes East Bay Street. Turn left on Market Street and right on Concord Street. Long-term parking is $15 per day for standard-size cars, $30 per day for vehicles over 20 feet long.

SAN JUAN, PUERTO RICO

In addition to being the embarkation port for a number of ships, San Juan is a major port of call, so see "Puerto Rico," in chapter 5, for all information.

5

The Ports of Call

The Caribbean is the classic cruise destination, tailored to people who want nice white-sand beaches, Tiki bars serving tropical drinks, some hot island music, and sun, sun, sun. Culture and history also have their place. In general, western Caribbean itineraries offer opportunities for visiting the ruins of Mayan cities and temple sites on the mainland, while eastern Caribbean itineraries are more likely to dock at ports that offer reminders of British, French, Spanish, and Dutch colonial history. Panama Canal itineraries mix the lore of that massive construction effort with access to rich Central American culture. And, of course, there's gorgeous scenery all over the Caribbean, from the lush jungles of Dominica to the arid moonscape of Aruba.

Here's the good news: There are hardly any lousy Caribbean islands, though, depending on your likes and dislikes, you'll appreciate some more than others. Some—especially St. Thomas and Nassau—are much more touristy and commercial than others, though their large variety of bustling stores will appeal to shoppers. Others—Virgin Gorda, St. John, Jost Van Dyke, and Les Saintes, for instance—are quieter and more natural, and will appeal to those who want to walk along a calm beach or take a drive along a lonely, winding road amid lush tropical foliage. Destinations like St. Barts and Bequia offer a low-key yachting-port atmosphere, while ports like Key West and Cozumel are all about whooping it up.

1 Port Strategies & Tips

SHORE EXCURSIONS VS. GOING IT ON YOUR OWN

Participating in the shore excursions offered by the cruise lines can be a wonderful and carefree way to get to know the islands and to experience everything from island tours, snorkeling, and sailing excursions (often with a rum-punch party theme) to more physically challenging pursuits like bicycle tours, hiking, kayaking, and horseback riding. But do you really *need* to sign up for them? The answer is: not everywhere. At some ports—Aruba, Bequia, Curaçao, and San Juan, Puerto Rico, for instance—your best bet is experiencing the island on your own. In this chapter, we'll advise you on which islands are good bets for solo exploring; tell you whether you should go it on foot or by taxi, motor scooter, ferry, or some other form of transportation; and detail the best sights to see. One downside to exploring independently is that you'll be forgoing the kind of narrative you'd get from a guide, so you may miss out on some of the historical, cultural, and other nuances of a particular island. On the other hand, you may find your own fascinating details, things that an organized tour might pass over. In some ports, touring on your own could be an inefficient use of your time, involving lots of hassles and planning, maybe costing more, and possibly incurring some risk (because of poor roads or driving conditions, for instance). In these cases,

> **Tips Booking Shore Excursions Early**
>
> If you want to arrange a private custom-designed excursion for your family or group of friends, or just want to save a little money on a snorkeling trip, Florida-based **Port Promotions** (www.shoreexcursions.com) organizes shore excursions and allows you to book them online as late as a week before your cruise. You'll get a confirmation via e-mail. Port Promotions often uses the same tour companies that the cruise lines do, though groups tend to be smaller and rates for Caribbean tours are about 10% cheaper. If you change your mind before the excursion, you can e-mail or call Port Promotions to get a refund.

the shore excursions offered by the cruise lines are the way to go. Under each port review, we'll describe the best excursions available. See p. 79 for a chart rating various aspects of each island—dining, shopping, activities close to the port, and beaches and watersports. This is a good tool for deciding which ports interest you at a glance.

Keep in mind that **shore excursion prices** vary from line to line, even for the exact same tour; the prices we've listed are typical and are adult rates; children's rates for many excursions are also offered, so just ask. Also note that some cruise lines may not offer all these tours, while others may offer even more. In some cases, the excursions fill up fast, especially on the megaships, so don't dawdle in signing up. When you receive your cruise documents, you'll probably receive a pamphlet with a listing of the excursions offered for your itinerary. Look it over, make your selections, and sign up ASAP. A few lines, like Royal Caribbean, Celebrity, and Princess, allow you to sign up before your cruise, using your booking code on their websites; where this is not the case, sign up on the first or second day of your cruise. Sometimes if a tour offered by your ship is booked up, you can try to book it independently once you get to port. The popular Atlantis submarine tour, for example—offered at Grand Cayman, Nassau, St. Thomas, and other islands—usually has an office or agent in the cruise terminals or nearby.

If you want to rent a car in port, make reservations in advance. **Avis** (© **800/ 331-1212;** www.avis.com), **Budget** (© **800/472-3325;** www.drivebudget.com), and **Hertz** (© **800/654-3001;** www.hertz.com) all have offices on most of the Caribbean islands in this chapter; **Dollar** (© **800/800-4000;** www.dollar.com) and **National** (© **800/227-7368;** www.nationalcar.com) are less well represented in the region. See "Getting Around" in the individual port listings to see which companies have offices there. Also note that in certain ports, we advise against renting at all.

DOCKING, DOLLARS & OTHER PORT DETAILS

ARRIVING IN PORT   Most cruise ships arrive in port sometime before 10am, though this will vary slightly from line to line and port to port. If you're a U.S. citizen, you'll rarely have to clear Customs or Immigration because your ship's purser has your passport or other ID and will have done all the paperwork for you. When local officials give the word, you just go ashore. In most cases, you can walk down the gangway right onto the pier, but occasionally (if your ship is too big for the island's docks, for example, or if you've arrived on a busy day and all the pier space is full) your ship will have to anchor offshore and ferry passengers to land via a small boat called a tender. In either case, you might have to wait in line to get ashore, but the wait will be longer if you have to tender in. Once ashore, even if you've come by tender, you aren't stuck there—tenders run back and forth on a regular basis, so you can return to the ship at any time for lunch, a nap, or whatever. Tenders all look pretty much alike, so you might be confused as to which one's heading to your ship, but officers are on duty to check your ID and make sure you get to the right boat.

SCHEDULING YOUR TIME ASHORE   All shore excursions are carefully organized to coincide with your time in port. If you're going it on your own, you can count on finding taxi drivers at the pier when your ship docks. In most cases, it's a good idea to arrange with the driver to pick you up at a certain time to bring you back to the port. In most ports, you can also rent a car, moped/scooter, or bicycle to get around.

CALLING HOME   Prices for calling home from a cruise ship are sky high ($4–$15 a min.), so it's a better idea to call from land when you're in port. Most phones in port will take any phone card, but for some phones you'll need to purchase a local calling card from a vendor. We've included information on where to find phones in all the port reviews. Country codes are as follows: United States and Canada, 1 (from most Caribbean islands, it's just like dialing between states); Australia, 61; New Zealand, 64; the United Kingdom, 44; and the Republic of Ireland, 353. Another option is using your ship's Internet center to keep in touch with folks at home via e-mail. It'll still cost you, but not nearly as much as you'd spend on phone calls. You'll also find Internet centers close to the docks in most ports.

SHOPPING TIPS   You'll find it all here, from jewelry (lots and lots of jewelry), perfume (ditto), and electronics to indigenous arts and handicrafts to the cheesiest tourist gimcracks. Prices vary by port. Some—such as the U.S. Virgin Islands, St. Barts, St. Martin, and Aruba—are pretty pricey, while ports like Cozumel, Jamaica, and the Grenadines are cheaper. **Duty-free merchandise** can save you as little as 5% to as much as 50%, so if you have particular goods you're thinking of buying this way, it pays to check prices at your local discount retailer before you leave home so you'll know whether you're really getting a bargain. Many ports offer particularly good deals on **liquor,** though keep in mind that you'll pay tax when coming back into the U.S. if you buy more than your legal limit (see p. 28 for more Customs info).

When shopping, be aware that some items you may see offered may not be allowed by U.S. Customs. You might be eyeing that gorgeous piece of **black-coral jewelry,** for instance, but laws prohibiting the trade in endangered species make it illegal to bring many products made from coral and other marine animals back to the United States. (Remember, corals aren't rocks: They're living animals—a single branch of coral contains thousands of tiny coral animals, called polyps.) Sea turtles, too, are highly endangered, and sea horses, while not yet protected by laws, are currently threatened with extinction. The shopkeeper selling items made from these creatures probably won't tell

---

Tips **Don't Forget Cash When Going Ashore**

It's happened to both of us and it's happened to our friends, so it can happen to you, too: After a few days of living cash-free aboard ship, it doesn't even cross your mind to grab the greenbacks when you're going ashore. You get there and realize you're penniless. It's soooo frustrating, especially if you've had to take a tender in from offshore. Don't let it happen to you.

Frommer's Ratings at a Glance: Caribbean Ports of Call

1 = poor 2 = fair 3 = good 4 = excellent 5 = outstanding

Port	Review on Page	Overall Experience	Shore Excursions Activities	Close to Port	Beaches & Watersports	Shopping	Dining/Bars
Antigua	87	4	3	4	5	2	4
Aruba	94	5	3	4	5	4	4
Freeport, Bahamas	109	3	2	2	3	3	3
Nassau, Bahamas	102	4	3	4	4	3	3
Barbados	114	4	3	3	3	3	3
Belize	120	4	5	2	4	2	3
Bequia	128	4	2	4	4	2	4
Bonaire	134	3	4	3	5	2	3
Tortola, British Virgin Islands	144	4	3	3	3	2	3
Virgin Gorda, British Virgin Islands	148	5	3	4	4	2	3
Cozumel, Mexico	154	4	5	4	2	4	3
Curaçao	164	4	3	4	2	3	3
Dominica	170	3	4	3	2	3	3
Grand Cayman	177	5	5	4	5	4	3
Grand Turk	181	5	4	5	5	5	3
Grenada	186	5	3	4	3	3	3
Guadeloupe	192	4	4	5	4	4	5
Montego Bay, Jamaica	205	4	5	4	3	3	3
Ocho Rios, Jamaica	200	4	5	4	3	2	3
Key West	208	4	4	5	2	3	4
Les Saintes	216	4	2	5	3	2	3
Martinique	221	4	3	3	4	3	3
Nevis	230	4	1	4	4	2	2
Playa del Carmen, Mexico	160	4	5	3	3	2	3
San Juan, Puerto Rico	236	5	2	5	3	4	4
St. Barts	250	4	3	4	5	4	4
St. Croix, U.S. Virgin Islands	297	4	4	4	4	5	3
St. John, U.S. Virgin Islands	292	4	3	4	4	2	2
St. Kitts	256	3	3	1	3	2	3
St. Lucia	261	4	4	3	4	2	3
St. Martin	268	3	3	4	4	4	3
St. Thomas, U.S. Virgin Islands	284	4	4	4	4	5	3
Tobago	281	4	3	1	4	2	2
Trinidad	278	2	2	1	2	2	3

you they're questionable from a Customs standpoint, but the Customs agent sure will, and may fine you or at the least confiscate the item if he catches you with it. Better to just buy a cheap underwater camera and take pictures of underwater beauties on a snorkeling expedition—you get the memories, the evidence, and a little exercise to boot.

Cuban cigars are also prohibited by U.S. Customs. You'll see them all over the islands, but be aware that, *legally* speaking, you have to smoke 'em before you head for home.

REBOARDING   Most passengers start heading back to the ship around 4pm or not much later than 5pm. By 6pm, you're often sailing off to your next destination. In some cases—for instance, in New Orleans, Nassau, St. Barts, and the British Virgin Islands—the ship may stay in port until after midnight so that passengers can stay ashore and enjoy the island's nightlife. When actually walking back aboard, you'll have to present your shipboard ID to be scanned (except aboard some small ships, which are less formal).

If a shore excursion runs late, the ship will be held until the excursion's participants are back on board. It occasionally happens, though, that a passenger goes off on his or her own, has a little too much fun, and misses the boat. If it happens to you, don't panic: The cruise line's port agent (whose offices will be at or close to the pier) will be able to get you back aboard, though it'll cost you—you'll have to either charter a boat or pay for a flight to the next port of call.

2 A Brief History of the Caribbean

Caribbean history reads like a Hollywood blockbuster—brutal conquests, devastating plagues, swashbuckling pirates, new frontiers, monumental sea battles, slave insurrections, and violent revolutions. Grab your popcorn.

PRE-COLUMBIAN CULTURES   Every schoolchild learns that in 1492 Columbus sailed the ocean blue. He was a Johnny-come-lately, of course—people lived in the Caribbean for hundreds, even thousands, of years before Europeans arrived. Three major groups, all originally from South America, were there when Columbus arrived.

The least advanced of the native peoples, the **Ciboney,** were probably the first to arrive. Living primarily in rock shelters and caves, they formed small family groups, hunted turtles and reptiles, and collected shellfish, wild fruits, and herbs. Their rudimentary tools were made of stone.

The more advanced **Arawak** and **Carib** peoples had frequent contact with each other and shared many of the same material technologies. They farmed, hunted, and fished, and both groups used similar methods to construct canoes, build huts, weave cloth, and make pottery. Both peoples cultivated root plants—yucca, yams, arrowroot, peanuts, peppers, and gourds—and seed crops like maize, beans, and squash. Pineapple and guava, shellfish, fish, iguanas, birds, and snakes provided additional sustenance. Men generally hunted and fished, while women farmed, cooked, wove cloth, and made household pottery and baskets.

The Arawak, by all accounts, were peaceful, gentle, and friendly. Women enjoyed considerable status, religion was based on the belief that spirits inhabited both humans and natural objects, and islands were divided into provinces ruled by chiefs.

Carib authority was less centralized. Independent villages were presided over by village chiefs, who came together to elect war chiefs for each island. Men lived together in communal houses and kept their wives, who they treated as servants, in separate huts. Because they resisted Spain's efforts to enslave them, the Carib were vilified as bloodthirsty savages by the Spanish. In fact, the word *cannibal* comes from the Spanish name for the tribe—*caribal.* There is no evidence that the Carib practiced cannibalism—the Spanish may have made the claim to justify their assault on the tribe. The Carib were more aggressive than the Arawak, who were frequently on the receiving end of Carib raids. However, when the French and English settled the Lesser Antilles (most of the Caribbean islands except Cuba, Jamaica, and Hispaniola) in the 1630s, the Carib were friendly and provided food for the starving adventurers—they became violent only after the Europeans attacked them.

EUROPEAN "DISCOVERY" OF THE ISLANDS   On October 12, 1492, Columbus became the first European to reach the New World, landing on Watling's Island in the Bahamas. This exploratory first voyage was followed in 1493 by a second and much larger expedition to establish a permanent foothold in the islands. On his second expedition, along with 1,500 men, Columbus brought horses, sheep, cattle, and hogs, as well as plants grown in Europe such as wheat, barley, grapes, and sugar cane. Landing first on Dominica, the fleet passed through and named the islands of the Lesser Antilles before arriving in Hispaniola (where Haiti and the Dominican Republic are located) in November 1494. Before returning to Spain, Columbus sighted Jamaica and explored Cuba.

ENSLAVEMENT OF THE INDIANS   The Spanish crown distributed land on the islands to individual settlers, who were expected to cultivate it for 4 years. In return, they received the use of the property in perpetuity. By the time Columbus returned on his third voyage in 1498, the system had been distorted considerably, with Indian communities forced to work the land as slave laborers. Without this slave system, the colonial economies certainly would have failed. The Spanish not only enslaved the local population, but eventually, if unintentionally, almost completely obliterated it by bringing in diseases to which the native islanders had no immunity.

DISEASE & DECIMATION   Prior to the 15th century, the peoples of Europe and Africa rarely mingled, and the indigenous peoples of the Americas existed in total isolation. Consequently, a distinctive disease environment developed on each continent. Until the Europeans and Africans arrived, a host of illnesses—among them smallpox, measles, typhus, yellow fever, malaria, and tuberculosis—were unknown in the New World. The native peoples had no natural immunity to these diseases, and when exposed to them, they died in staggering numbers. In 1492, as many as six million Arawak and Carib Indians lived in the Caribbean. Within 20 years, almost all were dead. Europeans and African slaves gave each other diseases as well, and as many as a third of both groups died during their first 2 years on the islands.

GOLD FEVER   The Spanish were interested in only one thing in the New World: gold. Wherever gold was found, settlers rushed in, and the meager gold sources on any given island were quickly exhausted. Undaunted, the Spanish moved on to another island, with Indian slaves in tow. Eventually, they searched farther into Mexico, Panama, and Peru, where they hit the jackpot: the unparalleled treasures of the Aztec and Inca.

Once the enormous value of the gold and silver in Mexico and Peru became clear, the Spanish ignored the Antilles except as a source of slaves. King Ferdinand authorized slaving expeditions to the Lesser Antilles and the Curaçao group in 1511. By

1520, the northern (or Leeward) islands from the Virgins to Barbuda (located next to Antigua), except for St. Kitts and Nevis, were depopulated. The inhabitants of the Curaçao group, Barbados, St. Lucia, and Tobago, were also forcibly removed, and on the remaining islands, the Carib retreated to the mountainous interiors, where they resisted would-be enslavers with considerable skill.

TREASURE SHIPS & PIRATES   The islands remained important to Spain not only as sources of slaves, but also because Spanish treasure fleets had to pass by them on their way from Mexico and Peru to Seville, the sole port in Spain authorized to receive the gold, silver, and other riches from the New World. Rulers of other European states, envious of Spain's wealth, encouraged their subjects to plunder Spanish ships. Piracy became an accepted business, and thousands of buccaneer ships, sailing from ports in France, Britain, and the Netherlands, attacked Spanish ships, as well as ports in the Caribbean and along the coast of Central America. **Sir Francis Drake** took the greatest booty, capturing an entire year's yield of Peruvian silver in 1573. To protect its treasure fleets from pirates, Spain closed its American empire to outside trade, forbidding its American colonies from trading with any other European powers. Spain also limited ocean crossings to Europe—only two heavily guarded convoys made the trip each year. While great forts were built on gold- and silver-loaded islands along the fleet route, other island settlements remained unprotected and had to fend for themselves when buccaneers came onto their shores to help themselves to food, water, and any other supplies that they needed on their long journey. Spain's focus on Peru and Mexico precluded state development of the Caribbean colonies, and for 3 centuries, most inhabitants of the forgotten islands earned modest livings as farmers and ranchers.

COLONISTS FROM NORTHERN EUROPE   The Dutch, French, and British established permanent colonies on the islands in the 1620s, initially concentrating on the smaller, still unoccupied islands of the eastern Caribbean, and moving west into the Greater Antilles (Cuba, Jamaica, and Hispaniola) after 1650. The success of these efforts often depended on events in Europe, and islands, like chips in a poker game, frequently changed hands during wars on the Continent. Governments, more interested in European affairs and with no money to spend on colonial development, played only a limited role in the initial settlement and economic development of the islands. Individual adventurers, often acting for groups of merchants, established the first Dutch, French, and British colonies. Governments gave adventurers exclusive licenses to exploit specific areas in return for a share of the profit.

In 1618, the Dutch began to challenge Spanish control of the Caribbean by establishing its own colonies and trade in the region. During the 17th century, the Netherlands led all other European nations in manufacturing, commerce, and finance capitalism, and the nation soon dominated trade with the Far East, Africa, and the Caribbean. The **Dutch West India Company,** chartered in 1621, had a state-granted 25-year monopoly in the Americas. Between 1625 and 1635, Dutch maritime forces changed the balance of power in the Caribbean, making it possible for Dutch traders to control most of the region's commerce for decades. The Dutch established colonies on Sint Maarten, St. Eustatius, Saba, Curaçao, Aruba, and Bonaire. Eventually, the Dutch West India Company's fortunes waned and its monopoly expired after investors became displeased by the venture's profits. Individual traders then moved in to fill the void, and the company reorganized to focus on the trade in West African slaves and goods to Caribbean colonies settled and controlled by other European powers.

New waves of British and French marauders followed the Dutch to the Caribbean. Tropical products such as **tobacco** and **sugar** were fetching high prices in Europe, and few investments at home promised comparable profits. The prospect of economic gain was the primary lure, but adventurers, fame seekers, and religious nationalists had their own motives for going to the Caribbean. The British and French claimed many of the same islands, but speaking in very general terms, the British settled St. Kitts, Barbados, Nevis, Antigua, Montserrat, Anguilla, the British Virgin Islands, and Jamaica, while the French established colonies on Guadeloupe, Martinique, St. Christophe (the French name for St. Kitts), and what is today Haiti. The Danish (St. Thomas, St. John, and St. Croix) and Swedish (St. Barts) came later and in much smaller numbers.

ENORMOUS SUGAR PROFITS   The Caribbean enjoyed relative peace and prosperity for much of the 1700s, and the region's economy—especially the sugar industry—grew rapidly. During the 18th century, the islands produced 80% to 90% of the sugar consumed in western Europe. Demand encouraged planters to develop large-scale plantations, which ushered in a new era of slavery. Profits and associated tax revenues convinced British and French politicians that both sugar and slavery were essential to their national economies.

SLAVERY ON AN UNPRECEDENTED SCALE   Economically, socially, and politically, slavery dominated the sugar islands to an extent never matched in human history. By the 1750s, nearly 9 out of 10 people on all the islands where sugar was grown were slaves. Conditions were brutal: Heat, disease, and backbreaking work killed slaves before they could reproduce, and sugar estates could operate only by constantly importing enormous numbers of new slaves from Africa. Except for the Spanish, all the colonial powers supported and were directly involved in the slave trade. The genocide began even before the human cargo from Africa arrived on the islands. The trip across the Atlantic—known as the Middle Passage—claimed the lives of millions. Shackled together, subsisting on tainted water and food of minimal nutritional value, and exposed to disease, 20% of the slaves died aboard ship. As many as another third, already weakened by confinement and malnutrition, perished in their first few years on the islands. And three out of four babies born to slaves died before the age of 5.

ENGLAND & FRANCE COMPETE FOR DOMINANCE   From 1740, Great Britain and France fought throughout the world to gain commercial and colonial supremacy. The Caribbean was a major theater of battle, but the struggle was worldwide in scope, affecting Europe, North America, Africa, and India as well. Caribbean islands, often used as bargaining chips, changed flags frequently as the balance of world power shifted between France and England. But the swing of the pendulum affected Caribbean societies and economies only superficially. Soldiers rather than civilians fought battles. Crops and plantations were largely unscathed, and planters essentially maintained power over island politics, regardless of which flag happened to be flying at any particular time. And slaves remained slaves whether an island was designated as British or French.

Islands held by both sides were vulnerable to attack, as neither the British nor the French were willing to spend the huge sums needed to protect them. The British maintained two permanent ports in the region; France had none, electing instead to send ships from Europe for specific purposes. The French fleets arrived fresh from the dockyard and in good shape, while the British ships quickly rotted under the tropical conditions. Once they arrived in the region, however, the French fleets quickly ran out of food, while British ships obtained provisions from their permanent naval stations. Disease also played a role: Any victory had to be won almost immediately, as a long siege would lead to staggering death rates from illnesses.

SLAVE RESISTANCE During the height of the slave era, blacks outnumbered whites 10 to 1 on most islands. Individual slaves frequently ran away, and groups of slaves planned escapes and uprisings. In fact, slaves rebelled much more frequently in the Caribbean than in the United States, and thousands joined in widespread insurrection on dozens of occasions, destroying plantations and killing slave owners. But only the 1791 revolt on Saint-Domingue (now Haiti), led by **Toussaint L'Ouverture,** culminated in permanent liberation, with the establishment of an independent Haiti in 1804. On other islands, maroons—escaped slaves who banded together and formed their own independent communities—sought refuge in mountains and areas of dense brush and broken terrain. As planters cut down forests to create new cane estates, maroons fled to Dominica and St. Vincent, two lush, mountainous islands designated as Carib territory. Escaped slaves on the flatter, drier islands had no hiding places at all.

ABOLITION OF SLAVERY & INFLUX OF INDENTURED SERVANTS Slavery dominated every facet of life in the Caribbean islands—it made sugar plantations possible, shaped social and familial relations, and dominated the laws and politics of the region. The abolition of slavery, therefore, represented a cataclysmic change in island life. In 1833, pressured by more frequent slave rebellions and by the large segment of the British population who increasingly found slavery morally repugnant, cruel, and economically inefficient, England permanently ended slavery in its Caribbean colonies. Inspired by the success of British abolitionists, French intellectuals pressed for emancipation, winning the fight in 1848. The Dutch abolished slavery in 1863. Many freed slaves moved off the plantations to squat on vacant land, and the loss of free labor temporarily crippled sugar production. To fill the labor void, planters recruited indentured workers (who labored under contract) primarily from India, but also from China, Indochina, and Africa's west coast.

INDEPENDENCE & ECONOMIC CHALLENGES At the end of the 19th century, the United States succeeded the European powers as the main economic and political force in the Caribbean. Under the centralized political systems in place until the 1950s, laws governing the region continued to be made in London, Paris, and the Hague, but after almost a century of economic decline on the islands, it was American capital that provided the means to rebuild the sugar, coffee, and banana industries. And American military power, protecting American commercial interests in the region, intervened in Cuba, Haiti, and the Dominican Republic.

In the years between the two world wars, islandwide political movements developed, paving the way for independence. Since World War II, some islands have become integral parts of larger nations, with constitutional arrangements that give their peoples management of local affairs. Puerto Rico and the U.S. Virgin Islands entered into relationships with the United States, the French Antilles were integrated into France, and the Dutch West Indies became an autonomous part of the Kingdom of the Netherlands. The major British colonies have become totally independent states, while smaller islands remaining within the British sphere enjoy home rule.

The Caribbean islands have different languages, political systems, and cultural traditions, but all face similar economic problems as they search for new sources of income to replace the declining sugar industry. Tourism is now the region's main business.

3 The Cruise Lines' Private Islands

Costa, Disney, Holland America, Norwegian, Princess, and Royal Caribbean all have private islands (or parts of islands) that are included as port of calls on many of their Caribbean and Bahamas itineraries. While few offer any kind of true Caribbean culture, they do offer cruisers a guaranteed beach day with all the trimmings and a more private experience than you'd get at most ports' public beaches. Note that aside from Disney's Castaway Cay, none of the islands has a large dock, so passengers are ferried ashore by tender.

CELEBRITY CRUISES   See "Royal Caribbean," below.

COSTA CRUISES   Passengers on Costa's eastern Caribbean itineraries spend a day at **Catalina Island,** off the coast of the Dominican Republic. This relaxing patch of paradise offers a long beach fringed by palm trees, with activities such as volleyball, beach Olympics, and snorkeling. The area adjacent to the tender dock is the busiest spot, as is to be expected, but if you walk down the beach a bit, you'll find a more private, quiet area (though the coastline gets a little rocky when you get farther out from the dock). The island has a strip of shops hawking jewelry, beachwear, and other souvenirs; a local island vendor rents jet skis and offers banana-boat rides; and the ship's spa staff sets up a cabana to do massages on the beach. Locals often offer massages as well; for $25 each—a fraction of what the ship charges—a local woman gave us a great foot and shoulder massage. Locals also sell coconuts for $2 apiece, hacking off the end and plunking in a straw or two so you can get at the milk. After you're finished, take it back to the vendor and they'll whack the thing to pieces with a machete and scrape out the tender coconut meat for you. Music and a barbecue round out the day.

DISNEY CRUISE LINE   A port of call on all *Disney Magic* and *Disney Wonder* cruises, 405-hectare (1,000-acre), 4.8×3.2km (3×2-mile) **Castaway Cay** is rimmed with idyllically clear Bahamian water and fine sandy beaches. Disney has developed less than 10% of the island, but in that 10%, guests can swim and snorkel, rent bikes and boats, get their hair braided (for $2!), shop, send postcards, enjoy a massage, or just lounge in a hammock or on the beach. Barbecue burgers, ribs, fish, and chicken are available at Cookie's Bar-B-Q, and several bars are scattered near the beaches.

The island's best quality is its accessibility. Unlike the other private islands, which require ships to anchor offshore and shuttle passengers back and forth on tenders, Castaway Cay's dock allows *Magic* and *Wonder* guests to step right off the ship onto the island. Visitors can then walk or take a shuttle tram to the island's attractions. Families head to their own beach, lined with lounge chairs and pastel-colored umbrellas, where they can swim, explore a 4.8-hectare (12-acre) snorkeling course, climb around on the offshore water-play structures, or rent a kayak, paddleboat, banana boat, sailboat, or other beach equipment. Teens have a beach of their own, where they can play volleyball, soccer, or tetherball; go on a "Wild Side" bike, snorkel, and kayak adventure; or design, build, and race their own boats. Parents who want some quiet time can drop the kids at **Scuttle's Cove,** a supervised children's activity center for ages 3 to 12, where activities include arts and crafts, music and theater, and scavenger hunts. An "excavation site" at Scuttle's Cove allows kids to go on their own archeological digs and make plaster molds of what they find—including a 35-foot reproduction of a whale skeleton. Meanwhile, Mom and Dad can walk or hop the shuttle to quiet, secluded **Serenity Bay,** a mile-long stretch of beach in the northwest part of the island, at the end of an old airstrip decorated with vintage prop planes for a 1940s feel. Available here are 25- and

50-minute massages given in private cabanas open to a sea view on one side (sign up for your appointment at the onboard spa on the first day of your cruise to ensure that you get a spot), and the Castaway Air Bar serves up drinks.

Adult- and child-size bicycles can be rented on the island for $6. A 4km (2½-mile) round-trip biking/walking path begins at Serenity Bay, but don't go looking for scenery or wildlife—the most you'll see is the occasional bird or leaping lizard. Parasailing is available for $70 for 45 minutes (over age 8 only). Beach wheelchairs and all-terrain strollers with canopies are available free of charge.

HOLLAND AMERICA LINE   Located on the Bahamian island of San Salvador, 2,500-acre **Half Moon Cay** is a port of call on most of HAL's Caribbean and Panama Canal cruises. Passengers can take it easy on one of the many beach chairs or under a blue canvas cabana (a boon to shade-worshipers), or do a little windsurfing, snorkeling, kayaking, scuba diving, deep-sea fishing, parasailing, sailboarding, aqua-cycling, or horseback riding. The ship's activities staffs also organize volleyball matches, tug-of-war competitions, and other games for adults, plus sandcastle building and treasure hunts for kids and teens. Facilities around the island include a food pavilion, a few bars, an ice-cream stand, a kids' play area that was expanded recently as part of the line's "Signature of Excellence" initiative, a post office selling exclusive Half Moon Cay stamps, a cute chapel for vow-renewal ceremonies, and several "tropical mist stations" to help keep you cool. For a special treat, you can get a massage on the beach from the Steiner spa therapists, who set up a pair of tents on the sand. Choose from options including full-body, half-body, and scalp massages. Chair massages are also available on the beach at $1 per minute (10-min. minimum).

NORWEGIAN CRUISE LINE   NCL's private island, **Great Stirrup Cay,** is a stretch of palm-studded beachfront in the southern Bahamas. This was the very first private resort developed by a cruise line in the Caribbean. Loaded with bar, lunch, and watersports facilities, the sleepy beach turns into an instant party whenever one of the NCL vessels is in port. Music is either broadcast or performed live, barbecues are fired up, hammocks are strung between palms, and rum punches are spiced and served. Passengers can ride paddleboats, sail one-person Sunfish sailboats, go snorkeling or parasailing, hop on a banana boat, get a massage at one of the beachside stations, or do nothing more than sunbathe all day long.

PRINCESS CRUISES   Most of Princess's eastern and western Caribbean itineraries offer a stop at **Princess Cays,** the line's "private island" (a misnomer; since it's really a 40-acre strip off the southwestern coast of Eleuthera in the Bahamas, pretty much cut off from the rest of the island). A half-mile of shoreline allows passengers to swim, snorkel, and make use of Princess's fleet of Hobie Cats (catamarans), Sunfish sailboats, banana boats, kayaks, and paddle-wheelers. (If you want to rent watersports equipment, be sure to book it aboard the ship or even online before your cruise to ensure that you get what you want.) There's live music, a dance area, and a beach barbecue on the island, and anyone who wants to get away from it all (or sleep off too many rum punches) can head for the several dozen terrific tree-shaded hammocks at the far end of the beach. Princess's local shop sells T-shirts and other clothing, plus souvenirs of the mug-and-key-chain variety, and local vendors set up stands around the island to sell conch shells, shell anklets, straw bags, and other crafts, as well as to offer hair braiding.

ROYAL CARIBBEAN & CELEBRITY CRUISES   Many ships of sister lines Royal Caribbean and Celebrity stop for a day at one of the line's two private beach resorts, CocoCay and Labadee.

At **CocoCay** (also called Little Stirrup Cay), an otherwise uninhabited 56-hectare (140-acre) landfall in the Bahamas' Berry Islands, you'll find lots of beach, hammocks, food, drink, and watersports, plus such activities as limbo contests, water-balloon tosses, relay races, and volleyball tournaments. For snorkelers, they've even built and sunk a replica of one of Bluebeard's schooners.

Labadee, an isolated, sun-flooded, 108-hectare (270-acre) peninsula along Haiti's north coast, is so completely tourist oriented that you'd never know it was attached to the rest of poverty-stricken Haiti. Labadee is a rarity among cruise lines' private islands, in that it gives you a real glimpse of the island's culture. At the straightfor-wardly named "Folkloric Show," a large, colorfully costumed troupe performs Haiti's distinctly African brand of dancing, drumming, and song, while bands at the various bars and restaurants perform the kind of acoustic guitar, banjo, and percussion "mento" music that was a precursor to reggae and other Caribbean styles. It's happy stuff, creating a wonderfully relaxed soundtrack for the whole island. Five beaches are spread around the peninsula; they're progressively less crowded the farther you walk from the dock, where enormous tenders make the short trip to and from the ship. In the Columbus Cove area, a children's aqua-park called Arawak Cay is full of floating trampolines, inflatable iceberg-shaped slides, and water seesaws. Kayaking and para-sailing are offered from a dock nearby. At the center of the peninsula, the Haitian Market and Artisans' Market are the port's low points, full of cheesy Africanesque stat-ues and carvings, with touts trying to lure you in with "Sir, let me just show you some-thing over here." Steer clear unless you're desperate for a souvenir. When we were here last, a painter near the dock had much more interesting work for sale.

On both Labadee and Coco Cay, organized children's activities include beach par-ties, volleyball, seashell collecting, and sand-castle building.

4 Antigua

Though it's the largest of the British Leeward Islands, Antigua (pronounced An-*tee*-gah) is still only 23km (14 miles) long and 18km (11 miles) wide, and offers little of the polish or glitz of some Caribbean islands. And that's its greatest asset: serenity. Nice, relaxing beaches are close to port; **St. John's,** the island's capital and main town, is sleepy and undemanding; and the locals, usually friendly, sometimes wary, are easy-going. Sure, there are things to do, but nothing will raise your blood pressure. Close to port, you can shop lazily in historic, restored warehouses that now feature bou-tiques and restaurants, spend half an hour or so at a museum to get a sense of Antigua's past, or climb a gentle hill to the massive cathedral overlooking town. Not all of St. John's is charming, but the town is full of cobblestone sidewalks, weather-beaten wooden houses, and louvered Caribbean verandas. The island's British legacy is clearly evident: Antigua has been independent since 1981, but driving is on the left, half of the tourists are subjects of the queen, every little village has an Anglican church, and the island's greatest passion is for the sport of cricket.

Away from St. John's, the rolling, rustic island boasts important historic sites and lots of pretty beaches. On the southern coast, **Nelson's Dockyard,** once Britain's main naval station in the Lesser Antilles, is now a well-maintained national park. Tucked away in the arid, grassy interior, **Betty's Hope,** with its picturesque windmills, conjures up Antigua's sugar-plantation past. And the **Wallings Conservation Area,** in the island's southwestern region, is the best example of the moist forests that covered Antigua before Europeans cleared the land for agriculture.

Antigua cashed in on sugar and cotton production for years. Today, tourism is the main industry. Most Antiguans are descendants of African slaves brought over centuries ago to labor in the fields. People of European, Asian, and Middle Eastern extraction are also represented in the population of 68,000.

COMING ASHORE   Most cruise ships dock at **Heritage Quay** (pronounced *Key*) in St. John's, the island's only town of any size. Heritage Quay and the adjacent **Redcliffe Quay** are the main shopping areas, but duty-free stores, restaurants, taxis, and other services can be found in the surrounding blocks as well. When several ships are in port, some dock at the **Deep Water Harbour Terminal,** 1.6km (1 mile) from St. John's. From there, you can either walk or take a short taxi ride into town. A handful of smaller vessels drop anchor at **English Harbour,** on the south coast.

Phone booths that take credit cards can be found on the dock, at both quays, and at Deep Water Harbour. If you want a more comfortable, air-conditioned place to make calls, try the Kinko's-like **Comet,** 14 Redcliffe St., in Redcliffe Quay (② **268/ 462-1040**), where you can also check your e-mail (US$3 for 15 min.). **Cable & Wireless,** at Long and Thames streets (② **268/480-4237**), sells prepaid phone cards for as little as US$4. You'll find ATMs at both quays and at the corner of Thames and St. Mary streets.

LANGUAGE   Antigua is a former British colony, so the official language is English, often spoken with a musical West Indian lilt.

CURRENCY   Although the **Eastern Caribbean dollar** (EC$2.70 = US$1; EC$1 = US37¢) is Antigua's official currency, the U.S. dollar is readily accepted by most shopkeepers and cab drivers, and almost all businesses post their prices in U.S. currency. Credit cards and traveler's checks are accepted by most tourist-oriented businesses as well. Unless otherwise specified, prices quoted in this section are in U.S. dollars.

INFORMATION   The **Antigua and Barbuda Department of Tourism,** at the Government Complex on Queen Elizabeth Highway in St. John's (② **268/462-0480;** www.antigua-barbuda.org), is open Monday through Thursday from 8am to 3pm. If you want to get information before you leave home, the Department of Tourism also has a New York office (② **888/268-4227** or 212/541-4117).

CALLING FROM THE U.S.   When calling Antigua from the U.S., simply dial "1" before the numbers listed throughout this section.

GETTING AROUND

BY TAXI   Taxis meet every cruise ship. Although meters are nonexistent, rates are fixed by the government and are posted at the taxi stand at the end of Heritage Quay's pedestrian mall. From the cruise ship dock, it's US$10 to Dickenson Bay, US$20 to Betty's Hope, US$22 to Nelson's Dockyard, and US$25 to Devil's Bridge. Settle on a fare (and the currency) before hopping in. Drivers often double as tour guides: For this added service, expect to pay about US$20 per hour for up to four people, with a 2-hour minimum. Tip between 10% and 15% for all rides.

BY BUS   Buses are cheap (little more than US$1 to almost anywhere on the island), but service is erratic. The privately operated vehicles, mostly 12-seat vans (all have

ATLANTIC OCEAN

Hodges Bay
Jabberwock Beach
Dutchman's Bay
Dickenson Bay
Cedar Grove
Long Island
Runaway Bay
Cedar Valley Golf Club
Fort James Beach — Fort James
V.C. Bird Airport
Galley Bay
Guiana Island
Hawksbill Beaches
Five Islands
St. John's
Long Bay
Parham
Pineapple Beach
Indian Town Point
Devil's Bridge
Jennings
Betty's Hope Plantation
Willikies
Megaliths
Harmony Hall
Jolly Harbour
Bolans
All Saints
Potworks Dam
Freetown
Darkwood Beach
Boggy Peak
Wallings Conservation Area
Half Moon Bay
Turner's Beach
Urlings
Falmouth
Willoughby Bay
Old Road
Falmouth Bay
English Harbour
Morris Bay
Mamora Bay
Carlisle Bay
Pigeon Point
Nelson's Dockyard National Park
Shirley Heights
Rendezvous Bay
Caribbean Sea

Fig Tree Dr.

✈	Airport
↖	Beach
⚓	Cruise Ship Dock
▲▲	Mountain

0 — 5 mi
0 — 5 km

license plates beginning with "A" or "B"), run from early morning until about 6pm. If you're adventurous and want to chew the fat with Antiguan villagers, give it a whirl.

There are two bus stations in St. John's: East Bus Station, on Independence Avenue, serves the north and east; West Bus Station, near St. John's market, is the terminus for routes to the south and west (and English Harbour).

BY RENTAL CAR　Driving is on the left side. Most roads are decent, but some are narrow and chock-full of potholes. Inadequate signage is a problem islandwide. On the bright side, you'll never have to worry about traffic jams. **Avis, Budget, Hertz,** and **National** all operate on the island. Your valid driver's license and a local temporary driving permit (US$20, available from all rental agencies) are required.

BEST CRUISE LINE SHORE EXCURSIONS

Nelson's Dockyard at English Harbour (US$49, 3 hr.): The tour begins with a drive through the capital of St. John's and stops at Antigua's national park. A guided tour of Nelson's Dockyard includes the admiral's house, the officers' quarters, and a stop at an 18th-century inn. A short drive brings you to the Blockhouse ruins, Indian Creek, the St. James Club, and Shirley Heights, atop a rugged cliff offering spectacular views.

Helicopter to Montserrat Volcano (US$248, 2 hr.): In December 1997, the Soufriere Hills Volcano on Antigua's neighboring island of Montserrat blew its top,

Frommer's Favorite Antigua Experiences

Sand, Sun, and Sloth: It's your choice: a bustling, social strand or a tranquil, private refuge. Both are within easy reach of the dock. (See "Beaches," below.)

Nosing around Nelson's Dockyard: Located on Antigua's southern coast, this is a must for history buffs. Colonial forts guard the narrow passage into the protected harbor where the British maintained their most important naval station in the Lesser Antilles, beginning in the 1700s. Like a Caribbean version of Colonial Williamsburg, the national park, with its many restored buildings, evokes another era. (See "On Your Own: Beyond the Port Area," below.)

spewing lava and ash over a huge area and burying large swaths of the island, including the former capital, Plymouth. This trip takes you over both the volcano and the charbroiled highlights of Montserrat's exclusion zone, the area declared off-limits to ground transportation.

Four-Wheel-Drive Island Tour (US$66, 3 hr.): Tour the island's only remaining rainforest in a four-wheel-drive vehicle, stopping at the ruins of forts, sugar mills, and plantation houses. The excursion includes beach time.

Hiking Safari (US$49, 3 hr.): This 6.4km (4-mile) uphill/downhill hike takes you through Antigua's rainforest, offering panoramic views from one of the island's highest peaks (360m/1,181 ft.).

Bird Island Catamaran Sail (US$82, 5 hr.): Sail along the reef-protected north coast of Antigua into the sheltered bay of Bird Island, a designated national park, perfect for the beginning snorkeler. Venture up the trail for a fantastic view of the Atlantic Ocean from 30m (100-ft.) cliffs, and then relax on the beach.

EXCURSIONS OFFERED BY LOCAL AGENCIES

Catamaran Cruises: Every day except Monday, **Wadadli Cats** (℅ 268/462-4792) offers different all-day catamaran cruises. Prices, which include an open bar, buffet lunch, live music, and snorkeling equipment, range from US$70 to US$100 (children under 12 pay half, and those under 2 are free). Check, though, to make sure you'll be back in time to reboard your cruise ship before it leaves. Private catamaran charters are also available.

Miscellaneous Tours: Several reputable operators offer outback eco-adventures, jeep safaris, kayak and snorkeling excursions, and bus tours of the island. Prices are reasonable, and discounts for children under 12 are common. Inquire at **Antigua Destination Planners** (℅ 268/463-1944), **Paradise Island Tours** (℅ 268/462-7280), and **Wadadli Island Tours** (℅ 268/773-0367).

ON YOUR OWN: WITHIN WALKING DISTANCE

St. John's has a number of attractions that are easily accessible on foot. To your right, just as you pass through immigration formalities, is **Redcliffe Quay,** Antigua's most interesting shopping complex. Most of the sugar, coffee, and tobacco produced on the island in years past was stored in the warehouses here, and before slavery was abolished on the island in 1834, the area witnessed slave auctions. The restored buildings, with their stone foundations, wooden-slat sidings, colorful shutters, and red corrugated-metal roofs, now house an array of boutiques and restaurants.

For more local color, turn right (south) once you've reached Market Street and walk 5 blocks to the **Public Market.** The roof of the enclosed structure casts a strange color on the vendors' wares below, but this is the best place to sample locally grown fruits and vegetables, and to pick up some Antiguan pottery or baskets. The market is at its most animated early in the morning, especially on Friday and Saturday. Across the street, next to the West Bus Station, fishermen hawk their catch every morning at the waterfront **Fish Market.** Chances are slim that you'll buy anything here, but stop by for the salty and sometimes saucy scene.

Next, retrace your steps on Market Street, walking north to the intersection of Long Street, where you'll find the **Museum of Antigua and Barbuda** (© 268/462-1469). Although it's not the plushest exhibition space in the Caribbean, the museum traces the history of the nation from its geological birth to the present day. Housed in a former courthouse, a neoclassical structure built in 1750, its exhibits include pre-Columbian tools and artifacts, a replica of an Arawak wattle-and-daub hut, African-Caribbean pottery, and sections dedicated to the island's naval, sugar, and slavery eras. It's open Monday through Friday from 8:30am to 4pm, Saturday from 10am to 2pm. Admission is free, but a donation of US$2 is requested.

A couple of blocks uphill from the museum, bordered by Church, Long, and Newgate streets, **St. John's Anglican Cathedral** dominates St. John's skyline with its 21m-high (69-ft.), aluminum-capped twin spires. The original St. John's, a simple wooden structure built in 1681, was replaced in 1720 by a brick building, which was destroyed during an 1843 earthquake. Upon its completion in 1847, the present baroque structure was not universally appreciated: Ecclesiastical architects criticized it as being like "a pagan temple with two dumpy pepperpot towers." The cavernous interior is entirely encased in pitch pine, a construction method intended to secure the building from hurricanes and earthquakes.

ON YOUR OWN: BEYOND THE PORT AREA

One of the major historical attractions of the eastern Caribbean, **Nelson's Dockyard National Park** (© 268/481-5021 or 268/481-5022) lies 18km (11 miles) southeast of St. John's, along one of the world's best-protected natural harbors. English ships used the site as a refuge from hurricanes as early as 1671, and the dockyard played a major role during the 18th century, an era of privateers, pirates, and great sea battles. Admiral Nelson's headquarters from 1784 to 1787, the restored dockyard today remains the only Georgian naval base still in use. At its heart, the **Dockyard Museum,** housed in a former Naval Officers' House built in 1855, traces the history of the site from its beginnings as a British Navy stronghold through its development into a national park and yachting center. You'll find plenty of nautical memorabilia. Uphill and east of the Dockyard, the **Dow's Hill Interpretation Center** (© 268/481-5045) features an entertaining 15-minute multimedia overview of Antiguan history and an observation platform that affords a 360-degree view of the park. Farther uphill, Palladian arches mark the **Blockhouse,** a military fortification built in 1787 that included officers' quarters and a powder magazine. For an eagle's-eye view of English Harbour, continue to the hill's summit, where you'll discover the **Shirley Heights Lookout.** Fortified to defend the precious cargo in the harbor below, Fort Shirley's barracks, arched walkways, batteries, and powder magazines are scattered around the hilltop. The Lookout, with its view of the French island of Guadeloupe, was the main signal station used to warn of approaching hostile ships. The grounds of the national park, which represent 10% of Antigua's total land area, are well worth exploring. Bordered on one side by sandy beaches, the park is blanketed in cactus, tamarind, cinnamon, and turpentine trees, as well as mangroves that shelter African cattle egrets. An array of **nature trails,** which take anywhere from 30 minutes to 5 hours to walk, meander through the vegetation and offer vistas of the coast. One trail climbs to **Fort Berkeley,** built in 1704 to protect the harbor's entrance. Admission to the park is US$5 for adults and free for children under 12. The complex, open daily from 9am to 5pm, is within walking distance of the dock at English Harbour. Free guided tours of the dockyard last 15 to 20 minutes; tipping is discretionary.

To see what's billed as the only operational 18th-century sugar mill in the Caribbean, visit **Betty's Hope** (© 268/462-1469), not far from Pares village on the island's east side. On site are twin mills, the remnants of a boiling house, and a small visitor center, which opens its doors Tuesday through Saturday from 10am to 3pm. Gardeners should be able to spot golden seal bushes, neem trees, and wild tamarinds on the rolling hills. Serene cows saunter lazily on the grounds.

Not far from Betty's Hope, on the extreme eastern tip of the island, **Devil's Bridge** is one Antigua's most picturesque natural wonders. Over the centuries, powerful Atlantic breakers, gathering strength over the course of their 4,830km (2,995-mile) run from Africa, have carved out a natural arch in the limestone coastline and created blowholes through which the surf spurts skyward at high tide.

Another attraction for nature lovers, **Wallings Conservation Area** is Antigua's largest remaining tract of tropical rainforest. Located in the southwest, this lush wilderness area features three hiking trails and numerous opportunities to spot some of Antigua's nonhuman inhabitants: birds (purple-throated caribs, Antillean crested hummingbirds, broadwinged hawks), mammals (mongooses, bats), amphibians (tree frogs), and reptiles (lizards, snakes). Vegetation includes strangler fig, hog plum, black loblolly, mango, and silk cotton trees, as well as numerous epiphytes. If you've spent your day at Nelson's Dockyard, pass through the area on the way back to your ship via the circular **Fig Tree Drive.** Although full of potholes in places, this is the island's most scenic drive. It winds through the tropical forest, passing fishing villages, frisky goats, and old sugar mills along the way.

SHOPPING

Most shops of interest in St. John's are clustered in Heritage Quay and Redcliffe Quay, and on St. Mary's Street, all within easy walking distance of the cruise ship docks. Duty-free items include English woolens and linens, as well as local pottery, straw work, and rum.

Redcliffe Quay, to your right as you pass through Customs, was a slave-trading and warehouse district before abolition. Tastefully renovated, it now contains interesting specialty shops, including **Jacaranda,** on Redcliffe Street (© 268/462-1888), which sells spices and Caribbean art; the **Goldsmitty,** also on Redcliffe Street (© 268/462-4601; www.goldsmitty.com), which offers handmade gold jewelry; and the **Map Shop,** on St. Mary's Street (© 268/462-3993), which stocks old and new map prints, sea charts, and Caribbean literature.

Located at the cruise dock, **Heritage Quay** is a run-of-the-mill shopping center with 40 duty-free shops and a vendors' hall.

BEACHES

Antiguans claim that the island is home to 365 beaches, one for each day of the year. True or not, all of them are public, and quite a few are spectacular.

Closest to St. John's, **Fort James Beach,** located 5 minutes and a US$7 cab fare from the cruise ship dock, is popular with both locals and visitors. The cordoned area of the water is always safe, but farther from shore, undercurrents are occasionally strong. Volleyball and cricket are played daily. You can rent umbrellas and beach chairs, and the open-air restaurant/bar allows you to spend every minute outdoors. For a change of pace, hike up the hill to explore the authentically derelict ruins of Fort James, which once protected St. John's harbor. Another restaurant/bar at the summit offers splendid views of the area.

A bit farther north, a US$10 cab ride from the dock, the .8km-long (½-mile) beach at **Dickenson Bay** is the island's most bustling strand, with numerous hotels, restaurants, and watersports. It's the place to watch people, try out some watersports equipment, or just bake in a social environment. The water is calm, drinking and eating options abound, and chairs and umbrellas are available for rent.

Pleasant, picturesque spots on the less-developed southwest coast include unspoiled **Darkwood Beach** and nearby **Turner's Beach.** Showers, snorkeling equipment, and chairs are available. Restaurants serve fresh seafood, while bars keep you hydrated.

If you crave complete peace and quiet, head to Antigua's most beautiful beach, at **Half Moon Bay.** Isolated at the island's southeast extreme, this expanse is virtually undeveloped. Waves at the beach's center are great for bodysurfing, while the quieter eastern side is better for children and for snorkeling. A restaurant and bar are near the parking lot.

SPORTS

GOLF   The 18-hole, par-70 **Cedar Valley Golf Club,** Friar's Hill Road (© 268/462-0161), is a 10-minute, US$10 taxi ride from the cruise dock. The 6,142-yard golf course has panoramic views of the northern coast. Greens fees for 18 holes are US$35; use of a cart is an additional US$30. Club rental is US$20.

SCUBA DIVING & SNORKELING   Antigua's dive sites include reefs, wall drops, caves, and shipwrecks. To arrange a dive, contact **Dive Antigua,** at the north end of Dickenson Bay (© 268/462-3483; www.diveantigua.com). A two-tank dive is US$79; reef snorkeling is US$25.

WATERSPORTS   Tony's Watersports (© 268/462-6326) and **Sea Sports** (© 268/462-3355;** www.seasports.com), both at Dickenson Bay Beach, offer a full range of watersports equipment. Prices are negotiable depending on season and demand, but sample fares are US$45 per half-hour for jet skis and US$30 per "figure 8" lap for water-skiing.

WINDSURFING   Windsurfing Antigua Watersports (© 268/461-9463), also at Dickenson Bay Beach, specializes in 2-hour introductory lessons (US$60) that are limited to four people. Experienced wind sailors can rent a full rig for US$50 a day or US$40 for half a day. The operation also rents Sunfish sailboats (US$20 per hour), kayaks (US$10 per hour), and snorkel gear (US$10 for the day).

GREAT LOCAL RESTAURANTS & BARS

Lunch menus on the island focus on West Indian cuisine, though you can get sandwiches, salads, and burgers as well. Antigua's local beer is **Wadadli,** the island's Carib name. The local rum is **Cavalier.**

There's no better place to watch the street life of St. John's than the second-floor wraparound veranda at **Hemingway's,** on St. Mary's Street (✆ **268/462-2763**). Across from Heritage Quay, on the main road leading from the dock, it serves tasty salads, sandwiches, burgers, seafood, and refreshing tropical drinks.

If you've opted to spend all day at the beach, your best bet at Dickenson Bay is **Coconut Grove Restaurant** (✆ **268/462-1538**), a quiet, open-air beachside refuge at the strand's southern extreme, complete with palm trees and superb seafood. Lunch is about US$19.

If you're in English Harbour, stop for a lunch break at the rustic **Admiral's Inn,** in Nelson's Dockyard (✆ **268/460-1027**). Built in 1788, this restored brick building originally stored barrels of pitch, turpentine, and lead used to repair ships. The menu changes daily but usually features pumpkin soup and main courses such as local red snapper, grilled steak, and lobster. Lunch is around US$25.

5 Aruba

More of a desert island than a rainforest, Aruba has unwaveringly sunny skies, warm temperatures, and cooling breezes, along with some of the best beaches in the Caribbean—or in the world, for that matter: miles of white sugary sand; turquoise and aqua seas; warm, gentle surf; and plenty of space.

If you tire of lolling on the beach, there's scuba diving, snorkeling, great windsurfing, and all the other watersports you expect from a sun-and-sea vacation. On land, you can golf, ride a horse, or drive an all-terrain vehicle over the island's wild-and-woolly outback. Away from the beach, Aruba is full of cactus, iguanas, and strange boulder formations. Contrasting sharply with the southern shoreline's beaches, the north coast features craggy limestone cliffs, sand dunes, and crashing breakers.

Focused on shopping? The collection of stores and malls in **Oranjestad,** the island's capital, can compete with the most impressive offerings in the Caribbean. In between purchases, try your luck at one of the island's **casinos;** two are just steps away from your ship. Or grab a bite to eat: Unlike the so-so fare found in much of the Caribbean, Aruba's culinary offerings are diverse, inventive, and often outstanding.

Aruba is still part of the Netherlands, so there's a Dutch influence, which adds a nice European flavor. Though it has a few small museums and some centuries-old indigenous rock glyphs and paintings, nobody comes to Aruba for culture or history.

Only 32km (20 miles) long and 9.7km (6 miles) across at its widest point, the island is slightly larger than Washington, D.C. It's the westernmost of the Dutch ABC islands—Aruba, Bonaire, and Curaçao—and lies fewer than 32km (20 miles) north of Venezuela. Aruba's largest city, Oranjestad, is on the island's southern coast, pretty far to the west. The Aruban people are as friendly as can be. With little history of racial or cultural conflicts, locals have no cause for animosity.

COMING ASHORE   Cruise ships arrive at the **Aruba Port Authority,** a modern terminal with a tourist information booth, phones, ATMs, and plenty of shops. From the pier, it's a 5-minute walk to the shopping districts of downtown Oranjestad.

LANGUAGE   The official language is Dutch, but nearly everybody speaks English. The language of the street is often Papiamento, a local patois that combines various European, African, and indigenous American languages. Spanish is also widely spoken.

CURRENCY   The **Aruban florin** (AWF) is the official currency, but U.S. dollars are widely accepted, and most items and services are priced in both currencies. Traveler's

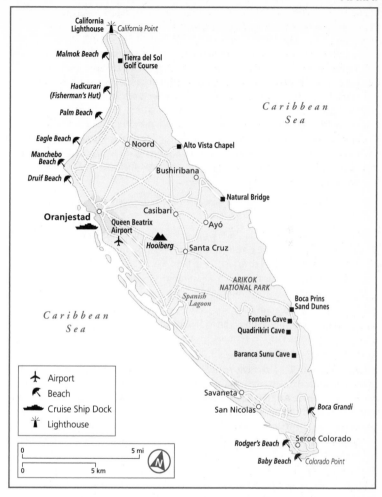

checks and major credit cards are almost universally accepted. The exchange rate is relatively stable, at about 1.8 AWF to US$1 (1 AWF = US56¢). Prices quoted in this section are in U.S. dollars.

INFORMATION   For information, go to the **Aruba Tourism Authority,** 172 L. G. Smith Blvd., Oranjestad (② **297/582-3777;** www.aruba.com). It's open Monday through Friday from 7am to 4:30pm.

CALLING FROM THE U.S.   When calling Aruba from the U.S., dial the international access code (011) before the numbers listed in this section.

GETTING AROUND

BY TAXI   Taxis line up at the dock to take you wherever you want to go. If you need to call for a cab, the dispatch office number is ② **297/582-2116.** Cabs don't have

Frommer's Favorite Aruba Experiences

Pretend You're Neil Armstrong: Alien boulders and stark terrain mark Aruba's northern coast, making you feel like a visitor to the moon. The roads are unpaved but easy to navigate in an all-terrain vehicle. You can stop at a lighthouse, an old chapel, and the ruins of a gold-smelting factory, but the major attractions are supplied by nature. (See "Best Cruise Line Shore Excursions" and "On Your Own: Touring by Rental Jeep," below.)

Make Like Captain Nemo: Submerge yourself 45m (148 ft.) beneath the sea in a modern submarine to marvel at nature's underwater splendor. (See "Best Cruise Line Shore Excursions," below.) Or ditch the sub and dive the amazing reef and wrecks.

meters, but fares are fixed, and every driver has a copy of the official rate table. Ask what the fare will be before getting in the car. The trip from the cruise terminal to the beach resorts will be US$8 to US$10. Tip between 15% and 20%. Most drivers speak good English and are eager to give you a tour of the island; expect to pay US$40 per hour for a maximum of five passengers.

BY BUS Aruba has good daily bus service beginning at 6am. The same-day round-trip fare between the beach hotels and Oranjestad is US$2; a one-way ride is US$1.15. Have exact change. The bus terminal is across the street from the cruise terminal on L. G. Smith Boulevard.

BY RENTAL CAR Excellent roads connect major tourist attractions, and all the major rental companies accept valid U.S. or Canadian driver's licenses. Rent a four-wheel-drive vehicle for the rough roads in the outback. **Avis, Budget, Dollar, Hertz,** and **National** all have offices here.

BY MOTORCYCLE OR BICYCLE Scooters and motorcycles are practical only if you plan to stick to paved roads. They're available at **Melchior Cycle Rental,** Bubali (© **297/587-1787**). Scooters rent for US$40 per day, while ATVs go for US$100 per day and Harleys are US$125. At **George's All-Terrain Vehicles, Scooters & Motorcycle,** in Oranjestad (© **297/993-2202**), you can rent scooters for US$40, motorcycles for US$60, and ATVs from US$85 per day. Mountain bikes are available at **Eagle Beach Bike Rental,** Eagle Beach (© **297/587-8655**), where rates start at US$15 per half-day and US$20 for the full day.

BEST CRUISE LINE SHORE EXCURSIONS
In addition to the options described here, cruise lines typically offer about a dozen snorkeling, diving, sailing, and other water-oriented tours.

Offroad Adventure (US$98, 7½ hr.): Take off into Aruba's backcountry in a convoy of four-passenger SUVs. You'll be behind the wheel and have radio contact with your guide. A stop is made for lunch and swimming.

Island Bike Adventure (US$54, 3½ hr.): Explore Aruba's undeveloped northeast coast by mountain bike, pedaling 16km (10 miles) and visiting the Natural Bridge (cut by the sea and wind and eventually collapsed), the Bushiribana Gold Mine, the Alto Vista Chapel, and the California Lighthouse.

Aruba Beach and Snorkel Cruise (US$65, 5 hr.): Travel by catamaran to snorkel at different spots, including a reef and an amazing shallow shipwreck, and then head to the beach for some swimming, sunbathing, rum punch, and a tasty lunch.

Atlantis Submarine Journey (US$89, 1½ hr.): Cruise 45m (148 ft.) below the sea in a submarine. During the gentle descent, you'll pass by scuba divers, coral reefs, shipwrecks, and hundreds of curious sergeant majors, damselfish, parrotfish, and angelfish.

Aruba Bus Tour (US$34, 3 hr.): This air-conditioned bus tour rolls along part of Aruba's wild and woolly windward coastline to the (now collapsed) Natural Bridge and the Casibari rock formations, followed by a swing through Aruba's hotel strip.

ON YOUR OWN: WITHIN WALKING DISTANCE

Aruba's capital, Oranjestad, has a sunny Caribbean atmosphere, with Dutch colonial buildings painted in vivid colors. The main thoroughfare, **L. G. Smith Boulevard,** runs along the waterfront and is crowded with marinas, shopping malls, restaurants, and bars. **Caya G. F. Betico Croes,** or Main Street, is another major shopping street running roughly parallel to the waterfront several blocks inland. The harbor is packed with fishing boats and schooners docked next to stalls where vendors hawk fruits, vegetables, and fish. On the other side of the Seaport Marketplace shopping mall, **Queen Wilhelmina Park,** named after one of Holland's longest-reigning monarchs, features manicured lawns, views of colorful fishing boats, and lush tropical vegetation.

If you're looking for a little culture, Oranjestad has a handful of museums that are worth a bit of your time. Squeezed between St. Franciscus Roman Catholic Church and the parish rectory, the small **Archaeological Museum of Aruba,** J. E. Irausquinplein 2A (© **297/582-8979**), illustrates the island's Amerindian heritage with pottery vessels, shell and stone tools, burial urns, and skulls and bones. Free admission; open Monday through Friday from 8am to noon and 1 to 4pm.

To defend the island against pirates, the Dutch erected Fort Zoutman in 1796. In 1867, Willem III Tower, named after the then-reigning Dutch monarch, was added. Since 1992, the complex has housed the modest **Museo Historico Arubano,** Zoutmanstraat 4 (© **297/582-6099**), which displays island history from the colonial period through the present, prehistoric Amerindian artifacts, and relics from the Dutch-colonial period. Admission is US$6; open Monday through Friday from 9am to 3pm.

The small **Numismatic Museum of Aruba,** Westraat s/n (that is, without a number; © **297/582-8831**), has meticulous homemade exhibits that tell the history of the world through coins. Dedicated numismatists can spend the better part of the morning perusing the 35,000 different specimens from more than 400 countries, and anyone with a passing interest in coins or history will appreciate this labor of love. Admission is US$5; open Monday through Friday from 9am to 1pm.

ON YOUR OWN: TOURING BY RENTAL JEEP

The best way to see Aruba's desertlike terrain is to rent a four-wheel-drive vehicle. Car-rental companies have maps highlighting the best routes to reach the island's attractions. Here's one of the most popular routes:

Following the system of roads that traces the perimeter of the island, start clockwise from Oranjestad. Drive past the hotel strip, toward the island's northwesternmost point. Here, the **California Lighthouse** affords sweeping 360-degree views of spectacular scenery—gentle sand dunes, rocky coral shorelines, and turbulent waves. The picturesque lighthouse got its name from the *California,* a passenger ship that sank off the nearby coast in 1916. Incidentally, the story that this vessel was the only ship to have heard (and ignored) the *Titanic*'s distress signal is malarkey. In fact, the *Californian* (with a final *n*) of *Titanic* infamy was torpedoed by a German submarine off the coast of Greece in 1915.

From here on, your adventure will take you onto the island's moonlike terrain, past heaps of giant boulders and barren rocky coastline. The well-maintained road that links the hotel strip with Oranjestad deteriorates abruptly into a band of rubble, and the calm, turquoise sea turns rough and rowdy.

By the time you reach the **Alto Vista Chapel,** about 8km (5 miles) from the lighthouse, chances are you'll already be coated with red dust. Don't let that stop you from peeking inside the quaint pale-yellow church that was built in 1750 and renovated 200 years later. Radiating serenity from its cactus-studded perch overlooking the sea, the chapel, Aruba's first, was built by native Indians and Spanish settlers before the island had its own priest.

Farther along the northern coast, you'll approach the hulking ruins of the **Bushiribana Gold Smelter.** Built in 1872, its massive stone walls are reminders of the importance of gold-mining on the island in the 19th century. Unfortunately, the walls have been marred with artless graffiti. Climb the multitiered interior for impressive sea views.

Within sight of the smelter, **Natural Bridge** is Aruba's most photographed attraction. The former Natural Bridge collapsed in 2005, but luckily the **Baby Natural Bridge,** right next to the former one, is just as pretty. Rising 7.5m (25 ft.) above the sea and spanning 30m (98 ft.) of rock-strewn waters, this limestone arch has been carved out over the centuries by the relentless pounding of the surf. Because the bridge acts as a buffer between the sandy beach and open ocean, many people come here to swim and picnic.

Next, head toward the center of the island and the bizarre **Ayó and Casibari rock formations.** Looking like something out of the Flintstones, the gargantuan Ayó rocks served Aruba's early inhabitants as a dwelling or religious site. The reddish-brown petroglyphs on the boulders suggest mystical significance. Although the Casibari boulders weigh several tons each, they look freshly scattered by some cyclopean dice roller. Look for the formations that resemble birds and dragons, and climb the trail to the top of the highest rock mound for a panorama of the area.

Farther east, back along the northern coast, **Arikok National Park,** Aruba's showcase ecological preserve, sprawls over roughly 20% of the island. Its premier attractions are a series of caves that punctuate the cliff sides of the area's mesas. The most popular, **Fontein Cave,** has brownish-red drawings left by Amerindians and graffiti etched by early European settlers. Stalagmites and stalactites here look like human heads and bison; park rangers stationed at the cave will point them out. The cave is an important roosting place for long-tongued bats, which nap in the damp inner sanctum. Nearby **Quadirikiri Cave** boasts two large chambers with roof openings that allow sunlight in, making flashlights unnecessary. Hundreds of small bats use the 30m-long (98-ft.) tunnel to reach their nests deeper in the cave. You'll need a flashlight to explore the 90m-long (295-ft.) passageway of **Baranca Sunu,** another cave in the area commonly known as the Tunnel of Love because of its heart-shaped entrance. Helmets and lights can be rented at the entrance for US$6.

Heading southeast toward Aruba's behemoth oil refinery, you'll eventually come to **Baby Beach,** at the island's easternmost point. Like a great big bathtub, this shallow bowl of warm turquoise water is protected by an almost complete circle of rock, and is a great place for a dip after a sweaty day behind the wheel.

SHOPPING

Although Aruba boasts plenty of shopping, don't expect prices to be fabulously cut-rate: The days of Caribbean bargains are waning. Nevertheless, the island's low 3.3% duty can make prices on items such as jewelry and fragrances attractive. What's more, there's no sales tax.

Because the island is part of the Netherlands, Dutch goods, such as Delft porcelain, chocolate, and cheese, are especially good buys. Items from Indonesia, another former Dutch colony, are reasonably priced, too. If you're looking for big-ticket items, Aruba offers the usual array of watches, cameras, gold and diamond jewelry, Cuban cigars, premium liquor, English and German china, porcelain, French and American fragrances, and crystal. Skin and hair-care products made from locally produced aloe are also popular and practical, and can be bought at **Aruba Aloe,** Pitastraat 115 (© **297/ 588-3222**).

Aruba's retail activity centers on Oranjestad. About 1km (½ mile) long, **Caya G. F. Betico Croes,** better known as Main Street, is the city's major shopping venue. Downtown also teems with several contiguous shopping malls that stretch for several blocks along the harbor. **Renaissance Mall** and **Renaissance Marketplace** feature more than 130 stores, 2 casinos, 20 restaurants and cafes, and a movie theater. Just down the road, **Royal Plaza Mall** is chock-full of popular restaurants and upscale boutiques.

BEACHES

All of Aruba's beaches are public, but chairs and shade huts are hotel property. If you use them, expect to be charged. Shade huts located at beaches where there are no hotels, such as Baby Beach, Arashi, and Malmok, are free of charge. Visitors can rent chairs at Eagle and Bay beaches.

Palm Beach, home of Aruba's glamorous high-rise hotels, is the best spot for people-watching. This stretch of sea and white sand is also great for swimming, sunbathing, sailing, fishing, and snorkeling. It can get crowded, and with two piers and numerous watersports operators, it's also busier and noisier than Aruba's other beaches.

Separated from Palm Beach by a limestone outcrop, **Eagle Beach** stretches as far as the eye can see. The sugar-white sand and gentle surf are ideal for swimming, and although the nearby hotels offer watersports and beach activities, the atmosphere on the beach is relaxed and quiet. A couple of bars punctuate the expansive strand, and shaded picnic areas are provided for the public.

Baby Beach, at Aruba's easternmost tip, is a prime destination for families with young children. The protection of rock breakwaters makes this shallow bowl of warm turquoise water perfect for inexperienced swimmers. Giant sea-grape bushes offer shade from the sun. The beach has a refreshment stand and washrooms, but no other facilities.

SPORTS

SCUBA DIVING & SNORKELING   Aruba is no Bonaire, but it still offers enough coral reefs, marine life, and wrecks to keep scuba divers and snorkelers busy. The best snorkeling sites are around Malmok Beach and Boca Catalina, where the water is calm and shallow, and marine life is plentiful. Dive sites stretch along the entire southern coast, but most divers head for the German freighter *Antilla,* which was scuttled during World War II off the island's northwestern tip, near Palm Beach. The island's largest watersports operators, **Pelican Adventures** (© **297/587-2302**) and **Red Sail Sports** (© **297/586-1603**), offer sailing, windsurfing, and water-skiing in addition to snorkeling and scuba diving. Two-tank dives are US$80; one-tank dives are US$58. Two-and-a-half-hour snorkeling trips are US$33; half-day (4½ hr.) snorkeling excursions are US$59.

WINDSURFING   Aruba's world-class windsurfing conditions attract wind sailors from around the world. Malmok Beach is the island's most popular windsurfing spot. Used by novices and pros alike, it has slightly gusty offshore winds, minimal current, and moderate chop. Boca Grandi, on the extreme eastern coast, is for advanced wave sailors only. **Vela Windsurf and Kiteboard Center** (© **297/586-6900** or 297/586-4760) offers beginner lessons with equipment for US$55; rentals are US$40 for 2 hours.

GAMBLING

Aruba boasts 11 casinos, most of them casually elegant. Slot machines gear up at 10am; table games, such as baccarat, blackjack, poker, roulette, and craps, can start as early as noon; and bingo starts in the afternoon.

Two casinos are steps from the dock. At the Aruba Renaissance Beach Resort, the **Crystal Casino,** L. G. Smith Blvd. 82 (© **297/583-6000**), is one of Aruba's only 24-hour casinos and probably its most elegant. The **Seaport Casino,** L. G. Smith Blvd. 9 (© **297/583-6000**), also in downtown Oranjestad, fits in well with the surrounding shopping mall; you might think it's just another store. In addition to slots and an array of table games, it features a race- and sports-book room with a satellite linkup and wagering based on Las Vegas odds.

GREAT LOCAL RESTAURANTS & BARS

Opulence and first-rate French cuisine make **Chez Mathilde,** Havenstraat 23 (© **297/583-4968**), the perfect choice for special occasions. Main courses include pan-fried trout, wild boar, and ostrich. It's pricey, but you deserve it. Lunch is about US$30.

Hip and happy **Cuba's Cookin',** Wilhelminastraat 27 (© **297/588-0627**), serves flavorful Cuban dishes that are expertly prepared. Kid-friendly **Waterfront Crabhouse,** Renaissance Marketplace, L. G. Smith Boulevard (© **297/583-5858**), offers grilled-cheese sandwiches and "psketti." The more sophisticated adult fare includes red snapper, Maine lobster, and crab. Lunch is about US$12.

6 Bahamas: Nassau & Freeport

Technically, the 700 islands of the Bahamas aren't in the Caribbean—they're in the Atlantic Ocean, just north of the Caribbean and less than 161km (100 miles) from Miami. However, because they're an important port of call on the cruise ship circuit and are part of the West Indies, they're almost always lumped together with their island neighbors to the south.

If you're a seasoned cruiser, chances are you've been to the Bahamas already and might prefer an itinerary that includes more far-flung ports. If you're new to the region, the Bahamas are a great introduction, with everything you'd expect from a fun-in-the-sun vacation—postcard-perfect beaches, a full range of water activities, and warm temperatures year-round. There's a well-developed tourist infrastructure—things work here—and economic conditions are the envy of most other West Indian islands, so you won't see the kind of poverty that plagues some Caribbean islands. In many ways, the Bahamas aren't much different from, say, some parts of Florida, but if you're looking for something on the exotic side, you'll still be able to see and experience colonial sights,

Nassau

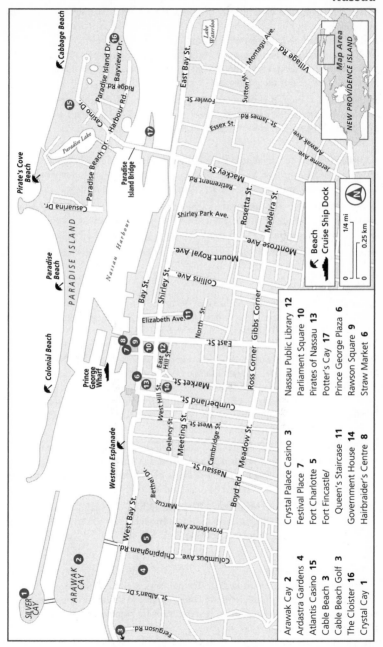

Arawak Cay **2**
Ardastra Gardens **4**
Atlantis Casino **15**
Cable Beach **3**
Cable Beach Golf **3**
The Cloister **16**
Crystal Cay **1**

Crystal Palace Casino **3**
Festival Place **7**
Fort Charlotte **5**
Fort Fincastle/
  Queen's Staircase **11**
Government House **14**
Hairbraider's Centre **8**

Nassau Public Library **12**
Parliament Square **10**
Pirates of Nassau **13**
Potter's Cay **17**
Prince George Plaza **6**
Rawson Square **9**
Straw Market **6**

British influences, and West Indian color—you'll know right away you're not in Kansas anymore.

The Bahamas became an independent commonwealth of Great Britain in 1973. Tourism and offshore banking account for the islands' current prosperity. About 85% of Bahamians are descended from African slaves; people of European extraction make up most of the rest of the population.

LANGUAGE   English is the official language of the Bahamas. Most people in the tourism industry speak a standard American version of the language at work. You'll also hear an island lilt and a vocabulary that reflects British, Arawak, and African influences.

CURRENCY   The legal tender is the **Bahamian dollar** (B$1), whose value is always the same as that of the U.S. dollar. Both currencies are accepted everywhere on the islands, and most stores accept traveler's checks and major credit cards.

INFORMATION   For information before you go, call the **Bahamas Tourism Board** in New York at ✆ **800/4-BAHAMAS** or go to www.bahamas.com.

CALLING FROM THE U.S.   Calling the Bahamas from the United States is as simple as phoning between states: Just dial "1" before the numbers listed throughout this section.

NASSAU

Located 298km (185 miles) southeast of Miami, the town of Nassau is the cultural, social, political, and economic center of the Bahamas. With its beaches, shopping, resorts, casinos, historic landmarks, and water and land activities, it's also the island chain's most visited destination—one million travelers a year make their way to the town, and Nassau is one of the world's busiest cruise ship ports. The Nassau/Paradise Island area comprises two separate islands. Nassau is on the northeastern shore of the 34km-long (21-mile) island of New Providence, while tiny Paradise Island, linked to New Providence by bridges, protects Nassau harbor for a 4.8km (3-mile) stretch. Although the area accounts for only 2% of the nation's land area, its 175,000 residents represent 60% of the Bahamian population.

COMING ASHORE   The cruise ship docks at **Prince George Wharf** are in the center of town, near Rawson Square and adjacent to the main shopping areas. Your best bet for making long-distance phone calls is the **Bahamas Telecommunications (BATELCO)** phone center on East Street, about 4 blocks inland from Rawson Square.

INFORMATION   The **Ministry of Tourism Office,** at Bolam House on George Street (✆ **242/302-2000**), is open Monday through Friday from 9am to 5pm. A smaller booth at Rawson Square is near the dock. You can also check out www.nassau. bahamas.com.

GETTING AROUND

Unless you hire a horse-drawn carriage, the only way to see Old Nassau is on foot. The major attractions and stores are pretty concentrated, so walking is the most convenient mode of transportation anyway. If you're really fit, you can even trek over to Cable Beach or Paradise Island.

BY TAXI   Taxis are practical for longer trips. The cabs are required to have working meters, but some drivers insist on flat rates. The initial meter fare is $3, and each additional ¼-mile for the first two passengers is 40¢; for third and fourth passengers, add

Frommer's Favorite Nassau Experiences

Gorging on Fresh Conch at Arawak Cay: This small man-made island across the West Bay Street shore has the freshest conch around. For a true island experience, wash it down with the local cocktail—coconut water, milk, and gin. (See "Great Local Restaurants & Bars," below.)

Taking a Walk through Colonial History: Nassau has numerous forts, government buildings, and private establishments that keep the flavor of the islands' colonial past alive. Shops and boutiques abut the historic attractions, so you can get some culture and feed your shopping addiction at the same time. (See "On Your Own: Within Walking Distance," below.)

$3 each to the meter reading. A surcharge is added for luggage stowed in the trunk. Tip your driver 15%. You can hire a five-passenger cab at $45 per hour. Taxis can be hailed on the street or taken from stands. **Motor cabs** can be ordered by calling © **242/323-5111.**

BY JITNEY Jitneys, medium-size buses that travel set routes throughout the city, are the least expensive means of transport. The fare is $1 for adults and 75¢ for children; exact change is required. Buses operate from 6:30am to 6pm except on weekends, when service is reduced.

BY FERRY Ferries run from the end of Casuarina Drive on Paradise Island across the harbor to Rawson Square for $3 per person. Water taxis also operate during the day between Paradise Island and Prince George Wharf for $4 per person.

BY HORSE-DRAWN CARRIAGE Horse-drawn surreys are the regal (if touristy) way to see Nassau. Agree on a price before you start your ride. The average charge for a 25-minute tour is $10 per person. The maximum load is two adults plus one child under 12 (or three small adults—if you've been spending too much time at the ship's buffet, you don't qualify). The colorfully painted surreys are available daily from 9am to 4:30pm, except when the horses rest—usually from 1 to 3pm May through October, 1 to 2pm November through April. You'll find surreys in front of the cruise port building.

BY RENTAL CAR Most vehicles have left-hand steering, and driving is British style. If you're used to driving on the right, it may take some time to adjust. Thankfully, traffic is seldom heavy except downtown near the port. Rental-car license plates carry the letters SD (which stands for "suicide driver," according to joking Bahamians). **Avis, Budget, Dollar,** and **Hertz** all have offices here.

BY MOTOR SCOOTER To rent a motor scooter (also known as a moped), contact **Fathia Investment,** Prince George Wharf (© **242/356-5739**). Mopeds run about $20 an hour or $50 for a full day.

BEST CRUISE LINE SHORE EXCURSIONS
In addition to the excursions below, cruise lines typically offer a variety of snorkeling, diving, and boat tours. Avoid the city bus tours, which are dull, dull, dull.

Harbor Cruise & Atlantis Resort ($42, 2½ hr.): A tour boat with a local guide shows you the sights (such as they are) from the water, then drops you at the fanciful Atlantis

Resort for a brief tour that includes a visit to Predator Lagoon, home to sharks, barracuda, and other toothy fish.

Thriller Powerboat Tour ($42, 1 hr.): This is a thrill-seeker's excursion, with high-speed boats roaring around the waters off Nassau, scaring the fish out of their wits. Not our personal favorite way to see . . . well, anything, but it sure is fast. Vroom.

EXCURSIONS OFFERED BY LOCAL AGENCIES

Guided Walking Tours: These 1-hour tours, arranged by the **Ministry of Tourism** (© 242/302-2000), depart from the Welcome Center on Prince George Wharf and usually begin every hour from 10am to 2pm. Make reservations in advance. The tours include descriptions of some of the city's oldest buildings, with information on Nassau's history, customs, and traditions. The cost is $10.

Scuba Diving, Sea Scootering & Shark Dives: Try **Stuart Cove,** Southwest Bay Street, South Ocean (© 800/879-9832 in the U.S., or 242/362-4171; www.stuart cove.com), which offers many options, including personal submarine excursions that allow nondivers to move about underwater without scuba equipment ($105). The operation can be a mob scene, though. The company also offers two-tank dives for certified divers ($82–$130) and snorkel excursions ($52). All programs are 3½ hours long. We recommend that you reserve ahead.

Walking on the Ocean Floor: If you loved *Captain Nemo* and *20,000 Leagues Under the Sea,* you won't want to miss **Hartley's Undersea Walk,** East Bay Street (© 242/ 393-8234; www.underseawalk.com). As part of a 3½-hour yacht cruise ($125 per person), you'll don a breathing helmet and spend about 20 minutes walking along the ocean bottom through a "garden" of tropical fish, sponges, and other undersea life. You don't have to be able to swim, and you can wear your glasses, but some people find the high-pitched pinging noise annoying. Ships depart from the Nassau Yacht Haven Tuesday through Saturday at 9:30am and 1:30pm. Check-in times are 9am and 1pm, respectively.

ON YOUR OWN: WITHIN WALKING DISTANCE

Walking is the best way to see the major sights of Nassau and to get a feel for the city's character and history (and to shop, shop, shop). Start at Prince George Wharf, where your ship is docked.

As you exit from the cruise ship wharf into the main port area, you'll have no choice but to pass through **Festival Place,** a barnlike hall full of little shops and stalls selling arts and crafts, T-shirts, hot sauces, and other touristy items. Outside, hawkers will encourage you to have your hair braided at the **Hairbraider's Centre.** This government-sponsored open-air pavilion attracts braiding experts from all over the island. If you're looking for a Bo Derek look, here's your chance. If you're not, a simple "no, thanks" keeps the touts at bay.

Just across Bay Street from Rawson Square (inland from the wharf) are the flamingo-pink government buildings of **Parliament Square,** constructed in 1815. The House of Assembly, old colonial Secretary's Office, and Supreme Court flank a statue of Queen Victoria, while a bust on the north side of the square honors Sir Milo B. Butler, the Bahamas's first governor-general.

Built as a prison in 1798, the **Nassau Public Library,** located a block inland from Parliament Square, facing Shirley Street, is one of the city's oldest buildings and surely one of the more interesting libraries anywhere. Its octagonal shape was copied from a munitions storage facility, and the decidedly unpenitentiary pink paint was added after 1889, when the building reopened as a library. The books, historical prints, colonial documents, and Arawak Indian artifacts are kept in former cells.

Slaves carved the **Queen's Staircase** out of a solid limestone cliff in 1793. Originally designed as an escape route for soldiers at Fort Fincastle, each step now represents a year in Queen Victoria's 65-year reign. Lush plants and a waterfall stand guard over the staircase, which is located a few blocks up from the library on East Street. The staircase leads to **Fort Fincastle,** on Elizabeth Avenue, built in 1793 by Lord Dunmore, the royal governor. At the fort, an elevator climbs a 38m-high (125-ft.) water tower; from the top, you can look down on the entire arrowhead-shaped fort. Walk around on your own or hire a guide. *Note:* You may find some of the guides aggressive.

Walking downhill from Fort Fincastle and back toward the waterfront, turn left on East Hill Street past Market Street. On the left stands **Government House,** the official residence of the governor-general, built in 1801. Tropical foliage lines the grounds leading to the colonial mansion, and a statue of Columbus stands over the hillside steps.

This one's for kids, but young-at-heart parents may also enjoy the **Pirates of Nassau Museum,** at King and George streets (© **242/356-3759;** www.pirates-of-nassau. com), downhill from Government House. Step aboard an embattled pirate ship and come face to face with Captain Teach and his fearsome crew as they guide you through the age of piracy in the lawless Nassau of 1716. Friendly guides will entertain and engage children and adults alike. It's open daily from 9am to 5:30pm, except on Sunday, when it closes at 1pm; admission is a steep $12 for adults—worth it only if you're with kids, as each adult may bring two children under 12 for free (each additional child is $6). Admission includes a 45-minute self-guided tour.

On Bay Street, not far from the Pirates of Nassau, is the **Straw Market,** full of stalls selling some authentic Bahamian items and lots and lots of objects that are actually made in Asia. There are better places to get the real thing (see "Shopping," later in this section), but enjoy the scene anyway. Hours are roughly 7:30am to 7pm.

If you're up for more walking, **Potter's Cay,** under the Paradise Island Bridge, provides more market color. Sloops from the less populated Out Islands bring in their fresh catch. Freshly grown herbs and vegetables are also sold, along with limes, papayas, pineapples, and bananas. Stalls sell conch in several forms: raw and marinated in lime juice, as spicy deep-fried fritters, and in salad and soup.

ON YOUR OWN: BEYOND THE PORT AREA

About 1.6km (1 mile) west of downtown Nassau, just off West Bay Street, **Fort Charlotte** covers more than 40 hilltop hectares (99 acres). The largest fort in the Bahamas, it offers impressive views of Paradise Island, Nassau, and the harbor. The complex, constructed in 1788, features a moat, dungeons, underground passageways, and 42 cannons.

Parading pink flamingos are the main attraction at the lush 2-hectare (5-acre) **Ardastra Gardens, Zoo & Conservation Center,** Chippingham Road, about 1.6km (1 mile) west of downtown Nassau (© **242/323-5806;** www.ardastra.com). The graceful birds obey their drillmaster's orders, and with their long-legged precision and discipline, they give the Rockettes a run for their money. The performances, accompanied by informative commentary, are presented daily at 10:30am, 2:10pm, and 4pm. Lory parrot feedings can be viewed at 11am, 1:30pm, and 3:30pm. The other exotic wildlife here—boa constrictors, honey bears, macaws, and capuchin monkeys—are less talented but still fascinating in their own right. Paths meander through tropical foliage that's sure to enchant gardeners. Open daily from 9am to 5pm, with gates closing at 4:30pm. Admission is $12 for adults and $6 for children 4 to 12.

The **Cloister,** on Casino Drive on Paradise Island (© 242/363-3000), is part of a monastery built in the 13th century by French monks. In the 1920s, William Randolph Hearst bought it, had it disassembled, and moved it from France to his estate in San Simeon, California. The stones were stored for years because no one knew how to properly reassemble them. In 1962, Huntington Hartford, the A&P grocery-store heir and developer of Paradise Island, bought the structure from Hearst and hired a sculptor to reconstruct it on the island. It's quite an anomaly on tropical Paradise Island, but it's a serene spot. The adjacent **Versailles Gardens** feature formal vistas, tropical flowers, and classic bronze and marble statuary. The Cloister is open only to guests staying at the Ocean Club, Comfort Suites Paradise Island, Atlantis Paradise Island, and Harborside Resort at Atlantis. Visitors are welcome to walk through when no wedding ceremonies are taking place. There is no admission fee.

The mythical lost city of Atlantis submerged under Bahamian waters? Sure, it sounds hokey, and all the grandiloquent hype makes you want to hate the place, but the **Dig** and **Marine Habitat** at the Atlantis Paradise Island megaresort actually end up exceeding expectations. Drawing on age-old myths of the lost city, the Dig is a fantastic world of faux ancient ruins flooded by the sea. The interconnected passageways, boulevards, and chambers, now inhabited by piranhas, hammerhead sharks, stingrays, and morays, are visible through huge glass windows. Purported to be the largest manmade marine habitat in the world—"second only to Mother Nature"—the resort's sprawling 11-million-gallon lagoon system boasts more than 200 sea species and 50,000 individual creatures. Tickets for the guided "Discovery Tour" of the marine attractions are available at the resort's guest services desks for $29 per adult, $21 per child under 12. **Note:** This tour does not include use of the resort's beach or water slide, which are reserved for guests only. For information, call © **242/363-3000** or check out www.atlantis.com.

SHOPPING

In 1992, the Bahamas abolished import duties on 11 luxury-good categories, including china, crystal, fine linens, jewelry, leather goods, photographic equipment, watches, and fragrances. Even so, you can end up spending more on an item in the Bahamas than you would at home. True bargains are rare, as is finding much that's really worth buying. The principal shopping areas are **Bay Street** and the adjacent blocks, which are almost the first places you see when you leave your ship. Here you'll find duty-free luxury-goods stores, such as Colombian Emeralds and Solomon's Mines, plus hundreds of other shops selling T-shirts, tourist gimcracks, duty-free booze and cigars, and recordings of Junkanoo music.

In the crowded aisles of the **Straw Market** on Bay Street, you can watch craftspeople weave and plait straw hats, handbags, dolls, place mats, and other items; be aware, though, that many of the items for sale here aren't of the best quality, nor even made locally (much of the stock is imported from Asia). Welcome to the global market, folks! It's tourist central, so most shopkeepers are willing to bargain, though some won't budge. If you want really beautiful handmade straw work, walk a few blocks to the **Plait Lady,** at Victoria and Bay streets, where the merchandise is vastly superior to what's peddled in the Straw Market—and it's 100% Bahamian-made.

For Bahamian arts and crafts, Junkanoo masks, and jewelry, try both **Island Tings,** Bay Street between East Street and Elizabeth Avenue, and **Seagrape,** West Bay Street at the Travelers' Rest restaurant (10 min. west of Cable Beach by car).

Marlborough Antiques, across the street from the Hilton British Colonial on Marlborough Street, has an eclectic and interesting collection of antiques and books.

Bahamas Rum Cake Factory, 602 E. Bay St., carries an array of Bahamian food products, including hot sauces, spices, and the eponymous dessert, which you can buy as they come out of the oven. If you can't get enough of the local rum, try a milkshake with a shot. And if you get home and want more, you can arrange worldwide cake delivery through www.bahamasrumcakefactory.com.

BEACHES

On New Providence Island, sun worshippers make the pilgrimage to **Cable Beach,** which offers various watersports and easy access to shops, a casino, bars, and restaurants. The beach stretches for 6.4km (4 miles), and the waters can change quickly from rough to calm and clear. It's 8km (5 miles) from the port—a $10 taxi ride or $1 on bus no. 10.

More convenient for cruise ship passengers but inferior to Cable Beach, the **Western Esplanade** sweeps westward from the Hilton British Colonial hotel. Facilities include restrooms, changing facilities, and a snack bar. In the months preceding the Junkanoo carnival (celebrated on the new year), local bands practice their carnival routines here.

Paradise Beach, on Paradise Island, is a ferry ride away from Prince George Wharf (see "By Ferry" under "Getting Around," above). The price of admission ($3 for adults, $1 for children) includes use of the showers and a locker. An extra $10 deposit is required for towels. Paradise Island has a number of smaller beaches as well, including **Pirate's Cove Beach** and **Cabbage Beach.** Bordered by casuarinas, palms, and sea grapes, Cabbage Beach's broad sands stretch for 3.2km (2 miles), but it's likely to be crowded with guests from the nearby resorts. Tranquillity seekers find something approaching solitude on the northwestern end of the island, accessible by boat or on foot only.

SPORTS

GOLF   **South Ocean Golf Course,** Southwest Bay Road (© **242/362-4391**), is the best course on New Providence Island and one of the best in the Bahamas. Located 30 minutes from Nassau, this 18-hole, 6,707-yard, par-72 beauty has some first-rate holes with a backdrop of trees, shrubs, ravines, and undulating hills. Greens fees are $100 per person with cart. Although not as challenging, the 6,453-yard, par-72 **Cable Beach Golf Course,** Cable Beach, West Bay Road (© **242/327-6000**), has lakes and ponds tucked picturesquely throughout, and the length encourages strong hitters to shave strokes with long, well-placed drives. Greens fees are $180 per person for 18 holes, including cart.

GAMBLING

If you think your ship's casino is as good as most land-based facilities, you haven't been to the impressive 9,290-sq.-m (100,000-sq.-ft.) **Atlantis Casino,** in the Atlantis Paradise Island megaresort (© **242/363-3000**). This is the largest gaming and entertainment complex in the Caribbean. Two astounding glass sculptures, the Temple of the Sun and the Temple of the Moon, anchor the vast facility and tie in with the resort's

"Lost City of Atlantis" theme. Open 24 hours daily, the casino boasts nearly 1,000 slot machines and 78 gaming tables for baccarat, roulette, craps, blackjack, and Caribbean stud poker. Unlike most other casinos, the Atlantis makes no attempt at hiding what's going on outside: Huge windows provide panoramas of the adjacent marina and lagoons.

The 3,250-sq.-m (34,983-sq.-ft.) **Crystal Palace Casino,** West Bay Street, Cable Beach (© **242/327-6200**), part of the Wyndham Nassau Resort, is the only casino on New Providence Island. Despite tough competition from the Atlantis Casino, it stacks up well against most other casinos in the Caribbean, with 750 slot machines and more than 50 gaming tables and live poker. The oval-shaped bar extends onto the gaming floor, and the lounge offers live entertainment. It's open 24 hours daily.

Taxis will take you to either casino from the cruise ship pier.

GREAT LOCAL RESTAURANTS & BARS

Conch, Bahamian "rock lobster," and boiled fish are local specialties; pigeon peas and rice are popular side dishes. The local beer is **Kalik,** and Nassau's local rum is **Bacardi.**

ON ARAWAK CAY You'll get all the conch you can eat on Arawak Cay, a small man-made island across West Bay Street from Ardastra Gardens and Fort Charlotte. Join the locals in munching on conch with hot sauce, and wash it down with a coconut-water-and-gin cocktail. Gorging on the cay is a local tradition and a real Bahamian experience.

IN NASSAU If you want fancy, **Graycliff Restaurant,** West Hill Street, next to Government House (© **242/322-2796**), is one of the most elegant restaurants in the West Indies. It was built in the 1740s by a former privateer and became Nassau's first inn in 1844. During the American Civil War, its cellar served as a jail for war prisoners. Polly Leach, a friend of Al Capone, owned the house some time later, as did Lord and Lady Dudley, friends of the Duke and Duchess of Windsor. Royalty and celebrities have dined in the elegant surroundings for decades, enjoying the extensive wine list and hand-rolled cigars. The Continental lunches and dinners are expensive but worth it if you've squirreled away for a really special meal. Call ahead for reservations. Lunch is about $30. Also at the Graycliff Hotel is **Humidor Churrascaria,** a Brazilian-style barbecue restaurant that opened in March 2005. It serves a wide variety of meats slow-roasted on a giant rotisserie hearth spit.

Much more modest, **Bahamian Kitchen,** Trinity Place, off Market Street, next to Trinity Church (© **242/325-0702**), is one of the best places for good, down-home Bahamian food. Specialties include lobster Bahamian style, fried red snapper, and curried chicken. Lunch is $8.

Try the boiled-fish breakfast at the **Shoal,** Nassau Street, near Ardastra Gardens (© **242/323-4400**). It's a local favorite and a featured restaurant in the Ministry of Tourism's "Real Taste of the Bahamas" program, which highlights independent establishments that serve indigenous cuisine. Every cab driver knows the place, which really hops on Sunday mornings. Lunch is $17.

Café Matisse, on Bank Lane at Bay Street, behind Parliament Square (© **242/356-7012**), is housed in an old colonial home and features antique tile floors, Matisse prints, and a serene outdoor courtyard. The extensive menu includes seafood, pastas, and pizzas. It's an unbeatable respite from shopping and sightseeing in downtown Nassau. Lunch is $15.

ON PARADISE ISLAND Among the 30-plus pricey restaurants and bars in the **Atlantis Paradise Island** resort, on Casino Drive (© **242/363-3000**), one merits special mention. **Seagrapes** serves an affordable buffet of tropical dishes, with a special emphasis on Cuban, Caribbean, and Cajun cuisines. Lunch is $20. For casual fare, head over to the new **Marina Village.**

FREEPORT/LUCAYA

Freeport/Lucaya, on Grand Bahama Island (often referred to as GBI), is the second most popular destination in the Bahamas. Technically, Freeport is the landlocked section of town, while adjacent Lucaya hugs the waterfront. Originally intended as two separate developments, the two have grown together over the years, and though they offer none of Nassau's colonial charm, they do boast plenty of sun, surf, golf, tennis, and watersports. The frenzy of the gambling and shopping scenes has been quelled in recent years by a triple punch of three hurricanes in only 2 years. While rebuilding is an ongoing process, the short-term effect is that the island's tourism sites have taken on a calmer and quieter feel

It wasn't until the 19th century that the first permanent settlers arrived on the island. Most earned a living as fishermen or by harvesting timber. GBI remained sparsely populated until 1955, when American developer Wallace Groves joined British industrialist Sir Charles Hayward to build the tax-free city of Freeport for tourism and manufacturing. Today, tourism remains the lifeblood of the island's 50,000 residents, but with the filming of all three *Pirates of the Caribbean* films on location here, the movie industry may become an even bigger source of revenue. Hollywood hounds, determined to trod in the footsteps of Johnny Depp and Orlando Bloom, meet locals hired to play extras, or ogle at the spectacular ships and other props that may be left behind, will no doubt add to an already booming tourism industry.

COMING ASHORE Your ship docks at a quiet port on Grand Bahama Island, where you'll find a small straw market, a cheery shopping area with phone banks, and hair-braiding stations in the middle of an industrial zone. You are best served by taking the $24 taxi ride to the **Port Lucaya Marketplace,** where you'll find most of the action. Closer to the pier, but not as bustling, is the **International Bazaar,** a $16 cab ride away.

INFORMATION Information is available from the **Grand Bahama Tourism Board,** located in the International Bazaar in the Lucaya area (© **800/448-3386** or 242/352-8044). Another information booth is located at Port Lucaya (© **242/373-8988**). You can also check out www.grand-bahama.com.

GETTING AROUND

Once you get to Freeport by taxi, you can explore the center of town on foot. If you want to make excursions to the west or east ends of the island, your best bet is to rent a car.

BY TAXI The government sets taxi rates, which start at $3 and increase 40¢ for each additional ¼ mile. Cabs wait at the dock, or you can call **Freeport Taxi Company** (© **242/352-6666**) or **Grand Bahama Taxi Union** (© **242/352-7101**).

BY BUS Public bus service runs from the International Bazaar to downtown Freeport, and from the Pub on the Mall to the Lucaya area. The typical fare is around 75¢ to $1.

Frommer's Favorite Freeport/Lucaya Experiences

Touring Lucayan National Park: About 19km (12 miles) from Lucaya, this park boasts one of the loveliest beaches on Grand Bahama, as well as caves, mangroves, and nature walks through various ecological zones. (See "Best Cruise Line Shore Excursions," below.)

Dining at the Ferry House: This restaurant is by far one of the finest places we've eaten at in the entire Caribbean. Understated from the outside, this hidden gem has a cozy yet elegant atmosphere, with artwork on the ceiling and the feeling of a wedding banquet held under a tent. The chef is from Iceland, but the food is straight from heaven. Every dish is simply divine. (See "Great Local Restaurants & Bars," below.)

BY RENTAL CAR Roads are good on GBI, and traffic is light. Remember that driving is on the left side. **Avis, Dollar,** and **Hertz** all have offices here.

BY MOTOR SCOOTER OR BICYCLE You can rent scooters or bicycles at the island's major hotels, including the **Royal Oasis Beach & Golf Resort,** West Sunrise Highway (© **242/350-7000**). A two-seat scooter requires a $100 deposit and rents for about $45 a day; bikes go for $20 a day.

BEST CRUISE LINE SHORE EXCURSIONS

Sanctuary Bay Dolphin Encounter ($80, 3¼ hr.): Pat a dolphin on the nose! On this excursion you can watch, touch, and photograph Flipper, or at least one of his relatives. See the UNEXSO information below for more elaborate dolphin excursions that you can arrange on your own.

Kayaking Nature Adventure ($75, 6 hr.): Visit a protected island creek, kayak through a mangrove forest, explore the island's caves, and take a guided nature walk into Lucayan National Park. The excursion includes lunch and beach time.

EXCURSIONS OFFERED BY LOCAL AGENCIES

Kayak & Bike Tours: Contact **Kayak Nature Tours** (© **242/373-2485;** www.gbn. com) to arrange one of the four worthwhile and recommended excursions that fit in a cruiser's time frame. The first, to Lucayan National Park, features sea kayaking through mangroves, a nature hike, a stop at two caves, and a swim and picnic lunch at Gold Rock Beach ($79, 6 hr.). The second, to Peterson Cay National Park, includes sea kayaking to the small offshore cay, guided snorkeling, beach time, and lunch ($79, 5 hr.). The third features a leisurely bicycle ride along Taíno Beach and the Settlement of Smith Point; it includes a visit to Sanctuary Bay, a guided walk through historic settlement areas, time to shop, and lunch ($79, 6 hr.). The newest trip involves an off-road jeep convoy through the pine forests, over the canal, and down to the beach for lunch and a swim ($99, 6 hr.). Guides on all tours are personable, informative, and professional.

Scuba, Snorkeling, Shark Dives & Dolphin Swims: In the Bahamas, reef diving takes a back seat to theme-park-style "adventure" programs, including shark-feeding dives and swim-with-dolphins adventures. One of the premier diving and snorkeling

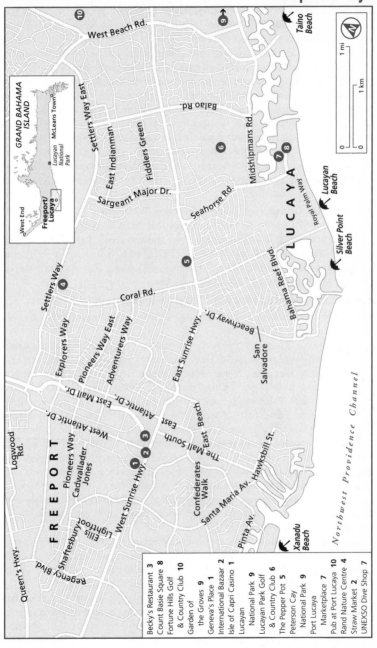

GRAND BAHAMA ISLAND

West End

McLeans Town

Lucayan National Park

Freeport/Lucaya

West Beach Rd.

Settlers Way East

Balao Rd.

East Indianman

Fiddlers Green

Settlers Way

Sargeant Major Dr.

Midshipmans Rd.

Seahorse Rd.

Coral Rd.

Explorers Way

Pioneers Way East

Adventurers Way

Settlers Way

East Sunrise Hwy.

Beachway Dr.

San Salvadore

Bahama Reef Blvd.

Royal Palm Way

L U C A Y A

Taino Beach

Lucayan Beach

Silver Point Beach

FREEPORT

Logwood Rd.

Queen's Hwy.

Regency Blvd.

Shaftesbury

Ellis

Lightfoot

Pioneers Way

Cadwallader Jones

West Atlantic Dr.

East Atlantic Dr.

East Mall Dr.

West Sunrise Hwy.

The Mall South

East Beach

Confederates Walk

Santa Maria Av.

Hawksbill St.

Pinta Av.

Xanadu Beach

Northwest Providence Channel

1 mi

1 km

Becky's Restaurant **3**
Count Basie Square **8**
Fortune Hills Golf & Country Club **10**
Garden of the Groves **9**
Geneva's Place **1**
International Bazaar **2**
Isle of Capri Casino **1**
Lucayan National Park **9**
Lucayan Park Golf & Country Club **6**
The Pepper Pot **5**
Peterson Cay National Park **9**
Port Lucaya Marketplace **7**
Pub at Port Lucaya **10**
Rand Nature Centre **4**
Straw Market **2**
UNEXSO Dive Shop **7**

outfitters in the Caribbean, the **Underwater Explorers Society (UNEXSO),** at Lucaya Beach (© **800/992-3483** or 242/373-1244; www.unexso.com), offers reef and wreck dives. Two-tank reef dives are $70, while 3-hour learn-to-dive courses are $85. UNEXSO also allows divers to swim alongside dolphins in the open ocean. Several different programs are available: During the **Close Encounter** ($75 adults, $35 children 4–12), you will observe the sea mammals from an observation deck while listening to an informative presentation; then you can wade into the waist-high water and touch the creatures. The highlight of **Swim with the Dolphins** ($169; minimum age 10; children younger than 16 must be accompanied by an adult) is swimming alongside the animals in protected waters after a briefing on dolphin behavior. The open-ocean **Ultimate Dolphins Experience** ($199; minimum age 10; children younger than 16 must be accompanied by an adult) allows you to dive with bottlenose dolphins in shallow open waters. These programs are exceedingly popular, so advance reservations are a must.

Party/Snorkel Cruises: In Freeport, **Superior Watersports** (© **242/373-7863**) offers daily 5-hour party/snorkeling cruises that include equipment, lunch, and unlimited rum punch ($59 for adults, $39 for children 2–12). **Paradise Watersport,** at Club Fortuna and Island Seas Resorts (© **242/374-6676** or 242/373-4001), offers snorkeling cruises on a 14m (46-ft.) catamaran ($35 adults, $18 children 3–12) and glass-bottom boat rides ($30 adults, $15 children).

ON YOUR OWN: BEYOND THE PORT AREA

Nothing of note is within walking distance of the port. You must take a cab over to Freeport/Lucaya for all attractions.

One of the island's top attractions, the 4.8-hectare (12-acre) **Garden of the Groves,** at Midshipman Road and Magellan Drive, in Freeport (© **242/373-5668**), was nearly destroyed due to hurricanes. It was once the private meditation garden of Freeport's founder, Wallace Groves, and featured waterfalls, flowering shrubs, around 10,000 trees, tropical birds, Bahamian raccoons, Vietnamese potbellied pigs, and West African pygmy goats. The serene hilltop chapel overlooking the pond was also a popular place for exchanging vows. The garden is scheduled to reopen in 2007, if not sooner.

A couple of miles east of downtown Freeport, the 40-hectare (99-acre) **Rand Nature Centre,** on East Settlers Way (© **242/352-5438**), serves as the regional headquarters of the Bahamas National Trust. Pineland nature trails meander past native flora and wild birds, including the Bahama parrot and other animals. Other highlights include native animal displays (don't miss the boa constrictors), an education center, and a gift shop. It's open Monday through Friday from 9am to 4pm; admission is $5 for adults and $3 for kids 5 to 12.

Peterson Cay National Park, approximately 24km (15 miles) east of Freeport and .8km (½ mile) offshore, is accessible by boat only. Coral reefs ringing the tiny island make for great snorkeling and diving, and the serene location is perfect for a picnic. For information, contact the Rand Nature Centre, described above.

If your ship's in port late, don't miss the free nightly concert at **Count Basie Square,** in the center of Port Lucaya's waterfront restaurant-and-shopping complex. The legendary jazz bandleader who lends his name to the square had a home on Grand Bahama, and the square's vine-covered bandstand attracts steel-drum bands, small Junkanoo groups, and gospel singers.

SHOPPING

The **International Bazaar,** at East Mall Drive and East Sunrise Highway, is pure 1960s Bahamian kitsch, and though relentlessly cheerful, it's rather long in the tooth. Each area of the 4-hectare (10-acre), 100-shop complex once attempted to capture the ambience of a different region of the globe, but since the last few hurricanes, it's become a bit of a patchwork in terms of which country-themed shops had to close its borders and retreat. Buses marked INTERNATIONAL BAZAAR deliver passengers to the center's much-photographed Torii Gate, a Japanese symbol of welcome.

The **Port Lucaya Marketplace,** on Seahorse Road near UNEXSO, is a 2.4-hectare (6-acre) shopping-and-dining complex that, in recent years, has eclipsed the International Bazaar. This is definitely where all the action is, and since it's so close to the Lucayan Beach just across the street, it's a great way to combine dining, shopping, and beach bumming in one spot. The gingerbread trim on the pink-painted shops adds to the festive atmosphere. Many of the restaurants and shops overlook a 50-slip marina, next to the **UNEXSO Dive Shop,** where you should stop if you're in need of a wet suit, snorkel, mask, fins, underwater camera, or more prosaic items such as swimsuits, sunglasses, and hats.

The **Straw Market,** beside the Port Lucaya Marketplace, features items with a Bahamian touch—baskets, hats, handbags, and place mats. Quality varies, so look around before buying.

BEACHES

Grand Bahama Island has miles of white-sand beaches. **Xanadu Beach,** immediately east of Freeport at the Xanadu Beach Resort, is the closest to the cruise pier, but two of the island's best are **Taíno Beach** and **Lucayan Beach,** both conveniently located on the Lucaya oceanfront. Of the two, Lucayan Beach is easiest to reach and closest to the Lucayan Marketplace. It also has plenty of beach-chair rentals, watersports, and restaurants. If total isolation is your thing, then **Gold Rock Beach,** a 20-minute ride east of Lucaya, may be the island's best. Hidden away in Lucayan National Park, it has barbecue pits, picnic tables, and a spectacular low tide. **Barbary Beach,** slightly closer to Lucaya, is great for seashell hunters, and white spider lilies in the area bloom spectacularly in May and June.

SPORTS

GOLF   **Our Lucaya Beach & Golf Resort,** Royal Palm Way, Lucaya (© **242/373-2002;** www.ourlucaya.com), offers two courses. The par-72 Lucayan course, designed by Dick Wilson, features well-protected elevated greens, fairways lined with tropical foliage, and doglegs. The par-72 links-style Reef course, designed by Robert Trent Jones, Jr., is 6,909 yards from the championship tees, with water traps on 13 of 18 holes. Greens fees are $140 for 18 holes, including cart. Club rentals are $45.

Fortune Hills Golf & Country Club, Richmond Park, Lucaya (© **242/373-4500**), was designed as an 18-hole course, but the back 9 holes were never completed. You can replay the front 9 for a total of 6,916 yards from the blue tees; par is 72. Greens fees are $61 per person, including cart.

WATERSPORTS   **Paradise Watersport,** at Island Seas (© **242/374-6676**), offers water-skiing ($30 for 30 min.) and parasailing ($50). Water-skiing lessons are $50 for 1 hour. **Lucayan Watersports** (© **242/373-6375**) and **Ocean Motion Watersports** (© **242/374-2425**), at Breakers Booth on Lucayan Beach, offer windsurfing (rentals for $30 per hour, or 2-hr. lesson for $100), kayaking ($20 per hour), banana-boat rides ($15 adults, $10 children), WaveRunners ($60 per half-hour), water-skiing ($40 for a 2-mile run), parasailing ($60), and day passes to use the water trampoline ($10 for a half-day, $20 for a full day).

GAMBLING

The **Isle of Capri Casino,** between the Westin and Sheraton resorts at Lucaya (© **242/ 350-7000**), offers gaming, dining, and live entertainment. Serious gamblers appreciate the variety of games: full-service race and sports book, craps, blackjack, minibaccarat, roulette, Caribbean stud poker, 350 slots, and 45 video poker games.

GREAT LOCAL RESTAURANTS & BARS

The most popular Bahamian beer is **Kalik.** Another brand, **Bahamian Hammerhead,** is brewed on Grand Bahama. GBI's local rums include **Don Lorenzo** and **Ricardo.**

The **Ferry House,** at Port Lucaya near the entrance to the Pelican Bay Resort (© 242/373-1595), is perhaps the island's best-kept secret. Its seafood dishes are as creative as they are irresistible. Lunch will set you back easily $30, but it's worth it.

The highest concentration of casual and not-so-casual eateries can be found near Count Basie Square at the Port Lucayan Marketplace. Pubs and restaurants abound, many serving traditional Bahamian and British favorites. The **Pub at Port Lucaya** (© 242/373-8450) is open all day and serves everything from New York–style deli sandwiches to shepherd's pie, plus tasty burgers, salads, and kids' meals. Lunch is $10.

On the waterfront at Lucayan Beach, the **Prop Club** (© 242/373-1333) has a sports-bar feel and features plenty of beach and ocean views from both indoor and outdoor tables. Pizzas and pastas dominate the menu. Lunch is $25.

Becky's Restaurant, East Sunrise Highway, near the International Bazaar (© 242/ 352-8717), offers authentic Bahamian cuisine prepared in the time-tested style of the Out Islands. Try the souse (a traditional soup), stewed fish, and johnnycakes. Lunch is $11.

The **Pepper Pot,** East Sunrise Highway, at Coral Road (© 242/373-7655), in a tiny shopping mall a 5-minute drive east of the International Bazaar, serves takeout portions of the best carrot cake on the island, as well as a savory conch chowder, fish, pork chops, chicken souse, sandwiches, and burgers. Lunch is $7.

7 Barbados

No port of call in the southern Caribbean can compete with Barbados when it comes to natural beauty, attractions, and fine dining. With all it offers, you'll think the island is much bigger than it is. But what really put Barbados on world travelers' maps is its seemingly endless stretches of pink- and white-sandy beaches, among the best in the entire Caribbean Basin.

This Atlantic outpost was one of the most staunchly loyal members of the British Commonwealth for over 300 years, and although it gained its independence in 1966, Britishisms still remain—the accent is British, driving is on the left, cricket is a popular sport, and Queen Elizabeth II is still officially the head of state.

Originally operated on a plantation economy that made its aristocracy rich, the island is the most easterly in the Caribbean, floating in the mid-Atlantic like a great coral reef. Topography varies from rolling hills and savage waves on the eastern (Atlantic) coast to densely populated flatlands, rows of hotels and apartments, and sheltered beaches in the southwest.

Barbados

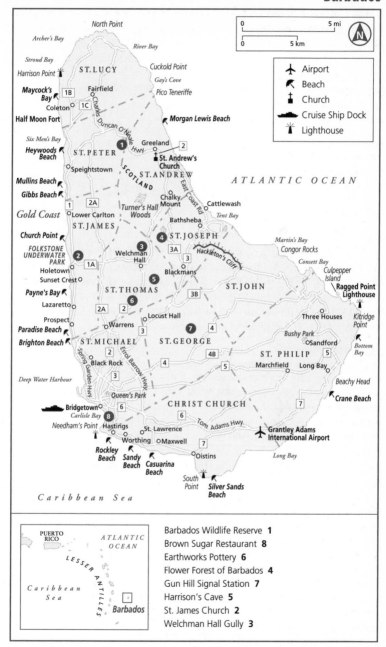

✈	Airport
⅄	Beach
⅃	Church
⚓	Cruise Ship Dock
⅄	Lighthouse

North Point
Archer's Bay
Stroud Bay
River Bay
Harrison Point
ST. LUCY
Cuckold Point
Gay's Cove
Pico Teneriffe
Maycock's Bay
1B
Fairfield
Coleton
1C
Half Moon Fort
Morgan Lewis Beach
Six Men's Bay
Greeland
2
Heywoods Beach
ST. PETER
1
St. Andrew's Church
ATLANTIC OCEAN
Speightstown
ST. ANDREW
SCOTLAND
Mullins Beach
Gibbs Beach
Chalky Mount
Cattlewash
1
2A
Turner's Hall Woods
Bathsheba
Tent Bay
Gold Coast
Lower Carlton
ST. JAMES
Church Point
4
ST. JOSEPH
Martin's Bay
Congor Rocks
FOLKSTONE UNDERWATER PARK
2
Welchman Hall
3
3A
Hackleton's Cliff
Consett Bay
Culpepper Island
1A
Holetown
Blackmans
3
Ragged Point Lighthouse
Sunset Crest
5
ST. JOHN
Payne's Bay
ST. THOMAS
Lazaretto
6
3B
Three Houses
Kitridge Point
2A
2
Locust Hall
7
4
Prospect
Warrens
Bushy Park
Bottom Bay
Paradise Beach
Brighton Beach
ST. MICHAEL
3
ST. GEORGE
Sandford
ST. PHILIP
5
2
4B
Marchfield
Long Bay
Black Rock
4
5
Beachy Head
3
Queen's Park
Deep Water Harbour
Crane Beach
Bridgetown
6
CHRIST CHURCH
7
Carlisle Bay
8
6
Needham's Point
Hastings
St. Lawrence
Tom Adams Hwy.
Worthing
Maxwell
7
Grantley Adams International Airport
Rockley Beach
Sandy Beach
Casuarina Beach
Oistins
Long Bay
South Point
Silver Sands Beach
Caribbean Sea

PUERTO RICO
ATLANTIC OCEAN
LESSER
Caribbean Sea
ANTILLES
Barbados

Barbados Wildlife Reserve **1**
Brown Sugar Restaurant **8**
Earthworks Pottery **6**
Flower Forest of Barbados **4**
Gun Hill Signal Station **7**
Harrison's Cave **5**
St. James Church **2**
Welchman Hall Gully **3**

The people in Barbados are called Bajans, and you'll see this term used everywhere.

COMING ASHORE   The cruise ship pier, a short drive from **Bridgetown,** the capital, is one of the best docking facilities in the southern Caribbean. You can walk right into the modern cruise ship terminal, which has car rentals, taxi services, sightseeing tours, a tourist information office, a huge phone center (where you can make credit card calls to the U.S., send faxes, and buy phone cards and stamps), and shops and scads of vendors (see "Shopping," below).

If you want to go into Bridgetown, about 1.6km (1 mile) from the port, instead of to the beach, you can take a hot, dusty 10- to 15-minute walk or simply catch a taxi. The one-way fare ranges from US$4 on up. Buses pass by the harbor frequently; the fare is BD$1.50 (US75¢).

LANGUAGE   English is spoken with an island lilt.

CURRENCY   The **Barbados dollar** (BD$) is the official currency. It's available in $100, $20, $10, and $5 notes; $1, 25¢, and 10¢ silver coins; plus 5¢ and 1¢ copper coins. The exchange rate is BD$2 to US$1 (BD$1 = US 50¢). Most stores take traveler's checks or U.S. dollars, so don't bother to convert money if you're here for only a day. Unless otherwise noted, prices in this section are given in U.S. dollars.

INFORMATION   The **Barbados Tourism Authority** is on Harbour Road, Bridgetown (© **888/BARBADOS** or 246/427-2623; www.barbados.org). Its cruise terminal office, which is very well run, is always open when a cruise ship is in port.

CALLING FROM THE U.S.   When calling Barbados from the United States, you need only dial a "1" before the telephone numbers listed here.

GETTING AROUND

BY TAXI   Taxis are not metered, but their rates are fixed by the government. Even so, drivers may try to get more money out of you, so make sure you settle on the rate before getting in. Taxis are identified by the letter Z on their license plates, and you'll find them just outside of the terminal.

BY BUS   Blue-and-yellow public buses fan out from Bridgetown every 20 minutes or so onto the major routes; their destinations are marked on the front. Buses going south and east leave from Fairchild Street, and those going north and west depart from Lower Green and the Princess Alice Highway. Fares are BD$1.50 (US75¢); exact change is required.

Privately owned minibuses run shorter distances and travel more frequently. These bright-yellow buses display destinations on the bottom-left corner of the windshield. In Bridgetown, board at River Road, Temple Yard, or Probyn Street. Fare is about BD$1.50 (US75¢).

BY RENTAL CAR   While it's a good way to see the island if you've got an adventurous streak and an easygoing attitude, before you decide to rent a car, keep in mind that driving is on the left side of the road and that signs are totally inadequate (boy, could we tell you stories!). Rental cars all have an H on their license plates (meaning "hired"), so everyone will know you're a visitor. **Hertz** has an office here.

BEST CRUISE LINE SHORE EXCURSIONS

It's not easy to get around Barbados quickly and conveniently, so a shore excursion is a good idea here.

Frommer's Favorite Barbados Experiences

Renting a Car for a Barbados Road Trip: Seventeenth-century churches, tropical flowers, snorkeling, great views, and more are just a rental-car ride away. (See "On Your Own: Beyond the Port Area," below.)

Visiting Gun Hill Signal Station: If you've got less time, hire a taxi or rent a car and go to Gun Hill for panoramic views of the island. (See "On Your Own: Beyond the Port Area," below.)

Taking a Submarine Trip: Sightseeing submarines make several dives daily. (See "Best Cruise Line Shore Excursions," below.)

Kayak & Turtle Encounter (US$75, 3½ hr.): A boat ride along the west coast brings you to the beach, where you'll clamber into your kayak for a 45-minute paddle along the shore. Once at the snorkel site, you'll be able to swim with and join your guide in feeding sea turtles.

Mount Gay Rum Distillery & Banks Beer Tour (US$42, 3½ hr.): Talk about getting in the spirit. This excursion takes you for a tour and tipple at Barbados's number-one rum distillery; it then heads for the Banks Brewery for the yeasty side of things.

Horseback Riding (US$100, 3½ hr.): Horse treks through the heart of the island wind past old plantation houses, sugar cane fields, old sugar factories, small villages, and, if you're lucky, green monkeys scouting for food.

EXCURSIONS OFFERED BY LOCAL AGENCIES

Island Tours: Since most cruise lines don't really offer a comprehensive island tour, many passengers rely on one of the local tour companies. **Johnson's Tours,** Brownes Gap, Hastings (℡ 246/426-5181; www.johnsonstours.com), offers several tours that cost about US$60 per person. Call ahead for information and reservations.

Taxi Tours: If you can afford it, touring by taxi is far more relaxing than the standardized bus tour. Nearly all Bajan taxi drivers are familiar with their island and like to show off their knowledge to visitors. The standard rate is about US$20 per hour per taxi, for up to four passengers. You might want to try contacting taxi owner/driver **Aaron Francis** (℡ 246/431-9059). He's a gem: friendly, reliable, and knowledgeable. **Johnson's Tours** (℡ 246/426-5181; www.johnsonstours.com) also offers private tours for about US$40 per person per hour.

ON YOUR OWN: WITHIN WALKING DISTANCE

About the only thing you can walk to is the cruise terminal. The modern, pleasant complex has an array of duty-free shops and retail stores, plus many vendors selling arts and crafts, jewelry, liquor, china, crystal, electronics, perfume, and leather goods.

ON YOUR OWN: BEYOND THE PORT AREA

We don't recommend wasting too much time in Bridgetown—it's hot, dry, and dusty, and the honking horns of traffic jams only add to its woes. So, unless you want to go shopping, you should spend your time exploring all the beauty the island has to offer. The tourist office in the cruise terminal is very helpful if you want to go somewhere on your own.

Welchman Hall Gully, in St. Thomas (© 246/438-6671), is a lush tropical garden owned by the Barbados National Trust. It's 13km (8 miles) from the port (reachable by bus) and features some plants that were here when the English settlers landed in 1627. If you're driving, take Highway 2 from Bridgetown.

All cruise ship excursions visit **Harrison's Cave,** Welchman Hall, St. Thomas (© 246/438-6640), Barbados's top tourist attraction. Here you can see a beautiful underground world from aboard an electric tram and trailer. Admission is US$16 for adults and US$7 for children. If you'd like to go on your own, a taxi ride takes about 30 minutes and costs at least US$40 round-trip.

About 1.6km (1 mile) from Harrison's Cave is the **Flower Forest,** Richmond Plantation, St. Joseph (© 246/433-8152). This old sugar plantation stands 255m (836 ft.) above sea level near the western edge of the "Scotland district," in one of the most scenic parts of Barbados. The entrance fee is US$7.

Built in 1818, the strategically placed **Gun Hill Signal Station,** Highway 4, St. George (© 246/429-1358), one of two such stations owned and operated by the Barbados National Trust, commands a wonderful panoramic view from east to west. It's 19km (12 miles) from the port; the one-way taxi ride costs about US$15, and the entrance fee is US$4.60 for adults and US$2.30 for kids 6 to 12. It's open Monday through Saturday from 9am to 5pm.

If it's wildlife you want, head for the **Barbados Wildlife Reserve,** in St. Peter (© 246/422-8826), on the northern end of the island. It's not exactly Animal Kingdom, but you'll see turtles, rabbits, iguanas, peacocks, green monkeys, and a caged python on this 1.6-hectare (4-acre) site. The entrance fee is about US$11.60 for adults, US$5.80 for kids 3 to 12.

Maybe it's the party life you crave. If so, don't miss the **Mount Gay Rum Tour,** in Bridgetown (© 246/425-9066; www.mountgay.com). You'll get a 40-minute soup-to-nuts introduction to rum in an air-conditioned rum shop (rumor has it that of all the rum shops on the island, this is the only one with air-conditioning). Tours are offered Monday through Friday every hour from 9:30am to 3:45pm. The cost is US$6 per person. There's also a "with lunch" tour option for US$14.

Ocean Park Barbados, in Christ Church (© 246/420-7405; www.oceanpark barbados.com), is a new underwater marine park that displays a collection of freshwater and tropical marine life of the Caribbean. Miniature golf is also available. A family ticket, which admits up to two adults and three children, costs US$50.

SHOPPING

The shopping-mall-size cruise terminal contains duty-free shops, retail stores, a convenience store, and a plethora of vendors selling arts and crafts, jewelry, liquor, china, crystal, electronics, perfume, and leather goods. Vendors sell great local hot sauce, as well as yummy **Punch de Crème,** a creamy rum drink (you can get a free sample before buying). For rum cake, an island specialty, go to the family-owned **Calypso Island Bakery** (© 246/426-1702). The shrink-wrapped cakes last up to 6 months and make great gifts. In general, though, you'll find a wider selection of merchandise and better prices in Bridgetown—last time we were here, T-shirts in the terminal were going for US$15 apiece, a roll of film was US$5, and a liter of J&B (yellow label) was anywhere from US$11 to US$15.

Good duty-free buys include cameras, watches, crystal, gold jewelry, bone china, cosmetics and perfumes, and liquor (including locally produced Barbados rum and liqueurs), along with tobacco products and British-made cashmere sweaters, tweeds, and sportswear. **Cave Shepherd,** Broad Street, Bridgetown (© **246/431-2121**), is the largest department store on Barbados and the best place to shop for duty-free merchandise.

Among Barbados handicrafts, you'll find lots of black-coral jewelry, but beware—because black coral is endangered, it's illegal to bring it back to the United States. We suggest looking but not buying. Local clay potters turn out different products, some based on designs that are centuries old. Check out **Earthworks Pottery,** Edgehill Heights, St. Thomas (© **246/425-0223;** www.earthworks-pottery.com). Crafts include wall hangings made from grasses and dried flowers, straw mats, baskets, and bags with raffia embroidery. Bajan leatherwork includes handbags, belts, and sandals.

In Bridgetown, **Articrafts,** on Broad Street, is a standout for Bajan arts and crafts, straw work, handbags, and bamboo items.

BEACHES

Beaches on the island's western side—the luxury resort area called the Gold Coast—are far preferable to those on the surf-pounded Atlantic side, which are dangerous for swimming. The government requires that there be access to all beaches, via roads along the property line or through the hotel entrance, so all Barbados beaches are open to the public, even those in front of the big resort hotels and private homes.

ON THE WEST COAST (GOLD COAST)   Take your pick of the beaches on the west coast, which are about a 15-minute, US$8 taxi ride from the cruise terminal. A good beach for watersports, especially snorkeling, is **Payne's Bay,** with access from the **Coach House** (© **246/432-1163**) or **Mannie's Suga Suga restaurant** (© **246/419-4511**). There's a parking area here. It can get rather crowded, but the beautiful bay makes it worth it. Directly south of Payne's Bay, at Fresh Water Bay, is a trio of fine beaches: **Brighton Beach, Brandon's Beach,** and **Paradise Beach.**

Church Point lies north of St. James Church, opening onto Heron Bay, site of the **Colony Club Hotel** (© **246/422-2335**). Although this beach can get crowded, it's one of the most scenic bays in Barbados, and the swimming is ideal. Retreat under some shade trees when you've had enough sun. You can also order drinks at the Colony Club's beach terrace.

Snorkelers in particular seek out the glassy blue waters by **Mullins Beach.** There are some shady areas, and you can park on the main road.

ON THE SOUTH COAST   Depending on traffic, south-coast beaches are usually easy to reach from the cruise terminal. Figure on a US$10 taxi fare. **Sandy Beach,** reached from the parking lot on the Worthing main road, has tranquil waters opening onto a lagoon. This is a family favorite, with lots of screaming and yelling, especially on weekends. Food and drink are sold here.

Windsurfers are particularly fond of the trade winds that sweep across **Casuarina Beach** even on the hottest summer days. Access is from Maxwell Coast Road, across the property of the **Casuarina Beach Hotel** (© **246/428-3600**), which, at press time, is closed for business until January 2007. This is one of the wider beaches on Barbados.

Silver Sands Beach is to the east of the town of Oistins, near the very southernmost point of Barbados, directly east of South Point Lighthouse. This white-sand beach is a favorite with many Bajans, who probably want to keep it a secret from as many visitors as possible. Windsurfing is good here, but not as good as at Casuarina Beach.

ON THE SOUTHEAST COAST   The southeast coast is known for its big waves, especially at **Crane Beach,** a white-sandy stretch backed by cliffs and palms that often appears in travel-magazine articles about Barbados. The **Crane Beach Hotel** (℡ 246/ 423-6220) towers above it from the cliffs, and Prince Andrew owns a house here. The beach offers excellent bodysurfing—but this is real ocean swimming, not the calm Caribbean, so be careful. At US$20 from the cruise pier, the one-way taxi fare is relatively steep, so try to share the ride with other cruise passengers.

SPORTS

GOLF The 18-hole, par-72 championship course at the west coast's **Sandy Lane Golf Club,** St. James (℡ 246/444-2500; www.sandylane.com), is open to all. Greens fees are US$220 for 18 holes or US$195 for 9 holes. Carts and caddies are included. Make reservations the day before you arrive in Barbados or before you leave home for your cruise. The course is a 20- to 25-minute taxi ride from the cruise terminal; the one-way fare is about US$20.

WINDSURFING Experts say that Barbados windsurfing is as good as any this side of Hawaii. In fact, it's a very big business between November and April, when thousands of windsurfers from all over the world come here. **Silver Sands** is rated the best spot in the Caribbean for advanced windsurfing (skill rating 5–6). **Club Mistral,** at the Silver Sands Resort in Christ Church (℡ 246/428-6001, ext. 4227; www.clubmistral barbados.com), gives lessons and rents boards. Windsurfing rentals are US$40 for 3 hours, or US$75 for a full day (add US$5 if you want insurance). To reach the club, take a taxi from the cruise terminal; it's about a US$15 one-way fare. Or go to **Club Mistral Oistins** (℡ 246/428-7277), which is better suited for beginning windsurfers.

GREAT LOCAL RESTAURANTS & BARS

Two tips: Be sure to try the tasty local delicacy, **flying fish** (you can even get it in burger form). And remember that because this is a British-flavored island, it is customary in restaurants for waitstaff to hold onto your bill until you ask for it.

Brown Sugar, Aquatic Gap (off Bay St.), St. Michael, just below Bridgetown on Carlisle Bay (℡ 246/426-7684), is an alfresco restaurant in a turn-of-the-20th-century bungalow. The chefs prepare some of the tastiest Bajan specialties on the island. Of the main dishes, Creole-broiled pepper chicken is popular, as are the stuffed crab backs. There's a great lunch buffet Monday through Friday for less than US$25 per person.

For pub grub, try the hopping **Whistling Frog Pub** (℡ 246/420-5021), located at the Gap Hotel facing Dover Beach. Lunch will run you about US$12.

8 Belize

Located on the northeastern tip of Central America, bordering Mexico on the north, Guatemala to the west and south, and the Caribbean to the east, Belize combines Central American and Caribbean cultures. The area offers both ancient Mayan ruins and a 298km (185-mile) coral reef that runs the entire length of the country—it's the largest in the Western Hemisphere and the second-largest in the world, supporting a tremendous number of patch reefs, shoals, and more than 1,000 islands called cays (pronounced *keys*), the largest and most populous being Ambergris Caye. (Both **Ambergris Caye** and **Caye Caulker** are popular with visitors, offering a barefoot informality.) The country is noted for its eco-friendly ways and, unlike many other Caribbean countries, is serious in its dedication to conservation: One-fifth of Belize's total landmass is dedicated as nature reserves, and 7,770 sq. km (3,030 sq. miles) of its waters are protected as well.

THE TRAVELOCITY GUARANTEE

...THAT SAYS EVERYTHING YOU BOOK WILL BE RIGHT, OR WE'LL WORK WITH OUR TRAVEL PARTNERS TO MAKE IT RIGHT, RIGHT AWAY.

*To drive home the point,
we're going to use the word "right" in every single sentence.*

Let's get right to it. Right to the meat! Only Travelocity guarantees everything about your booking will be right, or we'll work with our travel partners to make it right, right away. Right on!

Here's a picture taken smack dab right in the middle of Antigua, where the Guarantee also covers you.

The Guarantee covers all but one of the items pictured to the right.

For example, what if the ocean view you booked actually looks out at a downright ugly parking lot? You'd be right to call – we're there for you. And no one in their right mind would be pleased to learn the rental car place has closed and left them stranded. Call Travelocity and we'll help get you back on the right track.

Now, you may be thinking, "Yeah, right, I'm so sure." That's OK; you have the right to remain skeptical. That is until we mention help is always right around the corner. Call us right off the bat, knowing our customer service reps are there for you 24/7. Righting wrongs. Left and right.

Now if you're guessing there are some things we can't control, like the weather, well you're right. But we can help you with most things – to get all the details in righting,* visit travelocity.com/guarantee.

*Sorry, spelling things right is one of the few things not covered under the Guarantee.

I'd give my right arm for a guarantee like this, although I'm glad I don't have to.

travelocity
You'll never roam alone.

Frommer's Favorite Belize Experiences

Visiting Lamanai: Satisfying to both the archaeology buff and the wildlife enthusiast, a visit to this Mayan site gives you both land and water experiences. And how could you pass up wonderful photo ops and howler monkeys? (See "Best Cruise Line Shore Excursions," below.)

Snorkeling or Diving at Hol Chan Marine Reserve & Shark Ray Alley: The reef is what it's all about when it comes to the waters of Belize: Friendly fish and playful stingrays make for an extremely memorable day. (See "Best Cruise Line Shore Excursions," below.)

Going Horseback Riding: Whether you're an experienced rider or have always wanted to give it a try, Banana Bank Lodge is definitely the place to go. (See "Excursions Offered by Local Agencies," below.)

Tubing in Caves: Glide down the Caves Branch River in an inner tube while wearing miner-style flashlight headbands. (See "Best Cruise Line Shore Excursions," below.)

Xunantunich: This Mayan site in western Belize boasts one of the largest temples in the country; if you're sturdy enough to climb to the top, you'll be rewarded with amazing panoramic views of Belize and nearby Guatemala. (See "Best Cruise Line Shore Excursions," below.)

GETTING AROUND

BY TAXI   Taxis are available at the pier, in town, and in resort areas, and are easily recognized by their green license plates. Although the taxis have no meters, the drivers do charge somewhat standard fares; ask what your fare will be prior to hiring a taxi.

BY WATER TAXI   From the **Marine Terminal,** in Belize City (© **501/203-1969**), water-taxi service runs to Ambergris Caye, Caye Caulker, and various other cays. Boats leave at 9am, 10:30am, noon, 1:30pm, 3pm, and 4:30pm. The ride from Belize City to San Pedro, the main town on Ambergris Caye, is approximately 80 minutes and costs US$28 round-trip.

BY PLANE   Local airlines **Tropic Air** (© **800/422-3435** or 501/226-2012; www.tropicair.com) and **Maya Island Air** (© **800/225-6732** or 501/226-2435; www.maya air.com) offer hourly flights to Ambergris Caye, Caye Caulker, Placencia, and Dangriga. The flight to Ambergris Caye takes approximately 20 minutes, and, because you fly so low, you get a breathtaking view of the surrounding cays and atolls. Keep your eyes open for stingrays and dolphins swimming below you. Flights leave from Belize City going to San Pedro approximately every 90 minutes from 7:40am until 5:40pm; the cost is approximately US$105 round-trip. The term "puddle jumper" really applies here: The planes can be as small as 14-seaters, and you may even get to sit next to the pilot. You can get a walk-up ticket, but it's best to reserve ahead.

BY RENTAL CAR   Not recommended. Although most of the major roads and highways are paved, lots of patches are in need of repair, which makes for a very bumpy ride.

BEST CRUISE LINE SHORE EXCURSIONS

Lamanai (US$87, 7½ hr.): Lamanai is one of the largest ceremonial centers in Belize. In the original Mayan language, its name means "submerged crocodile," and you will see various crocodile carvings throughout the site. Starting with a 45-minute drive up the Northern Highway to Tower Hill, you'll board a riverboat and head up the New River. Along the way, through the mangroves, your guide will point out crocodiles basking in the sun, a variety of birds (including jacanas and hawks), delicate water lilies, and other exotic flowers such as black orchids. You'll pass local fisherman and, surprisingly, Mennonite farms—Mennonites from Canada and Mexico began arriving in Belize in 1958 in search of land and a more isolated and simple life, and today their community numbers around 7,000. Landing at the Lamanai grounds, you'll enjoy lunch and then tour the series of temples. There are more than 700 structures, most of them still buried beneath mounds of earth. For a view above the thick jungle, you can climb some of the temples—look in the trees for toucans and spider monkeys playing or napping. You won't mistake the roar of the howler monkey. Your guide may tell you about the red gumbo-limbo tree, whose bark becomes red and then peels off—it's jokingly referred to as the tourist tree. A small archaeological museum is at the site, and there are a few stands to buy souvenirs.

Altun Ha (US$45, 4 hr.): Meaning "water of the rock," Altun Ha is a relatively small site of temples and tombs that was rediscovered in 1957 during expansion of the Northern Highway. This is one of the most extensively excavated sites and was an important trading post during the classical Mayan period. Many treasures were found here, including a carved jade head representing Kinich Ahau, the Mayan sun god (not on display). It has become one of the country's national symbols and is depicted on Belize's currency. The tour includes lunch. There is a small gift shop on site.

Xunantunich (US$89, 7 ½ hr.): This site, also called **Maiden of the Rock,** is located near the Guatemalan border, overlooking the Mopan River. Xunantunich was a major ceremonial center during the classic Mayan period. After crossing the river by hand-cranked ferry, you can explore six major plazas surrounded by more than 25 temples and palaces, including El Castillo (the castle), the largest of the temples. Be sure to climb to the top—it's well worth it for the amazing panoramic view. A new visitor center houses old excavation photos, a scale model, and a few exhibits and souvenir shops. Afterward, you'll head to San Ignacio for lunch and enjoy the sounds of a marimba band.

Hol Chan Marine Reserve & Shark Ray Alley (US$92, 8 hr.): You'll head north for an hour-long speedboat ride to Hol Chan (Mayan for "little channel"), 6.4km (4 miles) southeast of San Pedro on Ambergris Caye; snorkel the reef for about an hour; and then head off to the Shark Ray Alley dive site, about 5 minutes away, where you'll see and pet dozens of southern stingrays and nurse sharks. Guides bring goodies for them to eat, and they stick around till the food is gone. Remember to bring a disposable underwater camera—if you're going to pet a stingray, you may as well capture it on film! Lunch is on San Pedro, where you can find yourself a rum punch, go shopping, or just hang out at the beach.

Cave Tubing (US$98, 6½ hr.): Upon arrival at Jaguar Paw, you'll take a 45-minute hike down a jungle trail where your guide will point out various plants and trees used by the ancient Maya for medicinal purposes. When you get to the cave, your guide will hand out flashlights and inner tubes and set you afloat, propelled by the current, through the cave system. On several occasions, you'll emerge into the sunlight before entering another cave. The float lasts about 2 hours, after which you'll have lunch. Bring a change of clothes.

EXCURSIONS OFFERED BY LOCAL AGENCIES

Taxi Tours: Generally, the excursions offered by the cruise lines are the way to go in Belize, but if you crave a more personalized experience, you can hire a taxi driver who doubles as a guide (make sure you tell the driver that you want a tour before getting into the taxi and negotiating a price). Tour guides must be licensed by the Belize Tourism Board and are recognizable with a photo ID. Of the many operators, one of the larger ones is **Cruise Solutions** (© 501/223-0748; www.shorexbelize.com), which offers a wide variety of tours all around the country and can arrange custom tours as well. For a tour of Belize City, try to snag **Lasalle Tillet** of **S&L Travel & Tours** (© **501/227-7593** or 501/227-5145; fax 501/227-7594; www.sltravelbelize. com). Everyone in town seems to know him, and you'll enjoy his cheerful demeanor and insightful information.

Horseback Tours: Contact **Banana Bank Lodge** (© **501/820-2020;** www.banana bank.com), located in Belmopan, about an hour's drive from the pier. It offers 7-hour tours through the jungle, plains, and riverbank. Larger-than-life cowboy/owner John Carr greets each of his guests personally and makes your riding experience a memorable one. The US$90 per-person cost includes a delicious traditional lunch and a tour of the lodge's grounds. Well-trained horses are matched to each rider's ability.

Fishing Excursions: Belize is a fishing mecca, with an abundance of game fish that guarantees excellent sport. The estuaries, inlets, and mouths to the many rivers are known for their tarpon, snook, and jacks; the lagoons and grass flats are known for bonefish, permit, and barracuda; the coral reefs support grouper, snapper, jacks, and barracuda; and the deeper waters offshore are home to sailfish, marlin, bonito, and pompano. One of the largest operations is the **Belize River Lodge** (© **888/275-4843;** www.belizeriverlodge.com), which offers a half-day fishing package that includes lunch and drinks (US$388 for up to two guests). A favorite local fishing guide is **Richard Young, Jr.** (© **501/227-4385**), who charges US$250 for up to three guests for a half-day excursion.

ON YOUR OWN: WITHIN WALKING DISTANCE

Belize City is the hub of the country but is not home to the country's major attractions. The historic harbor district right around the pier is small and quaint. You'll find a few restaurants here, and the **Baron Bliss Park and Lighthouse** is just a short stroll away. After sailing from Portugal, Baron Bliss arrived sick with food poisoning and remained aboard his yacht for 2 months; local fisherman and administrators treated him kindly and taught him about Belize. He died soon after arriving, but not before changing his will and leaving $2 million to Belize in a trust fund. That money made possible the building of the Bliss Institute Library and Museum and a number of health clinics and markets around the country, as well as helping with the Belize City water system. The baron is considered Belize's greatest benefactor, and Baron Bliss Day, a national holiday, is celebrated on March 9.

Outside of the immediate port area, much of the rest of the city is run-down and poor, with narrow, crowded streets and many old colonial structures that are in need of repair. However, since tourism is an important industry in Belize, the country is making an effort to spruce up the city and reduce crime, instituting a squad of Tourism Police to patrol popular tourist areas. Its officers are dressed in brown uniforms.

ON YOUR OWN: BEYOND THE PORT AREA

A 20-minute flight will get you to **Ambergris Caye,** the largest of Belize's 200 offshore islands and the reputed inspiration for the Madonna song "La Isla Bonita." You know: "Last night I dreamt of San Pedro . . . tropical island breeze . . . all of nature wild and free . . . " blah blah blah? The thing is, she got it about right. Everyone drives around in golf carts, and you can, too (for about US$35 for an afternoon, from rental places located along the main streets and near the little airport). Once in San Pedro, the island's main town, the beach functions as the main street, offering plenty of shopping, restaurants, bars, and watersports.

Slightly smaller **Caye Caulker** is Belize's second-most-popular caye and is even more laid-back, with plenty of beachfront restaurants and bars. Despite the growth of tourism, the island retains a small-village feel not found in areas with large-scale tourist development. Almost all of the businesses are locally owned, and you'll rarely see vehicles larger than golf carts on the streets. You can just hang out on the beach or plunge into one of the island's watersports, which include snorkeling, scuba, fishing, kayaking, windsurfing, sailing, and manatee-watching. Birding is also popular.

The **Community Baboon Sanctuary,** about 48m (30 miles) west of Belize City off the Northern Highway in the Belize District (© **501/220-2181;** www.howlermonkeys. org), offers a guided tour along forest trails for US$5. Through a grassroots effort, the villagers and landowners have committed to preserving the habitat necessary to ensure a healthy population of black howler monkeys (known locally as baboons).

Birders should tour the **Crooked Tree Wildlife Sanctuary,** about 35 minutes from Belize City (© **501/614-5658**), which provides a habitat for more than 360 species of birds.

Another worthwhile venture is a visit to the **Belize Zoo,** along the Western Highway (© **501/220-8004;** www.belizezoo.org). First created as a haven for animals who were injured and couldn't be returned to the wild, the zoo now houses an impressive array of large cats, primates, reptiles, and birds in large, airy enclosures.

SHOPPING

In general, the best buys in Belize are wooden and slate carvings, Mayan calendars, pottery, ceramics, and furniture made by the Mennonites. At the pier, the new **Belize Tourism Village** offers shops specializing in local souvenirs such as mahogany bowls, jewelry, clothes, assorted carvings, and artwork. A local favorite is Marie Sharp's hot sauces and jams. They're served everywhere and can be purchased to take home. On Ambergris Caye, you'll find a variety of slightly upscale gift shops, and the excursion sites all have local goods available.

BEACHES

Compared to many other islands in the Caribbean, the beaches of Belize are neither the biggest nor the widest, but they are relaxing, with very clear water. Areas that offer the best beach sunbathing are in the cays, including **Ambergris Caye, Caye Caulker,** and **Tobacco Caye;** and on the mainland to the south, in **Dangriga** and **Placencia.** There are no beaches near Belize City.

SPORTS

WATERSPORTS If you don't opt for one of your ship's dive excursions, local dive shops can customize an experience for you. Hugh Parkey's **Belize Dive Connection** (© 888/223-5403 or 501/223-4526; www.belizediving.com) is conveniently located on the Radisson Pier and offers day scuba dives and snorkel trips with a yummy lunch. In San Pedro, **Aqua Dives** (© 800/641-2994 or 501/226-3415 or 501/226-3222; www.aquadives.com) is located on the beachfront and can plan your diving or snorkeling adventure. A one-tank dive will run about US$40; a two-tank reef dive, about US$90.

In the center of Lighthouse Reef Atoll, about 80km (50 miles) due east of Belize City, the **"Blue Hole"** was originally a cave. The roof fell in some 10,000 years ago as the land receded into the sea, leaving an almost perfectly circular hole 300m (984 ft.) in diameter and 124m (407 ft.) deep. Popularized by a Jacques Cousteau television special, it's become the most famous dive site in all of Belize.

Half Moon Caye, located at the southeast corner of Lighthouse Reef Atoll, was the first reserve to be established by the Natural Parks System Act of 1981, which specifically protected the Red-footed Booby bird and its rookery. Some 98 other species of birds have been recorded on the caye.

One of the newest national parks is **Laughing Bird Caye,** located 21km (13 miles) southeast of Placencia Village in the Stann Creek District. Although the caye was named for the large number of laughing gulls that used to live here, the birds have virtually abandoned their rookery because of excessive human encroachment. Since Laughing Bird Caye is a shelf atoll with deep channels, the scuba-diving and snorkeling opportunities are outstanding.

Many dive excursions include a barbecue lunch on **Goff's Caye.** Part of the Central Main Reef, it's a popular dive site itself.

GAMBLING

If you must do some gambling, the **Princess Hotel-Casino,** Newtown Barricks Road, Belize City (© 501/223-2670), is located 1 or 2 miles from the cruise pier. The casino is about 10 minutes and US$5 by taxi from the pier.

GREAT LOCAL RESTAURANTS & BARS

The local beer is **Belikan,** and you can order it most anywhere. If you visit Altun Ha, you'll recognize the site as the beer's logo (or vice versa).

IN BELIZE CITY Around the Belize Tourism Village, you'll find many pleasant restaurants within walking distance. Stroll to the Great House Hotel, 13 Cork St., to find the **Smokey Mermaid** (© 501/223-4759), situated in a lovely patio garden shaded by mango trees. One of its specialties is the yucca-crusted snapper with a fruity salsa topping. For dessert, be sure to try the coconut pie. The lunch special is US$10.

At the **Radisson Hotel** (© 800/333-3333 or 501/223-3333), you can pick from several dining choices, either inside or out on a deck overlooking the Caribbean. A buffet lunch is about US$12, while sandwiches and burgers can be had for about US$7.

Chateau Caribbean, 6 Marine Parade (© 501/223-0800), offers Caribbean and Asian specialties. Lunch runs approximately US$13.

IN SAN PEDRO, AMBERGRIS CAYE Most of the restaurants and bars here are on the beach, so you can just stroll along and stop at whatever place strikes your fancy.

ON CAYE CAULKER   Caye Caulker has about 25 restaurants, also mostly on the beach, offering Belizean and international cuisine, including fresh seafood. Lobster, conch, and red snapper are seasonal specialties.

FARTHER OUT   Heading west of Belize City, the very rustic **Cheers Bar & Restaurant** is kind of in the middle of nowhere, on the Western Highway at mile 31 (about 3km/1¾ miles from the Belize Zoo and 26km/16 miles from Banana Bank Lodge), but the food is good, it has a nice outdoor patio, and it's frequented by travelers and locals. Leave behind a memento T-shirt to say you were here—there are dozens of them from all over the world.

Still farther west, about 5km (3 miles) from Xunantunich, you'll find **Eva's Restaurant,** 22 Burns Ave., San Ignacio (© **501/804-2267**), where you can enjoy a tasty lunch and check your e-mail as well.

9 Bequia

Bequia (meaning "Island of the Cloud" in the original Carib, and inexplicably pronounced *Beck*-wee) is the largest island in the St. Vincent Grenadines, with a population of around 5,000. Sun-drenched, windswept, peaceful, and green (though arid), it's a popular stop for small-ship lines such as Clipper, ACCL, Star Clippers, Windjammer, and the more upscale Seabourn, SeaDream, and Windstar, which join the many yachts in Admiralty Bay throughout the yachting season.

Very much a tourism-oriented island, Bequia is nevertheless anything but touristy. You'll find a few of the requisite cheesy gift shops in the main town, **Port Elizabeth,** but none of the typical cruise port giants such as Little Switzerland. Instead, the town offers one of the most attractive port settings in the Caribbean, with restaurants, cozy bars, a produce market, and crafts shops strung along and around the **Belmont Walkway,** a path that skirts so close to the calm bay waters that at high tide you have to skip across rocks to avoid getting your feet wet. Many ships spend the night here or make late departures, allowing passengers to take in the nightlife.

The island has a rich seafaring tradition, including fishing, sailing, boat building (though most of the handmade boats that you'll see are scale models made for the yachting set), and even whaling, though this is whaling of a token, almost ritualistic sort—only about one whale is taken in any given year.

COMING ASHORE   Ships dock right in the center of the island's main town, Port Elizabeth, a stone's throw from the restaurants, bars, and shops that line the waterfront.

LANGUAGE   The official and daily-use language is English.

CURRENCY   The **Eastern Caribbean dollar** (EC$2.70 = US$1; EC$1 = US37¢) is used on Bequia; however, U.S. dollars are accepted by all businesses. It's always a good idea to ask if you're not sure which currency a price tag refers to. Prices quoted in this section are given in U.S. dollars.

INFORMATION   A small tourist information booth is right on the beach by the cruise dock, but frankly, you can see almost everything there is to do from the same spot. It's a pretty small island. For information before you go, contact the **Bequia Tourist Association** (© **784/458-3286;** www.bequiatourism.com) or the **St. Vincent & the Grenadines Department of Tourism** (© **800/729-1726** or 212/687-4981 in the U.S., or 784/457-1502; www.svgtourism.com).

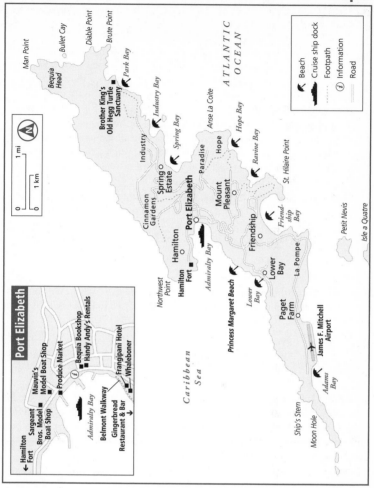

CALLING FROM THE U.S. To place a call to Bequia, you need only dial a "1" before the numbers listed in this section.

GETTING AROUND

Ships dock right in Port Elizabeth, putting you within walking distance of all the sights in town. The popular Princess Margaret Beach is within walking distance as well.

BY TAXI You'll find plenty of taxis lined up right at the cruise dock to take you around the island. The fare is approximately US$20 per hour, or US$5 per person per hour for groups of more than four.

BY WATER TAXI Water taxis can be picked up at the wharf. These are perfect for destinations in Admiralty Bay (Princess Margaret or Lower Bay Beach, as well as various

Frommer's Favorite Bequia Experiences

Strolling along the Belmont Walkway: In the evenings, this walkway at water's edge makes for a terrifically romantic stroll as you make your way from one nightspot to the next. You might even pick up the company of one of the friendly port dogs, who seem more interested in companionship than panhandling. (See "On Your Own: Within Walking Distance," below.)

Visiting Brother King's Old Hegg Turtle Sanctuary: Wanna see baby turtles? This is the place. You'll spot hundreds of the critters in the main swimming pool and in their own little private cubbyholes. You'll also hear about the sanctuary's conservation efforts. Donations are gladly accepted. (See "On Your Own: Beyond the Port Area," below.)

Visiting the Lower Bay & Princess Margaret Beach: South of Port Elizabeth, this stretch of sand is frequently described by cruisers as "the best beach I've ever experienced." It's a little chunk of paradise, backed by waving palms and fronted by yachts bobbing at anchor in the distance. (See "Beaches," below.)

bars and restaurants) or for just cruising the harbor. The fixed rate for one to four persons is about US$3.75 to Princess Margaret Beach, US$5.60 to Lower Bay Beach; other rates are negotiable.

BY MINIBUS Bequia's Main Road between the wharf and the airport is served by a fleet of small, unofficial dollar-cab minibuses that cruise regular routes, picking up passengers when flagged down (some obvious bus stops are also scattered around). Tell the driver where you want to go and he'll tell you a price.

BY RENTAL CAR Rentals are available at **Handy Andy's Rentals,** on the Main Road in Port Elizabeth, to the right of the dock if you're facing inland (© **784/458-3722;** http://handyandybequia.tripod.com). A Jeep Wrangler rents for US$80 daily. **Phil's Car Rental,** at the cruise ship dock (© **784/458-3304**), has Geo Trackers and Suzuki Sidekicks for approximately US$70 per day.

BY BICYCLE **Handy Andy's Rentals** (see above) also rents Mongoose mountain bikes for US$10.

BEST CRUISE LINE SHORE EXCURSIONS

Bequia is very much a "relax and have a drink" kind of island rather than one with a lot of definable, tourable attractions. Standard island tours (US$35, 3 hr.) offer an overview and still allow you plenty of time to poke around or go to the beach. Most other excursions are sailing trips around the island and to neighboring Mustique and Tobago, but we'd advise not missing Bequia. It's a lovely place.

Sailing Excursion to Mustique (US$90, 7–8 hr.): Sail aboard a schooner to exclusive (that is, rich people own it) Mustique, just southeast of Bequia, for strolling, shopping, snorkeling, or simply lying on the beach. Complimentary drinks are included aboard ship. A shorter version of this tour travels between islands by powerboat rather than sailing ship—less romantic, but speedier (US$70, 3–4 hr.).

ON YOUR OWN: WITHIN WALKING DISTANCE

In theory, almost the entire island of Bequia is within walking distance, but only for serious walkers. We decided to test out this theory by walking from Port Elizabeth to **Hamilton Fort,** just west of town, then backtracking through the port and down to the tiny old whaling village of **Paget Farm,** near the airport on Bequia's southern tip. As the crow flies it's not much of a distance, but curving roads and hilly terrain made it a real journey that took about 4 to 5 hours round-trip, with no significant stops. If your ship is in port late and you're in good shape, it's a great way to see the island (including lovely **Friendship Bay,** on the east coast) and meet some of the local people along the way. Bring water.

For those wanting something less strenuous, strolling around Port Elizabeth itself is close to idyllic. The **Belmont Walkway** runs south from the docks right at the water's edge (meaning at high tide, parts of it are actually under a few inches of water), fronting many restaurants, shops, and bars. This area is particularly romantic in the evenings.

Heading north from the docks along the Main Road, you'll find a homey produce market that also stocks some souvenir items. Across the street, **Mauvin's Model Boat Shop** (© 784/458-3669) is one of the visible reminders of the island's boat-building tradition, though now the money seems to lie in crafting scale models of real boats for sale to the yachting crowd. Farther along the Main Road, **Sargeant Bros. Model Boat Shop** (© 784/458-3344) is a larger shop offering the same type of merchandise. The workshop is a little more accessible here, so you can easily watch the craftsmen creating their wares (all the work is done by hand; no power tools are employed at all) and see models in various stages of construction. At both shops, the models are beautiful, lovingly constructed, and signed by the craftsman—but they're not what you'd call cheap: Prices start around US$110 for a tiny model and can go up as high as US$10,000 for something really fabulous. Farther along the Hamilton Main Road, in the section known as Ocar, Lawson Sargeant, descendant of one of the great trading schooner-building families, has opened the **Bequia Maritime Museum** (© 784/458-3896). Hours are Monday through Friday from 9am to 4:30pm, Saturday from 9am to noon, and by appointment. Admission is US$5.

If you continue walking along the Main Road, you'll pass through an area with many boating-supply stores and a few bars and food stands obviously geared to the local fishing and sailing trades. It's a quiet, pretty walk, even though it may well be the most "industrial" part of the island. Eventually you'll come upon a concrete walkway hanging above the water along the coast. From here, the going gets rough—many sections of the walkway have been cracked and heaved drastically off-kilter by hurricanes, and it's patched here and there with planks and other makeshift materials. At the end of the walkway, the road starts curving uphill and inland through a quiet residential area, and all the way up to **Hamilton Fort,** perched above Admiralty Bay and offering a lovely view of Port Elizabeth, though that's about all it offers—a few tiny fragments of battlements and five plugged canons are all that remain of the old fort. A taxi

---

Use Your Ship's Facilities

Since Bequia is an extremely dry island and is very conscious of water conservation, it has no public washrooms except in restaurants. You'd be well advised to use your ship's bathroom facilities before coming ashore.

can take you here by another route if you want to avoid the walk (a good idea unless you're in decent shape and very sure-footed).

ON YOUR OWN: BEYOND THE PORT AREA

At Park Beach, on the island's northeast coast, 3.2km (2 miles) east of Port Elizabeth, **Brother King's Old Hegg Turtle Sanctuary** (© 784/458-3245) offers a chance to see conservation in action. Founded in 1995 by the eponymous King and dedicated to raising and releasing Hawksbill turtle hatchlings, the sanctuary is a real labor of love. A main concrete swimming pool and small plastic kiddy pools allow maturing hatchlings to socialize. Brother King and his assistants are on hand to tell you about their conservation efforts. The sanctuary is open Sunday through Friday from 9:30am to 5pm; it charges a US$5 admission fee to help keep the place going.

Aside from this and the activities in Port Elizabeth, most of the island's other attractions are beaches, so turn to that section, below.

SHOPPING

You'll find most of the shopping that's worth doing within walking distance of the docks in Port Elizabeth. Several generic gift shops are located farther along, some fronting off the Belmont Walkway, including **Solana's**, for Caribelle batiks, T-shirts, and so on.

Heading south from the pier, one of the first businesses you'll come to is the **Bequia Bookshop** (© 784/458-3905), selling books on the island's and region's cultures and history, poetry and prose by local authors, yachting guides, and a selection of other fiction and nonfiction titles, as well as truly beautiful scrimshaw pocket knives, pendants, money clips, necklaces, and pins, all made from polished domesticated camel bone rather than the traditional whalebone.

Sam McDowell, the artist who creates these scrimshaw items, opens his **Banana Patch Studio** for visitors by appointment. Located in the little village of Paget Farm

---

Moments A Quiet Day on Union Island

Some small ships stop for a day at quiet, tranquil (very quiet, very tranquil) Union Island, the southernmost port of entry in the St. Vincent Grenadines. Think of your stop here as a "recovery day" rather than a whiz-bang exciting day in port: There are few facilities (none whatsoever in Chatham Bay, where ships usually tender passengers to land), few people, and few opportunities for anything more than swimming, snorkeling, and a little beach-combing. You'll likely see hundreds of conch-shell pieces along the beach, since a number of local fishermen are based here. (You can always tell if the conch was naturally thrown up on the beach or caught, since the latter have a small gash in the shell—the method the fishermen use to sever the muscle by which the conch beast holds onto its shell home.) Some enterprising fishermen set out the best shells they find (conch and otherwise) on small tables, offering them to tourists for a couple bucks—you miss out on the personal thrill of finding them yourself, but they're some mighty nice shells. The snorkeling is decent in Chatham Bay, though the waters don't yield the diversity you'll see elsewhere in the eastern Caribbean.

on the southern part of the island, near the airport, the studio displays Sam's scrimshaw and whaling-themed paintings, as well as his wife Donna's intricate mosaic shellwork. Call or fax © **784/458-3865** for an appointment.

Heading in the other direction in Port Elizabeth, north from the docks, you'll find the two model-boat shops described above, as well as a couple of open-air souvenir/crafts stalls, a produce market, and **Kennie's Music Shop,** for island sounds on CD.

Not to be missed is **Spring Pottery and Art Gallery** (© **784/457-3757**), built among the ruins of the old Spring sugar estate, where it offers decorative and functional pottery items created on site, as well as a permanent display of paintings by local and visiting artists. Open November through April.

Also of note is **Claude-Victorine's Atelier** (© **784/458-3150**), located up the hill from the far end of Lower Bay Beach. It's a working studio with magnificent hand-painted silks, cushion covers, pareus, and wall hangings.

BEACHES

Beaches are one of the big draws on Bequia, and all are open to the public. The best on the list is **Princess Margaret Beach,** a golden-sand stretch lying just south of Port Elizabeth. To get here, take the Belmont Walkway to its end at Plantation House; from there, take the dirt path over the hill. **Lower Bay Beach** is a little farther down along the same stretch of coast.

On the northeast coast, the beach at **Industry Bay** is, despite its name, windswept and gorgeous, a scene straight out of a romance novel. Trees on the hills surrounding the bay grow up to a certain height and then level out, growing sideways due to the constant wind off the Atlantic. The three-room **Crescent Beach Inn** (© **784/458-3400**) lies along this stretch, in case you want to come back after your cruise and stay a while.

Along the southeast coast is **Friendship Bay,** an area that draws many European visitors.

Warning: Do not under any circumstances pick or eat the small green apples you'll see growing in some spots; these are extremely poisonous.

SPORTS

Besides walking (see "On Your Own: Within Walking Distance," above) and biking (mountain bikes are available from Handy Andy's Rentals, right by the cruise dock), hiking the more inaccessible parts of the island can be interesting and rewarding. Some trails are marked, and special nature walks can be arranged through **Martine & Francois** (© **784/457-3898**), specialists in dry tropical ecosystems, flora, and fauna.

Most of the sports here, like the rest of life on the island, center on the water. **Dive Bequia** (© **784/458-3504;** www.dive-bequia.com) and **Bequia Dive Adventure** (© **784/458-3826;** www.bequiadiveadventures.com), located along Belmont Walkway right by the docks, specialize in diving and snorkeling. **Marlin's Water Sports** (© **784/526-6552**) offers rentals and lessons for those interested in windsurfing, water-skiing, laser sailing, and kayaking.

GREAT LOCAL RESTAURANTS & BARS

The coastal stretch along the Belmont Walkway is chockablock with restaurants and bars. The local beer of St. Vincent and the Grenadines is **Hairoun,** which is decent but not up to the level of St. Lucia's Piton. The local rum is **Sunset.**

The **Frangipani Hotel Restaurant & Bar** (© **784/458-3255**) is right on the water along the walkway. Lunch, which is served from 10am to 5pm, includes sandwiches, salads, and seafood platters. Dinner specialties include conch chowder, baked chicken with rice-and-coconut stuffing, and an array of fresh fish. On Thursday nights, the bar hosts an excellent steel band. It's a lovely scene, with yachters, locals, cruisers from ships that have stayed late in port, and a coterie of friendly local dogs all getting to know one another over drinks or settling down for the restaurant's special barbecue. Lunch is about US$9.

Farther along the walkway, the **Whaleboner Bar & Restaurant** (② 784/458-3233) serves a nice thin-crust pizza (with toppings such as lobster, shrimp, and generic "fish"), sandwiches, fish and chips, and cold beer, either indoors or at tables in its shaded, oceanview front yard. It's a perfect casual resting-up spot after walking around the island. Lunch is about US$10.

Also right along the waterfront is the **Gingerbread Restaurant & Bar** (② 784/458-3800), with a beautiful balcony dining room that's open throughout the day, plus a downstairs cafe that serves coffee, tea, and Italian ice cream at outdoor tables. Lunch is about US$12.

Continue along the walkway for **Mac's Pizzeria** (② 784/458-3474), famous for its lobster pizzas and specialty baked goods such as breads, cakes, cookies, and the best cheesecake. Next door, **L'Auberge des Grenadines** (② 784/458-3201) has a live lobster pool and specializes in French Creole dishes.

10 Bonaire

Ever wonder what's going on under all that water you've been cruising on for days? There's no better place to find out than the island of Bonaire: "Divers Paradise," as the slogan on the island's license plates says. Avid divers have flocked to this unspoiled treasure for years for its pristine waters, stunning coral reefs (which encircle the island just feet from shore), and vibrant marine life—it's simply one of the best places in the Caribbean for diving and snorkeling.

The island also offers other adventure activities such as mountain biking, kayaking, and windsurfing; if these options sound too strenuous, why not just marvel at the sun-basking iguanas, fluorescent lora parrots, wild donkeys, graceful flamingos, and feral goats? As for flora, you're likely to see more cacti in Bonaire than anywhere outside of the deserts of Mexico and the Southwest. Sprawling bushes of exotic succulents and permanently windswept divi-divi trees also abound. If you'd rather join the iguanas and just bake in the sun, Bonaire's beaches are intimate and uncrowded. In fact, the entire island is cozy and manageable. In no time at all, you'll feel it's your very own private resort.

Relying on your high-school language lessons, you might think Bonaire was colonized by the French and named for its "good air," but you'd be wrong: The name actually comes from the Caiquetio word *bonay*, which means "low country." Located 81km (50 miles) north of Venezuela and 48km (30 miles) east of Curaçao, this untrampled, boomerang-shaped refuge is one of the southernmost Caribbean islands, and forms the B in the ABC chain, along with Aruba and Curaçao. Thirty-nine kilometers (24 miles) long and 5 to 11km (3–6¾ miles) wide at various points, it's large enough to require a motorized vehicle if you want to explore, but small enough that you won't get lost.

The Caiquetios, members of the Arawak tribe who sailed from the coast of Venezuela a thousand years ago, were Bonaire's first human inhabitants. Europeans arrived 500 years later, in 1499, when Alonso de Ojeda and Amerigo Vespucci claimed

the island for Spain. The Spanish enslaved the indigenous people and moved them to other Caribbean islands. Later, the Europeans used the island to raise cows, goats, horses, and donkeys. The Dutch gained control in the 1630s, and on the back of African slave labor, Bonaire became an important salt producer.

With the discovery of oil in Venezuela early in the 20th century, Aruba and Curaçao became refining centers, and Bonaire, too, got a piece of the pie. Tourism, the island's major industry today, developed after World War II, when Bonaire won self-rule from the Netherlands (though it remains a Dutch protectorate). The people of Bonaire are a mix of African, Dutch, and South American ancestries. You'll also meet expatriates from the U.S., Britain, and Australia.

COMING ASHORE Cruise ships dock in the port of **Kralendijk** (*Crawl*-en-dike), the island's capital, commercial center, and largest town (pop. about 2,500). The dock leads to **Wilhelmina Park,** a pleasant public space named after a former Dutch queen. **Queen Beatrix Way,** the brick-paved path along the waterfront, is lined with open-air restaurants and bars. Most of the town's shopping is a block inland on **Kaya Grandi.**

Your best bet for making long-distance phone calls is **Telbo,** the central phone company office, located at Kaya Libertador Simón Bolívar 8. It's open Monday through Friday until 4pm, but closed from 11:45am to 1:30pm for lunch.

LANGUAGE   Almost everyone in Bonaire speaks English, which, along with Dutch, is a required course in the local schools. The local patois and language of the street is Papiamento, a rich blend of Dutch, Spanish, Portuguese, French, English, Caribbean Indian, and several African languages. Given the island's proximity to Venezuela, you're likely to hear Spanish as well.

CURRENCY   Bonaire's official currency is the **Netherland Antilles florin,** also called the **guilder** (exchange rate at press time: 1.75 NAF = US$1; 1 NAF = US56¢). Don't waste your time exchanging money, though, since the U.S. dollar is as widely accepted as the local currency. Change may be a mixture of dollars and guilders. If you need cash, several ATMs are located along Kaya Grandi. Traveler's checks and credit cards are also widely accepted. Unless otherwise noted, prices quoted in this section are in U.S. dollars.

INFORMATION   The **Tourism Corporation Bonaire** is located at Kaya Grandi 2, in Kralendijk (© **800/BONAIRE** in the U.S., or 599/717-8322; fax 599/717-8408; www.infobonaire.com).

CALLING FROM THE U.S.   When calling Bonaire from the United States, dial the international access code (011) before the numbers listed in this section.

GETTING AROUND

BY TAXI   Taxis greet cruise ship passengers at the pier. Although the cabs are unmetered, the government establishes rates, and drivers should produce a price list upon request. Most cabs can be hired for a tour of the island, with as many as four passengers allowed to go along for the ride. Negotiate a price before leaving, but expect to pay about US$30 per hour. You can get more information by calling the **Taxi Central Dispatch** office at © **599/717-8100.**

BY RENTAL CAR   Highway signs are in Dutch and sometimes English, with easy-to-understand international symbols. Driving is on the right, the same as in the States and most of Europe. A valid driver's license is acceptable for renting and driving a car. **Avis, Budget, Hertz,** and **National** all have offices here, as do a number of local companies.

BY SCOOTER, MOPED, OR MOTORCYCLE   If you plan to stick relatively close to the port area, scooters and mopeds are practical options. They can be rented from **Rento Fun Drive,** Kaya Grandi 47 (© **599/717-2408;** www.rentofun.com), or **Bonaire Motorcycle Shop,** Kaya Grandi 54 (© **599/717-7790** or 599/786-2131). Mopeds are about US$25 a day; two-seat scooters run about US$32. A motorcycle (with a valid motorcycle license) will cost you about US$50 per day, or US$75 for a three-wheel chopper.

BY BICYCLE   For getting around town or exploring the nearby coast, try bicycling. Note that the coastal terrain is essentially flat, but the sun can be brutal even before noon. Plan your excursion as early in the day as possible. **Cycle Bonaire,** at the Sand Dollar Condominium Resort, Kaya Gobernador N. Debrot 77A (© **599/717-2229**), rents 21-speed mountain bikes (US$15) and arranges half- (US$55) and full-day

Frommer's Favorite Bonaire Experiences

Scuba Diving: Diving in Bonaire is truly easier than anywhere else on earth. The island's leeward coast has more than 80 dive sites, and whether you're diving from a boat or right from shore, you'll see spectacular coral formations and as many types of fish as anywhere in the Caribbean. If you're not certified to dive, you can take a half-day resort course to see firsthand what divers rave about. If you'd rather just stick to snorkeling, abundant marine life is perfectly visible just beneath the crystal-clear water.

Mountain Biking along the Western Coast: Bike along the coast on a road bordered with cactus and carved through lava and limestone. The road north from the island's capital and main town, Kralendijk, is relatively flat and passes several uncrowded beaches—perfect for cooling off.

Exploring Washington-Slagbaai National Park: This preserve is home to a variety of exotic wildlife and vegetation, and offers spectacular coastal views. At times, the towering cacti, the iguanas, and the thousands of jittery lizards make you think you're in Arizona; but the humidity, flamingos, and beaches make it clear you're not. (See "On Your Own: Beyond the Port Area," below.)

Making New Friends at the Donkey Sanctuary: Donkeys were first brought to Bonaire centuries ago as beasts of burden. Today, more than 300 of them, many orphaned or injured by cars, call this oasis near the airport home. They'll greet you as you enter the gate and accompany you around the tidy, brightly colored grounds. After rehabilitation, they're returned to the wild. If you're moved by the animals' unconditional affection, you can adopt one; as a new parent, you'll receive photos and letters from your adoptee twice a year. The sanctuary is located down a bumpy dirt road just off the coastal road, south of the airport in Kralendijk (© **599/9-560-7607;** www.bonairenature.com/donkey), and is open daily from 10am to 4pm. There's no admission charge, but donations are appreciated. The souvenir shop has donkey shirts, donkey bags, donkey art, and very nice donkey-milk soap and lotions. Plans are "a-hoof" to make the entire reserve into a drive-through donkey safari.

(US$65) tours. **Rento Fun Drive,** Kaya Grandi 47 (© **599/717-2408** or 599/786-2131) rents beach cruisers and hybrids for about US$10 per day.

BEST CRUISE LINE SHORE EXCURSIONS

One-Tank Scuba Excursion for Certified Divers (US$129, 3½–4 hr.) or **Discover Scuba for Uncertified Divers** (US$119, 3 hr.): Dive in the island's famous Bonaire National Marine Park; it's the perfect place for beginners and experts alike.

Sail and Snorkel (US$59, 3 hr.): The snorkeling here is some of the best you'll find in the Caribbean, and this tour takes you to the famed Bonaire National Marine Park.

North Tour & Donkey Sanctuary (US$49, 3 hr.): This bus tour explores northern coastal Bonaire, visiting the flamingos at Goto Lake, the island's oldest settlement at

Rincón, and the Donkey Sanctuary (see "Frommer's Favorite Bonaire Experiences," above). If you've got a thing for donkeys, this is the tour for you.

Water Taxi to Klein Bonaire (US$29, 3 hr.): Take a 30-minute boat ride to a deserted tropical island for a serene day on the beach. Pack a snack and plenty of sunscreen; there are no facilities and little shade, but beverages are provided.

ON YOUR OWN: WITHIN WALKING DISTANCE

You can walk the length of **Kralendijk** in an hour or less. It's a sleepy town, but its residents like it that way, thank you. The **tourist office,** at Kaya Grandi 2, has walking-tour maps, but because Bonaire has always been off the beaten track, Kralendijk's highlights are modest and few. You'll probably want to stroll along the seafront with its views and restaurants, and along **Kaya Grandi,** the island's major shopping district. Just south of the town dock is **Fort Oranje,** a tiny fortress that has a cannon dating from the time of Napoleon. The town has some charming Dutch Caribbean architecture—gabled roofs you might see in Amsterdam, but painted in cheerful Caribbean colors, especially sunny ochre and terra cotta. If your ship arrives early enough, you can visit the tiny waterfront produce market.

ON YOUR OWN: BEYOND THE PORT AREA

As a day visitor, you'll probably choose to explore either the northern or southern part of the island. The coastal road north of Kralendijk is one of the most beautiful in the Antilles. Turquoise, azure, and cobalt waters stretch to the horizon on your left, while pink-coral and gray-limestone cliffs loom on your right. Towering cacti, intimate coastal coves, strange rock formations, and panoramic vistas add to the beauty. The north also boasts Washington-Slagbaai National Park, an impressive, 5,400-hectare (13,338-acre) preserve that occupies the northwestern portion of the island, as well as Rincón, Bonaire's "other" town and oldest settlement.

NORTH OF KRALENDIJK   Soon after leaving Kralendijk, you'll find **Barcadera,** on the coast road across from the Bonaire Caribbean Club. This old cave was once used to trap goats. Take the stone steps down to the cave and examine the stalactites.

Just past the Radio Nederland towers, **1,000 Steps Beach** and dive site offers lovely views: picturesque coves, craggy coastline, and tropical waters of changing hues. There are actually only 67 steps; it just feels like a thousand if you're schlepping dive gear.

At the Kaya Karpata intersection, you'll see a mustard-colored building on your right. It's what's left of the aloe-processing facilities of **Landhuis Karpata,** a 100-year-old former plantation. The modest exhibits here explain the cultivation, harvesting, and processing of aloe, once a major export crop.

Thirty or 40 arduous minutes after turning right on Kaya Karpata, you'll arrive in **Rincón,** the original Spanish settlement on the island, founded in 1527. The town eventually became the home of African slaves who worked the island's plantations and salt pans. Nestled in a valley away from either coast, Rincón was hidden from marauding pirates, who plagued the Caribbean for decades. Today, the quiet and picturesque village is home to Bonaire's oldest church, a handsome ochre-and-white structure.

The pride of Bonaire, located on the island's northern tip, **Washington-Slagbaai National Park** (© 599/788-9015; www.washingtonparkbonaire.com) was one of the Caribbean's first national parks. Formerly two separate plantations that produced aloe and charcoal and raised goats, it now showcases the island's geology, animals, and vegetation. The park boasts more than 190 species of birds; thousands of kadushi, yatu, and prickly pear cactus; and herds of wild goats, foraging donkeys, flocks of flamingos, and what seems like billions of lizards. The scenery includes stark, desertlike hills; quiet beaches; secluded caverns; and wave-battered cliffs. You have two options: the shorter 24km (15-mile) route around the park, marked with green arrows, or the longer 35km (22-mile) track, marked with yellow arrows. You'll have plenty of opportunities to hike, swim, or snorkel either way. The unpaved roads are well marked and safe, but rugged; jeeps trump small cars. Mountain bikes are allowed in the park, but motorcycles and scooters are not, so therefore must be left at headquarters while you hike the nearby trails. Admission is US$10 for adults and US$5 for children under 12; the park is open from 8am to 5pm daily except for major holidays, with the last entry at 2:45pm. Guide booklets and maps are available at the gate, where there's also a small museum and visitor center.

On your way back to Kralendijk, take the Kaminda Onima, which traces the island's northeastern coast to **Onima,** the site of 500-year-old Caiquetio Indian inscriptions. Some of the red-and-brown drawings depict turtles and rain; others appear to have religious significance. You'll be able to recognize snakes, human hands, and the sun among the roughly 75 inscriptions.

Before returning to Kralendijk, call on **Sherman Gibbs.** You'll find his monument to the beauty of common objects on Kaminda Tras di Montaña, the road leading back to Kralendijk. Eccentric is one way to describe Mr. Gibbs. Sherman, who's as gentle as his pet iguanas, combines old detergent bottles, boat motors, buoys, car seats, and just about anything else to create a wondrously happy sanctuary. The wind and old fan blades power his TV.

SOUTH OF KRALENDIJK   Just minutes south of town, dazzlingly bright salt pyramids dominate the horizon. These hills, looking more like alpine snowdrifts than sodium mounds, are created when seawater is forced into lakes by the tide and then evaporates, leaving crystallized salt behind. Farther from the road, abandoned saltworks have been set aside as a **flamingo sanctuary.** Bonaire is one of the world's few nesting places for pink flamingos, a species that until recently was seriously threatened by extinction. Thanks to the reserve, the island's flamingo population now swells to roughly 10,000 during breeding season, rivaling the island's human population of 13,000. The sanctuary is completely off-limits to the public because the birds are extremely wary of humans and disturbances of any kind. But even from the road, you can spot a pink haze on the horizon, and with binoculars, you can see the graceful birds feeding in the briny pink-and-purple waters.

At the island's southern tip, restored **slave huts** stand as monuments to the inhumanity of the island's slave era. Each hut, no bigger than a large doghouse, provided crude nighttime shelter for slaves brought from Africa by the Dutch West India Company to cut dyewood, cultivate maize, and harvest solar salt. On Friday afternoons, the slaves trekked 7 hours in the oppressive heat to their homes and families in Rincón for the weekend, returning to the salt pans on Sunday evenings.

Located on the eastern side of the island's southern tip, the classically picturesque **Willemstoren Lighthouse,** Bonaire's first, was built in 1837. It's fully automated today and usually closed to visitors, but its magnificent setting is the real draw. Odd little bundles of driftwood, bleached coral, and rocks in the area look like something out of *The Blair Witch Project,* but they were actually constructed by fishermen to mark where boats have been left.

A few minutes up the east coast is **Lac Bay,** a lagoon that's every bit as tranquil as the nearby windward sea is furious. The calm, shallow waters and steady breezes make the area ideal for windsurfing, and various fish come here to hatch their young. Deep inside the lagoon, mangrove trees with *Edward Scissorhands*-like roots lunge out of the water. If it weren't for the relentlessly cheerful sun, they might seem sinister. Wild donkeys, goats, and flamingos pepper the countryside along the way.

SHOPPING

You'll find most shops on **Kaya Grandi,** on the adjacent streets, and in small malls. But don't expect to be caught up in a duty-free frenzy in Bonaire. You'll be able to hit every store in Kralendijk before lunch, and you'll probably find greater selections and better prices at other ports. The island is a great place to buy certain items, though. Consider top-of-the-line dive watches and underwater cameras. Or how about jewelry with marine themes?

For an impressive array of unique gifts and hand-finished jewelry with a marine theme (the diamond-and-sapphire seahorse set in white gold was our favorite), check out **Jewel of Bonaire,** Kaya Grandi 38 (© **599/717-8890**). There's also a nice selection of jewelry and hand-blown glass plates at **Atlantis** (© **599/717-7730**).

For TAG Heuer dive watches, Cuban cigars, and Lladró porcelain, try **Littman Jewelers,** Kaya Grandi 33 (© **599/717-8160**), which also owns the eclectic crafts shop and art gallery across the arcade called **Anything Artistique.** A third shop in the centrally located **Harborside Mall** has silk neckties, Nautica menswear, blue Delft porcelain, and an array of Cuban cigars in a climate-controlled cigar room (with the likes of Montecristos, Punch, Romeo & Julietas, and Cohibas). **Perfume Palace,** in the same mall, carries perfume and other cosmetics, including Lancôme, Estée Lauder, Chanel, Calvin Klein, and Ralph Lauren.

Benetton, Kaya Grandi 49, has smart casual wear at discounts of 20% to 30%. If batik shirts, bathing suits, or souvenir T-shirts are what you want, try **Best Buddies,** Kaya Grandi 32, or **Island Fashions and Gifts,** Kaya Grandi 5 (© **599/717-7565**).

On a hot day, nothing beats the frozen-food section at **Cultimara Supermarket,** Kaya L. D. Gerharts 13 (© **599/717-8278**). The store offers a wide assortment of Dutch cheeses and chocolates, straight-from-the-oven breads and pastries, and various products from the Caribbean, Europe, South America, and the United States.

BEACHES

Bonaire's beaches are narrow and full of coral, but they're clean, intimate, and uncrowded. Swimming on the tranquil, leeward coast is never a problem, but the east coast is rough and dangerous.

South of Kralendijk, **Pink Beach** was Bonaire's best strand before Hurricane Lenny washed away most of its lovely sand. Now white-sand **Sorobon Beach,** near **Lac Bay,** is the island's best. The shallow water is especially popular with families; trees provide shade. The two windsurf concessions nearby mean that you have to contend with a bit of traffic, but they make for good entertainment, especially from a perch at one of the two beachside bars/snack shops. This is also next to the island's only nude beach, **Sorobon Beach Resort;** as a nonguest, you'll pay US$15 for the privilege of disrobing if you want to make your way past the discreet wooden fence that extends into the water and blocks the view.

North of Kralendijk, **Nukove Beach** is a small white-sand cove carved out of a limestone cliff. A narrow sand channel cuts through an otherwise impenetrable wall of elkhorn coral, giving divers and snorkelers access to the sea.

Washington-Slagbaai National Park has a number of beaches. **Boca Slagbaai,** once a plantation harbor, draws divers, snorkelers, and picnickers. Be careful venturing into the water barefoot, though: The coral bottom can be sharp. On one side of **Playa Funchi,** flamingos nest in the lagoon; on the other, there's excellent snorkeling. The island's northernmost beach, **Boca Cocolishi,** is a perfect spot to picnic. The calm, shallow basin is good for snorkeling, but stay very close to shore. Algae make the water purplish, and the sand, formed by coral and mollusk shells, is black. At **Playa Chikitu,** the water is too treacherous for swimming, but the cove is secluded, and the sand dunes and crashing waves are beautiful.

Klein Bonaire, the small uninhabited island about 1km (½ mile) west of Kralendijk, boasts **No Name Beach,** which features a 270m (886-ft.) white-sand strip. Parrotfish and yellowtail snappers patrol the finger, brain, and mustard hill corals, attracting snorkelers and divers. There are no facilities or shade on Klein Bonaire. A water taxi from the town pier will cost US$15 round-trip.

SPORTS

KAYAKING   For a peaceful, relaxing time, kayak through the mangroves in Lac Bay. Proceed at your own pace in the calm waters, but take time to observe the hundreds of baby fish and the bizarre tree roots. Bring protection from the sun and the ravenous mosquitoes. Divers and snorkelers can tow a lightweight sea kayak behind them as they explore the waters of the leeward coast.

Kayak rentals and guided trips through the mangroves are available from **Bonaire Dive & Adventure,** at the southern end of Sand Dollar Condominium Resort, Kaya Gobernador N. Debrot 77A (© **599/717-2229;** www.bonairediveandadventure. com), and from **Jibe City,** in Sorobon (© **599/717-5233;** www.jibecity.com). Half-day kayak rentals cost US$25 for one person and US$30 for two.

The **Mangrove Info & Kayak Center,** on Kaminda Lac, the road to Lac Bay Cai (© **599/790-5353;** www.mangrovecenter.com), provides ecological information about the mangrove forest in addition to offering guided mangrove tours that include an option to snorkel. Prices are US$25 for 1 hour and US$45 for 2 hours; drinking water and snorkel gear are provided.

MOUNTAIN BIKING   Bonaire has miles of roads, paved and unpaved, flat and hilly. The truly athletic can even follow goat paths. Take water, a map, a wide-brimmed hat, and plenty of sunscreen. **Bonaire Dive & Adventure** (see above) conducts guided bike tours through the *kunuku* (outback) and Washington-Slagbaai National Park for US$65 per person.

SCUBA DIVING & SNORKELING   Bonaire has more than 80 marked dive sites and a rich marine ecosystem that includes brain, elkhorn, staghorn, mountainous star, and gorgonian coral; anemones, sea cucumbers, and sea sponges; parrotfish, surgeonfish, angelfish, grouper, blennies, frogfish, and yellowtails; and morays and sea snakes. This is all within the boundaries of the **Bonaire National Marine Park,** which helps to ensure protection of the island's abundant marine life, as does the US$10 daily access fee (or US$25 for the whole year). Dive shops are numerous and highly professional. Expect to pay US$45 to US$55 for a one-tank boat dive (equipment extra) and around US$120 for an introductory resort course (equipment included).

The **Sand Dollar Condominium Resort,** Kaya Gobernador N. Debrot 77A (© **599/717-8738**), has a "Sand Penny" children's program that's a godsend for parents who want to dive without worrying about the kids.

Great Adventures Bonaire, at Harbour Village Beach Club, Kaya Gobernador N. Debrot 72 (© **599/717-7500,** ext. 286; www.harbourvillage.com), is the island's poshest operation, upscale but unpretentious and friendly. It offers two of Bonaire's most beautiful boats.

Captain Don's Habitat, Kaya Gobernador N. Debrot 103 (© **800/327-6709** or 305/438-4222 in the U.S. for Maduro Dive Fanta-Seas, Captain Don's North American representative, or 599/717-8290; www.habitatbonaire.com), attracts diving fanatics and disciples of Captain Don Stewart, an island icon and the driving force behind the Bonaire National Marine Park. The full-service outfitter offers a photo shop and lab, plus equipment repair.

Thanks to shallow-water coral reefs, snorkelers can also enjoy Bonaire's awesome marine environment. The island's **Guided Snorkeling Program** includes a slide-show introduction to reef fish, corals, and sponges; an in-water demonstration of snorkeling skills; and a guided tour of one of several snorkeling sites. The cost is US$25 per person. Equipment rental is about US$10 more. You can arrange a tour through any of the dive shops listed above, or at **Buddy Dive Resort,** Kaya Gobernador N. Debrot 85 (© **599/717-5080**), or **Dive Inn,** Kaya C. E. B. Hellmund 27 (© **599/717-8761;** www.diveinnbonaire.com).

WINDSURFING Shallow waters, steady breezes, and protection from choppy waters make Lac Bay perfect for beginners and pros. Sorobon has two equipment-rental centers: **Jibe City** (© **599/717-5233;** www.jibecity.com) and **Bonaire Windsurf Place** (© **599/717-2288;** www.bonairewindsurfplace.com). Boards and sails are US$45 for half a day, US$60 for a full day. Two-hour beginner's lessons are US$45, including equipment.

GREAT LOCAL RESTAURANTS & BARS

Kralendijk offers a variety of culinary options at generally reasonable prices. One of Bonaire's most popular restaurants, **Capriccio,** Kaya Isla Riba 1 (© **599/717-7230**), serves impeccably fresh northern Italian cuisine on the harbor front. Originally from Padua and Milan, the restaurateurs offer savory salads, homemade pastas, straight-from-the-oven focaccia, thin-crust pizzas, and more substantial fare such as mahimahi braised in onion, olives, and sun-dried tomatoes. Lunch is around US$12. **Zeezicht Seaside Restaurant,** Kaya Jan N. E. Craane 12 (© **599/717-8434**), is a local favorite, also on the downtown waterfront. Ceviche, conch sandwiches, and a gumbo of conch, fish, shrimp, and oysters are on the menu. Mermaids, fishing nets, and pirates adorn the walls. Lunch is about US$6. A popular place more for its waterfront location and crowd than its food is **City Café,** Caya Grandi 7 (© **599/717-8286**), which serves burgers, pasta, sandwiches, and salads. Lunch is US$9.

11 British Virgin Islands: Tortola & Virgin Gorda

With small bays and hidden coves that were once havens for pirates, the BVIs are among the world's loveliest cruising regions, consisting of some 60 islands located in the northeastern corner of the Caribbean, about 97km (60 miles) east of Puerto Rico. Only Tortola, Virgin Gorda, and Jost Van Dyke (plus Anegada, 26km/16 miles to the north) are of significant size. The other islets, most of them tiny rocks and cays, have names such as Fallen Jerusalem and Ginger. Norman Island is said to have been the prototype for Robert Louis Stevenson's *Treasure Island,* and Blackbeard inspired a

The British Virgin Islands

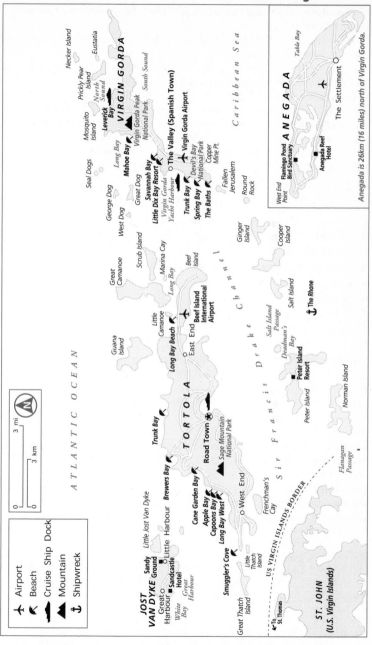

Legend:
- ✈ Airport
- ⚓ Beach
- 🚢 Cruise Ship Dock
- ▲ Mountain
- ⚓ Shipwreck

0   3 mi
0   3 km

ATLANTIC OCEAN

Caribbean Sea

ANEGADA

Table Bay

The Settlement

Flamingo Pond Bird Sanctuary
Anegada Reef Hotel

West End Point

Anegada is 26km (16 miles) north of Virgin Gorda.

VIRGIN GORDA

Necker Island
Eustatia
Prickly Pear Island
North Sound
South Sound
Mosquito Island
Leverick Bay
Mahoe Bay
Long Bay
Virgin Gorda Peak
Virgin Gorda Peak National Park
The Valley (Spanish Town)
Virgin Gorda Airport
Savannah Bay
Little Dix Bay Resort
Devil's Bay National Park
Copper Mine Pt.
Virgin Gorda Yacht Harbour
Trunk Bay
Spring Bay
The Baths
Fallen Jerusalem
Round Rock

Seal Dogs
George Dog
West Dog
Great Dog

Scrub Island
Great Camanoe
Marina Cay
Long Bay
Beef Island
Little Camanoe
Long Bay Beach
East End
Beef Island International Airport

Guana Island

D r a k e   C h a n n e l

Ginger Island
Cooper Island
Salt Island
Salt Island Passage
⚓ The Rhone
Deadman's Bay
Peter Island Resort
Peter Island
Norman Island

TORTOLA
Trunk Bay
Road Town ✈
Sage Mountain National Park
Brewers Bay
Cane Garden Bay
Apple Bay
Capoons Bay
Long Bay West
West End
Smuggler's Cove

S i r   F r a n c i s

Frenchman's Cay
Flanagan Passage

US VIRGIN ISLANDS BORDER

JOST VAN DYKE
Sandy Ground
Sandcastle Hotel
Great Harbour
Little Harbour
White Bay
Little Jost Van Dyke
Little Thatch Island
Great Thatch Island

← To St. Thomas

ST. JOHN
(U.S. Virgin Islands)

famous ditty by marooning 15 pirates and a bottle of rum on the rocky cay known as Deadman Bay. Yo-ho-ho.

Columbus came this way in 1493, but the British Virgins apparently made little impression on him. Although the Spanish and Dutch contested it, the English officially annexed Tortola in 1672. Today, these islands are a British territory, with their own elected government and a population of about 21,000.

The vegetation is varied and depends on the rainfall. Palms and mangoes grow in profusion in some parts, while other places are arid and studded with cacti.

Smaller cruise lines, such as Seabourn, Windstar, and Windjammer Barefoot Cruises, call at Tortola and the more scenic Virgin Gorda and Jost Van Dyke. Unlike port calls at St. Thomas and other major ports, visits here are less bound by rigid scheduling.

LANGUAGE   English is spoken here.

CURRENCY   The **U.S. dollar** is the legal currency, much to the surprise of arriving Brits who find no one willing to accept their pounds.

INFORMATION   For info before you go, call the **BVI Tourist Board** in New York at ℂ **800/835-8530** or 212/696-0400, or check out www.bvitourism.com.

CALLING FROM THE U.S.   When calling the BVIs from the United States, you need only dial a "1" before the numbers listed here.

TORTOLA

Road Town, the colony's capital, sits about midway along the southern shore of 62-sq.-km (24-sq.-mile) Tortola. Once a sleepy village, it's become a bustling center since **Wickhams Cay,** a 28-hectare (69-acre) landfill development and marina, brought in a massive yacht-chartering business.

Rugged mountain peaks characterize the island's entire southern coast. On the northern coast are beautiful bays with white-sandy beaches, banana trees, mangoes, and clusters of palms.

If your ship is scheduled to visit only Virgin Gorda but you want to see Tortola, you can catch a boat or ferry, or launch here and be on the island in no time, since it's only a 19km (12-mile) trip.

COMING ASHORE   Visiting cruise ships dock at **Road Town Harbour,** a pleasant 5-minute walk from Main Street in Road Town. You should have no trouble finding your way around.

INFORMATION   The **BVI Tourist Board,** in the Akara Building, Wickhams Cay 1 (ℂ **284/494-3134l;** www.bvitourism.com), is open Monday through Friday from 8:30am to 4:30pm. You can pick up a copy of the *Welcome Tourist Guide* here.

GETTING AROUND

BY TAXI   Open-air and sedan-style taxis meet every arriving cruise ship. To order a taxi in Road Town, call the **BVI Taxi Association** (ℂ **284/494-2322**). Two other local taxi services, **Road Town Taxi Association** (ℂ **284/494-8755**) and the **Waterfront Taxi Association** (ℂ **284/494-3456**), are within walking distance of the cruise pier.

BY BUS   **Scato's Bus Service** (ℂ **284/496-7541**) picks up passengers (mostly locals) who hail the bus. Fares for a trek across the island are about US$2 to US$4. Island tours are also available; a 3-hour tour costs about US$30 per person.

Frommer's Favorite Tortola Experiences

Visiting Bomba's Surfside Shack: The oldest, most memorable bar on Tortola may not look like much, but it's the best party on the island. (See "Great Local Restaurants & Bars," below.)

Spending a Day at Cane Garden Bay: It's the best beach on the island, with palm trees, sand, and a great local restaurant (shack) for lunch and drinks. (See "Beaches," below.)

Hiking up Sage Mountain: This is one of the best ways to learn about Tortola's natural character. Organized shore excursions usually include hiking trips to the 523m (1,715-ft.) peak, beginning with a ride along mountain roads in an open-air safari bus. (See "On Your Own: Beyond the Port Area," below.)

Taking an Island Tour: Open-air safari buses take you on a scenic journey around the extremely hilly island. Take your ship's organized tour (see "Best Cruise Line Shore Excursions," below), or opt for a 2- to 3-hour taxi tour from the pier, with beach stops, for about US$15 per person.

BY RENTAL CAR   We don't recommend renting a car here, as driving is on the left. But if you're intent on it, **Avis, Dollar, Hertz,** and **ITGO** (the local Budget operator) all have offices here.

BEST CRUISE LINE SHORE EXCURSIONS

Town & Country Tour (US$34, 3½ hr.): Tour the island in an open-air minibus, visiting the Botanical Gardens, Cane Garden Bay, Bomba's Surfside Shack at Capoons Bay, and Soper's Hole.

Norman Island Snorkeling (US$52, 3 hr.): Cross the Sir Frances Drake Channel by boat to Norman Island, one of the BVIs' prime snorkel sites, full of coral formations, colorful fish, and a group of caves at Treasure Point, where pirate treasure is reputed to have been hidden.

Scuba Diving at the RMS *Rhône* (US$138, 5½ hr.): This is a guided two-tank dive to a British ship sunk in an 1867 hurricane, her bow lying almost fully intact in 24m (79 ft.) of water. All divers must be certified and must have dived within the last 2 years.

EXCURSIONS OFFERED BY LOCAL AGENCIES

Bus Tours/Snorkeling Excursions/Glass-Bottom Boat Tours: Since the shore excursions here are very modest, you might consider calling **Travel Plan Tours,** Romasco Place, Wickham's Cay, Road Town (© 284/494-2872), which will take one to three people on a 3-hour guided tour of the island (about US$32 a person, if there is a minimum of two people), a snorkeling excursion (about US$32 a person for groups of 10 or more), or an all-day catamaran sailing excursion (US$105 per person, including lunch).

Taxi Tours: You can take a 2- to 3-hour taxi tour for about US$60 for up to three people. For a taxi in Road Town, call © 284/494-2322.

ON YOUR OWN: WITHIN WALKING DISTANCE

Besides the handful of shops on Main and Upper Main streets in Road Town, there's also a **Botanic Garden** (© 284/494-4557) right in the middle of town, across from the police station. It's open daily from 8am to 4:30pm.

ON YOUR OWN: BEYOND THE PORT AREA

You mainly have nature to look at on Tortola. The big attraction is **Sage Mountain National Park** (© 284/494-2069; www.bvinationalparkstrust.org), which rises to 523m (1,715 ft.)—the highest point in the BVIs and USVIs—and covers 37 hectares (91 acres). The park was established in 1964 to protect those remnants of Tortola's original forests not burned or cleared during the island's plantation era. It is both the oldest national park in the British Virgin Islands and the best present-day example of the territory's native moist forests. You'll find a lush forest of mango, papaya, breadfruit, birchberry, mountain guava, guavaberry, and coconut trees here, all of which have edible fruit. Many of the plants and trees are labeled. This is a great place to enjoy a picnic while overlooking neighboring islets and cays. Any taxi driver can take you to the mountain. Before going, stop at the tourist office (see above) and pick up a brochure with a map and an outline of the park's trails. The two main hikes are the **Rain Forest Trail** and the **Mahogany Forest Trail.** For a quiet beach day, head to **Smuggler's Cove,** a secluded spot with white sand and calm turquoise water.

SHOPPING

Shopping on Tortola is a minor activity compared to shopping at other Caribbean ports. Only British goods are imported without duty, and they are the best buys, especially English china. You'll also find West Indian art, terra-cotta pottery, wicker and rattan home furnishings, Mexican glassware, dhurrie rugs, baskets, and ceramics. Most stores are on Main Street in Road Town.

The **Pusser's Company Store,** Main Street, Road Town (© 284/494-2467; www.pussers.com), offers a selection of classic travel and adventure clothing, along with unusual accessories and Pusser's famous (though not terribly good) rum, which was served aboard British Navy ships for over 300 years. A good, cheap gift item is packets of Pusser's coasters, on which is written the recipe for that classic Caribbean rum specialty, the Painkiller.

The **Sunny Caribee Herb and Spice Company,** Main Street, Road Town (© 284/494-2178; www.sunnycaribbee.com), is a good spot for Caribbean spices, seasonings, teas, condiments, and handicrafts. You can buy two world-famous specialties here: West Indian Hangover Cure and Arawak Love Potion.

Soper's Hole Wharf & Marina, on the West End, has some shopping and restaurants. It's a short walk from the pier.

BEACHES

Most of the beaches are a 20-minute taxi ride from the cruise dock. Figure on about US$15 per person one-way (some will charge less, about US$5 per person if you've got a group), but discuss it with the driver before setting out. You can also ask the driver to pick you up at a designated time.

The finest beach is at **Cane Garden Bay,** which reminds us of the famous Magens Bay Beach on the north shore of St. Thomas. It's on the northwest side of the island, across the mountains from Road Town; it's worth the effort needed to get there and is so special, you might want to take a taxi here in the morning and not head back to your cruise ship until departure time. Plan to have lunch here at **Rhymer's**

(© 284/495-4639), where the chef will cook some conch or whelk, or perhaps some barbecue spareribs. The beach bar and restaurant is open daily from 8am to 8pm, serving breakfast, lunch, and dinner, with main courses ranging from US$15 to US$25. Showers are available, and Rhymer's rents towels.

Surfers like **Apple Bay,** also on the northwest side, but you'll have to watch out for sharks (no joke—on a recent trip, a friend saw one while surfing, and its dorsal fins were visible from the shore). A hotel here called **Sebastians** (© 284/495-4212) caters to the surfing crowd that visits in January and February, but the beach is ideal year-round.

Brewers Bay, site of a campground, is on the northwest shore near Cane Garden Bay and is good for beach strolling and swimming. Both snorkelers and surfers come here.

Smuggler's Cove (sometimes known as Lower Belmont Bay) is a wide crescent of white sand wrapped around calm, sky-blue water, located at the extreme western end of Tortola, opposite the offshore island of Great Thatch and very close to St. John's in the U.S. Virgin Islands. Snorkelers and surfers also like this beach.

SPORTS

SCUBA DIVING   *Skin Diver* magazine has called the wreckage of the RMS *Rhône,* which sank in 1867 near the western point of Salt Island, the world's most fantastic shipwreck dive. It teems with marine life and coral formations, and was featured in the motion picture *The Deep.*

Chikuzen, an 81m (266-ft.) steel-hulled refrigerator ship that sank off the island's east end in 1981, is another intriguing dive site off Tortola, although it's no *Rhône.* The hull, still intact under about 24m (79 ft.) of water, is now home to a vast array of tropical marine life, including yellowtail, barracuda, black-tip sharks, octopus, and drum fish.

Groups of three or more can charter a private dive boat for a half- or full day by contacting **UBS Dive Center** (© 284/494-0024; www.scubabvi.com). Two-tank dives for a group of three or more cost US$95 per person, including instruction, equipment, snacks, and drinks. After the dive, you can choose to snorkel, island-hop, have a land tour of the island, stop for lunch at an island restaurant, or go right back to your boat. The outfitter will pick you up at Village Cay Marina; call to make arrangements beforehand.

GREAT LOCAL RESTAURANTS & BARS

Right on the waterfront across from the ferry dock, **Pusser's Road Town Pub** (© 284/494-3897) serves Caribbean fare, English pub grub, and good pizzas. The drink to have here is the famous Pusser's rum, the same blend of five West Indian rums that the Royal Navy served to its men for more than 300 years. Honestly, it's not the world's greatest rum, but sometimes you just have to do things for the experience. Lunch is about US$22.

Capriccio di Mare, Waterfront Drive, Road Town (© 284/494-5369), is the most authentic-looking Italian cafe in the Virgin Islands, serving fresh pastas with succulent sauces, well-stuffed sandwiches, and great pizza. Lunch is about US$13.

Callaloo, at the Prospect Reef Resort (© 284/494-3311), is very romantic if it's a balmy day and the tropical breezes are blowing. Begin with the conch fritters or shrimp cocktail, and don't pass on the house salad, which has a zesty papaya dressing. Main dishes include fresh fish. Lunch is about US$15.

For a fine roti (curries wrapped in flatbread) sans atmosphere—it's sparsely furnished and not too attractive—try **Roti Palace,** in Road Town (© **284/494-4196**). Lunch is about US$8.

Over on Capoons Bay, **Bomba's Surfside Shack** (© **284/495-4148**) is the oldest, most memorable bar on Tortola, sitting on a 6m-wide (20-ft.) strip of coastline near the West End. It's the "junk palace" of the island, covered with Day-Glo graffiti and laced with wire and rejected odds and ends of plywood, driftwood, and abandoned rubber tires. The owners must've spent their decorating budget on the sound system, which thumps mightily. It's open daily from 10am to midnight (or later, depending on business). Lunch is about US$14.

Wash down your conch fritters and mahimahi burger with a daiquiri at **Myett's,** on Cane Garden Bay (© **284/495-9649**), where you can dine right on the beach among lush tropical foliage. Lunch is about US$15. **Quito's Gazebo,** also on Cane Garden Bay (© **284/495-4837**), is owned by local recording star Quito Rhymer. It's a good place for West Indian fish dishes. Quito performs Thursday through Sunday and Tuesday. Lunch is about US$14.

At **Pusser's Landing,** Frenchman's Cay, on the West End (© **284/495-4554**), you can enjoy grilled fish such as mahimahi, or perhaps some West Indian roast chicken. Try the mango soufflé for dessert. Lunch is about US$10.

VIRGIN GORDA

Instead of visiting Tortola, some small cruise ships put in at lovely Virgin Gorda, famous for its boulder-strewn beach known as the Baths. The third-largest island in the colony, it got its name ("Fat Virgin") from Christopher Columbus, who thought the mountain framing it looked like a protruding stomach. At 16km (10 miles) long and 3.2km (2 miles) wide, the island is about 19km (12 miles) east of Road Town, so it's easy to take a ferry here if your ship visits only Tortola (cruise lines offer shore excursions that do this trip, too).

The island was a fairly desolate agricultural community until Little Dix Bay Hotel opened here in the early 1960s. Other major hotels followed, but privacy and solitude still reign supreme on Virgin Gorda.

Frommer's Favorite Virgin Gorda Experiences

Visiting the Baths: House-size boulders and clear waters make for excellent swimming and snorkeling in a fabulous setting. (See "Best Cruise Line Shore Excursions" and "Beaches," both below.)

Spending a Beach Day in Spring Bay or Trunk Bay: Located near the Baths, Spring Bay has one of the best beaches on the island, with white sand, clear water, and good snorkeling. Trunk Bay, a wide, sandy beach that can be reached by boat or via a rough path from Spring Bay, is another good bet. (See "Beaches," below.)

Taking an Island Tour: Open-air safari buses do a good job of showing guests this beautiful island. (See "Best Cruise Line Shore Excursions," below.)

COMING ASHORE   Virgin Gorda doesn't have a pier or landing facilities to suit any of the large ships. Most vessels anchor offshore and tender passengers in to St. Thomas Bay, the port area and yacht harbor for Spanish Town. Ferries from Tortola also berth here.

GETTING AROUND

Taxis are available and will take visitors to the Baths and area beaches for about US$5 per person each way. For a tour of the island, contact Andy Flax of the **Virgin Gorda Tours Association,** c/o the Fischers Cove Beach Hotel (© 284/495-5252). It'll run you about US$40 per couple; you'll get picked up at the dock if you give at least 24-hour notice. Another good option is **Speedy's,** also known as Virgin Gorda Transport (© 284/495-5240).

BEST CRUISE LINE SHORE EXCURSIONS

The Baths Excursion (US$59, 4 hr.): All cruise lines stopping in Virgin Gorda offer a version of this trip. See "Beaches," below, for details.

Island Tour (US$55, 3–4 hr.): Open-air safari buses travel around this stunning island, traveling from Leverick Bay, ascending at least partway up Gorda Peak, and stopping at the quaint capital, Spanish Town.

ON YOUR OWN: WITHIN WALKING DISTANCE

The **Virgin Gorda Yacht Harbour** at St. Thomas Bay has several restaurants and shops.

ON YOUR OWN: BEYOND THE PORT AREA

You might also consider cabbing it up to glamorous **Little Dix Bay Hotel** (© 284/495-5555), established by Laurance Rockefeller in 1965, to enjoy a lunch buffet at an outdoor pavilion that shows off Virgin Gorda's beautiful hills, bays, and sky. Aside from this, most people head for the Baths, which really is a spectacular beach (see "Beaches," below).

SHOPPING

The only shopping of note here is right at the Virgin Gorda Yacht Harbor complex, with a few dive shops, boutiques, and handicraft shops. **DIVE BVI** (© 284/495-5513) sells diving equipment and offers diving instruction for all ability levels. **Margo's Jewelry Boutique** (© 284/495-5237) sells handcrafted gold and silver items. The **Virgin Gorda Craft Shop** (© 284/495-5137) features locally made items. The **Wine Cellar** (© 284/495-5250) offers oven-baked French bread and pastries, cookies, and sandwiches. The **Blue Banana Boutique** (© 284/495-6633) sells women's swimwear and beachwear.

BEACHES

The major reason cruise ships come to Virgin Gorda is to visit the **Baths,** where geologists believe ice-age eruptions caused house-size boulders to topple onto one another to form the saltwater grottoes we see today. The pools around the Baths are excellent for swimming and snorkeling (equipment can be rented on the beach), and a crawl between and among the boulders, which in places are very cavelike, is more than a little bit fun. A cafe sits just above the beach for a quick snack or a cool drink.

Just north of the Baths is **Spring Bay,** one of the best of the island's beaches, with white sand, clear water, and good snorkeling. Nearby is the **Crawl,** a natural pool

> ### *Moments* A Slice of Paradise: Jost Van Dyke
>
> Covering only 10 sq. km (4 sq. miles), mountainous Jost Van Dyke is truly an offbeat, rarely visited retreat—unless you count the small yachts dotting Great Harbour. With no cruise pier, passengers are shuttled ashore via tender. Small-ship lines, such as Windjammer Barefoot Cruises, will sometimes throw an afternoon beach party on the beach at White Bay, with the crew lugging ashore a picnic lunch for a leisurely afternoon of eating, drinking, and swimming. If your ship stays late, don't miss a trip to **Foxy's** (© **284/495-9258**), a well-known watering hole at the far end of Great Harbour that's popular with the yachting set as well as locals. It's your classic island beach bar, with music pounding and drinks flowing into the wee hours.

formed by rocks that's great for novice snorkelers; a marked path leads there from Spring Bay. **Trunk Bay,** just to the north, is a wide sand beach that can be reached via a rough path from Spring Bay.

Devil's Bay National Park can be reached by a trail from the Baths. The walk to the secluded coral-sand beach takes about 15 minutes through a natural setting of boulders and dry coastal vegetation.

SPORTS

WATERSPORTS Kilbrides Sunchaser Scuba, at the Bitter End Resort at North Sound (© **800/932-4286** in the U.S., or 284/495-9638; www.sunchaserscuba.com), offers diving at more than 20 BVI sites, including the wreck of the RMS *Rhône.* Morning two-tank dives go for US$105; afternoon dives are US$70. The excursions last about 4½ hours. Wet suits rent for US$5.

GREAT LOCAL RESTAURANTS & BARS

At the end of the waterfront shopping plaza in Spanish Town, **Bath and Turtle Pub,** Virgin Gorda Yacht Harbour (© **284/495-5239**), is the island's most popular bar and pub. You can join the regulars over midmorning guava coladas or peach daiquiris and order fried fish fingers, very spicy chili, pizzas, Reubens or tuna melts, steak, lobster, and daily seafood specials such as conch fritters. Lunch is about US$16. **Mad Dog** (© **284/495-5830**) is a hot-dog stop near the Baths that also serves BLTs, beer, and frozen piña coladas. Lunch is about US$7.

12 Cozumel & the Yucatán Peninsula

On some days, up to 16 ships visit Cozumel simultaneously, counting those that anchor offshore and tender passengers into shore. Despite the impact of Hurricane Wilma, this remains the number-one cruise ship destination in the Caribbean. All that activity can make the port town of **San Miguel** seem more like Times Square than the sleepy, refreshingly gritty Mexican port it once was. San Miguel has developed at a faster rate in recent years than just about any other Caribbean port on the map, so if you haven't been here in a while, you may not recognize the place. Watching the post-Wilma recovery was like watching a colony of ants rebuild a damaged nest; in this

The Yucatán's Upper Caribbean Coast

case, bigger, brighter, and glitzier than ever. Still, Cozumel's allure remains its proximity to the ancient Mayan ruins such as **Tulum** and **Chichén-Itzá** on the mainland of the Yucatán Peninsula. Besides the ruins, the island's beaches are a big draw, along with diving, shopping for silver jewelry and local handicrafts, and sampling of local tequila.

To see the ruins, you must take a rocky 45-minute ferry ride between Cozumel and **Playa del Carmen,** on the mainland, though a few cruise ships call directly on Playa del Carmen, anchoring just offshore. Recently a handful of other Yucatán ports have come onto the scene, including **Costa Maya,** near the sleepy fishing village of Mahajual, just over 161km (100 miles) south of Playa del Carmen. Details on both Playa and Costa Maya are included later in this section. A few ships also call at **Calica,** just south of Playa, where there's little more than a pier, and at **Progreso,** on the Gulf coast of the Yucatán, where the Mayan ruins and colonial architecture of nearby Merida are the big draw.

LANGUAGE   Spanish is the tongue of the land, although English is spoken in most places that cater to tourists.

CURRENCY   The Mexican currency is the **nuevo peso** (new peso). Its symbol is the $ sign, but it's hardly the equivalent of the U.S. dollar—the exchange rate is about $10 pesos to US$1 ($1 peso = about US10¢). The main tourist stores gladly accept U.S. dollars, credit cards, and traveler's checks. If you want to change money, you'll find many banks within a block or so of the downtown tender and ferry pier. Unless otherwise specified, prices in this section are given in U.S. dollars.

CALLING FROM THE U.S.   When calling from the U.S., you need to dial the international access code (011) and the country code for Mexico (52) before the local numbers listed here.

MAYAN RUINS & OTHER MAINLAND ATTRACTIONS

Because all of the sites listed here are quite far from the cruise piers, most cruise passengers visit them as part of **shore excursions.** Admission to the sites is included in the excursion prices, which typically runs from US$100 to US$130 for Chichén-Itzá and around US$75 for Tulum or Cobá. Chichén-Itzá and Cobá are all-day excursions. Visits to smaller Tulum are often paired with a visit to the Xel-Ha Eco Park, making it a full-day trek (US$99). Guests are usually served free and refreshingly coooollllldddd Mexican beer on the bus back after exploring the ruins.

CHICHEN ITZA   The largest and most fabled of the Yucatán ruins, Chichén-Itzá (meaning "Mouth of the Well of the Itza Family") was founded in A.D. 445 by the Mayans and later inhabited by the Toltecs of central Mexico. At its height, the city had about 50,000 residents, but it was mysteriously abandoned only 2 centuries after its founding. After lying dormant for 2 more centuries, the site was resettled and enjoyed prosperity again until the early 13th century, when it was once more relinquished to the surrounding jungle. The area covers 18 sq. km (7 sq. miles), so you can see only a fraction of it on a day trip. The following are some of the highlights:

The best known of Chichén-Itzá's ruins is the magnificent **El Castillo pyramid** (also called the Pyramid of Kukulkán), which was built with the Maya calendar in mind. The four stairways leading up to the central platform each have 91 steps, making a total of 364; when you add the top central platform, you get the 365 days of the solar year. On either side of each stairway are 9 terraces, which makes 18 on each face of the pyramid, equaling the number of months in the Maya solar calendar. On the facing of these terraces are 52 panels that represent the 52-year cycle when both the solar and religious calendars would become realigned. The pyramid's position is such that on the **spring** and **fall equinoxes,** light striking the pyramid gives the illusion of a snake slithering down the steps to join its gigantic stone head mounted at the base.

Northwest of El Castillo is Chichén's main **Ball Court (Juego de Pelota),** the largest and best preserved such Mayan ruin anywhere. Carved on both walls of the ball court are scenes showing Mayan figures dressed as ball players and decked out in heavy protective padding. The carved scene also shows a headless player kneeling with blood shooting from his neck; another player holding the head looks on. Players on two teams tried to knock a hard rubber ball through one of the two stone rings placed high on either wall, using only their elbows, knees, and hips. According to legend, the losing players paid for defeat with their lives. However, some experts say the victors were the only appropriate sacrifices for the gods. Note the lack of bleacher seating. As the games were played as a ritual, for the entertainment of the gods, only a single judge looked on.

Temples are located at both ends of the ball court. The **North Temple** has sculptured pillars and more sculptures inside, as well as badly ruined murals. The acoustics of the ball court are so good that from the North Temple, a person speaking can be heard clearly at the opposite end, about 136m (446 ft.) away. Near the southeastern corner of the main ball court is the **Temple of the Jaguars,** a small temple with serpent columns and carved panels showing warriors and jaguars. Up the steps and inside the temple, a mural was found that chronicles a battle in a Maya village. To the right of the ball court is the **Temple of the Skulls (Tzompantli).** Notice the rows of skulls carved into the stone platform. When a sacrificial victim's head was cut off, it was impaled on a pole and displayed in a tidy row with the others.

Follow the dirt road (actually an ancient *sacbé,* or causeway, made from a white, compacted, claylike soil that made the way visible at night) that heads north from the Platform of Venus. After about 5 minutes, you'll come to the **Sacred Cenote,** a great natural well that may have given Chichén-Itzá its name. This well was used for ceremonial purposes, not for drinking water. According to legend, sacrificial victims adorned with gold and other riches were drowned in this pool to honor the rain god Chaac. In the early 20th century, American consul and Harvard professor Edward Thompson bought the ruins of Chichén-Itzá and explored the cenote with dredges and divers, unearthing (and exporting) a fortune in gold and jade.

Due east of El Castillo is one of the most impressive structures at Chichén: the **Temple of the Warriors,** named for the carvings of warriors marching along its walls. It's also called the Group of the Thousand Columns for the rows of broken square pillars that flank it. A figure of high priest Chaac-Mool sits at the top of the temple, surrounded by impressive columns carved in relief to look like enormous feathered serpents. According to scholars, Chaac-Mool would tear out a sacrificial victim's heart here and then throw the body down the steps, where another priest would strip off his or her skin.

South of the temple is another group of columns (these are round) that were once an important **market,** controlling the trade in salt on the Yucatán. South of the market, a cluster of interesting ruins includes the **Observatory (El Caracol),** a complex building with a circular tower through whose slits astronomers could observe the cardinal directions and the approach of the all-important spring and autumn equinoxes; the **Edifice of the Nuns (Edificio de las Monjas),** which was named for its resemblance to a European convent; and the **Church (La Iglesia),** one of the oldest buildings at Chichén, named for its beautiful decorations. Its ceiling, with a Mayan false arch, is a stone replica of the thatched ceilings that were typical in Mayan homes of the period.

TULUM   About 130km (81 miles) south of Cancún and about a 30-minute drive from Playa del Carmen, the small walled city of Tulum is the single most visited Mayan ruin due to its proximity to the ports. It was the only Mayan city built on the coast and the only one inhabited when the Spanish conquistadors arrived in the 1500s. From its dramatic perch atop seaside cliffs, you can see wonderful panoramic views of the Caribbean. Though nowhere near as large and impressive as Chichén-Itzá, the two cities share a similar prominent feature: a ruin topped with a temple to Kukulkán, the primary Mayan/Olmec god. Other important structures include the Temple of the Frescoes, the Temple of the Descending God, the House of Columns, and the House of the Cenote, which is a well. There's also a sliver of silky beach at the site, so bring your bathing suit for a quick refreshing dip. Visitor facilities include a well-stocked bookstore and a soon-to-open museum.

COBA   A 35-minute drive northwest of Tulum puts you at Cobá, site of one of the most important city-states in the Mayan empire. Cobá flourished from A.D. 300 to 1000, with its population numbering perhaps as many as 40,000. Excavation work began in 1972, and archaeologists estimate that only 5% of this dead city has yet been uncovered. The site lies on four lakes. Its 32 rural hectares (79 acres) provide excellent exploration opportunities for hikers. Cobá's pyramid, Nohoch Mul, is the tallest in the Yucatán.

XCARET ECO-PARK   Lying about 6.4km (4 miles) south of Playa del Carmen on the coast, Xcaret (pronounced *Ish*-car-et) is a 100-hectare (247-acre) ecological theme park with small Mayan ruins scattered about the lushly landscaped acres. Visitors can put on life jackets for a river ride, which takes them through currents running through a series of caves, or don a Sea-Trek helmet and walk across the ocean floor. You can also snorkel through the caves (something we recommend highly) as well as swim with dolphins, though this is not included in the cost of the excursions. The park has a botanical garden, an aquarium, a sea-turtle breeding and release facility, a dive shop, a rotating observation tower, a Mayan village (complete with cemetery!), and two theaters that put on elaborate cultural shows. Excursions run about US$88 and take up a full day from Cozumel.

XEL-HA ECO-PARK   Farther south of Xcaret, Xel-Ha (pronounced *Shell*-ha) features a sprawling natural lagoon filled with sparkling blue-green water and surrounded by lush foliage. The use of inner tubes and life vests is included in the admission price, and you can spend a great couple of hours wending your way from one end of the snaking body of calm water to the other, accompanied by schools of tropical fish. Snorkeling gear is available for rental. Xel-Ha has dolphins, too. Knowledgeable, friendly, and very eco-minded guides will walk you along trails identifying local plants and take you to sacred sinkholes (called cenotes) where ancient Maya made offerings to the gods. You'll find shops, restaurants, and lots of beach chairs here.

COZUMEL

The ancient Mayans, who lived here for 12 centuries, would be shocked by the million cruise passengers who now visit Cozumel each year. Their presence has greatly changed San Miguel, which now has fast-food joints and a Hard Rock Cafe. With only one town, development has yet to destroy much of the island's natural beauty. Ashore, away from San Miguel, you'll see acres of low-lying scrub forest containing protected plant and animal species. Offshore, the government has set aside 32km (20 miles) of coral

Frommer's Favorite Cozumel Experiences

Visiting the Mayan Ruins at Chichén-Itzá or Tulum: Chichén-Itzá is the largest and most fabled of the Yucatán ruins—and the flight there, in a small plane, only adds to the experience of exploring the site. A few hours a day, you can climb a narrow staircase inside the main temple's inner pyramid to sneak a claustrophobic peek at a stunning jaguar throne inlaid with turquoise spots and eyes. Tulum is perched dramatically above the ocean (and in the middle of "iguana central"—they're everywhere), and tours there often include a stop at the beautiful Xel-Ha lagoon for some swimming. (See "Mayan Ruins & Other Mainland Attractions," above.)

Swimming with the Dolphins at Chankanaab: Book on your own for this once-in-a-lifetime opportunity to be kissed, splashed, towed, and pushed through the wake like a water-skier by some of the friendliest locals you'll ever meet. For the not-so-bold, the less expensive Dolphin Encounter (which is offered as a shore excursion) allows you to get up close and personal with two friendly dolphins, minus the aquatic acrobatics. The encounter program does not include the overpriced but irresistible video, complete with music and slow-motion close-ups. (See "On Your Own: Beyond the Port Area," below.)

Taking a Jeep Trek: Explore Cozumel's jungles and sandy back roads on a fun self-drive, caravan-style adventure, and then stop at a beach for lunch and swimming. (See "Best Cruise Line Shore Excursions," below.)

reefs as an underwater national park, including the stunning Palancar Reef, the world's second-largest natural coral formation.

COMING ASHORE   It seems like the whole coast of San Miguel is a cruise ship berth these days. The newest berth is **Punta Langosta,** right in the center of town, which puts you just steps from the shops, restaurants, and cafes across the street. (The ferries to Playa del Carmen dock about .4km/¼ mile away.) Other ships pull alongside the well-accoutered **International Pier** (3.2km/2 miles south of San Miguel) or the pier at **Puerto Maya** (another kilometer or so farther south), both a US$4 to US$5 taxi ride from town or a 30- to 45-minute walk from the heart of San Miguel. The beaches are close to the International Pier.

You can make telephone calls in Cozumel from the Punta Langosta pier, the Global Communications phone center on the International Pier, or a kiosk inside the terminal. Keep in mind that there are often lines for the phones. In town, try the **Calling Station,** Avenida Rafael Melgar 27, at the corner of Calle 3 in San Miguel, 3 blocks from the ferry pier.

INFORMATION   The **Department of Tourism Office,** on the second floor of Plaza del Sol (📞 **987/872-0972**), distributes the *Vacation Guide to Cozumel* and *Cozumel Island's Restaurant Guide;* both have island maps. It's open Monday through Friday from 9am to 7:30pm, Saturday from 9am to 1pm. There are also tourist booths at the ship piers and ferry pier, open daily from 8am to 8pm. For info before you go, call ☎ **800/44-MEXICO** or surf to www.islacozumel.com.mx.

GETTING AROUND

The town of San Miguel is so small, you can walk anywhere. Essentially, there's only one large road in Cozumel—it starts at the northern tip of the island, hugs the western shoreline, and then loops around the southern tip and returns through the middle of the island to the capital.

If you're driving in Cozumel, it's helpful to know that the roads parallel to the sea are called avenues, and these have the right of way. The ones running from the sea are called streets, and you have to stop at each avenue to give way.

BY TAXI Taxi service is available 24 hours a day; however, like many other things in the Miami of the Yucatán, it's no bargain. The average fare from San Miguel to most major resorts and beaches is about US$20; the trip between the International Pier and downtown is about US$10. More distant island rides cost US$25 and up. It's customary to overcharge cruise ship passengers, so settle on a fare before getting in—occasionally, you can bargain it down. It's easy to find a cab at the pier, but you can also call ☎ **987/872-0236.**

BY RENTAL CAR If you want to drive yourself, four-wheel-drive vehicles or open-air jeeps are the best rental choice. Located just 2 blocks from the ferry pier, **Budget,** Avenida 5A at Calle 20A (☎ **800/527-0700** in the U.S., or 987/872-5177), rents cars and four-wheel-drive vehicles. A four-door economy car costs about US$35 a day, with a Geo Tracker going for US$45 and up, plus insurance and gas. **Avis** and **Hertz** have offices here, too. *Note:* Most rental cars in the Caribbean have manual transmissions, so if you need an automatic, be sure to specify that when renting.

BY SCOOTER Scooters are a popular means of getting about despite heavy traffic, hidden stop signs, potholed roads, and a high accident rate. The best and most convenient rentals are at **Auto Rent,** in the Hotel El Cid La Ceiba (☎ **987/872-0844**), right next to the International Pier. The cost is about US$35 per day, including helmet rental; Mexican law requires that you wear a helmet.

BY FERRY A number of passenger ferries link Cozumel with Playa del Carmen, all of them with ticket booths at the main pier. The most comfortable are the big speedboats and water-jet catamarans run by **Cruceros Maritimos,** which make the trip in 25 to 45 minutes and run Monday through Saturday between 6am and 10pm. One-way fares cost about US$8 per person. You'll get a ferry schedule when you buy your ticket.

BEST CRUISE LINE SHORE EXCURSIONS

See "Mayan Ruins & Other Mainland Attractions," above, for details on the big mainland excursions. In addition to those below, the cruise lines offer dozens of different snorkeling, party-boat, and underwater excursions in Cozumel.

Palancar Reef Snorkeling (US$44, 4hr.): With some of the most spectacular reefs in the world, Cozumel is a diver's paradise, but even the snorkeling is almost unmatched. In addition to colorful fish, giant sponges, and large corals, one may also see eels, rays, or even turtles.

Horseback-Riding Tours (US$89, 3½ hr.): Worthwhile horseback-riding tours offer a chance to see Cozumel's landscape. However, although they tout visits to Mayan ruins, don't get your hopes up—there's little more than a few refrigerator-size rocks to be seen on this outing. A bus transports riders to a ranch, where the ride begins.

ON YOUR OWN: WITHIN WALKING DISTANCE

For walkers, the classic grid layout makes getting around the town of San Miguel easy, but with a twist—all odd-numbered streets are on the south side of the pier and all even-numbered streets head north. Directly across from the downtown tender docks, the main square—**Plaza del Sol** (also called *la plaza* or *el parque*)—is excellent for people-watching. The principal street along the waterfront is **Avenida Rafael Melgar,** which runs along the western shore of the island, site of the best resorts and beaches. Most of the shops and restaurants are on Rafael Melgar, although many well-stocked duty-free shops line the Malecón, the seaside promenade.

Only 3 blocks from the ferry pier, the **Museo de la Isla de Cozumel,** on Avenida Rafael Melgar between Calles 4 and 6 North (© **987/872-1434**), has two floors of exhibits displayed in what was Cozumel's first luxury hotel. Exhibits cover everything from pre-Hispanic times to the colonial era to the present. Included are many swords and nautical artifacts; one of the displays showcases endangered species. The highlight is a reproduction of a Mayan house. It's open daily from 9am to 5pm, and sometimes later; admission is US$3 for adults and free for children younger than 8.

ON YOUR OWN: BEYOND THE PORT AREA

You can rent a scooter and zip around most of the island, including its wild and natural side. Stop for a cool drink and a grilled-fish lunch at a beachside open-air seafood restaurant. Scooters can be rented from several outfits, including Auto Rent (see "Getting Around," above).

Outside of San Miguel is the **Chankanaab Nature Park,** where an archaeological park, botanical garden, and wildlife sanctuary complement a saltwater lagoon, offshore reefs, and underwater caves. More than 10 countries have contributed seedlings and cuttings to the botanical garden here. The lagoon is occupied by some 60 species of marine life, including sea turtles and captive dolphins (that you can swim with for a mere US$120). Reproductions of Mayan dwellings are scattered throughout the park. There's also a wide white-sand beach with thatch umbrellas and a changing area with lockers and showers. Both scuba divers and snorkelers enjoy examining the sunken ship offshore (there are four dive shops here). The park also has a restaurant and snack stand. It's all located at Carretera Sur, km. 9 (no phone); open daily from 9am to 5pm. Admission is US$11 for adults, free for children 9 and under. The 10-minute taxi ride from the downtown tender and ferry pier (Muelle Fiscal) costs about US$15.

Mayan ruins on Cozumel are very minor compared to those on the mainland. The most notable of the two is at **San Gervasio,** reached by driving east across the island to the well-marked turnoff, and then turning left and continuing north 6.4km (4 miles) to San Gervasio. This was once a ceremonial center and capital of Cozumel. The Mayans dedicated the area to Ixchel, the fertility goddess. The ruins cost US$6 to visit, for entrance to the access road. For US$30, guides will show visitors what's left, including several foundations and intact columns and lintels. It's open daily from 8am to 5pm.

Another meager ruin is **El Cedral,** which lies 3.2km (2 miles) inland at the turnoff at km. 17.5, east of Playa San Francisco. It's the island's oldest structure, with traces of original Mayan wall paintings. The Spanish tore much of it down, and the U.S. Army nearly finished the job when it built an airfield here in World War II. Little remains now except a Mayan arch and a few small ruins by the sea. Guides at the site will show you around for a fee.

SHOPPING

You can walk from the ferry pier to the best shops in San Miguel (they start right across the street from the Punta Langosta pier, and are 3.2–4.8km/2–3 miles by taxi or foot from the International and Puerto Maya cruise ship piers). Because of the influx of cruise ship passengers, prices are relatively high here, but you can and should bargain. Silver jewelry is big business, and it's generally sold by weight. You can find some nice pieces, but again, don't expect much of a bargain. **Heritage,** Avenida Rafael Melgar 341, is one of the most important jewelers in Cozumel and the exclusive distributor of Rolex watches on the Mexican Riviera. **Rachat & Romero,** Avenida Rafael Melgar 101, has a wide variety of loose stones, which they can mount while you wait.

Wall-to-wall shops along the waterfront in San Miguel offer all manner of souvenirs. Shops also line the perimeter of **Plaza del Sol,** adjacent to the downtown ferry pier (.4km/¼ mile or so north of the Punta Langosta pier), and several shopping arcades are accessible from the plaza, including the pleasant, tree-lined **Plaza Confetti** and the **Villa Mar** complex, with several good silver jewelry shops.

Agencia Publicaciones Gracia, Avenida 5A, a block from the downtown tender and ferry pier, is Cozumel's best source for English-language books, guidebooks, newspapers, and magazines. **Cinco Soleils,** at Avenida Rafael Melagar and Calle 8, is well stocked with beautiful, if pricey, handmade local goods. You'll also find a tequila bar, coffee shop, and outdoor restaurant to reenergize weary shoppers.

If you're docking at the **International Pier,** a bunch of nice shops in the terminal sell everything from Mexican blankets to jewelry, T-shirts, and handicrafts of all kinds. Again, prices aren't cheap—a roll of film went for US$10 the last time we were at the terminal. The pier at **Puerta Maya** has just undergone a major expansion and now boasts a wide selection of well-stocked gift shops.

BEACHES

Cozumel's best powdery white-sand beach, **Playa San Francisco,** stretches for some 4.8km (3 miles) along the southwestern shoreline. It was once one of the most idyllic beaches in Mexico, but resort development is threatening to destroy its old character. You can rent equipment for watersports here, as well as enjoy lunch at one of the many restaurants or bars on the shoreline. There's no admission to the beach, and it's about a US$15 taxi ride south of San Miguel's downtown pier. If you land at the International Pier, you're practically at the beach already.

Playa Mia (formerly **Playa del Sol**), about 1.6km (1 mile) south of Playa del San Francisco, is a fine beach but has a big reputation, so it's likely to be wall-to-wall with your fellow cruisers. It's also built up with bars, restaurants, watersports rentals, a miniature zoo, and so on, and charges a US$12 entrance fee.

Playa Bonita (sometimes called **Punta Chiqueros**) is one of the least crowded beaches; it lies on the east (windward) side of the island and is difficult to reach unless you rent a vehicle or throw yourself at the mercy of a taxi driver. It sits in a moon-shaped cove sheltered from the Caribbean by an offshore reef. Waves are only moderate, the sand is powdery, and the water is clear.

You may want to consider **Parque Chankanaab,** a parklike beach area lined with thatched umbrellas and contoured plastic chaise longues. While the water is rough here and not ideal for swimming, the beach and scenery are very nice and the place is popular with locals. Admission is US$10, and you can swim with dolphins (for a fee, of course) or rent snorkeling equipment. There's also a restaurant and bar. This beach is about a 10-minute US$15 taxi ride from the downtown pier.

If you don't want to go far, two hotel beaches are a stone's throw north of the International Pier (facing the water, they're on the right), and they welcome day visitors to use their small beach, cabanas, pools, and changing facilities. **El Cid La Ceiba** charges US$10 per person for the day (9am–5pm), while the **Park Royale** charges US$25 per person for the day, which includes all drinks, snacks, and lunch. At press time, both were closed for post-hurricane renovations, so check with the tourism booth before you head out.

SPORTS

SCUBA DIVING   Turtles and eagle rays in profusion, dozens of species of rainbow-hued tropical fish, and underwater visibility that averages 30m (98 ft.) make Cozumel one of the best (if not the best) diving destinations in the Caribbean. Cruisers might want to confine their adventures to the finest spot, **Palancar Reef.** Lying about 1.6km (1 mile) offshore, this fabulous water world features gigantic elephant-ear sponges and rare black coral, as well as deep caves, canyons, and tunnels. It's a favorite of divers from all over the world.

The best scuba outfitters are **Aqua Safari,** Avenida Rafael Melgar at Calle 5, next to the Vista del Mar Hotel (© **987/872-0101;** www.aquasafari.com), and **Diving Adventures,** Calle 51 Sur no. 2, near Avenida Rafael Melgar (© **888/338-0388** from the U.S., or 987/872-3009; www.divingadventures.net).

SNORKELING   The shallow reefs at Playa San Francisco and Chankanaab Bay are among the best snorkeling spots. You'll see a world of sea creatures parading by—everything from parrotfish to sergeant majors. The best outfitter is **Cozumel Snorkeling Center,** Calle Primera Sur (© **987/872-0539**), which offers a 3-hour snorkeling tour (US$40 per person), including all equipment and refreshments. It can also arrange parasailing. If you'd rather, you can also just rent snorkeling equipment at Chankanaab.

GREAT LOCAL RESTAURANTS & BARS

The local beer is **Sol,** though Corona, Tecate, and Dos Equis are favored, too. On a hot day, a bottle of the stuff is manna from heaven.

Right across from the Punta Langosta pier is **Carlos 'n Charlie's,** Avenida Rafael Melgar 551 (© **987/872-0191;** www.carlosn-charlies.com), Mexico's equivalent of the Hard Rock Cafe, but much wilder. Though it moved into these more sterile Houlihan's-style digs a few years ago, the music still blares, and dancing tourists pound back yard-long glasses of beer as if they're going out of style. Many a cruise passenger has stumbled back from this place clutching a souvenir glass as though it were the Holy Grail—dubious proof of a visit to Mexico. People come here for good times and the spicy, tasty ribs. You can dine surprisingly well on Yucatán specialties and the best chicken and beef fajitas in Cozumel.

Another party spot is the **Hard Rock Cozumel** itself, at Avenida Rafael Melgar 2A (© **529/872-5273;** www.hardrock.com), which serves the hard stuff as well as burgers and grilled beef or chicken fajitas. Yet another is **Fat Tuesday,** at the end of the International Pier (© **987/872-5130**), where you'll find lots of crewmembers on their day or night off (you can even hear their revelry from the ship). Join the fun and guzzle a 16-ounce margarita for US$5 a pop or a 24-ounce version for US$7. There's another Fat Tuesday near the ferry pier at the entrance to the Villa Mar complex, right next to Plaza del Sol.

Frommer's Favorite Playa del Carmen Experiences

Taking a Tour of Tulum or Chichén-Itzá: Both of the tours described in the Cozumel section, under "Mayan Ruins & Other Mainland Attractions," earlier in this chapter, are also offered from here.

Lazing Away in Xel-Ha: You'll find yourself floating around the lagoon on an inner tube without a care in the world or wandering a jungle trail and communing with nature. See "Mayan Ruins & Other Mainland Attractions," earlier in this chapter.

Spending a Day in Xcaret: How does snorkeling through a cool underwater cave followed by a massage and lounging in a hammock sound? See "Mayan Ruins & Other Mainland Attractions," earlier in this chapter.

A half block from the pier, **Las Palmeras,** Avenida Rafael Melgar (© **987/872-0532**), is ideal for casual eating. If you arrive in time, it serves one of the best breakfasts in town; at lunch, it offers tempting seafood dishes and Mexican specialties. On the main drag in town is **Lobster's Cove** (© **987/872-4022**), offering tasty seafood and Mexican dishes.

Just 5 blocks from the ferry pier, **El Capi Navegante,** Avenida 10A no. 312 at Calles 3 and 5 (© **987/872-1730**), offers the freshest fish in San Miguel, as well as a great lobster soufflé. Two blocks from the downtown tender and ferry pier is **La Choza,** Calle Rosado Salas 200 at Avenida 10A Sur (© **987/872-0958**), offering real local cooking that's a favorite of the town's savvy foodies.

PLAYA DEL CARMEN

The famed white-sand beach, washed away by Hurricane Wilma, is now back— thanks to an aggressive beach-recovery program that plopped tons of sand ashore at a rate of 1km (½ mile) of new beach per week. Shops, too, have bounced back with a vengeance. If you can tolerate the crowds, the snorkeling is still excellent over the offshore reefs. Turtle-watching is another local pastime.

COMING ASHORE   Some cruise ships spend a day at Cozumel and then anchor offshore at Playa del Carmen for another day, but most of them send passengers over from Cozumel to Playa by tender, enabling them to take tours to Tulum and Chichén-Itzá. The ships that do spend a day here dock at the **Puerto Calica Cruise Pier** (also a dock for freighters carrying cement), 13km (8 miles) south of Playa del Carmen. Taxis and buses meet each arriving ship to transport visitors into the center of Playa del Carmen—which is a good thing, since there's nothing to do at Calica, save for making a phone call or buying a soda.

GETTING AROUND

BY TAXI   Taxis are readily available to take you anywhere, but you can walk to the center of town, to the beach, and to most major shops.

BY RENTAL CAR   If you decide to rent a car for the day, **Budget, Hertz,** and **National** all have offices right next to the ferry pier.

BEST CRUISE LINE SHORE EXCURSIONS

Most visitors head for the Mayan ruins or one of the local eco-parks the moment they reach shore (see "Mayan Ruins & Other Mainland Attractions," on p. 152).

ON YOUR OWN: WITHIN WALKING DISTANCE

From the tender pier, you can walk to the center of Playa del Carmen, to the beach adjacent to the tender pier, and to the ever-expanding shopping district, which has a seemingly endless strip of trendy boutiques and hip restaurants.

ON YOUR OWN: BEYOND THE PORT AREA

Other than the beach and shopping, the only major attractions are the Xcaret and Xel-Ha eco-parks, both open daily. The easiest way to get to either is to sign up for your ship's organized excursion, which includes transportation; otherwise, if you're docked in Cozumel, you'll have to get ferry tickets on your own to travel between the island and Playa del Carmen.

If you come independently, general admission for **Xcaret** (© 998/881-2400; www.xcaret.net) is a steep US$59 for adults, US$41 for children 5 to 12. See "Mayan Ruins & Other Mainland Attractions," earlier in this section, for a full description of the park.

Just a few miles farther south of Xcaret is **Xel-Ha** (© 984/875-6000; www.xel-ha.com.mx), pronounced *Shell*-ha, which features a sprawling natural lagoon filled with sparkling blue-green water and surrounded by lush foliage. The use of inner tubes and life vests is included in the admission price, and you can spend a great couple of hours floating your way from one end of the calm body of water to the other, stopping to see schools of tropical fish. Snorkeling gear is available for rent. Xel-Ha also has dolphins in small enclosures. Shops, restaurants, and lots of beach chairs pepper the area. Admission is US$33 for adults and US$23 for kids 4 to 11, or you can purchase all-inclusive tickets at US$59 for adults and US$41for kids (since all meals and drinks are included, it's a better deal if you plan to stay all day). Buses from Playa del Carmen come here frequently; a taxi costs about US$40 one-way.

SHOPPING

At the tender pier, you'll be funneled like cattle through a chute right into the **Paseo del Carmen** shopping mall. Most shops are along **Avenida 5,** which runs parallel to the coast and has a pedestrian-only stretch not far from the dock. The **Rincón del Sol** plaza is a tree-filled courtyard between Calle 4 and Calle 6, built in the colonial Mexican style. It has the best collection of handicraft shops in the area, some of which offer much higher-quality items than the junky souvenirs peddled elsewhere.

GREAT LOCAL RESTAURANTS & BARS

El Chino, Calle 4, Avenida 15 (© 984/873-0015), is a pristine restaurant known locally for its regional Yucatán specialties, as well as standard dishes from throughout Mexico. **El Tacolote,** Avenida Juárez (© 984/873-1363), specializes in fresh seafood and the best grilled meats in town, brought to your table right from the broiler on a charcoal pan to keep the food warm.

If you want to stay in the thick of things, there's a **Señor Frog's** (© 984/873-0930) right at the ferry pier and a **Carlos 'n Charlie's** just up the street, for all the beer and shots you can stomach.

COSTA MAYA

While Cozumel gets the most traffic by far, a handful of other Yucatán ports have entered the scene, including Costa Maya, near the sleepy fishing village of Mahajual

Frommer's Favorite Costa Maya Experiences

Jungle Beach Break: A short bus ride lands you at small but charming Uvero Beach, where you can sunbathe, kayak, rent jet skis or a mini-speedboat, or snorkel on the pristine reef. Then again, you may just want to stroll out to the end of the long pier to gaze down at the colorful sea life in the crystal-blue water below. See "Best Cruise Line Shore Excursions," below.

Kohunlich Mayan Explorer: This fascinating Mayan site offers a noncommercial look at both excavated and unrestored Mayan ruins, including a ball court, foundations of residential buildings, and a monument returned to the site after being stolen by thieves. The high point (literally and figuratively) is a large temple with remarkably well-preserved stucco faces flanking the crumbling steps. Uncleared ruins near the ball courts, just waiting to be unearthed, make you feel like a bona fide explorer. See "Best Cruise Line Shore Excursions," below.

(just over 161km/100 miles south of Playa del Carmen). Don't confuse Costa Maya with Riviera Maya, which stretches between Cancún and Tulum. Technically, Costa Maya is the region between Punta Herrero and Xcalak, near the border with Belize. Millions of dollars have been invested in a pier that opened just a few years ago; there's also a lavish oceanfront shopping-and-restaurant complex that caters exclusively to the needs of cruise ship passengers (there are no hotels in the area). Princess, Royal Caribbean, Regal, Carnival, and Norwegian are among the lines that visit the port. The Mayan ruins of nearby Kohunlich and Chacchoben are popular attractions, along with silky white beaches and diving and snorkeling at the Chincorro, Mexico's largest coral atoll.

COMING ASHORE   Literally carved out of the jungle, this amenity-filled pier is the only major form of development for miles around, and has pretty much everything you want: sprawling restaurants (one with a balcony, the other with outdoor seating and a stage for live music), an amphitheater for cultural dance performances, two saltwater pools, a pool bar, a trampoline, and plenty of shops. And a free tram shuttles passengers from their ships down the loooooong .5km (¼-mile) pier to the port entrance.

GETTING AROUND

BY TAXI   A long line of shiny new taxis lines up just outside the pier. Unfortunately, because any attraction of note is far, far away and there are no alternative means of transportation, the prices are steep and non-negotiable. Visiting the Mayan ruins of Kohunlich will set passengers back US$65 per person round-trip, while a round-trip ride to Chacchoben comes in at US$45 per person. With prices like these, we highly recommend you book the cruise line shore excursions instead (see below). About the only reasonable fare is to the nearby sleepy fishing village of Mahajual (US$5 per person).

BY RENTAL CAR   No rental-car facilities are in the area, but with only one long, straight, flat road—which is still in the process of being paved—this does not seem to be too much of an inconvenience.

BEST CRUISE LINE SHORE EXCURSIONS

The Mayan Ruins of Kohunlich (US$82, 7 hr.): Located in a secluded jungle setting near the border of Belize, this Mayan city was built between A.D. 200 and 900, spanning the early through late-classical periods. The trail to the ruins is marked by a tree that was uprooted and replanted upside down—a means of marking sites used by the apparently brilliant, though obviously eccentric, Mexican archaeologist who first explored the site. Check out the Plaza of the Acropolis (where two temples are aligned with the equinox) and the Temple of the Masks from the 6th century, where 1.8m (6-ft.) stucco masks of the Mayan sun god are remarkably well preserved.

The Mayan Ruins of Chacchoben (US$69, 4 hr.): Opened to the public in 1999, this collection of temples dates back to A.D. 360, or the middle of the early classical period, and played an important role as a trading center for wood, jade, and colorful birds. There are more than two dozen structures; to date, less than 5% of the site has been excavated. The first temple that you'll encounter is the temple of Venus, a tribute to fertility. The pyramids are in an excellent state of preservation, and their distinctive curved edges and soft lines are particularly beautiful. Climbing to the first plateau affords an impressive view of the surrounding area.

Bike & Kayak (US$48, 3 hr.): Starting off on mountain bikes, you'll pedal along a dirt road past a small mangrove lagoon with views of the coastline, then through the village of Mahajual (don't blink or you'll miss it), and finally arrive at the beach. After a short refreshment break, trade in your helmet for a paddle and pair up with a partner for a kayak trip out along the nearby reef. The small two-person kayaks are easy to handle and to launch from shore. The bike ride back includes another beach stop.

Jungle Beach Break (US$38, no set time): A shuttle operates between the nearby Uvero Beach and the pier every 35 minutes, allowing you to come and go as you please. But would you ever want to leave the snow-white beaches and crystal-blue water, not to mention the chaise longues and umbrellas, open bar, free snorkel gear, paddleboats, and rental sea kayaks, jet skis, and powerboats? Facilities include changing rooms with showers and an on-site snack bar (food not included). Parasailing is also available.

ON YOUR OWN: WITHIN WALKING DISTANCE

If you choose, you could stay right at the one-stop-shop pier complex and forego a real taste of the Mayan coast. A 650-seat amphitheater here offers cultural shows daily, ranging from a pre-Hispanic dance to a Mexican folkloric performance. There are also activities throughout the day in and around the pier, from guacamole-making classes to aqua-aerobics, games, and contests. Check the daily entertainment schedule posted near the restrooms for performance times and activities.

Immediately next to the pier is a lovely private beach club with umbrellas, chairs, hammock swings, and a small restaurant and bar. There's a small fee for day passes. Enter from the parking lot near the bus departure point.

ON YOUR OWN: BEYOND THE PORT AREA

The only town in the area is the Mahajual fishing village, which, until quite recently, did not even have electricity. A single main road is lined with a short row of rustic, screened-in restaurants and a miniscule grocery; across the street is a long white beach with fishing boats—and noticeably devoid of beach umbrellas and sunbathers. Unless you're just curious, there's no real reason to go.

SHOPPING

Because the port at Costa Maya was constructed with the sole purpose of serving American and European cruise ship passengers, you can bet your last enchilada that shopping abounds. There are some 70 shops in a mall-like setting—some of them familiar to the seasoned cruiser, others unique. **Ultra Femme** specializes in fragrances and cosmetics cheaper than you'll find at the duty-free store. If it's gold and jewels you're after, head over to **Tanzanite International** for a wide selection and friendly staff, or to **Diamond International** for some great bargains. Next door, you can haggle over "art in silver" at **Taxco Factory.** For something different, head over to the two nearby *palapas* (small thatched-roof stands), where local artisans craft their wares as potential buyers look on.

GREAT LOCAL RESTAURANTS & BARS

Bandito's Lobster House, at the pier, serves some of the freshest seviche and tastiest guacamole around. The fish, shrimp, and lobster tacos can be ordered a la carte, so you can sample one of each, while the fire-roasted Baja lobster, whole sea bass, and Mayan fajitas are full meals and come with a slew of sides. Order a fruity tropical teaser or classic margarita to wash it all down. Next door, at **Mamacita's Taqueria,** you can enjoy casual dining and drinks while taking in the excellent views of the coast and port. Try the blackened chicken fundido to start, then the grande Baja burrito or the tres taco platter.

PROGRESO/MERIDA

Visited by a fraction of the ships that call at Cozumel, Progreso has one major advantage over its rival: proximity to Chichén-Itzá, which lies only 2 hours south by motorcoach. This makes excursions to the ruins considerably cheaper than they are from Cozumel, averaging about US$95 per person. Progreso itself is almost nothing but a port. Ships dock here at the end of a man-made causeway that juts several miles out into the Gulf of Mexico, making it very difficult to visit anything on your own. We recommend taking a tour: Aside from visits to Chichén-Itzá and the smaller Mayan ruins at Uxmal and Dzibilchaltun, cruise passengers can visit Merida, the capital of Yucatán state (about 32km/20 miles away); see pink flamingos in their natural habitat at the Celestun Estuary Nature Reserve; or take a jeep trek off-road to two local haciendas.

13 Curaçao

As you sail into the harbor of Willemstad, be sure to look for the quaint "floating bridge," the Queen Emma pontoon bridge, which swings aside to open the narrow channel. Welcome to Curaçao, the largest and most populous of the Netherlands Antilles, just 56km (35 miles) north of the Venezuelan coast.

Curaçao was first discovered by the Spanish around 1499, but in 1634, the Dutch came and prospered. Because much of the island's surface is an arid desert, the settlers ruled out farming and instead developed Curaçao into one of the Dutch empire's busiest trading posts. In 1915, when the Royal Dutch/Shell Company built one of the world's largest oil refineries to process crude from Venezuela, workers from 50 countries poured onto the island, and today it remains a melting pot, its population descended from a curious mixture of bloodlines, including African, Dutch, Venezuelan, and Pakistani. The oil refineries went into decline after World War II, and by the 1980s tourism had begun to develop, leading to the building of many new hotels.

Today, the island retains a Dutch flavor, especially in **Willemstad,** where the harbor is bordered by rows of picture-postcard, pastel-colored gabled Dutch-colonial houses. While these structures give Willemstad a storybook appearance, the rest of the island looks like the American Southwest, its desertlike landscape dotted with three-pronged cacti, spiny-leafed aloes, and divi-divi trees bent by trade winds.

COMING ASHORE   Cruise ships dock in Willemstad at a megapier just beyond the Queen Emma pontoon bridge, which leads to the duty-free shopping sector and the famous Floating Market. It's a 5- to 10-minute walk from here to the center of town, or you can take a taxi from the stand. A shopping/entertainment complex called Riffort Village recently opened in a restored fort nearby. The town itself is easy to navigate on foot. Most of it can be explored in 2 or 3 hours, leaving plenty of time for

Frommer's Favorite Curaçao Experiences

Visiting Christoffel National Park: Hike up 369m (1,210-ft.) St. Christoffelberg, passing cacti, iguanas, wild goats, many species of birds, and ancient Arawak paintings along the way. With 32km (20 miles) of roads, you can also see the park by car. (See "On Your Own: Beyond the Port Area," below.)

Gazing into the Mirrored Waters of the Hato Caves: Stalagmites and stalactites are mirrored in a mystical underground lake in these caves, whose limestone formations were created by water seeping through the coral. (See "On Your Own: Beyond the Port Area," below.)

beaches or watersports. Although the ship terminal has a duty-free shop, save your serious shopping for Willemstad. There's a phone center at the cruise terminal.

LANGUAGE Dutch, Spanish, and English are spoken on Curaçao, along with Papiamento, a patois that combines the three major tongues with Amerindian and African dialects.

CURRENCY The official currency is the **Netherland Antilles florin** (exchange rate at press time: 1.75 NAF = US$1; 1 NAF = US56¢). Each florin (also called a **guilder**) is divisible by 100 cents. Canadian and U.S. dollars, as well as euros, are accepted for purchases, so there's no need to change money. Unless otherwise noted, prices in this section are given in U.S. dollars.

INFORMATION Stop by the **Curaçao Tourist Board,** Pietermaai (© **599/9-434-8200**), open Monday through Friday from 8am to 5pm. For information before you go, call © **800/328-7222** or visit www.curacao.com.

CALLING FROM THE U.S. When calling Curaçao from the United States, you need to dial the international access code (011) before the numbers listed here.

GETTING AROUND

BY TAXI Taxis are metered, and the best place to flag one down is on the Otrabanda side of the floating bridge. You can also call © **599/9-869-0747** or 599/9-869-0752. Generally, there's no need to tip. Up to four passengers can share the price of an island tour by taxi, which costs about US$30 per hour.

BY BUS A fleet of buses operates from Wilhelmina Plein, near the shopping center, Punda, and Otrobanda, and runs to most parts of Curaçao. You can hail a bus at any designated bus stop.

BY RENTAL CAR Driving is on the right, on paved roads. **Avis, Budget, Hertz, National,** and **Thrifty** all have offices here.

BEST CRUISE LINE SHORE EXCURSIONS

Many excursions aren't really worth the price here—you can easily see the town on your own and hop a taxi to the few attractions on the island outside of Willemstad.

Spanish Water Canoe Tour & Snorkeling (US$69, 3½ hr.): At Caracas Bay Island, you'll board canoes for a 45-minute paddle alongside mangroves and rock formations.

Then you'll arrive at Baya Beach, where instructors lead snorkeling sessions over a sunken tugboat.

Underwater Animal Encounter (US$89, 4 hr.): Ever wanted to hand-feed a shark? Here's your chance. Suit up in scuba gear and dive into the shallow (3.6m/12-ft.) water at the Curaçao Seaquarium, where sharks and sea turtles are behind fencing, with holes through which you can hand them their grub while stingrays, parrotfish, and other marine life swim around on your side. Since the water is so shallow, scuba certification isn't required.

ON YOUR OWN: WITHIN WALKING DISTANCE

The major attraction here is **Willemstad,** which you can see on foot. After years of restoration, the town's historic center and the island's natural harbor, Schottegat, have been inscribed on UNESCO's World Heritage List. Be sure to watch the **Queen Emma pontoon bridge** move. It's motorized and a man actually drives it to the side of the harbor every so often so that ships and boats can pass through the channel. It's exceedingly cool.

A statue of **Pedro Luis Brion** dominates the square known as Brionplein, at the Otrabanda end of the Queen Emma pontoon bridge. Born in Curaçao in 1782, Brion became the island's favorite son and best-known war hero. He was an admiral of the fleet under Simón Bolívar and fought for the independence of Venezuela and Colombia.

Fort Amsterdam, site of the Governor's Palace and the 1769 Dutch Reformed church, has the task of guarding the waterfront. The church here still has a British cannonball embedded in it. The arches leading to the fort were tunneled under the official residence of the governor. A corner of the fort stands at the intersection of Breedestraat and Handelskade, the starting point for a plunge into the island's major shopping district.

A few minutes' walk from the pontoon bridge, at the north end of Handelskade, is the **Floating Market,** where scores of schooners tie up alongside the canal. Boats arrive here from Venezuela and Colombia, and from other West Indian islands, to sell tropical fruits and vegetables, as well as handicrafts. The modern market's vast concrete cap has not diminished the fun of watching the activity here. Either arrive early or stay late to view marine merchants setting up or storing their wares.

Between the I. H. (Sha) Capriles Kade and Fort Amsterdam, at the corner of Columbusstraat and Hanchi di Snoa, is the **Mikve Israel-Emanuel Synagogue.** Dating from 1651, the Jewish congregation here is the oldest in the New World. Next door, the **Jewish Cultural Historical Museum,** Hanchi Snoa 29 (© 599/9-461-1633; www.snoa.com), is housed in two 1728 buildings that served as the rabbi's residence and the mikvah (bath), used for religious purification purposes. Entry is through the synagogue; admission is US$5. Hours are Monday through Friday from 9am to 4:30pm, Sunday from 10am to 4pm.

You can walk from the Queen Emma pontoon bridge to the **Curaçao Museum,** Van Leeuwenhoekstraat (© 599/9-462-3873). The building, constructed in 1853 by the Royal Dutch Army as a military hospital, has been carefully restored and furnished with paintings, objets d'art, and antique furniture, and now houses a large collection from the Caiquetio tribes. On the museum grounds is a gallery for temporary exhibitions of both local and international art. Hours are Monday through Friday from 8:30am to 4:30pm, Sunday from 10am to 4pm. Admission is US$3 for adults, US$1.75 for children under 15.

ON YOUR OWN: BEYOND THE PORT AREA

Cacti, bromeliads, rare orchids, iguanas, donkeys, wild goats, and many species of birds thrive in the 1,800-hectare (4,446-acre) **Christoffel National Park** (© 599/9-864-0363), located about a 30-minute taxi or car ride from the capital near the north-western tip of Curaçao. The park rises from flat, arid countryside to 369m-high (1,210-ft.) St. Christoffelberg, the tallest point in the Dutch Leewards. Along the way are ancient Arawak paintings and the Piedra di Monton, a rock heap piled by African slaves who cleared this former plantation. Legend said that the slaves could climb to the top of the rock pile, jump off, and fly back home across the Atlantic to Africa. If they had ever tasted a grain of salt, however, they would crash to their deaths. The park has 32km (20 miles) of one-way trail-like roads. The shortest is about 8km (5 miles) long but takes about 40 minutes to drive because of its rough terrain. One of several hiking trails goes to the top of St. Christoffelberg; it takes about 1½ hours to walk to the summit (come early in the morning before it gets hot). There's also a museum in an old storehouse left over from plantation days. The park is open Monday through Saturday from 7:30am to 4pm, Sunday from 6am to 3pm. Admission is US$10 per person. Guided tours are available.

The **Curaçao Seaquarium,** off Bapor Kibra (© 599/9-461-6666; www.curacao-sea-aquarium.com), displays more than 400 species of fish, crabs, anemones, and other invertebrates, sponges, and coral. The Shark & Animal Encounter allows divers, snorkelers, and experienced swimmers to feed, film, and photograph sharks, stingrays, lobsters, tarpons, parrotfish, and other marine life in a controlled environment. You can swim with the dolphins for US$149 or dive with them for a mere US$300. Non-swimmers can see the underwater life from a 14m (46-ft.) semisubmersible observatory. Curaçao's only full-facility, white-sand, palm-shaded beach is on the Seaquarium grounds. Admission is US$15 for adults and US$7.50 for children 5 to 14. Hours are daily from 8:30am to 4:30pm.

Stalagmites and stalactites are mirrored in a mystical underground lake in **Hato Caves,** F. D. Rosseveltweg (© 599/9-868-0379). Long ago, geological forces uplifted this limestone terrace, which was originally a coral reef. The limestone formations were created over thousands of years by water seeping through the coral. After crossing the lake, you enter two caverns known as the Cathedral and La Ventana ("The Window"), where you'll see ancient Indian petroglyphs. The caves are open daily from 10am to 4pm; professional local guides take visitors through every hour. Admission is US$6.50 for adults, US$5 for children 4 to 11, and free for kids 3 and under.

SHOPPING

Curaçao is a shopper's paradise, with some 200 stores lining Heerenstraat, Breedestraat, and other streets in the 5-block district called the **Punda.** Many shops occupy the town's old Dutch houses.

The island is famous for its 5-pound "wheelers" of Gouda and Edam cheese. Look for good buys on wooden shoes, French perfumes, Dutch-blue Delft souvenirs, finely woven Italian silks, Japanese and German cameras, jewelry, silver, Swiss watches, linens, leather goods, liquor, and island-made rum and liqueurs, especially Curaçao liqueur, some of which has a distinctive blue color. Some stores also offer good buys on intricate lacework imported from everywhere between Portugal and China.

If you're a street shopper and want something colorful, consider a carving or flam-boyant painting from Haiti or the Dominican Republic; both are hawked by street vendors at any of the main plazas.

Suggested shops include **Bamali,** Breedestraat 2 (© **599/9-461-2258**), for Indonesian-influenced clothing (mostly for women), and **Gandelman Jewelers,** Breedestraat 35, Punda (© **599/9-461-1854**), for a large selection of fine jewelry as well as Curaçaoan gold pieces.

BEACHES

Curaçao has some 38 beaches, ranging from hotel sand patches to secluded coves. The seawater remains an almost-constant 76°F (24°C) year-round, with good underwater visibility, but beaches here just aren't as good as others in the region. Taxi drivers waiting at the cruise dock will take you to any of the beaches, but you'll have to negotiate a fare. To be on the safe side, arrange to have your driver pick you up at a certain time and take you back to the dock.

The **Curaçao Seaquarium** has the island's only full-facility, white-sand, palm-shaded beach, but you'll have to pay the full aquarium admission to get in (see "On Your Own: Beyond the Port Area," above). The rest of the beaches here are public.

Southeast of Willemstad, **Curaçao Underwater Park** (© **599/9-462-4242**) stretches from the Breezes Resort to the eastern tip of Curaçao and includes some of the island's finest reefs.

Daaibooi is a good beach about 30 minutes from town, in the Willibrordus area on the west side of Curaçao. It's free, but there are no changing facilities.

Blauwbaai (Blue Bay) is the largest and most frequented beach on Curaçao, with enough white sand for everybody. Along with showers and changing facilities, there are plenty of shady places to retreat from the noonday sun. To reach it, take the road that goes past the **Holiday Beach Hotel & Casino** (© **599/9-462-5400**), heading in the direction of Julianadorp. Follow the sign that tells you to bear left for Blauwbaai and the fishing village of San Michiel.

Westpunt is known for its gigantic cliffs and the Sunday divers who jump from them into the ocean below. This public beach is on the northwestern tip of the island. Just south of Westpunt is **Knip Bay,** which has beautiful turquoise waters. On weekends, live music and dancing make the beach a lively place. Changing facilities and refreshments are available. **Playa Abao,** with crystal-turquoise water, is situated at the northern tip of the island.

Warning: Beware of stepping on the hard spines of sea urchins, which are sometimes found in these waters. While not fatal, their spines can cause several days of real discomfort. For temporary first aid, try the local remedies of vinegar or lime juice.

GREAT LOCAL RESTAURANTS & BARS

Curaçao's local beer is the very Dutch **Amstel.** The local drink is **Curaçao liqueur,** some of which has a distinctive blue color.

La Pergola, in the Waterfront Arches, Waterfort Straat (© **599/9-461-3482**), is an Italian restaurant where the menu items change virtually every day. Lunch is about US$25.

Rijsttafel Indonesia & Holland Club Bar, Mercuriusstraat 13, Salinja (© **599/9-461-2606**), is the best place on the island to sample the Indonesian *rijsttafel,* a traditional "rice table" with tons of zesty side dishes. Lunch is around US$13. You'll need a taxi to get to this restaurant, which is in the suburbs near Salinja, near the Super-Clubs Breezes Curaçao, southeast of Willemstad.

14 Dominica

First things first: It's pronounced "Dom-in-*eek*-a," not "Doe-*min*-i-ka." And it has nothing to do with the Dominican Republic. The Commonwealth of Dominica is an independent country, and English, not Spanish, is the official language. The only Spanish commonly understood in Dominica is *mal encaminado a Santo Domingo* ("accidentally sent to the Dominican Republic"), the phrase stamped on the many letters that make it to their proper destination only after an erroneous but common detour.

To be sure, Dominica has some rough edges. The island is poor, so don't expect luxury or up-to-the-minute technology around every corner, and not everything manmade is as beautiful as nature's handiwork. Balancing this, though, is the fact that Dominica is the lushest and most mountainous island in the eastern Caribbean. About 47km (29 miles) long and 26km (16 miles) wide, and lying between the French islands of Guadeloupe and Martinique, smack-dab in the center of the arc formed by the Antilles, it's blessed with astonishing natural wonders—crystal-pure rivers (one for every day of the year, they say), dramatic waterfalls, volcanic lakes (one gurgles and boils from the heat and tumult in the earth below), and foliage as gargantuan as any H. G. Wells ever imagined on Venus. Volcanic coral reefs, every bit as biologically complex as the rainforests onshore, ring the island, and a bit farther from land, whales mate and calve.

Much of Dominica's beauty is accessible to even the most sedentary visitor. Sitting in a rowboat, you can glide up a river through swampland crowded with mangroves and exotic birds; impressive waterfalls are minutes from paved roads. You can also wend through astonishingly verdant rainforests along undemanding nature trails.

The island's people—primarily descendants of the West Africans brought over to work the plantations, plus some descendants of Europeans and Indians—are another great natural resource. Friendly and proud of their national independence, Dominica's 71,000 citizens remain, for the most part, unchanged by tourism. Don't be surprised when you're greeted with a smile and an "okay," the island's equivalent of "hi." Unfortunately, in Roseau, the main city, drug dealers offering to sell you some of the local weed may also greet you—tourism might be a still-developing industry here, but some other trades are obviously a little further along.

One portion of the island's population has immeasurable ethnological significance: Concentrated in a territory in the northeast, Dominica's approximately 3,000 Carib Indians are the last remaining descendants of the people who dominated the region when Europeans arrived.

COMING ASHORE   Dominica has two cruise ship ports. The most frequented is in the heart of **Roseau,** the country's capital and largest town. The other is near the northwestern town of **Portsmouth.** Banks, restaurants, a market, a tourism office, and the recommended Dominica Museum line the road opposite Roseau's berth. Portsmouth's port has a tourist welcome center (with an auditorium for speakers and films), shops, and instant access to Fort Shirley and Cabrits National Park.

LANGUAGE   English is Dominica's official language. Almost everyone speaks Creole as well, a patois that combines elements of French, English, and African language. Dominica's Creole is similar to those spoken on the neighboring French islands of Guadeloupe and Martinique.

CURRENCY   The **Eastern Caribbean dollar** (EC$2.70 = US$1; EC$1 = US37¢) is Dominica's official currency, but U.S. dollars are accepted almost everywhere. You're

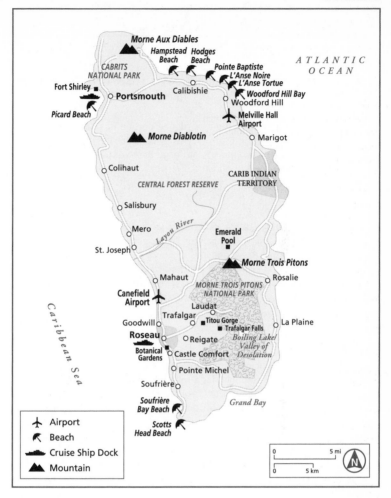

likely to receive change in the local currency. Several ATMs in Roseau, including one at the port, dispense both U.S. and EC dollars. Credit cards and traveler's checks are widely accepted. Unless otherwise specified, prices in this section are given in U.S. dollars.

INFORMATION   Dominica's **Division of Tourism** operates branches at the Roseau and Portsmouth cruise ship berths (the Roseau office is located a block from the waterfront at the old post office building, on Dame M. E. Charles Blvd.). For information before you leave home, contact the **Dominica Tourist Office** (*©* **888/ 645-5637;** www.dominica.dm). Several island businesses, including restaurants, tour operators, and other service providers, have joined forces to create another site, **www. delphis.dm/home.htm**, which has scores of links and helpful information.

CALLING FROM THE U.S.   When calling Dominica from the United States, simply dial "1" before the numbers listed here.

Frommer's Favorite Dominica Experiences

Hiking to the Emerald Pool: A 15-minute walk through a gorgeous forest brings you to this primeval pool, where you can swim or just take in the beauty of the picture-perfect waterfall, the moss-covered boulders, and the sunlight streaming through branches high overhead. (See "Best Cruise Line Shore Excursions," below.)

Experiencing Carib Culture: Along a rugged portion of Dominica's north-eastern coast, the 1,530-hectare (3,779-acre) Carib Territory is home to the world's last surviving Carib Indians. Kalinago Barana Aute, the "Carib Cultural Village by the Sea," honors the diversity, history, and heritage of the Kalinago people. Its features include traditional crafts demonstrations and dance performances, trails, scenic views, and more. (See "Best Cruise Line Shore Excursions," below.)

Exploring Fort Shirley/Cabrits National Park: On Dominica's northwestern coast, right by the cruise ship port of Portsmouth, the 324-hectare (800-acre) Cabrits National Park combines stunning mountain scenery, tropical deciduous forest and swampland, volcanic-sand beaches, coral reefs, and the romance of an 18th-century fort. (See "On Your Own: Within Walking Distance," below.)

GETTING AROUND

BY TAXI Taxis and public minivans are designated by license plates that begin with the letters H, HA, or HB. Also look for a round decal on the front of the car, which means the driver is a certified Tourism Operator. Fleets of both await cruise ship passengers at the Roseau and Portsmouth docks. Drivers are generally knowledgeable about sites and history, and the standard sightseeing rate is from US$20 per site per person. The vehicles are unmetered, so negotiate a price in advance and make sure everyone's talking about the same currency. You can get more information from the **Dominica Taxi Association** (© 767/449-8533). Two reputable operators are **Mally's Tour & Taxi Service** (© 767/448-3114) and **Alwyn's Taxi & Tour Service** (© 767/235-4260).

BY RENTAL CAR Dominica's road system is extensive and relatively well maintained, considering the frequent torrential rains, but driving is on the left side, and passage through the mountains can be harrowing. You'll need a valid driver's license and a Dominican driver's permit, which costs about US$12 and is available through rental agencies. Don't get annoyed when other drivers sound their horns; honking usually indicates an oncoming vehicle (especially at sharp curves) or is meant as a friendly greeting. Local agencies include **Valley Rent a Car,** with offices in both Roseau and Portsmouth (© 767/448-3233 in Roseau; 767/445-5252 in Portsmouth), and **Garraway Rent-a-Car,** 17 Old St., downtown Roseau (© 767/448-2891). Other options are **Auto Trade Car Rentals** (© 767/440-0415) and **Best Deal Rent a Car** (© 767/449-9204). **Budget** also has offices here.

BEST CRUISE LINE SHORE EXCURSIONS

Trafalgar Falls & Emerald Pool Nature Tour (US$45, 4 hr.): Drive to Morne Bruce for a panoramic view of Roseau and learn about local flora and fauna at the Botanical Gardens. Proceed to a lookout point for a majestic view of Trafalgar Falls. Another drive and a 15-minute walk along a relatively easy trail take you to the Emerald Pool, named for the moss-covered boulders that enclose it. You can splash in the refreshing water, if you like, floating on your back to see the thick rainforest canopy, the 15m (49-ft.) waterfall, and the bright-blue sky above you.

Carib Indian Territory (US$59, 5 hr.): Along a rugged portion of Dominica's northeastern coast, the 1,530-hectare (3,779-acre) Carib Territory is home to the world's last surviving Carib Indians. The Caribs today live like most other rural islanders—growing bananas and coconuts, fishing, and operating small shops—but their sturdy baskets of dyed and woven larouma reeds and their wooden canoes carved from the trunks of massive gommier trees are evidence of the people's links to the past. Kalinago Barana Aute, the "Carib Cultural Village by the Sea," honors the diversity, history, and heritage of the Kalinago people. Visitors can enjoy the traditional crafts demonstrations and dance performances, explore an herbal medicine garden, hike the trails, and stop in the arts-and-crafts gallery. Food and beverage concessions are available.

Rain Forest Aerial Tram (US$114, 3 hr.): Experience the flora and fauna from above the dense rainforest on this 1,400m (4,592-ft.) tram's scenic 70-minute journey. You'll glide through the treetops over streams and waterfalls and across the Breakfast River Gorge.

EXCURSIONS OFFERED BY LOCAL AGENCIES

See "Sports," below, for information on scuba, snorkeling, and kayaking trips.

Nature Tours: Dominica has several excellent tour operators who know the island's many features and intricate terrain like the backs of their hands. One truly outstanding and highly recommended operation is **Ken's Hinterland Adventure Tours,** Fort Young Hotel, Victoria Street, Roseau (© 767/448-4850 or 866/880-0508; www.kenshinter landtours.com), which offers tours that focus on botany, natural history, bird-watching, and whale-watching. Prices are US$60 for a full day and US$40 for a half-day.

Carib Indian Excursions: For trips through the Carib Territory, you might want to make arrangements with **NICE** (Native Indigenous Carib Excursions; © 767/445-8669). You can't miss with the firsthand knowledge of Carib traditions offered by NICE's operator, former Carib chief Irvince Auguiste.

Caribbean Cooking: The outfitter **Jungle Trekking Adventures & Safaris (JTAS;** © 767/440-JTAS; www.experiencescaribbean.com) offers several land tours with half- and full-day options, including "Cuisine a la Dominique," in which visitors are taught how to produce and present traditional Caribbean dishes by two of Dominica's hottest chefs.

Eco-Tourism Theme Park: The **Wacky Rollers Adventure Park** (© 767/440-4386; www.wackyrollers.com) is open daily from 10am to 4pm. There's a challenge course as well as river-tubing safaris, river-to-ocean kayak excursions, and jeep safaris. During the week, reservations are required.

ON YOUR OWN: WITHIN WALKING DISTANCE

IN ROSEAU   In the early 18th century, the French chose to build their largest settlement at what is now Roseau because the area had the largest expanse of flat land on the leeward coast and was well supplied with fresh water from the nearby Roseau River. The town's name comes from the river reeds (*roseaux* in French) that grow profusely around the estuary.

As you come ashore, you'll see the **Dominica Museum,** which faces the bay front. Housed in an old market house dating from 1810, the museum's permanent exhibit provides a clear and interesting overview of the island's geology, history, archaeology, economy, and culture. The displays on pre-Columbian peoples, the slave trade, and the Fighting Maroons—slaves who resisted their white slave owners and established their own communities—are particularly informative. Open Monday through Friday from 9am to 4pm, Saturday from 9am to noon; admission is US$2.

Directly behind the museum is the **Old Market Square.** Vendors of vegetables, fruits, and other merchandise have crowded this cobbled square for centuries, and over the years the location has also witnessed slave auctions, executions, and political meetings and rallies. Today, it primarily offers handicrafts and souvenirs. The **Public Market Place,** at the mouth of the Roseau River, to your left as you leave the ship, is the Old Market Square's successor as the town's center of commercial activity. It's most colorful on Saturday mornings, when farmers and country vendors from the hills artfully display their fruits, vegetables, root crops, and flowers across the courtyards, sidewalks, and stalls of the marketplace.

It took more than 100 years to build the **Roseau Cathedral of Our Lady of Fair Heaven,** on Virgin Lane. Made of cut volcanic stone in the Gothic-Romanesque revival style, it was finally completed in 1916. The original funds to build the church were raised from levies on French planters, and Caribs erected the first wooden ceiling frame. Convicts on Devil's Island built the pulpit, and one of the stained-glass windows is dedicated to Christopher Columbus. The **Methodist Church** stands next door to the Cathedral on land that once belonged to Catholics who later converted to Methodism. The Protestant church's location and the "conversion" of the land caused such discomfort in the late 1800s that a street riot ensued. Things are calmer today.

On the eastern edge of Roseau, the **Botanical Gardens** lie at the base of Morne Bruce, the mountain overlooking the town. The gardens were established at the end of the 19th century to encourage crop diversification and to provide farmers with correctly propagated seedlings. London's Kew Gardens provided exotic plants collected from every corner of the tropical world, and experiments conducted to see what would grow in Dominica revealed that everything does. Unfortunately, in 1979, Hurricane David destroyed many of the garden's oldest trees. One arboreal victim, an African baobab, still pins the bus it crushed, a monument to the power of the storm. At the garden's aviary, you can see sisserou and jacko parrots, part of a captive-breeding program designed to increase the ranks of these endangered species.

IN PORTSMOUTH The cruise ship dock at Portsmouth leads directly to 104-hectare (257-acre) **Cabrits National Park,** which combines stunning mountain scenery, tropical deciduous forest and swampland, volcanic-sand beaches, coral reefs, and the romance of 18th-century Fort Shirley overlooking the town and Prince Rupert's Bay. Previous visitors to the area included Christopher Columbus, Sir Francis Drake, Admiral Horatio Nelson, and John Smith, who stopped here on his way to Virginia, where he founded Jamestown. Fort Shirley and more than 50 other major structures make up one of the West Indies' most impressive and historic military complexes. Admission is US$2.

ON YOUR OWN: BEYOND THE PORT AREAS

Approximately 15 to 20 minutes by car from Roseau, **Trafalgar Falls** is actually two separate falls referred to as the mother and the father falls. The cascading white torrents dazzle in the sunlight before pummeling black-lava boulders below. The surrounding foliage grows in innumerable shades of green. To reach the brisk water of the natural pool at the base of the falls, you'll have to step gingerly along slippery rocks, so the nonballetic shouldn't attempt the climb. The constant mist that tinges the entire area beats any spa treatment. The rainbows are perpetual.

Titou Gorge, near the village of Laudat, offers an exhilarating swimming experience. Wending through the narrow volcanic gorge, you struggle against the cool current like a salmon swimming upstream to spawn. The sheer black walls enclosing the gorge loom 6m (20 ft.) above. At first, they seem sinister, but worn smooth by the water, they're ultimately womblike rather than menacing. Rock outcrops and a small cave provide interludes from the water flow, and eventually you reach the small but thundering waterfall that feeds the torrent. Scenes from *Pirates of the Caribbean* were filmed here.

Emerald Pool sits deep in the rainforest, not far from the center of the island. After walking 15 minutes along a relatively easy trail shaded by majestic trees, you reach a 15m (49-ft.) waterfall that crashes into the pool, named for the moss-covered boulders that enclose it. You can splash in the refreshing water, if you like, floating on your back to see the thick rainforest canopy and bright-blue sky arching over you.

About 6.4km (4 miles) from Portsmouth, in the midst of orange, grapefruit, and banana groves, the **Syndicate Nature Trail** provides an excellent introduction to tropical rainforests. The easy loop trail meanders through a stunningly rich ecosystem that features exotic trees such as the lwoyé kaka and the chantannyé.

Hard-core masochists have an easy choice—the forced march through the **Valley of Desolation** to **Boiling Lake.** Experienced guides say this 6-hour hike is like spending hours on a maximally resistant Stairmaster; one ex-Marine drill sergeant, a master of understatement, referred to it as "arduous." No joke, the trek is part of the Dominican army's basic training (of course, you won't have to carry one of your colleagues along the way). Why would any sane person endure this hell? To breathe in the harsh, sulfuric fumes that have killed all but the hardiest vegetation? Because the idea of baking a potato in the steam rising from the earth is irresistible? Maybe to feel the thrill that comes with the risk that you might break through the thin crust that separates you from hot lava? Or could it be the final destination, the 21m-wide (69-ft.) cauldron of bubbling, slate-blue water of unknown depth? Don't even think of taking a dip in this flooded fumarole: The water temperature ranges from 180°F to 197°F (82°C–92°C). Can we sign you up?

SHOPPING

In addition to the usual duty-free items—jewelry, watches, perfumes, and other luxury goods—Dominica offers handicrafts and art not obtainable anywhere else, most notably Carib Indian baskets made of dyed larouma reeds and balizier (heliconia) leaves. You can buy Carib crafts directly from the craftspeople in the Carib Territory or at various outlets in Roseau. A small, 12-inch basket will cost about US$10, and you can get a bell-shaped model about 22 inches high for US$30 or US$35. Floor mats made from vertiver grass are another Dominican specialty.

At **Tropicrafts,** at Queen Mary Street and Turkey Lane, in Roseau, you can watch local women weave grass mats with designs as varied and complex as those you made as a child with your Spirograph. This large store also stocks Carib baskets, locally made soaps and toiletries, rums, jellies, condiments, woodcarvings, and masks made from the trunks of giant fougère ferns. The **Rainforest Shop,** at 12 Old St., Roseau, is dedicated to the preservation of Dominica's ecosystem and offers colorful hand-painted items made from recycled materials such as oil drums, coconut shells, and newspapers.

The **Crazy Banana,** at 17 Castle St., Roseau, features Dominican arts and crafts, including straw and ceramic items, as well as jewelry and Cuban cigars. For unique and sometimes whimsical objects, try **Balisier's,** at 35 Great George St., Roseau, where local artist Hilroy Fingal transforms throwaway items such as aluminum cans, perfume bottles, rocks, and coconut shells into things of beauty. His aesthetic is a little like Keith Haring's and every bit as fun.

Earl Etienne's Gallery, at 31 Cork St., Roseau, is one of the island's oldest crafts shops. Etienne, one of Dominica's leading artists, also showcases his paintings here. **Frontline Cooperative,** at 78 Independence St., Roseau, specializes in books about Caribbean peoples, issues, and cooking.

BEACHES

If your sole focus is beaches, you'll likely find Dominica disappointing. Much of the seacoast is rocky, and many beaches have dark, volcanic sand. But there are golden-sand beaches as well, primarily on the northern coast. Head for **Woodford Hill Bay, L'Anse Tortue, Pointe Baptiste,** or **Hampstead Beach;** all have honey-colored sand, palm trees, and azure waters protected by reefs or windswept headlands. **Castaways Hotel (℡ 767/449-6245),** 2.4km (1½ miles) north of the mouth of the Layou River and about a half-hour drive from Roseau, rents out lounge chairs for US$3.

SPORTS

SCUBA DIVING   Dominica's lush, beautiful scenery above water is echoed underwater in the surrounding Caribbean and Atlantic. Although the island is drained by hundreds of rivers and streams, the jagged volcanic undersea-scape prevents runoff sediment from clouding the water. Visibility ranges from 18m (59 ft.) to more than 30m (98 ft.).

Most local dive operations surpass international standards set by PADI, NAUI, and SSI, and small, uncrowded excursions are the norm. **Dive Dominica (℡ 888/262-6611** in the U.S., or 767/448-2188) is perhaps the island's best operator. Single-tank boat dives run about US$45. First-time dives with instruction run about US$130.

Cabrits Dive Centre (℡ 767/445-3010; www.cabritsdive.com) is Dominica's only PADI five-star dive center, and the only dive operation on the north of the island, which means yours will be the only dive group—and you'll have access to many untouched sites, pristine reefs, and an array of colorful sponges. The abundant marine life includes rarer species that are at home in Dominica, like seahorses, flying gunards, and batfish. The dive center will provide boat or car pick-up service to/from the Cabrits cruise ship dock. It will also arrange transportation for passengers on ships docked in Roseau (about an hour's drive) for US$120 for up to four people. Single-tank dives are US$61; two-tank dives are US$94. First-time dives with instruction are US$109. Snorkeling is also offered.

SNORKELING   Dominica offers nearly 30 top-notch snorkeling areas, including the popular Champagne site. Snorkelers can join a dive-boat party, participate in special snorkel excursions, or explore the coast in a sea kayak, periodically jumping overboard for a look below. The calm water on the island's leeward side is perfect for viewing the riotous colors of the sponges, corals, and 190-plus fish species native to the area. Off-shore snorkeling and equipment rental can be arranged through the dive operators listed above. Prices start at approximately US$25.

GREAT LOCAL RESTAURANTS & BARS

Seafood, local root vegetables referred to as "provisions," and Creole recipes are among the highlights of Dominican cuisine. *Crapaud* ("mountain chicken" in English, though it's really mountain frog) is the national delicacy. For a local beer, try **Kubuli;** for a local rum, try **Soca** or **Macoucherie.**

IN ROSEAU   Try **La Robe Créole,** 3 Victoria St. (© **767/448-2896**), which gets top marks for its callaloo soup (made from the spinachlike leaves of a local vegetable called dasheen, plus coconut), lobster and conch crepes, and mango chutney. The decor features heavy stone walls, solid ladder-back chairs, and colorful madras table-cloths. Lunch is about US$25.

Guiyave, 15 Cork St. (© **767/448-2930**), an airy restaurant on the second floor of a pistachio-colored wood-frame house, features steamed fish, conch, octopus, and spareribs. Take a table on the veranda and cool off with one of the fresh-squeezed juices. How about soursop, tamarind, sorrel, cherry, or strawberry? The downstairs takeout counter offers chicken patties, spicy rotis, and delectable tarts and cakes. Lunch is about US$18.

The **Sutton Grille,** in the Sutton Place Hotel, 25 Old St. (© **767/449-8700**), boasts an airy dining area ensconced in 100-year-old stone walls. You can choose a table a few steps up from the bustle of downtown Roseau or one set back from the action. The menu, a veritable primer of Creole and other West Indian cookery, also offers a gener-ous sprinkling of international and vegetarian dishes. Lunch is about US$13.

IN PORTSMOUTH   If you disembark in Portsmouth, get a table at the **Coconut Beach Restaurant,** near Picard Beach (© **767/445-5393**). It overlooks the Caribbean Sea and the twin peaks of Cabrits National Park across Prince Rupert's Bay. The fresh seafood and Creole dishes taste even better with the tang of salt in the air. Lunch is about US$23.

The **Purple Turtle** (© **767/445-5296**) is closer to the dock and features lobster and crayfish, as well as lighter fare such as rotis, sandwiches, and salads. Lunch is about US$15.

15 Grand Cayman

Grand Cayman is the largest of the Cayman Islands, a British colony 773km (479 miles) due south of Miami (Cayman Brac and Little Cayman are the others). It's the top of an underwater mountain, whose side—known as the Cayman Wall—plum-mets straight down for 150m (492 ft.) before becoming a steep slope that falls away for 1,800m (5,904 ft.) to the ocean floor.

Despite its "grand" name, the island is only 35km (22 miles) long and 13km (8 miles) across its widest point. Flat, relatively unattractive, and full of scrubland and swamp, Grand Cayman and its sister islands nevertheless boast more than their share of upscale, expensive private homes and condos, owned by millionaire expatriates from all over who come because of the tiny nation's lenient tax and banking laws. (Enron, the poster child of shady business dealings, reportedly had more than 690 different subsidiaries here to help it avoid paying U.S. taxes.) Grand Cayman is also popular because of its laid-back civility—so civil that ships aren't allowed to visit on Sunday. **George Town** is the colony's capital and its commercial hub, and many hotels line the sands of the nation's most famous sunspot, **Seven Mile Beach.** Scuba divers and snorkelers come for the coral reefs and other formations, some of which lie within swimming distance of the shoreline.

COMING ASHORE   Cruise ships anchor off George Town and ferry their passengers to a pier on **Harbour Drive.** The short tender ride can be choppy, but the landing point couldn't be more convenient: You're let off right in the heart of the shopping district. There's a tourist information booth at the pier, and taxis line up to meet cruise ship passengers. You'll find a phone center for credit card calls and Internet access centers on Cardinal Avenue, right downtown.

LANGUAGE   English is the official language of the islands.

CURRENCY   The legal tender is the **Cayman Islands dollar** (CI82¢ = US$1; CI$1 = US$1.25), but U.S. dollars are commonly accepted. Be sure to note which currency is referred to on price tags before making a purchase. Unless otherwise specified, prices in this section are given in U.S. dollars.

INFORMATION   The **Department of Tourism** is in Regatta Business Park, Leeward Two, Safehaven (✆ **800/346-3313** or 345/949-0623). It's open Monday through Friday from 9am to 5pm. To get info before you go, contact the New York office of the **Cayman Islands Department of Tourism** (✆ **212/889-9009;** www. caymanislands.ky).

CALLING FROM THE U.S.   When calling Grand Cayman from the U.S., you need only dial a "1" before the numbers listed here.

GETTING AROUND

BY TAXI   Taxi fares are fixed; typical one-way fares range from US$12 to US$20. **Holiday Taxi** (✆ **345/947-1066**) offers 24-hour service.

BY RENTAL CAR   The roads are good by Caribbean standards, so driving around is relatively easy, as long as you remember to drive on the left side of the road. **Avis, Budget, Dollar,** and **Hertz** all have offices here.

BY MOTOR SCOOTER OR BICYCLE   The terrain is relatively flat, so motor scooters and bicycles are another way to get around. **Island Scooter Rental,** at Bernard Drive in Industrial Park (✆ **345/949-2046**), offers shuttle service to/from George Town and rents scooters for US$30 per day.

Frommer's Favorite Grand Cayman Experiences

Swimming with Stingrays: At Stingray City, you can hop into the water with dozens of these weird-looking but gentle sea creatures, which will swim right into your arms, like dogs. (See "Best Cruise Line Shore Excursions," below.)

Taking in the Scene on Seven Mile Beach: Grand Cayman's famed stretch of sand is known for its watersports and its translucent aquamarine waters. (See "Beaches," below.)

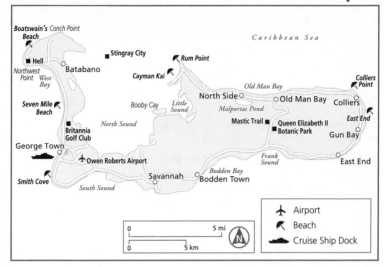

Grand Cayman

BEST CRUISE LINE SHORE EXCURSIONS

Cruise lines typically offer about 30 shore excursions here, most of them of the swimming, snorkeling, sailing, submarine, and glass-bottom boat variety.

Stingray City (US$45–US$55, 2–3 hr.): The waters off Grand Cayman are home to Stingray City, one of the world's most unusual underwater attractions. Set in the very shallow waters of North Sound, about 3.2km (2 miles) east of the island's northwestern tip, the site was discovered in the mid-1980s when local fishermen noticed that scores of stingrays were showing up to feed on the offal they dumped overboard. Today, anywhere from 30 to 100 relatively tame stingrays swarm around the hundreds of visiting snorkelers like so many aquatic basset hounds, eager for handouts. Stingrays are terribly gentle creatures and love to have their bellies rubbed, but never try to grab one by the tail—their barbed stingers can inflict a lot of pain.

Atlantis Submarine Excursion (US$94, 1½ hr.): Those looking for some underwater adventure can sign up for a deep-sea dive on a 48-passenger sub, which takes you down to 30m (100 ft.) through coral canyons, with an automatic fish feeder drawing swarms of colorful marine creatures.

Island Bicycle Tour (US$69, 3 hr.): A great way to really get a feel for an island—and get some exercise—is via bicycle. You'll pick up your touring mountain bike at the Beach Club Colony Hotel, ride along the coastline for views of Seven Mile Beach, and then journey inland en route to the north side of the island to ride along the coast again.

EXCURSIONS OFFERED BY LOCAL AGENCIES

Stingray City: If the tours on your ship get booked, about half a dozen entrepreneurs lead expeditions to Stingray City, and usually a few tour agents wait around the terminal in George Town to snare cruise passengers as they debark. **Moby Dick Tours** (© 480/626-5429; www.mobydicktours.com) will pick you up from the terminal and take you to the Stingray City sandbar for a morning of snorkeling. The price is US$35 for adults and US$30 for children under 12.

Taxi Tours: If you want to see the island, you can grab a taxi in port and take a tour. Taxis should cost about US$45 per hour and can hold up to five people. A 3-hour tour covers all the sights in a leisurely fashion. Make sure to stop in the town called Hell and send a postcard home.

ON YOUR OWN: WITHIN WALKING DISTANCE

In George Town, the **Cayman Islands National Museum,** Harbour Drive (© 345/ 949-8368; www.museum.ky), is housed in a veranda-fronted building that once served as the island's courthouse. The museum is currently undergoing restoration, but the cafe and gift shop are open. Hours are Monday through Friday from 9am to 5pm, Saturday from 10am to 2pm.

The **National Gallery of the Cayman Islands,** Harbour Place, South Church Street (© 345/945-8111; www.nationalgallery.org.ky), is a nonprofit educational organization that supports the growth of the Cayman Islands art scene. It offers an average of eight exhibitions per year of both local and international art. Open Monday through Friday from 9am to 5pm, Saturday from 11am to 4pm. Admission is free.

ON YOUR OWN: BEYOND THE PORT AREA

North of George Town, at Northwest Point, **Boatswain's Beach** (© 345/949-3894; www.boatswainsbeach.ky), pronounced "*boe*-suns," is a newly renovated 9-hectare (22-acre) marine park that includes a snorkeling lagoon, a predator tank full of sharks and green moray eels, a separate tank for dolphin swims, an aviary, a nature trail, three restaurants, and other mostly marine-oriented displays. At press time, the facility is scheduled for completion in mid-2006, when it will also encompass what's long been one of Grand Cayman's most popular attractions, the **Cayman Turtle Farm** (© 345/ 949-3894; www.turtle.ky), the only green-sea-turtle farm of its kind in the world. Once upon a time, a multitude of turtles lived in the waters surrounding the Cayman Islands, but today these creatures are an endangered species. The turtle farm's purpose is twofold: to replenish the waters with hatchlings and yearling turtles, and, at the other end of the spectrum, to provide the local market with edible turtle meat. You can peer into 100 circular concrete tanks containing turtles ranging in size from 6 ounces to 600 pounds, or sample turtle dishes at the **Turtle Crawl Deli.** The farm is open daily from 8:30am to 5pm. Admission is US$6 for adults, US$3 for children 6 to 12.

On 26 hectares (64 acres) of rugged wooded land, **Queen Elizabeth II Botanic Park,** off Frank Sound Road, North Side (© 345/947-3558), offers visitors a 1-hour walk along a short (1.2km/.75-mile) trail through wetlands, swamps, dry thicket, and mahogany trees. If you're lucky, you may spot a blue iguana, a species endemic to Grand Cayman, with fewer than 15 left in the wild. You may also see hickatees (the freshwater turtles found only on the Caymans and in Cuba), the rare Grand Cayman parrot, or the anole lizard, with its cobalt-blue throat pouch. There are six rest stations along the trail, plus a visitor center and a canteen, a heritage garden, a floral garden, and a lake. Hours are daily from 9am to 6:30pm.

The **Mastic Trail,** west of Frank Sound Road, is a restored 200-year-old footpath through a 2-million-year-old woodland area in the heart of the island. Named for the majestic mastic tree, the trail showcases the reserve's natural attractions, including a native mangrove swamp, traditional agriculture, and an ancient woodland area. You can follow the 3.2km (2-mile) trail on your own, but we recommend taking a 3-hour guided tour for $15 per person. Call © 345/945-6588 to make a reservation. The trail, adjacent to the Botanic Park, is about a 45-minute drive from George Town.

SHOPPING

There's duty-free shopping here for silver, china, crystal, Irish linens, and British woolen goods, but we've found most prices to be similar to those in the U.S. You'll also find rum and cigar shops. Please don't succumb and purchase turtle or black-coral products. You'll see them everywhere, but it's illegal to bring them back into the United States and most other Western nations.

Some standout shops include **Artifacts Ltd.,** Harbour Drive, on the harbor front across from the landing dock (℃ 345/949-2442), for back issues of Cayman stamps; the **Jewelry Centre,** Cardinal Avenue (℃ 345/949-0070), one of the largest jewelry stores in the Caymans; and the **Kennedy Gallery West Shore Centre** (℃ 345/949-8077), specializing in paintings and sculptures by local artists.

BEACHES

Grand Cayman's **Seven Mile Beach,** which begins north of George Town, is an easy taxi ride from the cruise dock and has sparkling white sands with a backdrop of casuarina trees. The beach is really about 8.9km (5½ miles) long, but who are we to quibble with tradition? It's lined with condominiums and plush resorts, and is known for its array of watersports and its translucent aquamarine waters. The average water temperature is a balmy 80°F (27°C).

SPORTS

SCUBA DIVING & SNORKELING   Coral reefs and other formations encircle the island and are filled with marine life. It's easy to dive close to shore, so boats aren't necessary, but plenty of boats and scuba facilities are available, as well as many dive shops renting scuba gear to certified divers. An easily accessible dive operation is **Red Sail Sports** (℃ 877/733-7245 or 345/945-5965; www.redsailcayman.com), which offers full-day resort courses as well as excursions for experienced divers. The staff is helpful and highly professional.

GREAT LOCAL RESTAURANTS & BARS

A favorite local beer is **Stingray,** and a favorite local rum is **Tortuga.**

A short walk (less than 1km/½ mile) south of the pier is **Paradise Bar & Grill,** on Harbour Drive (℃ 345/945-1444). It's a great open-air seaside cafe for a sandwich, chicken fingers, and a couple of cool Stingray beers or a frozen drink.

Near Boatswain's Beach, **Cracked Conch by the Sea,** West Bay Road (℃ 345/945-5217), serves some of the island's freshest seafood, including the inevitable conch, plus meat dishes such as beef, jerk pork, and spicy combinations of chicken. Lunch is about US$15.

Fisherman's Reef Bar & Grill, Morgan's Harbour (℃ 345/945-5879), is one of the island's top restaurants for dinner, offering such dishes as Bavarian cucumber soup; bouillabaisse; French pepper steak; Wiener schnitzel; and chicken Trinidad, stuffed with grapes, nuts, and apples, rolled in coconut flakes, sautéed golden brown, and served in orange-butter sauce.

16 Grand Turk

Welcome to the Caribbean's newest cruise port. Just 11km (6¾ miles) long and about 2km (1¼ miles) wide, with 3,700 residents, Grand Turk has long been known as a one of the top five diving destinations in the world, owing to the fact that, just a few hundred yards from shore, the shallow continental shelf suddenly plunges 2,133m

(6,996 ft.) straight down, with healthy coral reefs and great visibility making conditions absolutely perfect. The whole western shore of the island is a protected underwater park. Above water, things are practically perfect as well, with an average temperature of 28°C (83°F) and an amazing 350 days of sunshine a year. The temperature can climb pretty high in the summer, but the surprisingly strong trade winds keep things comfy.

While ships have visited Grand Turk in the past, the island really wasn't equipped to handle a massive influx of passengers until the Grand Turk Cruise Center opened in February 2006, its deepwater pier able to accommodate even the largest megaships. Carnival was the prime mover behind the project, leasing 15 hectares (37 acres) from the government and developing less than half of them, building a transportation center, restaurant, shopping area, crafts stalls, fountains, and duty-free building. The cruise center will welcome all ships, not just Carnival lines.

About 4.8km (3 miles) from the pier is charming downtown **Cockburn Town,** a sleepy half-mile stretch that also happens to be the administrative capital of the Turks and Caicos Islands. Along its streets, Bermudan-influenced colonial buildings mix with simple gift shops, guest houses, and a couple of laid-back bars, plus miles of public powder-white beaches. Islanders describe the ambience here as the way the rest of the Caribbean was 25 years ago. A bit neglected over the years, Grand Turk received a $7 million boost from Carnival for infrastructure improvements, ranging from pedestrian crossings to the creation of ready-made tourist attractions based on the island's substantive history.

So far, Grand Turk retains its air of quaintness, but the developers are moving in, and plans call for 370,000 cruise visitors a year by the end of 2007—about a hundred times as many people as actually live on the island. This is one port you may want to make a special effort to visit as soon as you can.

COMING ASHORE   Located on the south side of Grand Turk, the **Grand Turk Cruise Center** may seem to arriving passengers like one of the cruise lines' private islands, with its carefully placed landscaping between the dock and the beach. Its advantages, of course, are that (a) it's part of a real country, and (b) passengers don't have to tender ashore, since the cruise pier can accommodate the largest ships. At the cruise center beyond, you can get visitor info, rent a car, make phone calls, shop, or catch a taxi or water taxi into Cockburn Town, 4.8km (3 miles) away.

LANGUAGE   English is spoken everywhere.

CURRENCY   The official currency is the **U.S. dollar,** but there's a local currency called the TCI crown (of equal value with the dollar) and a quarter, both of which make nice souvenirs.

INFORMATION   Visitor centers can be found right in the cruise center and on Front Street in Cockburn Town. For info before you go, call ✆ **800/241-0824** in the U.S. or go to www.turksandcaicostourism.com.

CALLING FROM THE U.S.   No country calling code is required—just dial as you do from home, with a "1" and the area code.

GETTING AROUND

BY TAXI   Taxi fares from the port to Cockburn Town run about US$10, but get a quote from the driver before you commit.

Grand Turk

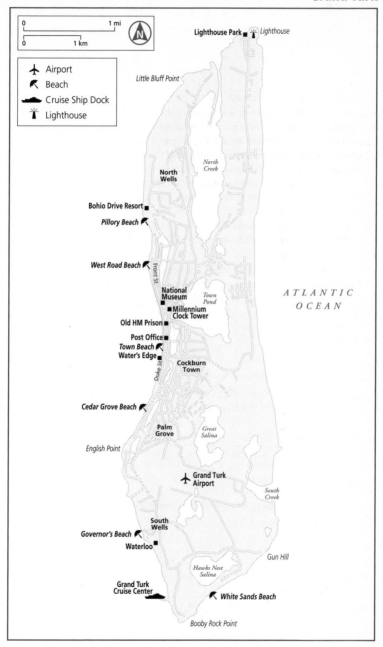

0   1 mi
0   1 km

✈ Airport
⦅ Beach
⬛ Cruise Ship Dock
⚊ Lighthouse

Lighthouse Park ⬛ ☼ Lighthouse

Little Bluff Point

North Creek

North Wells

Bohio Drive Resort ⬛

Pillory Beach ⦅

West Road Beach ⦅

Front St

National Museum ⬛

Town Pond

ATLANTIC OCEAN

Millennium Clock Tower ⬛

Old HM Prison ⬛

Post Office ⬛

Town Beach ⦅

Water's Edge ⬛

Cockburn Town

Duke St

Cedar Grove Beach ⦅

Palm Grove

Great Salina

English Point

Grand Turk Airport ✈

South Creek

South Wells

Governor's Beach ⦅

Waterloo ⬛

Gun Hill

Hawks Nest Salina

Grand Turk Cruise Center ⬛

⦅ White Sands Beach

Booby Rock Point

Frommer's Favorite Grand Turk Experiences

Getting Below the Surface: While Grand Turk has a rich history and a gem of a downtown, it's the ocean topography that really makes it so grand. With the continental shelf plunging just 275m (902 ft.) offshore, you can scuba right from the beach. Many consider this the best diving in the Caribbean, and it's on many lists of the top five diving destinations in the world. (See "Best Cruise Line Shore Excursions," below.)

Standing on Top of the World: Walking out on the eastern trail leading from the lighthouse at the northern end of the island, you can brace yourself against the strong trade winds, marvel at the beautifully eroded cliff faces below, perhaps spot giant manta rays or humpback whales in the turquoise waters, and let your mind drift back to a time when the islanders stood near where you're perched, waving lanterns and guiding ships to their doom on the rocks below so they could plunder their treasures. (See "Hop-On, Hop-Off Island Tour" under "Best Cruise Line Shore Excursions," below.)

Looking for the Green Flash: After your day in Grand Turk, once you're back aboard ship, keep your eyes peeled for the Green Flash, a solar phenomenon in which the sky flashes green for about 10 to 20 seconds after the sun goes down. There are not many places in the world where you can see the flash, but Grand Turk is one of them—at least on days when the sky conditions are very calm.

BY BUS   There's no public transportation on the island, but one shore excursion offered by the cruise lines is a bus loop, which allows you to hop off and on at will (see below).

BY RENTAL CAR   Car-rental desks are located at the cruise terminal—but if you want one, be sure to book ahead, as supplies are limited. Also be prepared to drive on the left side of the road.

BEST CRUISE LINE SHORE EXCURSIONS

In addition to the excursions listed here, **whale-watching** will be added to ships' offerings on an ad-hoc basis. It has to be the right season and the right weather, but the Atlantic humpback whales travel down Turk's Passage trench on the western side of the island every year, heading for their breeding grounds south of Grand Turk, where they take care of their calves from January to April. Aside from looking for whales, the main thing to do in Grand Turk is get underwater.

Scuba Diving (US$109–US$119, 2½–4 hr.): You won't get better conditions anywhere in the Caribbean than Grand Turk, with its tranquil, crystal-clear waters and protected reef. Experienced divers will be wowed by the manta rays, whale sharks, sea turtles, and beautiful colors of the third-largest coral reef in the world. Even a first-timer can get to the reefs via a resort course, with intensive one-on-one instruction followed by a half-hour of diving.

Snorkeling (US$49, 2½ hr.): If you're not up for scuba, you can at least go snorkeling to experience the beauty of Grand Turk's undersea world. Snorkeling trips departing from the cruise terminal visit two sites, typically Horseshoe Reef (with depths averaging 1.8–3.7m/6–12 ft.) and a reef off Round Cay, one of Grand Turk's best dive locations.

Grand Turk Semi-Sub Tour (US$49, 1 hr.): If you don't want to get your feet wet at all, sign up for this semi-submersible excursion, which takes you 2.4m (7¾ ft.) below the surface to view sea life and get a glimpse of Grand Turk's famous coral reefs.

Hop-On, Hop-Off Island Tour (US$39, duration varies): Air-conditioned buses loop around the island whenever there's a ship in port, letting booked excursioners see things at their leisure. A wristband allows entry to various tourist venues along the route, including Cockburn Town's Millennium Clock Tower and restored 1800s prison; Lighthouse Park, with its namesake 1852 light and two nature trails; the Turks and Caicos National Museum, which has some information on John Glenn's splashdown off Grand Turk in 1962; and the Philatelic Bureau. Anyone who's ever collected stamps will know that Turks and Caicos is well known for its beautiful stamps, created almost solely for collectors. Stops are located approximately every half-mile along the route, with many sited close to island attractions. Buses arrive at each stop approximately every 15 minutes.

EXCURSIONS OFFERED BY LOCAL AGENCIES

The only local tour operators are the dive shops. For instance, on Duke Street, you'll find **Oasis Divers** (© 800/892-3995) and **Sea Eye Diving** (© 800/786-0669). Diving can range from US$110 for a resort course for beginners to US$400 for an open-water two-tank dive. You might want to consider an experience unique to the area—such as diving with the stingrays at Gibb's Cay or with the humpback whales (in season).

ON YOUR OWN: WITHIN WALKING DISTANCE

Passengers could easily spend their whole day just hanging out at the cruise center, whose biggest structure by far is the two-story, 1,580-square-meter (17,007-sq.-ft.) **Margaritaville Cafe,** the largest stand-alone Jimmy Buffett franchise in the Caribbean. Wastin' away again? Behind the restaurant is a giant amoeba-shaped swimming pool with swim-up bar, slide, cabanas, and infinity-edge view. It's open to the public and, because it's only 1m (3¼ ft.) deep, makes a great place to hang out with the younger kids.

ON YOUR OWN: BEYOND THE PORT AREA

Cockburn Town's historic district is centered on Duke and Front streets, where some houses built of wood and limestone stand along the waterfront. Historic government buildings surround a small plaza where canons and a bronze plaque mark the spot where Christopher Columbus allegedly first set foot in the New World, on October 14, 1492. Columbus's logbook notes landfall at a bean-shaped island, but there's no absolute proof that said bean was Grand Turk.

Also on Front Street is the **Turks and Caicos National Museum** (© 649/946-2160; www.tcmuseum.org). Housed in 180-year-old Guinep House, the museum includes wreckage from a Spanish caravel that sank in shallow offshore waters sometime before 1513, plus exhibits on the island's natural history, salt industries, plantation economy, and pre-Columbian inhabitants. Open Monday through Friday from

9am to 4pm, until 5pm on Wednesday, plus Saturday from 9am to 1pm. Admission is US$5.

SHOPPING

Grand Turk isn't particularly known for its arts and crafts, though you will find shops at the cruise center and at the island's various attractions and museums, plus a couple along Duke Street, which borders the western beach in the downtown area.

BEACHES

The cruise terminal's powder-white sandy beach is just steps from the pier, and you'll find lounge chairs, hammocks, and bartending staff coming by to take your drink order. For US$19 a day, you can rent a clamshell that provides shade for two lounge chairs. You can also get a taste of the underwater view that makes Grand Turk famous by snorkeling, with equipment available for rent or purchase.

On the island's southwest coast, below Cockburn Town, **Governor's Beach** is one of the few blue-flagged beaches in the Caribbean, which means it's passed stringent tests for water quality, cleanliness, and lifeguard availability. It's also reputed to have the best snorkeling on the island. Right next door is **Waterloo**, the governor's mansion, a pretty structure with the curved stucco architecture characteristic of Bermudan buildings.

SPORTS

BIKING Bikes are available for rent at the cruise center and in town. Apart from the Ridge (which is where all the fancy accommodations are springing up), the roads are quite flat, and most of the attractions and sights are an easy bike ride away.

BIRD-WATCHING Grand Turk plays host to over 190 species of birds, but the most impressive sight has to be the greater flamingos fishing in the salt ponds of the island in spring and summer.

In Cockburn Town, just behind the historic waterfront, the island in the town's salt-water pond was once used to quarantine sick sailors. Today it's a favorite of birders who come to see flamingos, pelicans, and herons feeding in the shallow waters.

WATERSPORTS Because of the delicate reef system, watersports like jet-skiing and banana-boating are not allowed. Snorkeling and scuba, which can be done right from shore, are the water activities not to be missed. Deep-sea and flats fishing are also fabulous in these waters.

GREAT LOCAL RESTAURANTS & BARS

Water's Edge, on Duke Street (© **649/946-1680**), is hard to miss, sitting on stilts right over the beautiful white-sand beach. With a view like that, what you're eating hardly matters (though the fish and conch are fresh and tender). Lunch runs US$8 to US$15.

For something with a slightly more upscale feel, head toward the other end of Duke Street to the **Guanahani Restaurant,** in Bohio Dive Resort (© **649/946-2135**). You'll find juicy jerk chicken, an eclectic menu featuring fish (of course), and some delicious desserts. Lunch runs US$12 to US$15.

17 Grenada

The southernmost nation of the British Windwards, Grenada (Gre-*nay*-dah) is one of the lushest places in the Caribbean. Called the "Spice Island," it has extravagant fertility—a result of the gentle climate and volcanic soil—that produces more spices than anywhere else in the world: clove, cinnamon, mace, cocoa, tonka beans, ginger, and a

Grenada

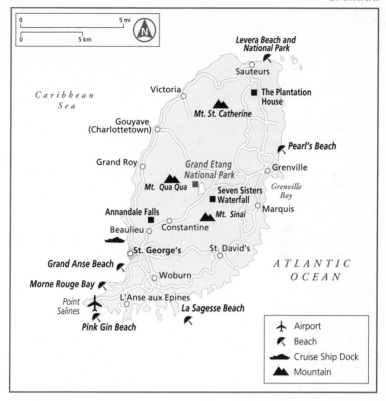

0   5 mi
0   5 km

Caribbean Sea

Levera Beach and National Park

Sauteurs

Victoria

The Plantation House

Mt. St. Catherine

Gouyave (Charlottetown)

Pearl's Beach

Grand Roy

Grand Etang National Park

Grenville

Mt. Qua Qua

Seven Sisters Waterfall

Grenville Bay

Annandale Falls

Mt. Sinai

Marquis

Beaulieu   Constantine

St. George's

St. David's

ATLANTIC OCEAN

Grand Anse Beach

Woburn

Morne Rouge Bay

Point Salines

L'Anse aux Epines

La Sagesse Beach

Pink Gin Beach

✈ Airport
🗡 Beach
⛴ Cruise Ship Dock
▲▲ Mountain

third of the world's supply of nutmeg. The beaches are white and sandy, and the populace (a mixture of English expatriates and islanders of African descent) is friendly. Once a British crown colony but now independent, the island nation also incorporates two smaller islands: Carriacou and Petite Martinique, neither of which has many tourist facilities.

Crisscrossed by nature trails, Grenada's interior is a jungle of palms, oleander, bougainvillea, purple and red hibiscus, crimson anthurium, bananas, breadfruit, birdsong, ferns, and palms. The island's tropical scenery and natural bounty attract visitors who want to snorkel, sail, fish, hike on jungle paths, or loll the day away on the 3.2km (1¾-mile) white-sand Grand Anse Beach, one of the best in the Caribbean.

St. George's, the country's capital, was one of the most colorful ports in the West Indies before Hurricane Ivan struck in 2004. Nearly landlocked in the deep crater of a long-dead volcano, and flanked by old forts, it once reminded many visitors of Portofino, Italy. Many of its charming Georgian colonial buildings have red-tile roofs (the tiles were brought by European trade ships as ballast) and pastel walls. Sadly, many of the roofs on the buildings and churches dotting the hillside of the harbor were seriously damaged by the hurricane. In addition to the lovely frangipani and flamboyant trees, expect to see a lot of construction in town.

Frommer's Favorite Grenada Experiences

Hiking to the Seven Sisters Waterfalls: This is a hearty walk along a muddy path that winds through the thick, pristine jungle. At the end of the approximately 1.6km (1-mile) trail, there's a set of beautiful waterfalls. You can even jump from the tops of two of them into the pools below. (See "Best Cruise Line Shore Excursions," below.)

Visiting Levera National Park: With beaches, coral reefs, a mangrove swamp, a lake, and a bird sanctuary, this is a paradise for hikers, swimmers, and snorkelers alike. (See "On Your Own: Beyond the Port Area," below.)

Taking the Rainforest and Grand Etang Lake Tour: Take a bus to an extinct volcanic crater some 530m (1,738 ft.) above sea level. On the way, drive through rainforests and stop at a spice estate. (See "Best Cruise Line Shore Excursions," below.)

Picnicking at Annandale Falls: A 15m (49-ft.) cascade is the perfect backdrop for a picnic among tropical flora—and you can swim in the falls afterward. (See "On Your Own: Beyond the Port Area," below.)

COMING ASHORE   Grenada recently unveiled a new deepwater cruise ship port, **St. George's Cruise Ship Terminal,** complete with a welcome center, a duty-free shopping mall, and restaurants. Ships either dock here (on Melville St.) or anchor in the much-photographed harbor and send their passengers to the pier by tender. The Carenage (St. George's main street) is only a short (but steep) walk away from the pier; a taxi into the center of town costs about US$6. To get to Grand Anse, you can take a regular taxi or a water taxi (see "Getting Around," below).

There are about five or six pay phones inside the cruise terminal and about six Lon-don-style red phone booths midway around the Carenage, less than a half-mile from the terminal. **Java Kool Café,** on the Carenage (© 473/435-3506), has Internet access.

LANGUAGE   English is commonly spoken on this island. Creole English, a mix-ture of African, English, and French, is spoken informally by a small percentage of the population.

CURRENCY   The official currency is the **Eastern Caribbean dollar** (EC$2.70 = US$1; EC$1 = US73¢). Always determine which dollars—EC or U.S.—you're talk-ing about when discussing a price. Credit cards and traveler's checks are commonly accepted in tourist areas. Unless otherwise specified, all prices in this section are given in U.S. dollars.

INFORMATION   Go to the **Grenada Board of Tourism,** on the Carenage in St. George's (© **800/927-9554** or 473/440-2279), for maps and information. Open Monday through Friday from 9am to 5pm. To get information before you go, call the Florida office at © **561/588-8176** or check out www.grenadagrenadines.com.

CALLING FROM THE U.S.   When calling Grenada from the United States, you need only dial a "1" before the numbers listed here.

GETTING AROUND

St. George's can easily be explored on foot, although parts of the town are steep as the streets rise up from the harbor.

BY TAXI   Taxi fares are set by the government. Most cruisers take a cab from the pier to somewhere near St. George's. You can also tap most taxi drivers as a guide for a day's sightseeing. The charge is about US$25 per hour for a group of one to four persons; be sure to negotiate a price before setting out, and make sure you're both talking about the same currency. The ride from the pier to Grand Anse Beach is about US$12 per carload.

BY MINIVAN   Minivans, used mostly by locals, charge EC$2 to EC$6 (US75¢–US$4.40). Most minivans depart from Market Square or from the Esplanade area of St. George's. The most popular run is between St. George's and Grand Anse Beach.

BY WATER TAXI   Water taxis are an ideal way to get around the harbor and to Grand Anse Beach (the round-trip fare is about US$6), or from one end of the Carenage to the other (for another US$2). Look for them on the Carenage by the cruise ship welcome center.

BY RENTAL CAR   We don't recommend driving here, as the roads are very narrow and winding.

BEST CRUISE LINE SHORE EXCURSIONS

Because of Grenada's lush landscape, we recommend spending at least a few hours touring its interior, one of the most scenic in the West Indies.

Hike to Seven Sisters Waterfalls (US$64, 3½ hr.): After a 40-minute hike along a muddy path in the lush Grand Etang rainforest, passengers are free to take a swim in the natural pools or hop off the edge of the cascading waterfalls. It's gorgeous and lots of fun. Don't forget to wear your bathing suit and maybe a pair of Teva-type sandals.

Rainforest/Grand Etang Lake Tour (US$39, 4 hr.): This is a great way to experience Grenada's lush, cool, dripping-wet tropical interior. Via bus, you travel past the red-tiled roofs of St. George's en route to the bright-blue Grand Etang Lake, set within an extinct volcanic crater some 530m (1,738 ft.) above sea level. On the way, you drive through rainforests and stop at a spice estate. Some tours include a visit to Annandale Falls and Fort Frederick.

EXCURSIONS OFFERED BY LOCAL AGENCIES

Island Tours: Contact **Sunsation Tours** (© 473/444-1594; www.grenadasunsation. com), which offers full-day, half-day, and private tours to the island's homes and gardens, markets, and more. Guided hikes and tours are also available from **Grenada Tours** (© 473/440-1428; www.grenadatours.com).

ON YOUR OWN: WITHIN WALKING DISTANCE

In St. George's, you can visit the **Grenada National Museum,** at Young and Monckton streets (© 473/440-3725), set in the foundations of an old French army barracks and prison built in 1704. Small but interesting, it houses ancient petroglyphs and other archaeological finds, a rum still, and various Grenada memorabilia, including the island's first telegraph and two notable bathtubs: the wooden barrel used by the fort's prisoners and the carved marble tub used by Joséphine Bonaparte during her adolescence on Martinique. The most comprehensive exhibit illuminates the native culture of Grenada. Open Monday through Friday from 9am to 4:30pm, Saturday from 10am to 1pm. Admission is US$2.50 for adults and US$1 for children.

If you're up for a good hike, walk around the historic Carenage from the cruise terminal and then head up to **Fort George,** built in 1705 by the French and originally called Fort Royal. (You can pick up a rudimentary walking-tour map from the cruise terminal to help you find interesting sites along the way.) While the fort ruins and the 200- to 300-year-old cannons are worth a peek, it's the 360-degree panoramic views of the entire harbor area that are most spectacular.

ON YOUR OWN: BEYOND THE PORT AREA

You can take a taxi up Richmond Hill to **Fort Frederick,** which the French began building in 1779. The British retook the island in 1783 and completed the fort in 1791. From its battlements, you'll have a panoramic view of the harbor and the yacht marina.

Don't miss the mountains northeast of St. George's. If you don't have much time, **Annandale Falls,** a tropical wonderland where a 15m-high (49-ft.) cascade drops into a basin, is just a 15-minute drive away, on the outskirts of the **Grand Etang Forest Reserve.** The overall beauty is almost Tahitian. You can have a picnic surrounded by liana vines, elephant ears, and other tropical flora and spices. Annandale Falls Centre offers gift items, handicrafts, and samples of the island's indigenous spices. Nearby, a trail leads to the falls, where you can enjoy a refreshing swim.

If you've got more time and want a less crowded spot, the even better **Seven Sisters Waterfalls** are farther into Grand Etang, an approximately 30-minute drive and then a 1.6km (1-mile) or so hike along a muddy trail. It's well worth the trip and you'll really get a feel for the power and beauty of the tropical forest here. The falls themselves are lovely—you can even climb to the top and jump off into the pool below. Be careful, though: It's awfully slippery on those rocks. If you want to skip the jumping, you can still enjoy a relaxing swim in the cool water after your sweaty hike.

Opened in 1994, 180-hectare (445-acre) **Levera National Park** has several white-sand beaches for swimming and snorkeling, although the surf is rough. Offshore are coral reefs and sea-grass beds. Inland, the park contains a mangrove swamp, a lake, and a bird sanctuary. It's a hiker's paradise. About 24km (15 miles) from the harbor, the park can be reached by taxi, bus, or water taxi.

SHOPPING

The local stores sell luxury imports, mainly from England, at prices that are not quite down at duty-free level. This is no grand Caribbean merchandise mart, so if you're cruising on to such islands as Aruba, St. Martin, or St. Thomas, you might want to postpone serious purchases. On the other hand, you can find some fine local handicrafts, gifts, and art here.

Spice vendors besiege you wherever you go, including just outside of the cruise terminal. If you're not interested, a polite "I just bought some from another vendor" usually works. But you really should take at least a few samples home with you. The spices here are fresher and better than any you're likely to find in your local supermarket, so nearly everybody comes home with a hand-woven basket full of them. Nutmeg products are especially popular. The Grenadians use every part of the nutmeg: They make the outer fruit into a tasty liqueur and a rich jam, and ground the orange membrane around the nut into a different spice called mace. You'll see the outer shells used as gravel to cover trails and parking lots.

Arawak Islands, No. 15 Building in Frequente Industrial Park, St. George's (© 473/444-3577), has different fragrances distilled from such island plants as frangipani, wild lilies, cinnamon, nutmeg, and cloves. You'll also find body oils, soaps, an all-natural insect repellent, and some mighty fine hot sauce. We regretted not buying more the last time we were here, but then we found the shop's mail-order website at www.arawak-islands.com.

Some other worthwhile shops include **Art Fabrik,** Young Street (© 473/440-0568), for batik shirts, shifts, shorts, skirts, T-shirts, and the like; **Sea Change Bookstore,** the Carenage (© 473/440-3402), for recent British and American newspapers; and **Tikal,** Young Street (© 473/440-2310), for handicrafts from Grenada and around the world.

BEACHES

Grenada's **Grand Anse Beach,** with its 3.2km (1¾ miles) of wide sugar-white sands, is one of the best beaches in the Caribbean. The calm waters and a great view of St. George's make the scene complete. There are several restaurants beachside, and you can join a banana-boat ride or rent a Sunfish sailboat. From the port, it's about a 10-minute, US$10 taxi ride, although you can also take a water taxi from the pier for only US$4 round-trip.

SPORTS

SCUBA DIVING & SNORKELING   Grenada offers an underwater world rich in marine gardens, exotic fish, and coral formations. Visibility is often up to 36m (118 ft.). Off the coast is the wreck of the nearly 180m (590-ft.) ocean liner *Bianca C.* Novice divers should stick to the west coast; the more experienced might search out the sites along the rougher Atlantic side. *Note:* Grenada doesn't have a decompression chamber. In the event of an emergency, divers must be taken to the facilities on Barbados or Trinidad.

Aquanuts (© 473/444-1126), the premier diving outfit on Grenada, has three locations on the island and also offers snorkeling trips. American-run **Eco-Dive,** at Coyaba Beach Resort and the Grenada Grand Beach Resort, both on Grand Anse Beach (© 473/444-7777), offers diving and snorkeling jaunts to reefs and shipwrecks teeming with marine life. Diving instruction is available.

GREAT LOCAL RESTAURANTS & BARS

A favorite local beer is **Carib;** a favorite local rum is **Clarkecourt.**

Your last chance to enjoy food from old-time island recipes, many now fading from cultural memory, may be at the **Plantation House** (aka the Betty Mascoll Morne Fendue Plantation House), at St. Patrick's (© 473/442-9330), 40km (25 miles) north of St. George's. The house was built in 1912 of chiseled river rocks held together by a mixture of lime and molasses. Betty Mascoll was born that same year and lived here right up until her recent death. Guests dine as an upper-class family did in the 1920s. Lunch is likely to include a yam-and-sweet-potato casserole or curried chicken with lots of island-grown spices. The most famous dish is the legendary pepper-pot stew, which includes pork and oxtail, tenderized by the juice of grated cassava. The proprietor, Dr. Jean Thompson, and the veteran staff need time to prepare, so it's imperative to call ahead. They serve a three-course, fixed-price (US$45) lunch Monday through Saturday from 12:30 to 3pm.

The **Nutmeg,** the Carenage, right on the harbor over the Sea Change Shop (*©* **473/ 440-2539**), is a casual hangout for the yachting set and a favorite of expatriates and visitors. The menu is extensive. Lunch is about US$15.

Tout Bagay, the Carenage (*©* **473/440-1500**), offers fresh fish prepared with West Indian flair, accompanied by a gorgeous view of the harbor. Lunch is about US$22.

If you're an adventurous eater, take the steep hike up to **Deyna's Tasty Food,** on Melville Street (*©* **473/440-6795**), where you can order "Deyna's Fix Up," a small sampling of everything on the menu. This might include tatou, a relative of the armadillo, and titiri, minnow-sized fish. Wash everything down with bush tea, made from black sage leaves, or Lime Squash, a local drink. Lunch will cost you about US$10.

18 Guadeloupe

Take the things you love about France: sophistication, great food, and an appreciation of the good things in life. Add the best of the Caribbean: nice beaches, a relaxed pace, and warm, friendly people. Finally, combine with efficiency and modern convenience. *Voilà!* Guadeloupe. And once you leave the crowded, narrow streets of Pointe-à-Pitre, the commercial center and main port, you'll see that the island is more developed and modern than many others in the region.

Guadeloupe's Creole cuisine, a mélange of French culinary expertise, African cooking, and Caribbean ingredients, is reason enough to get off the ship, regardless of how much you're enjoying the food on board. And if shopping is your favorite sport, you'll have ample opportunity to stock up on French perfumes, clothes, and other luxury products. For the more adventurous, there's a volcano, scuba diving, surfing, and hiking to spectacular mountain waterfalls. Of course, you can always work on your tan at one of the island's many beaches. Or maybe you'll just want to sit at a sidewalk cafe, sip your espresso while glancing through a copy of *Le Monde,* and watch the world go by.

Guadeloupe, the political entity, is an overseas region of France that includes the islands of St. Barts, Les Saintes, La Désirade, Marie-Galante, St. Martin (at press time, St. Martin has appealed for independence from France; a decision is expected by the end of 2006), and Guadeloupe itself. The name *Guadeloupe,* however, usually refers to two contiguous islands—Basse-Terre and Grande-Terre—separated by a narrow seawater channel, the Rivière Salée. Nestled between Antigua and Dominica, these two islands are shaped like a 1,373-sq.-km (535-sq.-mile) butterfly. The eastern wing, the limestone island of **Grande-Terre,** is known for its white-sand beaches, rolling hills, sugar cane fields, and resort areas. Pointe-à-Pitre, your port of debarkation, is here. The butterfly's larger, volcanic western wing, **Basse-Terre,** is dominated by the national park of Guadeloupe, a mountainous rainforest replete with waterfalls and La Soufrière, a brooding, still occasionally troublesome volcano. The capital of Guadeloupe, also called Basse-Terre, is at the southern tip of this western wing.

Of Guadeloupe's population of 440,000, about 80% are descended from African slaves, with those of European and East Indian ancestry making up most of the remaining 20%. Sugar, rum, bananas, and melons are the island's main exports today.

COMING ASHORE Cruise ships dock at the modern **Centre Saint-John Perse,** adjacent to downtown Pointe-à-Pitre, Grande-Terre's main city. The terminal has shops, restaurants, cafes, a small tourist office, and phones.

LANGUAGE French is the official language, but you'll often hear islanders speaking a local Creole among themselves. Don't expect to get too far with only English

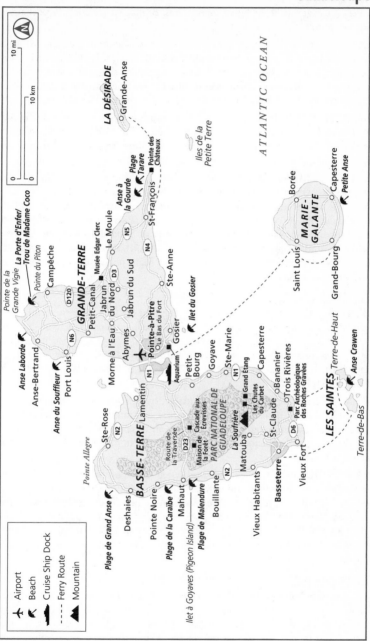

unless you're at one of the busier tourist areas. Bring a phrase book. Guadeloupeans are nice people; meet them halfway.

CURRENCY   Guadeloupe is an overseas region of France, so the **euro** (€) is now the official currency (exchange rate at press time: .82€ = US$1; 1€ = US$1.22). Each euro is divisible by 100 cents. You'll have no trouble using your credit cards here. There are also numerous *distributeur de billets* (ATMs) in downtown Pointe-à-Pitre. Unless otherwise specified, prices in this section are given in U.S. dollars.

INFORMATION   In Pointe-à-Pitre, the main **tourist office** (Comité du Tourisme des Iles de Guadeloupe) is at 5 Square de la Banque (© 590/82-09-30), a 5-minute walk from the port. Open Monday through Friday from 8am to 5pm, Saturday from 8am to noon. For advance information, visit www.lesilesdeguadeloupe.com.

CALLING FROM THE U.S.   When calling Guadeloupe from the United States, dial the international access code (011) and 590 before the numbers listed in this section. The numbers listed already have a 590 prefix, but that's not the same 590: You have to dial 590 twice (bureaucracy in France is just as inscrutable as anywhere). **Telecartes** phone cards make local and international calls easier and less expensive. They're sold at post offices and other outlets marked TELECARTE EN VENTE ICI, and are used in phone booths (marked TELECOM) found all over. Many phones also accept credit cards for long-distance calls.

GETTING AROUND
BY TAXI   Metered taxis await cruise passengers at the Pointe-à-Pitre pier. Rates are regulated, but they can be expensive. Taxis can be hired for private tours, but you'll have a hard time finding a driver who speaks English. Negotiate a price before setting out, and make sure all terms are clear, to avoid an unpleasant scene later. General radio cab–dispatch numbers include © **590/20-74-74, 590/83-86-90, 590/21-12-21,** and **690/35-18-02.**

BY BUS   Buses are inexpensive, comfortable, and efficient. Almost all play zouk, an upbeat local music (at reasonable decibel levels), and some have videos. Signs (ARRET-BUS) indicate bus stops, but you can wave down a driver anywhere along the road. Pay the driver or the conductor as you get off. The fare from Pointe-à-Pitre to Gosier is about US$1.20.

BY RENTAL CAR   Guadeloupe's road system is one of the best in the Caribbean, and traffic regulations and road signs are the same as elsewhere in France. Driving is on the right. Reserve a car before leaving home, especially during high season. **Avis, Budget, Hertz,** and **Thrifty** all have offices on the island. Your valid driver's license from home will be honored. Almost all rentals have standard transmissions. Be forewarned that Guadeloupeans are skillful but aggressive drivers; don't tarry in the passing lane.

BEST CRUISE LINE SHORE EXCURSIONS
La Soufrière Volcano Trek (US$59, 5½ hr.): Located in the Parc National de la Guadeloupe, the still-simmering La Soufrière volcano rises to 1,440m (4,723 ft.), flanked by banana plantations and lush vegetation. In 1975, ashes, mud, billowing smoke, and tremors proved that the volcano is still active, and today, you can smell sulfurous fumes and feel the heat through the soil as steam spews from the fumaroles. An hour-long uphill hike takes you to the summit, which looks like another planet.

Frommer's Favorite Guadeloupe Experiences

Climbing a Volcano: Draped in thousands of banana trees and other lush foliage, La Soufrière rises 1,440m (4,723 ft.) above the surrounding sea and dominates the island of Basse-Terre. You can drive to a parking area at La Savane à Mulets, then hike the final 450m (1,476 ft.) right to the mouth of the volcano. It'll take a couple of arduous hours to get to the top. (See "On Your Own: Beyond the Port Area," below.)

Touring Grande-Terre's Atlantic Coast: Drive out to Grande-Terre's eastern extreme, La Pointe des Châteaux, to watch the Atlantic and Caribbean vent their fury on the rocky shore. Continue up the coast to La Porte d'Enfer and La Pointe de la Grande Vigie for splendid views of limestone cliffs and sparkling aquamarine waters. (See "On Your Own: Beyond the Port Area," below.)

Soaking Up the French-Caribbean Ambience: Walk the streets of Pointe-à-Pitre. Browse the stores and perhaps buy some perfume or "thigh-reducing cream" from one of the upscale pharmacies (look for the neon green cross). Pick up a newspaper; find a shady table at a sidewalk cafe; order a cold, fresh fruit juice; and luxuriate in your blessed life.

Carbet Falls (US$44, 4 hr.): After driving through the banana plantations and rain-forests of Basse-Terre's south side, hike 30 minutes to picturesque Carbet Falls, where you're free to swim in the refreshing water. Wear sturdy walking shoes.

Pigeon Island (US$55, 4½ hr.): First pass through Guadeloupe's national park, a lush and mountainous tropical rainforest, on the Route de la Traversée. At Pigeon Island, board a glass-bottom boat for a 90-minute ride around a beautiful coral reef now designated the Cousteau Underwater Reserve. Marvel at the numerous fish, corals, and other marine life.

EXCURSIONS OFFERED BY LOCAL AGENCIES

Hiking Tours: Basse-Terre's **Parc National** (national park) has 322km (200 miles) of well-marked trails. Some meander through tropical rainforests to waterfalls and mountain pools; others focus on the La Soufrière volcano, geology, animals, and vegetation. Free maps and brochures in English can be obtained from the **National Park Office,** Habitation Beausoleil, Montéran, Boite Postal 13, St-Claude 97120 (© 590/80-86-00 or 590/99-03-15). The park office will also provide visitors with a list of local agencies offering excursions.

Snorkeling Tours: To snorkel in the Cousteau Underwater Reserve, contact **Nautilus** (© 590/98-89-08), located at the Bouillante town dock, south of Malendure. It offers 90-minute guided tours in glass-bottom boats several times daily; at least 15 minutes are reserved for snorkeling and refreshments. The cost is US$25 to US$30.

ON YOUR OWN: WITHIN WALKING DISTANCE

Walking is the best way to browse, shop, and visit the museums. Pointe-à-Pitre's narrow streets and congested sidewalks are bustling with activity, and its markets are among the Caribbean's most colorful. The largest, **Marché St. Antoine,** at the corner of rues Frébault and Peynier, is well known for its playful, sassy vendors, who sell tropical produce and spices in madras bags. **Marché de la Darse,** on the waterfront at the foot of place de la Banque, offers exotic fruits, vegetables, and souvenirs. The **place Gourbeyre flower market,** next to the cathedral, is ablaze with tropical blooms, including roses de porcelaine and alpinias.

Lined with royal palms, scarlet flamboyants, and travelers palms, the renovated **place de la Victoire** commemorates Victor Hugues's defeat of the English in 1794. It's the largest public space in town and is bordered with restaurants and cafes. The nearby **Cathedral of St-Pierre and St-Paul,** built in 1871, has an iron framework designed to withstand earthquakes and hurricanes. Three churches destroyed by successive earthquakes form its foundation.

The **Musée Municipal Saint-John Perse,** 9 rue de Nozières, near rue Achille-René Boisneuf (© **590/90-01-92**), chronicles the life of native son Alexis Léger, who won the Nobel Prize for literature under the nom de plume Saint-John Perse in 1960. The museum is housed in one of the city's most beautifully restored colonial mansions, an urban chalet with ornate friezes, voluted consoles, and wrought-iron galleries. Open windows allow breezes into the main parlor, which is furnished with bourgeois furniture. In addition to many of the poet's personal effects, the museum displays photographs documenting Guadeloupean life from the turn of the 20th century through the 1930s; you can buy postcards of some of them in the gift shop. The museum is open Monday through Friday from 9am to 5pm, Saturday from 8:30am to 12:30pm. Admission is about US$2 for adults, half-price for students.

The **Musée Schoelcher,** 24 rue Peynier (© **590/82-08-04**), tells the story of Victor Schoelcher, the key figure in the move to abolish slavery in Guadeloupe. The powerful exhibits, housed in a renovated mansion, include a slave-ship model, a miniature guillotine, china from Bordeaux with scenes from *Uncle Tom's Cabin,* and racist caricatures published in Parisian journals. Particularly moving is an 1845 census document that lists slaves as nothing more than plantation animals. Open Monday through Friday from 9am to 5pm; admission is US$2 for adults, half-price for students and children.

ON YOUR OWN: BEYOND THE PORT AREA

Guadeloupe is too large to tour in a single day. You'll have to choose among Grande-Terre, northern Basse-Terre, and southern Basse-Terre.

ON GRANDE-TERRE   The **Aquarium de la Guadeloupe,** near the Bas du Fort Marina just east of Pointe-à-Pitre (© **590/90-92-38**), is compact but has an impressive collection of exotic fish, corals, and sponges from the Caribbean and the Pacific. Come face to face with hugging sea horses, sleeping nurse sharks, and graceful sea turtles. Don't miss the polka-dot grouper known as *mérou de Grace Kelly.* Explanatory markers are in both French and English. The souvenir shop sells hand-painted folk art, jewelry, and fish- and sea-themed trinkets and T-shirts. Open daily from 9am to 7pm; admission is about US$8 for adults, US$2.75 for children under 4.

La Pointe des Châteaux (Castle Point), at Grande-Terre's easternmost point, is an impressive seascape spectacle. Angry Atlantic waves bash black-limestone rocks and jagged cliffs with a roughness reminiscent of Brittany's Finistère coast or England's Land's End. For the best views of the island of La Désirade, follow the path leading to the point where the land falls off abruptly to the ocean.

Farther north, **La Porte d'Enfer** is a quaint little cove and beach protected from the furious Atlantic by an outcrop of limestone cliffs. The name means "Hell's Gate," but swimming close to shore in the turquoise water is usually safe. Don't venture out too far, though; the next cove, **Le Trou de Madame Coco** (Madame Coco's Hole), is where (according to legend) the sea stole Madame Coco and her parasol as she promenaded along the edge. **La Pointe de la Grande Vigie,** at the northernmost tip of the island, has paths that lead to the edge of spectacular cliffs with dramatic views of Porte de l'Enfer and, on a clear day, the island of Antigua. Cacti and other succulents grow everywhere.

Along the northern coasts of Grande-Terre and Basse-Terre, **La Réserve Naturelle du Grand Cul-de-Sac Marin** is one of the Caribbean's largest marine reserves.

ON BASSE-TERRE   Basse-Terre's greatest attraction is the **Parc National de la Guadeloupe,** 29,600 hectares (73,112 acres) of tropical rainforests, mountains, waterfalls, and ponds. UNESCO designated the park a World Biosphere Reserve in 1992. Its 322km (200 miles) of well-marked trails make it one of the best places for hiking in the entire Caribbean. Pick up information and maps at park entrances. **La Maison de la Forêt** (Forest House) is 30 minutes from Pointe-à-Pitre on the Route de la Traversée, which bisects the park; it's the starting point for easy walking tours of the surrounding mountainous rainforest. English-language trail-guide booklets describe the plant and animal life. It's closed on Monday. Nearby, the **Cascade aux Ecrevisses** (Crayfish Falls), a slippery 10-minute walk from the roadside, is nice for a cooling dip. To the south, the steep hike to the three falls of **Les Chutes du Carbet** (Carbet Falls) is among Guadeloupe's most beautiful excursions (one of the falls drops 20m/66 ft., the second 108m/354 ft., the third 123m/403 ft.). The middle fall, the most dramatic, is the easiest to reach. On the way up, you'll pass **Le Grand Etang** (Great Pond), a volcanic lake surrounded by tree-size ferns, giant vining philodendrons, wild bananas, orchids, anthuriums, and pineapples.

The park's single greatest feature is the still-simmering volcano **La Soufrière,** rising to 1,440m (4,723 ft.) and flanked by banana plantations and lush vegetation. In 1975, ashes, mud, billowing smoke, and tremors proved that the volcano is still active, and today you can still smell sulfurous fumes and feel the heat through the soil as steam spews from the fumaroles. The summit is like another planet: Steam rises from two active craters, large rocks form improbable shapes, and roars from the earth make it difficult to hear your companions. Go with an experienced guide (see "Hiking Tours" under "Excursions Offered by Local Agencies," above). On your way down, don't miss **La Maison du Volcan,** the volcanology museum in St-Claude.

Gardeners should save a couple hours to visit the **Domaine de Valombreuse** (© **590/95-50-50**), a 2.4-hectare (6-acre) floral park with exotic birds, spice gardens, and 300 species of tropical flowers. Created in 1990, and close to the town of Petit Bourg, the park has a riverside restaurant and a superior gift shop. It's open daily from 9am to 6pm; admission is about US$10 for adults and US$5 for children 6 to 12.

Parc Archéologique des Roches Gravées, on Basse-Terre's southern coast in the town of Trois-Rivières (© **590/92-91-88**), has the West Indies' largest collection of Arawak Indian petroglyphs. The animal and human images etched on boulders date from between A.D. 300 and 400. Paths and stone stairways meander through the tranquil grounds. Open daily from 8:30am to 4:30pm; admission is about US$1.50.

SHOPPING

Parlez-vous Chanel? Hermès? Saint Laurent? Baccarat? If you do, you'll find that Guadeloupe has good buys on almost anything French—scarves, perfumes, cosmetics, crystal, and other luxury goods—and many stores offer a 20% discount on items purchased with foreign currency, traveler's checks, or credit cards. You can also find local handcrafted items, madras cloth, spices, and rum at any of the local markets.

Right at Pointe-à-Pitre's port, the **Centre Saint-John Perse** has about 20 shops that frequently offer lower prices than can be found elsewhere in town. **L'Artisan Parfumeur** sells French and American perfumes, as well as tropical scents.

Rue Frébault, directly in front of the port, is one of the best shopping streets for duty-free items. **Rosébleu,** 5 rue Frébault, offers china, crystal, and silver from Christofle, Kosta Boda, and other high-end manufacturers. **Phoenicia,** 8 rue Frébault and 121 bis rue Frébault, has large selections of French perfumes and cosmetics. For men's and women's fashions, as well as for cosmetics and perfumes, browse through **Vendôme,** 8–10 rue Frébault. If you find yourself overdosing on froufrou, duck into **Tati,** at rues Frébault and Abbé Grégoire; this venerable old department-store chain is France's answer to Kmart. It's famous for its antifashion pink-plaid shopping bags and makes a great stop for inexpensive basics.

The French Antilles are where the *beguine* began, so if you're in the market for French Antillean music or French-language books, visit **Librairie Général,** 46 rue Schoelcher. It has a small selection of English-language books as well.

BEACHES

Beaches on Grande-Terre's southern coast have soft white sand. Those on the Atlantic coast have wilder water and are less crowded. The convenient **Bas du Fort/Gosier hotel area** has mostly man-made strips of sand with rows of beach chairs, watersports shops, and beach bars. Changing facilities and chairs are available for a nominal fee. The tiny, uninhabited **Ilet Gosier,** across Gosier Bay, is a quieter option popular with those who want to bare it all. You can take a fishing boat to the island from Gosier's waterfront. The wide strip of white sand at **Ste-Anne,** about 30 minutes from Pointe-à-Pitre, is lined with shops and food stands. **Plage Tarare,** just before the tip of Pointe des Châteaux, is the most popular nude beach.

On Basse-Terre, the **Plage de Grande Anse** is a long expanse of ochre sand. A pleasant walk north from Deshaies, it offers changing facilities, watersports, boutiques, and outdoor snack bars. Farther south, the gray expanse of **Plage de Malendure** is alive with restaurants, bars, and open-air boutiques. It's the departure point for snorkeling and scuba trips to the **Cousteau Underwater Reserve,** off Pigeon Island.

SPORTS

SNORKELING Beachside stands at virtually all the resorts on Grande-Terre's southern coast rent snorkeling equipment for about US$10 a day. The St-François reef and the Ilet de Gosier are especially recommended.

GREAT LOCAL RESTAURANTS & BARS

Many restaurants change their hours from time to time and from season to season, so call in advance for reservations and exact hours. Most, but not all, restaurants accept major credit cards.

The local beer is **Corsaire,** while the local coffee is **Bonka.** Local rums come in a variety of flavors—such as *bois bandé* (made with the bark of the bois bandé tree), shrubb (orange and vanilla), and lemon—and are painstakingly nurtured at small rum estates such as **Séverin, Longueteau, Damoiseau, Bologne,** and **Montebello.** Local producers compare their slow, time-honored process to that used to make cognac.

ON GRANDE-TERRE   Cafes and bistros line the marina in St-François, and you can't go wrong at any of the lunch spots. On the waterfront, try the rustic and charming **Les Pieds dans l'Eau,** on rue de la République (✆ **590/88-60-02**), where you can get a grilled lobster for under US$20. Another option is **Man Michel** (✆ **590/88-72-79**), where lunch will cost about US$40.

The marina area of Bas du Fort in Gosier is also lined with restaurants. If you enjoy people-watching, park yourself at any French cafe and feast your eyes on the beautiful people—French tourists and yachties—mingling with one another. At **La Route du Rhum** (✆ **590/90-77-97**), lunch is about U$S35.

ON BASSE-TERRE   In Deshaies, Lucienne Salcède's family has run **Le Karacoli** (✆ **590/28-41-17**), one of Guadeloupe's best seaside restaurants, for almost 30 years. Sit on the beachfront terrace in the shadow of almond and palm trees, and let the waves hypnotize you. The island of Montserrat is visible in the distance. Try a rum aperitif or two, then bliss out on cod fritters, stuffed christophine, and avocado *féroce* (a peppery purée) before moving on to Creole lobster or conch. It's open daily from noon to 2pm (closed the entire month of Sept). Reservations are imperative on weekends. Lunch is about US$35.

19 Jamaica

A favorite of North American honeymooners, Jamaica is a mountainous island 145km (90 miles) south of Cuba and about 161km (100 miles) west of Haiti. It's the third largest of the Caribbean islands, with some 11,396 sq. km (4,444 sq. miles) of predominantly green terrain, a mountain ridge peaking at 2,220m (7,281 ft.) above sea level, and, on the north coast, many beautiful white-sand beaches rimming the clear blue sea.

One of the most densely populated nations in the Caribbean, with a vivid sense of its own identity, Jamaica has a history rooted in the plantation economy and some of the most impassioned politics in the Western Hemisphere, all of which leads to a sometimes turbulent day-to-day reality. You've probably heard, for instance, that the island's vendors and hawkers can be pushy and the locals not always the most welcoming to tourists, and while there's some truth to this, we've had nothing but positive experiences on many visits to Jamaica.

Most cruise ships dock at **Ocho Rios,** on the lush northern coast, although more and more are opting to call at the city of **Montego Bay** ("Mo Bay"), 108km (67 miles) to the west. These ports offer comparable attractions and some of the same shopping possibilities. Don't try to do both ports in a single day, however, since the 4-hour round-trip ride leaves time for only superficial visits to each.

LANGUAGE   The official language is English, but most Jamaicans speak a richly nuanced patois that's primarily derived from English but includes elements of African, Spanish, Arawak, French, Chinese, Portuguese, and East Indian languages.

CURRENCY   The unit of currency is the **Jamaican dollar,** designated by the same symbol as the U.S. dollar ($). For clarity, we use the symbol J$ to denote prices in Jamaican dollars. The exchange rate is usually J$60 = US$1; J$1 = US2¢. Visitors can pay in U.S. dollars, but always find out if a price is being quoted in Jamaican or U.S.

dollars—there's a big difference! Unless otherwise specified, prices in this section are given in U.S. dollars.

INFORMATION   For info before you go, contact the **Jamaica Tourist Board** (*(℗)* **800/233-4582** or 305/665-0557; www.visitjamaica.com). Information booths in the ports are discussed below.

CALLING FROM THE U.S.   When calling Jamaica from the United States, you need only dial a "1" before the numbers listed here.

SHORE EXCURSIONS OFFERED IN BOTH PORTS

Since there's little besides shopping near the docks at either Ocho Rios or Montego Bay, most passengers sign up for shore excursions. The following are usually offered from both ports.

Dunn's River Falls Tour (US$44, 4 hr.): These falls cascade 180m (590 ft.) to the beach and are the most visited attraction in Jamaica, which means they're hopelessly overcrowded when a lot of cruise ships are in port. Visitors are allowed to climb the falls, and it's a ball to slip and slide your way up with the hundreds of others, forming a human chain of sorts. Wear a bathing suit under your clothes, and don't forget your waterproof camera and your aqua-socks. (If you do, most cruise lines will rent you aqua-socks for an extra US$5.) The prettiest part of the falls, known as the Laughing Waters, were used in the James Bond classics *Dr. No* and *Live and Let Die*. This tour usually visits other local attractions as well, with time allocated for shopping. (*Note:* The falls are much closer to Ocho Rios than to Mo Bay, so tours from the latter typically cost around US$75 and require a 2¼-hr. drive each way, for a total of 7½ hr.)

River Tubing Safari (US$75, 3½ hr.): This is one of the best excursions we've ever taken. After a scenic van ride deep into the pristine jungles, the group of 20 or so passengers and a couple of guides sit back in big black inner tubes (they have wooden boards covering the bottom so your butt doesn't get scraped on the rocks) and glide a few miles downriver, passing by gorgeous, towering bamboo trees and other lush foliage. It's sometimes peaceful and sometimes exhilarating—especially when you hit the rapids! If you're docking in Ocho Rios, this tour is usually on the White River. If in Montego Bay, it's on the Great River. *Note:* We find this trip much more interesting than the popular **Martha Brae River Rafting,** which takes you down the river on two-seat bamboo rafts. The cost is a little more, but we think it's worth it.

Horseback-Riding Excursion (US$89, 3 hr.): Riders will love this trip; after a 45-minute ride from the stables through fields, you'll gallop along the beach and take your horse bareback into the surf for a thrilling ride.

OCHO RIOS

Once a small banana and fishing port, Ocho Rios is now Jamaica's cruise ship capital, welcoming a couple of ships every day during high season. Though the area has some of the Caribbean's most fabled resorts, and Dunn's River is just a 5-minute taxi ride away, the town itself is not much to see, despite there being a few outdoor local markets within walking distance. Don't expect to shop in the markets without a lot of hassle and a lot of very pushy hawking of merchandise—some of which is likely to be ganja, the locally grown marijuana. (Remember, it may be readily available, but it's still illegal.) In recent years, the government has been making an effort to keep things saner around the markets, employing a veritable army of blue-uniformed "resort patrol" officers on bikes to help keep order.

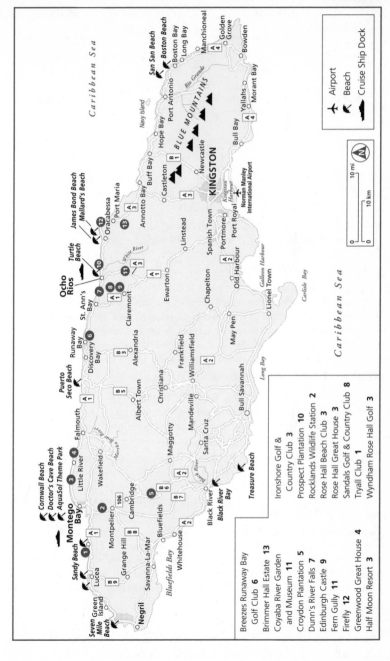

Jamaica

Caribbean Sea

Cornwall Beach
Doctor's Cave Beach
AquaSol Theme Park
Montego Bay
Sandy Beach
Seven Mile Beach
Negril

Puerto Seco Beach
Treasure Beach
Black River Bay

Turtle Beach
Ocho Rios
James Bond Beach
Mallard's Beach

San San Beach
Boston Beach

BLUE MOUNTAINS

KINGSTON

Caribbean Sea

Airport
Beach
Cruise Ship Dock

N

10 mi
0
10 km
0

Lucea
Green Island
Grange Hill
Savanna-La-Mar
Whitehouse
Bluefields
Bluefields Bay
Cambridge
Montpelier
Wakefield
Little River
Falmouth
Maggotty
Albert Town
Christiana
Mandeville
Santa Cruz
Black River
Long Bay
Bull Savannah
Williamsfield
Frankfield
Alexandria
Discovery Bay
Runaway Bay
St. Ann's Bay
Claremont
Ewarton
Chapelton
May Pen
Old Harbour
Lionel Town
Carlisle Bay
Spanish Town
Linstead
Annotto Bay
Port Maria
Oracabessa
Castleton
Newcastle
Buff Bay
Hope Bay
Port Antonio
Rio Grande
Boston Bay
Long Bay
Manchioneal
Golden Grove
Bowden
Morant Bay
Yallahs
Bull Bay
Port Royal
Kingston Harbour
Norman Manley International Airport
Portmore
Galleon Harbour
Galleon Bay
White River
Marth River
Great River
Martha Brae River
Rio Cobre
Rio Minho

Breezes Runaway Bay
Golf Club **6**
Brimmer Hall Estate **13**
Coyaba River Garden
and Museum **11**
Croydon Plantation **5**
Dunn's River Falls **7**
Edinburgh Castle **9**
Fern Gully **11**
Firefly **12**
Greenwood Great House **4**
Half Moon Resort **3**

Ironshore Golf &
Country Club **3**
Prospect Plantation **10**
Rocklands Wildlife Station **2**
Rose Hall Beach Club **3**
Rose Hall Great House **3**
Sandals Golf & Country Club **8**
Tryall Club **1**
Wyndham Rose Hall Golf **3**

Frommer's Favorite Ocho Rios Experiences

Tubing on the White River: Offered by most cruise lines, this trip is just a downright fantastic experience. (See "Shore Excursions Offered in Both Ports," above.)

Riding Horseback through the Surf: An excursion by horseback includes a ride along the beach and through the surf. (See "Shore Excursions Offered in Both Ports," above.)

COMING ASHORE   Most cruise ships dock at the **Port of Ocho Rios,** near Dunn's River Falls and adjacent to Island Village and several shopping options. The terminal has bathrooms and a phone center.

INFORMATION   You'll find the Ocho Rios office of the **Jamaica Tourist Board** at the Ocean Village Shopping Centre (© **876/974-2582**); open Monday through Friday from 8:30am to 4:30pm, and Saturday from 9am to 1pm. There's also a small information stand right at the dock.

GETTING AROUND

BY TAXI   Taxis are your best means of transport. Your safest bet is to get a taxi from the pier; there will be lots of them waiting, and fixed rates are posted. The official Jamaica Tourist Board taxis, which are licensed by the government, display JTB decals. All others are gypsy cabs, which you should avoid. If you're getting into a taxi from somewhere else on the island, always agree on a fare before you get in.

BY RENTAL CAR   We don't recommend renting a car here.

BEST CRUISE LINE SHORE EXCURSIONS

In addition to the excursions offered from both Jamaican ports (see "Shore Excursions Offered in Both Ports," above), tours to the following nearby attractions are also offered from Ocho Rios.

Prospect Plantation & Dunn's River Falls (US$82, 4½ hr.): About 4.8km (3 miles) east of town, Prospect Plantation offers a taste of Jamaica's colonial days (sans slavery), with a tractor-drawn jitney taking you among seasonal crops that include bananas, sugar cane, coffee, pineapple, and papaya. The trip includes a stop at Dunn's River Falls (see "Shore Excursions Offered in Both Ports," above).

Coyaba River Garden & Dunn's River Falls (US$59, 3 hr.): About a mile from town, Coyaba River Garden and Museum was built on the grounds of the former Shaw Park plantation; it displays artifacts from the Arawak, Spanish, and English settlements in the area. The gardens are filled with native flora, a cut-stone courtyard, and fountains. Like many of the other tours in Ocho Rios, it hits Dunn's River Falls on the way back.

Dolphin Cove (US$34–US$89, 2 hr.): Various excursions to this beachfront site allow you to gander at, touch, or swim with the resident dolphins. For about US$10 more, you can add on 1½ hours at (you guessed it) Dunn's River Falls.

ON YOUR OWN: WITHIN WALKING DISTANCE

Adjacent to the cruise pier, **Island Village** (www.islandjamaica.com) is a 1.6-hectare (4-acre) entertainment-and-shopping complex developed by Island Records' Chris

Blackwell. Attractions include the ReggaeXplosion museum, a museum of Jamaican art, a casino, an outdoor concert venue, an indoor theater, a beach with watersports, shopping (lots of it), and a branch of Jimmy Buffett's Margaritaville.

ON YOUR OWN: BEYOND THE PORT AREA

South of Ocho Rios, **Fern Gully** was originally a riverbed. Today, the main A3 road winds some 210m (689 ft.) through a rainforest filled with wild ferns, hardwood trees, and lianas. For the botanist, there are hundreds of varieties of ferns; for the less plant-minded, roadside stands sell fruits and vegetables, carved-wood souvenirs, and basket-work. The road runs for about 6.4km (4 miles).

Near Lydford, southwest of Ocho Rios, are the remains of **Edinburgh Castle.** This was the lair of one of Jamaica's most infamous murderers, a Scot named Lewis Hutchinson, who used to shoot passersby and toss their bodies into a deep pit. The authorities got wind of his activities, and although he tried to escape by canoe, he was captured by the navy and hanged in 1773. Rather proud of his achievements (evidence of at least 43 murders was found), he left £100 and instructions for a memorial to be built. It never was, but the 1763 castle ruins remain. To get to Lydford, take the A3 south until you reach a small intersection directly north of Walkerswood, and then follow the signposts west.

The 1817 **Brimmer Hall Estate,** Port Maria, St. Mary's (© **876/994-2309**), 34km (21 miles) east of Ocho Rios, is a working plantation where you're driven around in a tractor-drawn jitney to see the tropical fruit trees and coffee plants. Knowledgeable guides tell you about the processes necessary to produce the fine fruits of the island. Afterward, you can relax beside the pool and sample a wide variety of drinks, including an interesting one called "Wow!" The Plantation Tour Eating House offers typical Jamaican dishes for lunch. There's also a souvenir shop with a good selection of ceramics, art, straw goods, woodcarvings, rums, liqueurs, and cigars. Tours run daily if there are enough people. Hours are Monday through Friday from 8am to 4pm. Admission is US$15 for adults, US$7.50 for children, and free for kids under 5.

About 1.6km (1 mile) from the center of Ocho Rios, at an elevation of 126m (413 ft.), **Coyaba River Garden and Museum,** Shaw Park Road (© **876/974-6235;** www.coyabagardens.com), was built on the grounds of the former Shaw Park planta-tion. The Spanish-style museum displays artifacts from the Arawak, Spanish, and Eng-lish settlements in the area. The gardens are filled with native flora, a cut-stone courtyard, and fountains. Open daily from 8am to 6pm. Admission is US$5 for adults, US$2.50 for children.

At the 180m (590-ft.) **Dunn's River Falls,** on the A3 (© **876/974-2857**), you can relax on the beach, splash in the waters at the bottom of the falls, or climb with a guide to the top and drop into the cool pools higher up between the cascades of water. The beach restaurant provides snacks and drinks; dressing rooms are also available. If you're planning to climb the falls, wear aqua-socks or sneakers to protect your feet from the sharp rocks and to prevent slipping. At the prettiest part of Dunn's River Falls, known

---

Cruise Booze

If you step inside the small cruise "terminal" in Ocho Rios, you'll find a shop called Cruise Booze, which sets up a tasting station where you can sample a ton of different rums, including a 150-proof white rum.

as the Laughing Waters, scenes were shot for the James Bond classics *Dr. No* and *Live and Let Die.*

About 4.8km (3 miles) east of Ocho Rios along the A3, adjoining the 18-hole Prospect Mini Golf Course, the working **Prospect Plantation** (© **876/974-2373**) is often a shore-excursion stop. On your leisurely ride by covered jitney, you'll readily see why this section of Jamaica is called the "garden parish of the island." You'll see pimiento (allspice), banana, cassava, sugar cane, coffee, cocoa, coconut, pineapple, and the famous leucaena "Tree of Life"—plus, for what it's worth, Jamaica's first hydroelectric plant. Horseback riding is available on three scenic trails. The rides vary from 1 to 2¼ hours; you'll need to book a horse at least an hour in advance. Rates are US$20 per person per hour.

Firefly, Grants Pen (© **876/725-0920**), 32km (20 miles) east of Ocho Rios above Oracabessa, was the home of Sir Noël Coward and his longtime companion, Graham Payn, who, as executor of Coward's estate, donated it to the Jamaica National Heritage Trust. The recently restored house is as it was on the day Sir Noël died in 1973. Open Monday through Thursday from 9am to 5pm. Admission is US$10 for adults, free for children under 12.

SHOPPING

Shopping in Ocho Rios is not as good as in Montego Bay and other ports, but if your money's burning a hole in your pocket, you can wander around the Ocho Rios Craft Park, opposite the **Ocean Village Shopping Centre,** off Main Street. Some 150 stalls stock hats, handbags, place mats, woodcarvings, and paintings, plus the usual T-shirts and jewelry. More luxurious items can be found at **Soni's Plaza,** on Main Street (© **876/974-6455**). For more local craft items, try **Coconut Grove Shopping Plaza,** a collection of low-slung shops linked by walkways and shrubs. Right in the heart of Ocho Rios, the **Island Plaza** shopping complex has paintings by local artists, local handmade crafts (be prepared to do some haggling), carvings, ceramics, and even kitchenware—plus T-shirts, of course. At all of these places, prepare yourself for aggressive selling and fierce haggling. Every vendor asks too much for an item at first, which gives him or her the leeway to negotiate the real price.

> *Tips* **Deal or No Deal?**
>
> Some so-called duty-free prices are indeed lower than stateside prices, but then the Jamaican government hits you with a 16.5% "general consumption tax." Buyers, beware.

To find local handicrafts or art without the hassle of the markets, head for **Beautiful Memories,** 9 Island Plaza (© **876/974-2374**), which has a limited but representative sampling of Jamaican art, as well as local crafts, pottery, woodwork, and hand-embroidered items.

If you'd like to flee the hustle and bustle of the Ocho Rios bazaars completely, take a taxi to **Harmony Hall,** Tower Isle, on the A3 (© **876/975-4222**), about 6.4km (4 miles) east of Ocho Rios. One of Jamaica's great houses, the restored house is now a gallery selling paintings and other works by Jamaican artists. The arts and crafts here are of high quality—not the usual junky assortment you might find at the beach.

BEACHES

The **Sunset Jamaica Grande Resort,** on Main Street (© **876/974-2201**), has two beaches, shared by hotel guests and cruise ship passengers. The beaches, located at the

North and South Towers, can sometimes be overcrowded. You might also want to check out the big **James Bond Beach** in Oracabessa, at the east end of Ocho Rios.

SPORTS

GOLF   SuperClubs' 18-hole, par-72 **Breezes Runaway Bay,** at Runaway Beach near Ocho Rios (*C* **876/973-7319**), is one of the better courses in the area, although it's nowhere near the courses at Montego Bay. Call ahead to book tee times. Greens fees are US$80 for 18 holes, US$35 for carts, and US$14 for clubs.

The 18-hole, par-71 **Sandals Golf & Country Club,** at Ocho Rios (*C* **876/975-0119**), is also open to the public, charging a special cruise rate of US$45 for 18 holes. Clubs are an additional US$30 to US$45, while carts are an extra US$40. Caddies, which are required, are US$12 for 9 holes and US$17 for 18 holes. The course lies about 210m (689 ft.) above sea level. To get here from the center of Ocho Rios, travel along the main bypass for 3.2km (2 miles) until Mile End Road; turn right at the Texaco station and drive for 8km (5 miles).

GREAT LOCAL RESTAURANTS & BARS

The favorite local beer is **Red Stripe;** a favorite local rum is **Appleton.** Jamaica probably has more great rum bars than churches. Among the best is **Bibi Bips,** 93 Main St. (*C* **876/974-7438** or 876/865-7482).

Ocho Rios Jerk Centre, on DaCosta Drive (*C* **876/974-2549**), serves up lip-smacking jerk pork and chicken. Don't expect anything fancy; just come for platters of meat. Lunch is about US$14.

For a special lunch, **Almond Tree Restaurant,** in the Hibiscus Lodge Hotel, 83 Main St., 3 blocks from the Ocho Rios Mall (*C* **876/974-2813**), is a two-tiered patio restaurant overlooking the Caribbean, with a tree growing through its roof. Lobster thermidor is the most delectable item on the menu. Lunch is about US$20.

Evita's Italian Restaurant, Eden Bower Road, 5 minutes south of Ocho Rios (*C* **876/974-2333**), is run by a flamboyant Italian and is the premier Italian restaurant in Ocho Rios. It serves pastas and excellent fish dishes, as well as unique choices such as jerk spaghetti and pasta Viagra (don't ask). Lunch is around US$20.

MONTEGO BAY

Montego Bay (also referred to as "Mo Bay") is sometimes less of a hassle to explore than the port at Ocho Rios, plus it has better beaches, shopping, and restaurants, as well as some of the best golf courses in the Caribbean (superior even to those in Puerto Rico and the Bahamas). Like Ocho Rios, Montego Bay has its share of crime, traffic, and annoyances, but there's much more to see and do here.

There's little of interest in the town itself except shopping, although the good stuff in the environs is easily reached by taxi or shore excursion.

COMING ASHORE   Montego Bay has a modern cruise dock with lots of conveniences, including duty-free stores, phones, tourist information, and plenty of taxis to meet all ships.

INFORMATION   You'll find the **Jamaica Tourist Board** office at Cornwall Beach, St. James (*C* **876/952-4425**); open Monday through Friday from 9am to 5pm.

GETTING AROUND

BY TAXI   If you don't book a shore excursion, a taxi is the way to get around. See "Getting Around" under "Ocho Rios," above, for taxi information, as the same conditions apply to Mo Bay.

Frommer's Favorite Montego Bay Experiences

In addition to the following, our favorite shore excursions from Ocho Rios (described on p. 202) are also offered from Montego Bay.

Visiting Rocklands Wildlife Station: This is the place to go if you want to feed small doves and finches from your hand or have a Jamaican doctor bird perch on your finger. (See "On Your Own: Beyond the Port Area," below.)

Spending a Day at the Rose Hall Beach Club: With a secluded beach, crystal-clear water, a full restaurant, two beach bars, live entertainment, and more, it's well worth the US$8 admission. (See "Beaches," below.)

BEST CRUISE LINE SHORE EXCURSIONS

In addition to the tours offered from both Jamaica ports (see "Shore Excursions Offered in Both Ports," earlier in this section), Mo Bay is the starting point for excursions to several interesting plantations and great houses.

Rose Hall Great House (US$39, 3½ hr.): This is the most famous plantation home in Jamaica. Built about 2 centuries ago by John Palmer, it gained notoriety from the doings of "Infamous Annie" Palmer, wife of the builder's grandnephew, who supposedly dabbled in witchcraft and took slaves as lovers, killing them when they bored her. Annie was also said to have murdered several of her husbands while they slept, and eventually suffered the same fate herself. For what it's worth, many Jamaicans insist the house is haunted.

Greenwood Great House (US$39, 3½ hr.): More interesting to some than Rose Hall, the Georgian-style building was the residence of Richard Barrett, a first cousin of Elizabeth Barrett Browning. On display are the family's library, portraits, antiques, and period musical instruments.

Croydon Plantation Tour (US$64, 6 hr.): A guided tour of this mountain estate includes a ¼-mile walk over gently sloping terrain, with a lot of great views. Stops are made for refreshments and seasonal fresh fruits, and at the end you get a traditional Jamaican-style lunch.

ON YOUR OWN: WITHIN WALKING DISTANCE

There's nothing really. You'll have to take a taxi to the town for shopping or else sign up for an excursion.

ON YOUR OWN: BEYOND THE PORT AREA

It's a unique experience to have a Jamaican doctor bird perch on your finger to drink syrup, or to feed small doves and finches from your hand, or simply to watch dozens of birds flying in for the evening at **Rocklands Wildlife Station,** Anchovy, St. James (© **876/952-2009**). Lisa Salmon, known as the "Bird Lady of Anchovy," established this sanctuary. It's perfect for nature lovers and bird-watchers alike. Rocklands is about 1.2km (¾ mile) outside Anchovy on the road from Montego Bay. Open daily from 9am to 5:30pm; admission is US$8 for adults and US$4 for children 5 to 12.

SHOPPING

The main shopping areas are at **Montego Freeport,** within easy walking distance of the pier; **City Centre,** where most of the duty-free shops are, aside from those at the large hotels; and **Holiday Village Shopping Centre.**

While you're browsing the Holiday Village Shopping Centre, stop by **Blue Mountain Gems Workshop** (© **876/953-2338**), where you can take a tour to see the process from raw stone to finished product, available for purchase later.

Old Fort Craft Market, a shopping complex with nearly 200 vendors licensed by the Jamaica Tourist Board, fronts Howard Cooke Boulevard up from Gloucester Avenue in the heart of Montego Bay, on the site of Fort Montego. With a varied assortment of handicrafts, this is browsing country. You'll see a selection of wall hangings, hand-woven straw items, and hand-carved wood sculptures; you can also get your hair braided. Vendors can be extremely aggressive, so be prepared for some major hassles, as well as some serious negotiation. Persistent bargaining on your part will lead to substantial discounts.

You can find the best selection of handmade souvenirs at the **Crafts Market,** near Harbour Street in downtown Montego Bay. Straw hats and bags, wooden platters, baskets, musical instruments, beads, carved objects, and toys are all available here. That "jipijapa" hat will come in handy if you're going to be out in the island sun.

Try the **Gallery of West Indian Art,** 11 Fairfield Rd. (© **876/952-4547**), for the best selection of local folk art—as well an absolutely fantastic, and reasonably priced, collection of Cuban, Jamaican, and Haitian fine art. **Ambiente Art Gallery,** 9 Fort St. (© **876/952-7919**), stocks more local artwork. And the nearby **Klass Kraft Leather Sandals,** 44 Fort St. (© **876/952-5782**), offers sandals and leather accessories made on location.

BEACHES

Doctor's Cave Beach (© **876/952-2566**), on Gloucester Avenue across from the **Doctor's Cave Beach Hotel** (© **876/952-4355;** www.doctorscave.com), helped launch Mo Bay as a resort in the 1940s. Admission to the beach is about US$4 for adults, half-price for children up to 12. Dressing rooms, chairs, umbrellas, and rafts are available.

One of the premier beaches of Jamaica, **AquaSol Theme Park** (www.aquasol jamaica.com) is at Walter Fletcher Beach in the heart of Mo Bay. It's noted for tranquil waters, which makes it a particular favorite for families with children. Changing rooms are available, and lifeguards are on duty. There's also a restaurant for lunch. The beach is open daily, with an admission price of about US$5 for adults and US$3 for children.

You may want to skip the public beaches and head for the **Rose Hall Beach Club** (© **876/680-0969**), on the main road 18km (11 miles) east of Montego Bay. It sits on .8km (½ mile) of secure, secluded, white-sandy beach, with crystal-clear water. The club offers a full restaurant, two beach bars, a covered pavilion, an open-air dance area, showers, restrooms, and changing facilities, plus beach volleyball courts, various beach games, and a full watersports activities program. There's also live entertainment. The club is open daily from 9am to 5pm; admission fees are about US$8 for adults and US$3 for children under 12.

SPORTS

GOLF   Rose Hall Resort & Country Club, at Rose Hall (© **876/953-2650;** www. rosehallresort.com), has a noted 18-hole, par-71 course with an unusual and challenging seaside and mountain layout, designed by Robert Von Hagge. The 90m-high

(295-ft.) 13th tee offers a rare panoramic view of the sea, and the 15th green is next to a 12m (39-ft.) waterfall, once featured in a James Bond movie. A fully stocked pro shop, a clubhouse, and a professional staff are among the amenities. Greens fees are US$120.

The excellent, regal 18-hole, par-72 course at the **Tryall Club,** 19km (12 miles) from Montego Bay (© **876/956-5660;** www.tryallclub.com), has often been the site of major golf tournaments, including the Jamaica Classic Annual and the Johnnie Walker Tournament. Greens fees are about US$115, plus US$30 for a cart.

The **Half Moon Resort,** at Rose Hall (© **876/953-2560;** www.halfmoongolf.com), features an 18-hole, par-72 championship course designed by Robert Trent Jones, Sr. Greens fees are about US$130, plus US$25 for a mandatory caddy.

Ironshore Golf & Country Club, Ironshore (© **876/953-3681**), a well-known, 18-hole, par-72 course, is privately owned but open to the public. Greens fees are a flat rate of about US$40, cart included, plus US$16 for a mandatory caddy for 18 holes ($11 for 9 holes).

HORSEBACK RIDING   The best horseback riding is offered by the helpful staff at the **Rocky Point Riding Stables,** at the Half Moon Resort, Rose Hall (© **876/953-2286**). The stables, built in the colonial Caribbean style in 1992, are the most beautiful in Jamaica.

RAFTING   Mountain Valley Rafting, 31 Gloucester Ave. (© **876/956-4920**), offers excursions on the Great River, departing from the Lethe Plantation, about 16km (10 miles) south of Montego Bay. Bamboo rafts are designed for two, with a raised dais to sit on. In some cases, a small child can accompany two adults on the same raft, although you should exercise caution when doing so. A half-day experience includes transportation to and from the pier, an hour's rafting, lunch, a garden tour of the Lethe property, and a taste of Jamaican liqueur.

GREAT LOCAL RESTAURANTS & BARS

The open-air **Pork Pit,** 27 Gloucester Ave., near AquaSol Theme Park (© **876/952-1046**), is the best place for the famous Jamaican jerk pork and jerk chicken. Many beachgoers come here for a big, informal lunch at picnic tables encircling the building. Order half a pound of jerk meat with a baked yam or baked potato and a bottle of Red Stripe beer. Prices are very reasonable; lunch is about US$10.

The **Native Restaurant,** Gloucester Avenue (© **876/979-2769**), continues to win converts with such appetizers as jerk reggae chicken, ackee and saltfish (an acquired taste), smoked marlin, and steamed fish. The boonoonoonoos, billed as "A Taste of Jamaica," is a big platter with a little bit of everything, including meats and several kinds of fish and vegetables. Lunch is about US$20.

The **Brewery,** Miranda Ridge Plaza (© **876/940-2433**), is more a bar than a full-scale restaurant, but lunch and dinner are served. Basic burgers, salads, and sandwiches are available; there's also a special daytime buffet on Monday, Wednesday, and Friday for US$5. You can enjoy drinks and a meal on the patio overlooking the ocean. Happy hour is daily from 4 to 6pm.

20 Key West

No other port of call offers such a sweeping choice of fine dining, easy-to-reach attractions, street entertainment, and roguish bars as does this heavy-drinking, fun-loving town at the very end of the fabled Florida Keys. It's America's southernmost city,

Key West

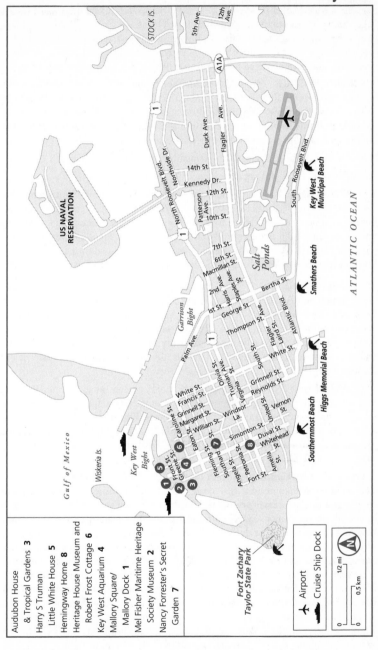

Audubon House
& Tropical Gardens **3**

Harry S Truman
Little White House **5**

Hemingway Home **8**

Heritage House Museum and
Robert Frost Cottage **6**

Key West Aquarium **4**

Mallory Square/
Mallory Dock **1**

Mel Fisher Maritime Heritage
Society Museum **2**

Nancy Forrester's Secret
Garden **7**

✈ Airport

⚓ Cruise Ship Dock

STOCK IS.

A1A

US NAVAL
RESERVATION

5th Ave.

12th Ave.

Duck Ave.

Flagler Ave.

14th St.

Kennedy Dr.

12th St.

Patterson Ave.

10th St.

South Roosevelt Blvd.

North Roosevelt Blvd.

Northside Dr.

Key West
Municipal Beach

7th St.

6th St.

Macmillan St.

2nd St.

Harris Ave.

Staples St.

Bertha St.

Salt
Ponds

Smathers Beach

ATLANTIC OCEAN

Garrison
Bight

George St.

Thompson St.

Palm Ave.

White St.

Flagler Ave.

Laird St.

Atlantic Blvd.

South St.

White St.

Southernmost Beach

Higgs Memorial Beach

Gulf of Mexico

Wisteria Is.

Key West
Bight

White St.

Francis St.

Grinnell St.

Margaret St.

Caroline St.

Front St.

Greene St.

Eaton St.

William St.

Fleming St.

Southard St.

Angela St.

Fort St.

Olivia St.

Truman Ave.

Virginia St.

Windsor La.

Simonton St.

Petronia St.

Whitehead St.

Duval St.

Amelia St.

United St.

Vernon St.

Grinnell St.

Reynolds St.

1

5

2

3

4

6

7

8

Fort Zachary
Taylor State Park

0   1/2 mi

0   0.5 km

located at Mile Marker 0, where U.S. Route 1 begins, but it feels more like a colorful Caribbean outpost mixed with a dash of New Orleans.

You have only a day here, so flee the busy cruise docks and touristy Duval Street for a walk through hidden and more secluded byways, such as Simonton, Olivia, or William streets. Or you might want to spend your day playing golf, diving, or snorkeling.

COMING ASHORE   Ships dock at **Mallory Square** (Old Town's tourist central), at the nearby Hilton Resort's **Pier B,** and at the U.S. Navy base's **"Outer Mole" pier.** All are on the Gulf side of the island. Passengers arriving at the Navy pier must take an official shuttle bus the short distance to and from Mallory Square, as individuals are not permitted to transit the base on their own.

LANGUAGE   Speak English here. Remember, you're in the U.S. of A.

CURRENCY   **U.S. dollars** are used here.

INFORMATION   Right near the cruise docks, the **Greater Key West Chamber of Commerce,** 402 Wall St. (© **305/294-2587;** www.keywestchamber.org), provides information on tours and fishing trips. *Pelican Path* is a free walking guide that documents the history and architecture of Old Town, while *Solares Hill's Walking and Biking Guide to Old Key West* contains a bunch of walking tours. For advance info, contact the **Florida Keys & Key West Tourism Council** (© **800/FLA-KEYS;** www.fla-keys.com).

GETTING AROUND

The island is only 6.4km (4 miles) long and 3.2km (2 miles) wide, and getting around is so easy that many locals do without cars, using "conch cruisers" (in other words, bicycles) instead. The most popular attractions, including the Harry S Truman Little White House and the Key West Art & History Museum, are all within walking distance of Mallory Square—even the farthest attraction (Hemingway House) is only about a mile down Duval.

BY TAXI   Island taxis operate around the clock, but are small and not suited for sightseeing tours. They will, however, take you to the beach and arrange to pick you up at a certain time. You can call one of four services: **Florida Keys Taxi** (© **305/294-2227**), **Maxi-Taxi Sun Cab System** (© **305/294-2222**), **Pink Cabs** (© **305/296-6666**), and **Florida Keys Taxi** (© **305/296-1800**). Prices are uniform; the meter starts at about US$2.75 and adds 55¢ per ⅓ mile.

BY TRAM   The **Conch Tour Train** (© **305/294-5161;** www.conchtourtrain.com) is a narrated 90-minute tour that takes you up and down all the most interesting streets and offers commentary on 100 local sites, giving you lots of lore about the town. It's the best way to see Key West in a short time. The depot is located at Mallory Square, near the cruise ship docks. Trains depart every 30 minutes. Most ships sell this as an excursion, but you can also do it on your own; departures are daily from 9am to 4:30pm and cost US$25 for adults, US$12 for children 4 to 12. The trip has only one stop where passengers can get on and off (at the Historic Seaport).

If you want more flexibility and are booking on your own, try the **Old Town Trolley** (© **305/296-6688;** www.trolleytours.com). It's less popular than the Conch Tour Train, but it lets you get off to explore a particular attraction, and then reboard another of its trains later. Professional guides spin tall tales about Key West throughout the 90-minute route. The trolleys operate daily from 9am to 4:30pm, with departures every 30 minutes from convenient spots throughout town. You can board the

Frommer's Favorite Key West Experiences

Viewing the Sunset from Mallory Dock: More than just a sunset, it's a daily carnival. If your ship is in port late enough, don't miss it. (See "On Your Own: Within Walking Distance," below.)

Taking a Catamaran Party Cruise: Catamarans take passengers snorkeling and then back to shore, with music, booze, and a good time for all. (See "Shore Excursions Offered by the Cruise Lines," below.)

trolley near the cruise docks (look for signposts). Tours cost about US$25 for adults, US$12 for children 4 to 12.

BY BUS   The cheapest way to see the island is by bus, which costs only about 75¢ for adults, 35¢ for seniors and children 6 and older.

BY MOTOR SCOOTER OR BICYCLE   One of the largest and best places to rent a bicycle or motorbike is **Keys Moped and Scooter Rental,** 523 Truman Ave., about a block off Duval Street (✆ **305/294-0399**). Cruise ship passengers might opt for a 3-hour motor-scooter rental for about US$15, the 9am-to-5pm rental for US$22, or the all-day (24-hr.) rental for US$30. One-speed, big-wheeled "beach-cruiser" bicycles, with soft seats and big baskets for toting beachwear, rent for about US$10 for 8 hours.

BY RENTAL CAR   Walking or cycling is better than driving in Key West, but if you do want to rent, **Avis, Budget, Dollar, Thrifty,** and **Hertz** all have offices here, as do **Tropical Rent-a-Car,** 1300 Duval St. (✆ **305/294-8136**), and **Enterprise Rent-a-Car,** 2834 N. Roosevelt Blvd. (✆ **800/325-8007** or 305/292-0220; www.enterprise. com). If you're visiting in winter, make reservations at least a week in advance.

SHORE EXCURSIONS OFFERED BY THE CRUISE LINES
In addition to the Conch Train Tour described above, most lines offer walking tours and sometimes bike tours for those who like the services of a guide. But this is really a port to explore on your own.

Catamaran Party Cruises (US$48, 3 hr.): The popular Fury catamarans take passengers to a reef for some snorkeling. This excursion finishes the trip back to shore with lots of music and booze.

EXCURSIONS OFFERED BY LOCAL AGENCIES
Glass-Bottom Boat Tours: The MV *Discovery* (✆ **800/262-0099** or 305/293-0099; www.discoveryunderseatours.com), a 78-foot motor craft, has 20 large viewing windows that are angled at 45 degrees and set below the water line to allow passengers to view reef life in comfort from below deck. Two-hour tours depart daily at 10:30am, 1:30pm during winter, 11:30am and 2:30pm in summer, and sunset from Land's End Village & Marina at the western end of Margaret Street, a 6-block walk from the cruise ship docks. The cost is US$35 for adults, US$16 for children 5 to 11.

ON YOUR OWN: WITHIN WALKING DISTANCE
The **Harry S Truman Little White House,** 111 Front St. (✆ **305/294-9911;** www. trumanlittlewhitehouse.com), is part of the 41.7-hectare (103-acre) Truman Annex,

near the cruise ship docks. Originally the home of the Navy base commander, Truman commandeered it for use as a vacation home during his presidency. Today it remains just as he left it, decorated in perfect late-1940s style. By the time the guides get through their well-organized hour-long tour, you'll feel as if you've gone back in time. Admission is US$11 for adults, US$5 for children.

The **Hemingway Home,** 907 Whitehead St. (© 305/294-1575; www.hemingway home.com), provides a similar if less formal look back at the island's old days. "Papa" lived here with his second wife, Pauline, completing *For Whom the Bell Tolls* and *A Farewell to Arms* in the studio annex out back. Hemingway had some 60 polydactyl (many-toed) cats, whose descendants still live on the grounds. Open daily from 9am to 5pm; admission is US$11 for adults and US$6 for children.

Audubon House & Tropical Gardens, 205 Whitehead St., at Greene Street (© 877/281-2473 or 305/294-2116; www.audubonhouse.com), is dedicated to the 1832 Key West sojourn of the famous naturalist John James Audubon. The ornithologist didn't live in this three-story building, but it's filled with his engravings. The main reason to visit is to see how wealthy sailors lived in Key West in the 19th century. And the lush tropical gardens alone are worth the admission of US$10 for adults, US$6.50 for students, and US$5 for children 6 to 12.

You can wander the grounds, look at the antique-filled rooms, and inspect the exotic treasures collected by six generations of the Porter family at the **Heritage House Museum and Robert Frost Cottage,** 410 Caroline St. (© 305/296-3573; www.heritagehousemuseum.org). Jessie Porter Newton, known as "Miss Jessie" to her friends, was once the grande dame of Key West, inviting the celebrities of her day to this house. Visitors included Tennessee Williams and her girlhood friend Gloria Swanson, as well as family friend Robert Frost, who stayed in a cottage out back.

On the waterfront at Mallory Square, the **Key West Aquarium,** 1 Whitehead St. (© 305/296-2051; www.keywestaquarium.com), in operation since 1932, was the first tourist attraction built in the Florida Keys. The aquarium's special feature is a touch tank where you can feel a horseshoe crab, sea squirt, sea urchin, starfish, and, of course, conch, the town's mascot and symbol. It's worth taking a tour, as the guides are both knowledgeable and entertaining—and you'll get to pet a shark, if that's your idea of a good time. Open daily from 10am to 6pm; admission is US$10 for adults and US$5 for children 4 to 12.

The late treasure hunter Mel Fisher used to wear heavy gold necklaces, which he liked to say were worth a king's ransom. He wasn't exaggerating. After long and risky dives, Fisher and his associates plucked more than $400 million in gold and silver from the shipwrecked Spanish galleons *Santa Margarita* and *Nuestra Señora de Atocha,* which were lost on hurricane-tossed seas some 350 years ago. Now this extraordinary Spanish treasure—jewelry, doubloons, and silver and gold bullion—is displayed at the **Mel Fisher Maritime Heritage Society Museum,** 200 Greene St. (© 305/294-2633; www.melfisher.org), near the docks. Open daily from 9:30am to 5pm. Admission is US$11 for adults, US$9.50 for students, and US$6 for children 6 to 12.

Nancy Forrester's Secret Garden, 1 Free School Lane, off Simonton between Southard and Fleming streets (© 305/294-0015; www.nfsgarden.com), is the most lavish and verdant garden in town. Some 150 species of palms and thousands of other plants, including orchids, climbing vines, and ground covers, are planted here, creating a blanket of lush, tropical magic. It's a 20-minute walk from the docks, near Key West's highest point, Solares Hill. Pick up a sandwich at a deli and then picnic at the tables in the garden. Open daily from 10am to 6pm; admission is US$6.

If your ship leaves late enough, you can take in a unique local celebration: viewing the sunset from **Mallory Dock.** Sunset-watching is good fun all over the world, but in Key West it's been turned into a carnival-like, almost pagan celebration. People from all over begin to crowd Mallory Square even before the sun starts to fall, bringing the place alive with entertainment—everything from string bands to a unicyclist wriggling free of a straitjacket to a juggler tossing around machetes and flaming sticks. The main entertainment, however, is that massive fireball falling out of view, a sight that's always greeted with hysterical applause.

ON YOUR OWN: BEYOND THE PORT AREA

Nothin'. That's the beauty of Key West: Everything worthwhile is accessible on foot.

SHOPPING

Within a 12-block radius of Old Town, you'll find mostly tawdry and outrageously overpriced merchandise, but if you're in the market for some Key West kitsch, this is the neighborhood for you. Shopping by cruise ship passengers has become a joke among Key West locals, but that's their problem. We say be proud of your flamingo snow globe and floppy straw hat. What else says "vacation" better?

Among the less kitschy alternatives, a few standouts are located much farther along **Duval Street,** the main drag leading to the Atlantic, and on hidden back streets. You can reach all these stores from the cruise ship docks via a 15- to 20-minute stroll.

Key West Aloe, Inc., 540 Greene St. (© 800/445-2563 or 305/294-5592; www. keywestaloe.com), is aloe, aloe, and more aloe; the shop's stock includes shaving cream, aftershave lotion, sunburn ointments, and fragrances for men and women based on tropical essences such as hibiscus, frangipani, and white ginger. **Key West Hand Print Fashions and Fabrics,** 201 Simonton St. (© 800/866-0333 or 305/ 292-8951; www.keywestfashions.com), sells bold, tropical prints—hand-printed scarves with coordinated handbags and rack after rack of busily patterned sundresses that will make you look jaunty on deck.

Haitian Art Company, 600 Frances St. (© 305/296-8932), claims to inventory the largest collection of Haitian paintings in the U.S. Prices range from US$15 to US$5,000. **Key West Island Bookstore,** 513 Fleming St. (© 305/294-2904), is well stocked with books on Key West and has Florida's largest collection of works by and about Hemingway. In the rear is a rare-book section where you may want to browse, if not buy.

BEACHES

Beaches are not too compelling here. Most are man-made, often with sand imported from the Bahamas or mainland Florida. Those mentioned below are free and open to the public daily from 8am to sunset. There are few facilities—just locals hawking beach umbrellas, food, and drinks.

The beach at **Fort Zachary Taylor State Park** (© 305/292-6713) is the best and the closest to the cruise ship docks, a 12-minute walk away. This 20.6-hectare (51-acre) man-made beach is adjacent to historic Fort Taylor, once known as Fort Forgotten because it was buried under tons of sand. The beach is fine for sunbathing and picnicking, and is suitable for snorkeling. To get here, go through the gates leading into Truman Annex. Watering holes near one end of the beach include the raffish **Green Parrot Bar** (© 305/294-6133) and **Meteore Smokehouse Barbecue** (© 305/ 294-5602).

A 25-minute walk from the harbor near the end of White Street, one of the main east-west arteries, leads to **Higgs Memorial Beach,** where you'll find lots of sand, picnic tables sheltered from the sun, and fewer of your fellow cruise ship passengers.

In the 1950s, **Southernmost Beach** drew Tennessee Williams, but today it's more likely to fill up with visitors from the area motels. Except for a nearby restaurant, facilities are nonexistent. The beach lies at the foot of Duval Street on the Atlantic side, across the island from the cruise ship docks. It's about a 20-minute walk along Duval Street. The beach boasts some white sand but is not particularly good for swimming. Nevertheless, it's one of the island's most frequented.

Smathers Beach, named in honor of one of Florida's most colorful former senators, is the longest (about 2.4km/1½ miles) in town. Unfortunately, it's about a US$10 one-way taxi ride from the cruise docks. The beach borders South Roosevelt Boulevard. *Note:* There's no shade here.

SPORTS

FISHING As Hemingway, an avid fisherman, would attest, the waters off the Florida Keys are some of the world's finest fishing grounds. You can follow in his wake aboard the 40-foot *Linda D IV* and *Linda D V* (© 800/299-9798 or 305/296-9798; www.charterboatlindad.com), which offer the best deep-sea fishing here. Full-day charters for up to six people are US$875; half-day charters are US$575. Full-day shared charters go for US$195 per person. Make arrangements as far in advance as possible.

GOLF Redesigned in 1982 by architect Rees Jones, the 18-hole, par-70 **Key West Resort Golf Club,** 6450 E. Junior College Rd. (© **305/294-5232;** www.keywestgolf. com), lies 4km (2½ miles) from the cruise docks, near the southern tip of neighboring Stock Island. It features a challenging terrain of coral rock, sand traps, mangrove swamp, and pines. Greens fees are US$160, including cart. The course is a 10- to 15-minute, US$10 taxi ride from the dock one-way.

SCUBA DIVING The largest dive outfitter is **Captain's Corner,** 125 Ann St. (© **305/296-8865;** www.captainscorner.com), located half a block from the cruise docks. The five-star PADI operation has 11 instructors, a well-trained staff, and a 60-foot dive boat that was used by Timothy "James Bond" Dalton during the filming of *License to Kill.* To reach the departure point, walk to the end of Greene Street.

GREAT LOCAL RESTAURANTS & BARS

RESTAURANTS All of the restaurants listed below are within an easy 5- to 15-minute walk of the docks, except for Camille's and El Siboney, which are more than a mile away. Several raw bars near the dock area offer seafood, including oysters and clams, although the king here is conch—served grilled, ground into burgers, made into chowder, fried in batter as fritters, or simply raw in a conch salad. Even if you don't have lunch, at least sample the local favorites: a slice of Key lime pie with a Cuban coffee. The pie's unique flavor comes from the juice and minced rind of the piquant Key lime.

Cruise ship passengers on a return visit to Key West often ask for the Rose Tattoo, a historic old restaurant named for the Tennessee Williams film partially shot on the island. The restaurant, one of Key West's finest, is now the **Bagatelle,** 115 Duval St., at Front Street (© **305/296-6609**). Look for daily specials or stick to the chef's better dishes, such as conch seviche (thinly sliced raw conch marinated in lime juice and herbs). Lunch is about US$13.

Blue Heaven, 729 Thomas St. (© **305/296-8666**), is a dive that serves some of the best food in town, including fresh local fish, most often grouper or red snapper. Its hot and spicy jerk chicken is as fine as that served in Jamaica. Lunch is about US$12.

Key West's original raw bar is the **Half Shell Raw Bar,** Land's End Marina, at the foot of Margaret Street (© **305/294-7496**), offering fresh fish, oysters, and shrimp direct from its own fish market. Lunch is about US$15. To be honest, though, we prefer **Turtle Kraals Wildlife Bar & Grill,** Land's End Village, at the foot of Margaret Street (© **305/294-2640**). Try the tender Florida lobster, spicy conch chowder, or perfectly cooked fresh fish (often dolphin fish with pineapple salsa or baked stuffed grouper with mango-crabmeat stuffing). Lunch is around US$14.

Pepe's Cafe, 806 Caroline St., between William and Margaret streets (© **305/294-7192**), is the oldest eating house in the Florida Keys, established in 1909. Diners sit under slow-moving paddle fans at tables or dark pine booths with high backs. Choose from zesty homemade chili, perfectly baked oysters, fish sandwiches, and Pepe's deservedly famous steak sandwiches. Lunch (served noon–4pm) is about US$15.

Camille's, 1202 Simonton St., at Catherine Street (© **305/296-4811**), is a hip, unpretentious cafe that serves the best breakfast in town and offers the best lunch value. Try a sandwich made from the catch of the day and served on fresh bread; then finish off with some of the great Key lime pie. Lunch is about US$10.

El Siboney, 900 Catherine St. (© **305/296-4184**), is the place for time-tested Cuban favorites such as *ropa vieja* (shredded meat stew), roast pork with garlic and tart sour oranges, and paella Valenciana. Lunch is around US$12.

If something cool would go down better than a full meal, stop for ice cream at **Flamingo Crossing,** 1105 Duval St., at Virginia Street (© **305/296-6124**).

BARS   Key West is a bar town, and since many ships stay in town late, you'll likely have an opportunity to do some carousing. Most places recommended below offer fast food to go with their drinks. The food isn't the best on the island, but it usually arrives shortly after you order it, which suits most rushed cruise ship passengers just fine. Try some of the favorite local beer, **Hog's Breath,** or the favorite local rum, **Key West Gold** (even though it's a cheat—it isn't actually made on the island).

Heavily patronized by cruise ship passengers, **Captain Tony's Saloon,** 428 Greene St. (© **305/294-1838**), is the oldest active bar in Florida and is tacky as can be. The 1851 building was the original Sloppy Joe's, a rough-and-tumble fisherman's saloon. Hemingway drank here from 1933 to 1937, and Jimmy Buffett got his start here before opening his own bar and going on to musical glory. The name refers to Capt. Tony Tarracino, a former Key West mayor and rugged man of the sea who owned the place until 1988.

The current **Sloppy Joe's,** 201 Duval St. (© **305/294-5717**), is the most touristy bar in Key West, visited by almost all cruise ship passengers, even those who don't normally go to bars. It aggressively plays up its association with Hemingway, although the bar stood on Greene Street back then (see above). Marine flags decorate the ceiling, and the ambience and decor evoke a Havana bar from the 1930s.

Jimmy Buffett's Margaritaville, 500 Duval St. (© **305/296-3070**), is the third most popular Key West bar with cruise ship passengers. Buffett is the hometown boy done good, and his cafe, naturally, is decorated with pictures of himself. And, yes, it sells T-shirts and Margaritaville memorabilia in a shop off the dining room. His margaritas are without competition, but then they'd have to be, wouldn't they?

Open-air, very laid-back, and sometimes very loud, the **Hog's Breath Saloon,** 400 Front St. (© **305/296-HOGG**), near the cruise docks, has been a Key West tradition since 1976. Drinking is a sport here, especially among the fishermen who come in after a day chasing the big one, as well as the biker types who show up anytime. Live entertainment is offered from 1pm to 2am.

For a real local hangout within an easy walk of the cruise docks, head to **Schooner Wharf,** 202 William St., Key West Bight (© **305/292-9520**), the most robust and hardest-drinking bar in Key West. It draws a primarily young crowd, many of whom work in the tourist industry or on the local fishing boats.

21 Les Saintes

You want charming? The eight islets of Les Saintes (pronounced "Lay *Sant*") are irresistibly so: pastel-colored gingerbread houses with tropical gardens, sugarloaf hills that slope down to miniature beaches, and picturesque bays with pelicans, sailboats, and turquoise water. Only two of the islands in this French archipelago off the southern coast of Guadeloupe are inhabited: **Terre-de-Bas** and its more populous neighbor, **Terre-de-Haut** (more populous, in this case, meaning it has about 1,700 inhabitants). Terre-de-Haut (pronounced "T'air *d'Oh*"), with only one village—the straightforwardly named Le Bourg ("the town")—is the destination of most visitors. Some say it's what Saint-Tropez was like before Brigitte Bardot. For a U.S. point of reference, think Fire Island, Provincetown, Martha's Vineyard, or Sausalito with a French-Caribbean twist. *Nautical* and *quaint* are the watchwords.

But Les Saintes, also known as Iles des Saintes, isn't a fantasy park built to look enchanting. Although tourism is important to the island's economy, most people here still make their living from the sea. Les Saintois, as the locals are called, are widely regarded as the best fishermen in the Antilles, and it's this underlying saltiness that keeps the place from being cloyingly sweet.

COMING ASHORE   Cruise ships dock at **Le Bourg,** in Terre-de-Haut. The village has two main streets, both parallel to the bay and lined with cafes, restaurants, and souvenir shops. Telephones at the dock require a *telecarte,* a prepaid phone card sold at the post office (a 10-min. walk from the dock; take a right) and other outlets marked TELECARTE EN VENTE ICI. Some phones now accept U.S. calling cards or major credit cards for long-distance calls.

LANGUAGE   The official language is French, but many islanders speak Creole with one another. Few locals feel comfortable with English, though, so take the opportunity

---

Fun Fact   Tormented by Love? Have a Pastry

As you leave your ship, you'll spot local women selling Les Saintes' signature sweet, tartlets known as *tourments d'amour* ("love's torments"). Legend has it that young maidens baked these flaky-crusted, coconut-filled treats to present to their betrotheds as they returned from lengthy fishing expeditions. From time to time, the cruel and heartless sea claimed the life of a beloved, leaving a teary-eyed damsel at the dock with nothing but her pain and pastry. Is it the suffering that makes the *tourments d'amour* so tasty?

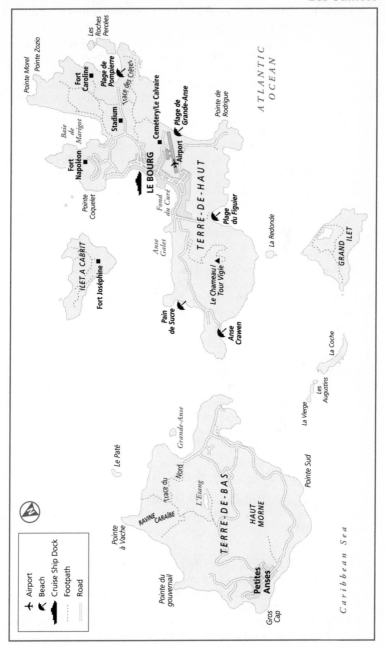

to practice your high-school French. Most everyone is helpful and friendly, especially if you smile and make an effort.

CURRENCY Les Saintes is part of the larger archipelago of Guadeloupe, an overseas region of France, so the **euro** (€) is now the official currency (exchange rate at press time: .82€ = US$1; 1€ = US$1.22). Each euro is divisible by 100 cents. You can withdraw euros from the ATM next to the tourism office (see "Information," below). Unless otherwise specified, prices in this section are given in U.S. dollars.

INFORMATION If you take a right on the main road after you leave the ship, you'll see signs for the **tourism office** (OFFICE DU TOURISME). It's less than a 5-minute walk. Most printed information available here is in French, but the maps are helpful even if you don't understand the lingo. For info before you go, call the **French Government Tourist Office** at ✆ 212/838-7800 or go to www.franceguide.com.

CALLING FROM THE U.S. When calling Les Saintes from the U.S., dial the international access code (011) and 590 before the numbers listed here. Yes, the numbers listed here already begin with 590, but an effort by the French telephone authorities to standardize procedures requires that you dial those three digits twice. Really.

GETTING AROUND

If you're reasonably fit, there's no reason you can't walk wherever you want to go. If you're the type who runs 8km (5 miles) a day, you can hike up Le Chameau, traipse around Fort Napoléon, head over to Plage de Pompierre, and complete the Trace des Crêtes, with time for a meal or swim before returning to the ship.

BY TAXI The island has a handful of minivans that serve as taxis. Each seats six to eight passengers, and most drivers offer 3-hour tours of the island for about US$40 (be aware, though, that fluent English is not widely spoken). You'll find the cabs parked directly in front of the cruise ship dock.

BY SCOOTER Terre-de-Haut is less than 6.4km (4 miles long) and 3.2km (2 miles) wide. Aside from tourist vans and the occasional private car, four-wheeled vehicles are rare (at last count, there were fewer than three dozen). Scooters rule the roads. Scores of them await you just off the dock along Le Bourg's main road. Expect to pay about US$31 for a two-seater for the day. A US$380 deposit (credit cards accepted) is required.

BY BICYCLE You can rent bicycles for between US$15 and US$20 along Le Bourg's main road. The island is hilly, though. You'd do better to rent a scooter or walk.

BEST CRUISE LINE SHORE EXCURSIONS

Don't expect any. This is a wander-around-at-your-own-pace kind of place. See "Sports," below, for scuba, snorkeling, and fishing excursions you can arrange through local agencies.

ON YOUR OWN: WITHIN WALKING DISTANCE

Everything is within walking distance of the dock. On the route to the tourism office and the ATM, you'll pass Le Bourg's **stone church.** It's humble, but worth the couple of minutes it takes to peek inside.

Fort Napoléon looms over Le Bourg's picturesque bay. The French started building this stone bastion after they regained Les Saintes from the British in 1815, but didn't complete it until 1867. Today, it houses engaging, detailed exhibits that cover the entire history of the islands, including life before Columbus, European expansion into the New World, early French settlements, the Battle of Les Saintes, and the development

Frommer's Favorite Les Saintes Experiences

Meandering around Fort Napoléon: The French built this impressive stone fortification after they regained Les Saintes in 1815, and today it houses interesting, informative exhibits covering the entire history of the islands. (See "On Your Own: Within Walking Distance," below.)

Trekking to the Top of Le Chameau: The highest point on Terre-de-Haut, Le Chameau is located in the southern part of the island and offers a tough (though shaded) 30- to 60-minute climb, for which you're rewarded with spectacular views. (See "On Your Own: Within Walking Distance," below.)

Climbing along the Trace des Crêtes: This trail across the center of Terre-de-Haut offers remarkable views of beaches, cliffs, the island's toylike airport, and neighboring islands. (See "On Your Own: Within Walking Distance," below.)

of the fishing industry. You can wander through barracks, dungeons, and the grounds, which feature an impressive array of cacti and succulents. Pick up the English-language brochure that describes the vegetation when you purchase your ticket; admission is about US$2.80 for adults and US$1.40 for children under 12. You can also rent a cassette that provides excellent English commentary as you walk through the museum. The fort is open a brief 3½ hours a day, from 9am to 12:30pm, so make it your first destination.

On the hill that leads to Fort Napoléon, visit **Jerome Hoff,** a fourth-generation Santois of Alsatian ancestry who paints religious icons in a heartfelt but slightly disturbing style. He has the wild-eyed air of a John the Baptist, but he's a gentle man, retired now, who loves to talk about his 50 years of singing in the church choir. You can't miss his modest home and studio—they're surrounded by numerous quirky signs that feature colorful saints and passionate prayers.

If you're up for some hiking, the **Trace des Crêtes trail** traces the spine of one of Terre-de-Haut's hills just north of the airport and offers remarkable views of beaches, cliffs, and neighboring islands. Although clearly marked, the path is rocky and challenging—you have an advantage if you're part goat. Wear sunscreen and bring water.

Be sure to stop for a few minutes at the **cemetery** next to the airport. You'll notice several graves adorned with conch shells, which signify a sea-related death. On Saturday nights, refrigerator-size speakers are brought in, makeshift food stands are set up, and the cemetery becomes a huge open-air disco. In the same vicinity is **Le Calvaire,** a giant Christ statue at the summit of a hill; numerous steps ascend to great panoramas.

Chameau means "camel" in French, and with a bit of imagination, you can see that **Le Chameau,** the highest point on Terre-de-Haut, looks sort of like the hump of a dromedary. The concrete road to the 300m (984-ft.) summit is off-limits to all motorized vehicles; mercifully, it's shaded much of the way. After 30 to 60 minutes of arduous climbing, you're rewarded with spectacular views of the entire archipelago, Guadeloupe, and Dominica. **Tour Vigie,** a military lookout dating from the time of Napoléon, crowns the mountain; unfortunately, it's usually locked.

SHOPPING

Little boutiques that sell beachwear, T-shirts, jewelry, and knickknacks line the streets. Be sure to stop by Pascal Foy's **Kaz an Nou Gallery,** behind the church. You can watch him make Cases Creoles, miniature carved wooden Creole houses in candy colors. They're becoming collectors' items. **Galerie Martine Cotten,** at the foot of the dock, features the work of an artist originally from Brittany who celebrates the natural beauty and fishing traditions of Les Saintes. Beyond the town hall, **Ultramarine** is a tiny cottage where you can buy unusual dolls, clothes, T-shirts, and handcrafted items from France, Haiti, and Africa. **Galerie Marchande Seaside,** a group of shops situated around a patio, is just up the street after you turn right from the pier. Art, gifts, antiques, jewelry, lace, beachwear, and ice cream are all available.

BEACHES

Beaches with golden sand are tucked away in almost all of the island's coves. Calm, crescent-shaped **Plage de Pompierre** (sometimes spelled Pont Pierre) is shaded by sea-grape bushes, as well as almond and palm trees. A 15-minute walk from the dock, it boasts soft white sand, shade from coconut palms, and quiet seclusion. The gentle water in the cliff-encircled cove is a stunning aquamarine. Because the bay is a nature preserve, fishing and anchoring are prohibited. It's the island's most popular sunbathing spot, so your best bet is to go early or late.

Grande Anse, near the airfield, is large, but there's no shade, and the rough surf has a strong undertow. Although swimming is discouraged, the cliffs at either end of the beach and the powerful breakers make for a dramatic seascape. The usually deserted **Figuier,** on the southern coast, has excellent snorkeling.

SPORTS

FISHING   Going out to sea with a local fisherman is one way to experience the nautical heritage of Les Saintes. Most of the local sailors will be delighted to take you out, if you can communicate well enough to negotiate a price. Most fishermen are stationed next to the cruise ship dock; just follow the waterfront to the fishing boats.

SCUBA, SNORKELING & OTHER WATERSPORTS   For scuba diving and snorkeling, go to **La Dive Bouteille Centre Nautique des Saintes** (© 590/99-54-25; www.dive-bouteille.com), at the Plage de la Colline, west of town past the market. One-tank dives run about US$65. You can also rent sea kayaks and windsurfing equipment here.

GREAT LOCAL RESTAURANTS & BARS

Virtually every restaurant in Terre-de-Haut offers seafood that couldn't be fresher, and many feature Creole dishes. A local favorite is *thazard fumé* (smoked kingfish).

L'Auberge les Petits Saints aux Anacardiers, on route de Rodrigue (© 590/99-50-99; www.petitssaints.com), is a hillside veranda restaurant overlooking the bay. It boasts a tropical garden and countless antiques. Lunch is US$38. Reservations are mandatory.

The terrace restaurant at the **Hôtel Bois Joli** (© 590/99-50-38), on the island's western tip, offers a view of Pain de Sucre, Les Saintes' petite version of Rio de Janeiro's Sugarloaf Mountain, and is fringed with palm trees.

For pasta, pizza, or salad, try the seaside terrace at **La Saladerie,** on the way to Fort Napoléon. Another option is **Café de la Marine,** on the bay and main street (© 590/99-53-78), which serves thin-crust pizzas and seafood. Lunch here is US$25.

The Goats of Love

Don't leave anything unattended while swimming at Plage de Pompierre. Savvy goats hide out in the scrub behind the beach, patiently scoping out the action. Once you go into the water, they'll make a beeline for your unattended picnic basket and treat themselves to anything edible. They're especially fond of those *tourments d'amour* you just bought at the dock. Who's crying now?

One of the island's best *boulangeries* (bakeries) is **Le Fournil de Jimmy** (*©* 590/99-57-73), on the same square as the town hall, across from the tourism office. If you stop in at the right time, you can get a crusty baguette hot from the oven. Or if you'd rather have something cold, try one of the Italian gelati at **Tropico Gelato** (*©* 590/99-88-12). Turn right off the dock; it's a couple of storefronts down on your right.

22 Martinique

Fairy-tale romance and horrific disaster: Who could resist such an enticing combination? As if being the birthplace and childhood home of Empress Joséphine, sweetheart and wife of Napoléon, weren't enough, Martinique mesmerizes with the epic tragedy that befell St-Pierre one fair day in 1902: bustling cosmopolitan capital one minute, devastated volcanic graveyard of 30,000 souls the next. Love and death make quite a one-two punch, but they're just the hook. Look a bit deeper to appreciate Martinique's subtler attractions—quaint seaside villages, colonial ruins, and captivatingly beautiful rainforests and beaches.

Madiana, or "island of flowers," was the Carib name for the island, and hibiscus, bougainvillea, and bird of paradise grow in lush profusion alongside mango, pineapple, banana, and papaya. Like Guadeloupe and St. Barts, Martinique is as French as Bordeaux, and you'll find everything from baguettes to Balenciaga here. But with African and New World roots forever entwined, Creole cuisine and traditions continue to flourish.

About 81km (50 miles) long and 35km (22 miles) wide, the island features a diverse topography. Rainforests drape the volcanic mountains of the north; small, rounded hills and enclosed valleys mark the central plain; and white-sand beaches ring the arid, flat south.

During the 18th and 19th centuries, France and England vied for the island. In 1946, Martinique became an overseas department of France, and in 1974, it achieved regional status—the French minister of the interior appoints a prefect, but the island's citizens elect representatives to the national legislature in Paris and the regional legislature in Fort-de-France.

Most of Martinique's 380,000 residents are descendants of African slaves, but others of European, Asian, and Middle Eastern ancestry add to the melting pot. Attesting to the generally amicable relations among the various peoples, every shade of skin color is represented.

COMING ASHORE   Most cruise ships dock in the heart of Fort-de-France, at the **Pointe Simon Cruise Dock,** which has quays for two large vessels. Because Martinique is a popular port of call, ships also dock at the **Passenger Terminal** at the main harbor, a cargo port on the north side of the bay, a US$10 cab ride from the center of town.

If you want to check your e-mail, go to **Cyber Club Caraibes,** 16 rue François Arago, Fort-de-France (✆ **596/71-43-21**). It's open Monday and Saturday from 8am to 8pm, Tuesday through Friday from 8am to 10pm. Internet access costs US$3 for 15 minutes—cheaper than aboard ship.

LANGUAGE   French is Martinique's official language, but you can get by with English at most restaurants and tourist attractions. You'll also hear the island patois, Creole, on the street. Because many of the island's service employees work hard to improve their English, cruisers who speak no French find Martinique easier to navigate than Guadeloupe, the other big French Caribbean island. Ask for English-language brochures and commentaries when sightseeing; most sites have them.

CURRENCY   Martinique is an overseas region of France, so the **euro** (€) is now the official currency (exchange rate at press time: .82€ = US$1; 1€ = US$1.22). Each euro is divisible by 100 cents. Unless otherwise specified, prices in this section are given in U.S. dollars.

There are numerous *distributeur de billets* (ATMs) in downtown Fort-de-France, and you'll have no trouble using your credit cards and traveler's checks as well. You can change money on the waterfront at **Change Caraïbe,** 4 rue Ernest Deproge (✆ **596/ 60-28-40**), or a block inland at **Change Point Change,** 14 rue Victor Hugo (✆ **596/ 63-80-33**).

INFORMATION   The **tourism office** (✆ 596/60-27-73) opens an office at the pier in Fort-de-France when ships come in. For info before you go, contact the **Martinique Promotion Bureau** (✆ 212/838-7800; www.martinique.org).

CALLING FROM THE U.S.   When calling Martinique from the U.S., dial the international access code (011) and 596 before the numbers listed here. The numbers listed here already begin with 596, but an effort by the French telephone authorities to standardize procedures requires that you dial those three digits twice.

GETTING AROUND

BY TAXI   Travel by taxi is convenient but expensive. Most cabs are metered, but they do offer flat rates for touring the island. Taxis wait for ships at the cruise pier, and several English-speaking drivers give tours of the island for roughly US$50 an hour for up to four passengers. For a radio taxi, call ✆ **596/63-63-62.**

BY BUS   For trips beyond Fort-de-France, collective taxi-minibuses are a cheap but iffy alternative. These privately owned minivans (look for the TC sign) generally seat eight and have flexible routes and unpredictable schedules. Often crowded and sometimes less than comfortable, they're widely used by adventurous tourists nonetheless, particularly those who speak some French. The reason? Price: A one-way ride to Grande Anse des Salines beach is about US$5. Vans leave from a parking lot at Pointe Simon, in the heart of Fort-de-France.

BY FERRY   To reach La Pagerie (Empress Joséphine's birthplace), the island's golf course, horseback-riding stables, and the resort area of Pointe du Bout, take one of the orange ferries operated by **Pyétrolettes du Soleil** or the white or blue ferries run by **Madinina Vedettes** from Quai d'Esnambuc, east of the cruise dock, in Fort-de-France. The ferry trip takes 15 minutes. Once you reach the other side of the bay, you will need to take a 3.2km (2-mile) taxi ride to Pointe du Bout. Round-trip ferry tickets are about US$6 per person; boats leave at least once an hour.

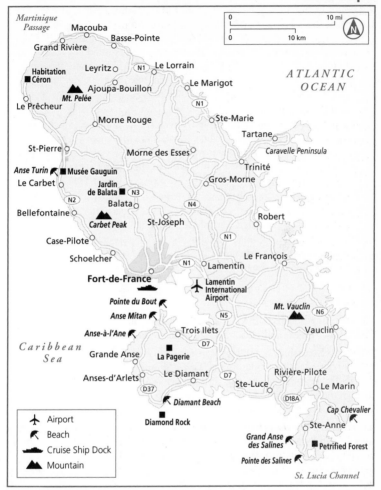

Martinique Passage

Macouba
Basse-Pointe
Grand Rivière
Habitation Céron
Leyritz
N1
Le Lorrain
Le Marigot
Ajoupa-Bouillon
Mt. Pelée
Le Prêcheur
N1
Morne Rouge
Ste-Marie
Tartane
St-Pierre
Morne des Esses
Caravelle Peninsula
Anse Turin
Musée Gauguin
Trinité
Le Carbet
Jardin de Balata
N3
Gros-Morne
N2
Balata
N4
Bellefontaine
Carbet Peak
St-Joseph
Robert
Case-Pilote
N1
Schoelcher
Le François
N1
Lamentin
Fort-de-France
Lamentin International Airport
Pointe du Bout
Anse Mitan
Mt. Vauclin
N6
Anse-à-l'Ane
Trois Ilets
N5
Vauclin
Caribbean Sea
D7
Grande Anse
La Pagerie
Anses-d'Arlets
Le Diamant
D7
Rivière-Pilote
Ste-Luce
Le Marin
D37
Diamant Beach
D18A
Diamond Rock
Cap Chevalier
Ste-Anne
Grand Anse des Salines
Petrified Forest
Pointe des Salines
St. Lucia Channel

ATLANTIC OCEAN

✈ Airport
🅚 Beach
⛴ Cruise Ship Dock
▲ Mountain

0 ——— 10 mi
0 ——— 10 km

BY RENTAL CAR Martinique's size and myriad attractions make renting a car especially worthwhile. You'll drive on the right on roads that are in excellent condition and almost always scenic. Renters need a valid driver's license and must be at least 21. **Avis, Budget,** and **Hertz** all have offices here.

BEST CRUISE LINE SHORE EXCURSIONS

Rainforest & Plantations 4WD Safari (US$99 4½ hr.): Take your off-road vehicle through tropical forests and sugar cane plantations (stopping to sample the crop) to a banana plantation and a distillery, where you'll do short tours.

Martinique Snorkeling (US$59, 3 hr.): Across the bay from Fort-de-France, the reef at Anse Dufour offers excellent snorkeling for experts and novices. It's filled with marine animals, including French grunts, blackbar soldierfish, and silversides. Snorkeling equipment is provided, as are professional instruction, supervision, and transportation.

Frommer's Favorite Martinique Experiences

Touring the "Pompeii of the Caribbean": Mt. Pelée erupted in 1902, killing all but one of St-Pierre's 30,000 residents. See the havoc this not-yet-dormant volcano wreaked on the town's church, theater, and other buildings, and view smaller relics at the volcano museum. (See "On Your Own: Beyond the Port Area," below.)

Traveling Back to the 17th Century: The estate ruins at Habitation Céron, near the island's northern Caribbean coast, are enormously evocative of early colonial times, when sugar was king. The old stone plantation buildings are covered with moss, and the wild gardens abound with lush vegetation and singing birds. (See "On Your Own: Beyond the Port Area," below.)

Eavesdropping on Imperial Romance: Empress Joséphine, the first wife of Napoléon Bonaparte, was born and reared at La Pagerie, her family's estate near the town of Trois Ilets. Part of the sugar plantation still stands, and the museum displays personal effects of the Martinican empress, including a passionate love letter from the Little Corporal to his Petite Creole. (See "On Your Own: Beyond the Port Area," below.)

EXCURSIONS OFFERED BY LOCAL AGENCIES

See "Sports," later in this section, for scuba diving and snorkeling.

Adventure Excursions & Hiking: Martinique's lush, mountainous northern half provides myriad adventure opportunities. **Cama Shipping** (© 596/71-31-00), based in Fort-de-France, offers many tours, including a 4-hour jeep adventure that takes you through the heart of Martinique, into the green forest, around the volcano Mt. Pelée, through banana plantations, and to a rum distillery. It costs US$61 per person.

Horseback Treks: Pros and novices are both accommodated on morning horseback rides offered by **Ranch Jack,** in Morne Habitué (© 596/68-37-69) and Trois Ilets (© 596/68-37-80). The daily promenades pass over hills, through fields, and onto beaches, as guides provide a running commentary on the history, fauna, and botany of the island. Transportation to and from the cruise dock can be arranged. The price of a half-day excursion with refreshments is about US$68.

ON YOUR OWN: WITHIN WALKING DISTANCE

Fort-de-France is a bustling, cosmopolitan town with 100,000 residents and an unmistakable French air. Part New Orleans, part French Riviera, it's full of ochre buildings, ornate wrought-iron balconies, cascading flowers, and tall palm trees. The town's narrow streets, cluttered with boutiques and cafes, climb from the bowl of the sea to the surrounding hills, forming a great urban amphitheater. There's plenty here to keep you busy.

At the eastern end of downtown, **La Savane** is a broad formal park with palms, mangoes, and manicured lawns, perfect for a promenade or a rest in the shade. Its most famous feature is the **Statue of Empress Joséphine,** carved in 1858 by Vital Dubray. Like a variation on the Venus de Milo, this white-marble empress is headless: Napoléon's Little Creole was unceremoniously decapitated and doused with red paint in 1995 by locals who remembered her role in reinstating slavery on the island in the early 1800s.

Across the street, the **Bibliothèque Schoelcher (Schoelcher Library),** 21 rue de la Liberté (© **596/70-26-67**), is one of Fort-de-France's great Belle Epoque buildings. Named in honor of Victor Schoelcher, one of France's most influential abolitionists, this elaborate structure, designed by French architect Henri Pick, was first displayed at the 1889 Paris Exposition. Four years later, the red-and-blue Romanesque portal, Egyptian lotus-petal columns, iron-and-glass cupola, and multicolored tiles were dismantled and then reassembled piece by piece at the present site. The interior light, mosaics, and tile floor are glorious. The proud repository of Schoelcher's 10,000-volume book collection, as well as an impressive archive of colonization, slavery, and emancipation documents, it's open Monday through Saturday and charges no admission.

Another Henri Pick masterpiece, **St-Louis Cathedral,** on rue Victor Schoelcher at rue Blénac, was built in 1895. A contemporary of Gustave Eiffel (of Eiffel Tower fame), Pick used massive iron beams to support the walls, ceiling, and spire. A grand example of Industrial Revolution architecture, it's been likened to a Catholic railway station. The organ, stained-glass windows, and ornamented interior walls are well worth a look and can be viewed every morning except Saturday.

Built in 1640, **Fort St-Louis,** Boulevard Alfassa, dominates the rocky promontory east of La Savane. A noteworthy example of 17th- and 18th-century military architecture, it first defended Fort-de-France in 1674 against Dutch invaders; beginning in 1762, it was the site of numerous battles between French and English forces. Today, the bastion remains the French navy's headquarters in the Caribbean. Guided tours leave daily every 30 minutes beginning at 9:30am. Bring a picture ID. The entrance fee, payable in dollars, is US$5 for adults and US$2.50 for students.

The best of Fort-de-France's many museums, the **Musée Départemental Archéologie Precolombienne Préhistoire,** 9 rue de la Liberté (© **596/71-57-05**), traces 2,000 years of Martinique's pre-Columbian past with more than a thousand relics from the Arawak and Carib cultures. Spread over three floors, the detailed exhibits document various pottery and tool styles, burial practices, agricultural methods, social and religious customs, and changes that occurred after the arrival of Europeans. Across the street from La Savane, it's open Monday from 1 to 5pm, Tuesday through Friday from 8am to 5pm, and Saturday from 9am to noon. Admission is about US$4 for adults, US$3 for students, and US$2 for children. The tiny gift stand sells pottery reproductions.

The **Musée Régional d'Histoire et d'Ethnographie**, 10 bd. du Général de Gaulle (© **596 72 81 87**), is housed in one of Fort-de-France's best-preserved examples of colonial architecture. The museum's permanent exhibition re-creates the interior of a bourgeois villa at the turn of the 20th century; various temporary photography exhibits depict life in Martinique over the last 150 years.

ON YOUR OWN: BEYOND THE PORT AREA

Martinique is much too large to tackle in a single day. You'll have to make some tough choices about which of its many museums, plantations, floral parks, and natural wonders to visit. Below are two suggested itineraries for the day.

NORTH OF FORT-DE-FRANCE   Less than 8km (5 miles) north of Fort-de-France, on the scenic Route de la Trace (N3), **L'Eglise Sacré Coeur de Balata** overlooks the capital and its bay. This quiet village church is anything but typical: Built in 1924, it's a one-fifth-scale replica of the wedding-cake-pretty Sacré Coeur Basilica that crowns Montmartre in Paris. Rather than the white stone of the Paris original, this unintentionally whimsical copy uses gray freestone.

Martinique's Carib name, Madiana, means "island of flowers." To see what the Caribs were talking about, stroll through the **Jardin de Balata** (© 596/64-48-73). Just minutes north of the Sacré Coeur church, this lush, Edenic garden showcases 200 species of plants, trees, and tropical flowers, including towering ferns, lotuses, alpinias, porcelain roses, anthuriums, and heliconias. The hillside oasis, which boasts resident hummingbirds, frogs, and lizards, is open daily from 9am to 5pm. Admission is about US$6 for adults, US$2.50 for kids under 12.

Yes, it's hot outside, but things could be worse. One of Martinique's must-see attractions, the village of **St-Pierre,** on the northwest coast, was the cultural and economic capital of Martinique until 8am on May 8, 1902, when Mt. Pelée, the hulking volcano that dominates the northern tip of the island, exploded in fire and lava. Three minutes later, all but one of St-Pierre's 30,000 inhabitants had been incinerated, buried in ash and lava, or asphyxiated by poisonous gas. The town once hailed as the "Paris of the Antilles" and the "Pearl of the West Indies" because of its beautiful buildings, imposing residences, and lively theaters suddenly became the "Pompeii of the Caribbean." It never regained its splendor, and today, it's no more than a sleepy fishing village, home to fewer than 5,000 souls. Ruins of a church, theater, and other buildings punctuate the town, memorials to St-Pierre's former glory and the horrific fury of Pelée. In lieu of walking from one ruin to another, you can hop on the rubber-wheeled trolley known as the Cyparis Express, which departs from the Musée Volcanologique (see below). The 1-hour tours operate Monday through Friday; half-hour tours run on the weekends. The fee is about US$8 for adults and US$4 for kids. (The trolley is named in honor of Cyparis, a prisoner locked behind thick cell walls, who was the sole human to survive the eruption. Found in his dungeon 4 days after the disaster, he later toured with P. T. Barnum's circus, showing his burn scars to curious folks around North America.)

The town's touristic potential hasn't been grotesquely exploited: Aside from the ruins, the only other point of interest is the **Musée Volcanologique,** rue Victor Hugo (© 596/78-15-16). Founded by American vulcanologist Franck A. Perret, this one-room exhibit traces the story of the cataclysm through pictures and relics excavated from the debris, including petrified spaghetti, lava-encrusted teapots, twisted musical instruments, a human skull, and distorted clocks that stopped at the hour of destruction. Open daily from 9am to 5pm; admission is about US$1.50 for adults and free for children under 8.

Part sugar-plantation ruins, part tropical paradise, **Habitation Céron** (© 596/52-94-53) is the most evocative of Martinique's historic agricultural sites. This sprawling 17th-century estate, 15 minutes north of St-Pierre, is almost as wild and tranquil as the surrounding rainforest, but its verdigris cisterns, moss-covered stone buildings, and archaic, still-functioning water mill are all haunted with the ghosts of a time when sugar was king, slaves toiled in the heat, and French colonists lived in languid comfort. The site is open daily from 9:30am to 5pm. Self-guided tours of the estate cost US$7.50. The on-site restaurant, housed in former slave quarters, serves crayfish, octopus, and other seafood.

A few miles south of St-Pierre, **Le Carbet** is where Columbus landed in 1502, the first French settlers arrived in 1635, and the French painter Paul Gauguin lived for 5 months in 1887. Too ill to return to France after a failed quest for "noble savages" in Panama, the artist wrote that "only in Martinique was I able to feel truly myself." An unassuming museum devoted to Gauguin and his Martinican works, the **Musée Paul Gauguin,** Anse Turin (② **596/78-22-66**), sits not far from the hut the painter once occupied. It boasts no original paintings, but it does have reproductions of the dozen pictures he composed on the island—precursors of his later, more famous Tahitian works. Also on display are biographical texts and whiny, self-pitying letters he wrote to his wife back in France. Other exhibits include Creole costumes and contemporary island art. The museum has extensive English commentary and is open daily from 9am to 5:30pm. Admission is about US$5 for adults, US$1 for children, and free for kids under 8.

SOUTH OF FORT-DE-FRANCE   Marie Josèphe Rose Tascher de la Pagerie was born in 1763 in the quaint little village of Trois Ilets, across the bay from Fort-de-France. As Joséphine, she became the wife of Napoléon Bonaparte in 1796 and Empress of France in 1804. Although reviled by some historians as ruthless and selfish, she's revered by some on Martinique as having been uncommonly gracious. Others, however, blame her for Napoléon's reintroduction of slavery. A small museum, the **Musée de la Pagerie** (② **596/68-33-06**), sits in the former estate kitchen building, where Joséphine gossiped with her slaves. Displays include the bed that she slept in until she departed for France at age 16, portraits of her and of Napoléon, invitations to Parisian balls, bills attesting to her extravagance as the empress, and letters, the most notable being a passionate missive from lovelorn Napoléon. The plantation house itself was destroyed in a hurricane, but the kitchen and partially restored ruins of the sugar mill and church remain (the latter is in the village itself). The museum is open Tuesday through Sunday from 9am to 3pm; an English-speaking guide is usually on hand. Admission is about US$6 for adults, US$2.50 for children under 16.

Diamond Rock, a craggy, multifaceted protrusion in the bay south of Trois Ilets, not only resembles a diamond, but was also once the jewel in the crown of the British Caribbean fleet. The British and French fought on so many fronts during the early 19th century that ships were sometimes in short supply. Only one ship was assigned to blockade the ports of Martinique, St-Pierre in the north and Fort-de-France in the south. Short of ships but not imagination, the British proclaimed Diamond Rock a man-of-war and proceeded to equip the islet with guns. No temporary gesture, it remained in service for 2 years. Birds have replaced Brits as the primary residents. On a misty day, the rock looks more like the Loch Ness Monster emerging from the depths than a diamond.

You'll have passed through a number of quaint coastal villages by this time, but none sweeter than **Ste-Luce.** Absurdly picturesque with its blindingly white stucco walls, red-tile roofs, turquoise sea, and multicolored fishing boats, this town is pure sun-drenched maritime serenity. Swim or snorkel off the small but pleasant beach, meditate on horizon-dominating Diamond Rock, or check out the village boutiques and cafes. For an unhurried taste of French island life, this is as good a place as any to spend the day.

SHOPPING

The main shopping district in Fort-de-France is bound by rue Ernest Deproge (on the waterfront), La Savane, rue Lamartine, and rue de la République, with **rue Victor Hugo** being the single most important stretch. Stores generally open at 9am and close at 5pm; most close for lunch, usually between 1 and 3pm. On Saturday, shops are open in the morning only; on Sunday, virtually all are closed.

Martinique offers a good selection of French luxury items—perfumes, fashionable clothing, luggage, crystal, and dinnerware—at prices that can be as much as 30% to 40% lower than those in the States. Unfortunately, because some luxury goods, including jewelry, are subject to a hefty value-added tax, the savings are ultimately less compelling. Paying in dollar-denominated traveler's checks or credit cards is sometimes good for a 20% discount. Duty-free divas invariably make **Nocibe/Roger Albert,** 7 rue Victor Hugo, their first stop. This well-known outlet frequently has the best buys on French perfume, china, and crystal. **Cadet-Daniel,** 72 rue Antoine Siger, is its chief competitor. Compare and save.

Martinican goods, such as rum, Creole jewelry, madras fabric, folk paintings, and hand-woven baskets, are good buys and more representative of the island. The open-air market in **La Savane,** at rue de la Liberté and rue Ernest Deproge, has the best selection of these items. For sheer Caribbean color, stroll through the enclosed produce market on **rue Isambert near rue Blénac;** built in 1901, it's another work of architect Henri Pick.

Centre des Métieres d'Art, rue Ernest Deproge, near the tourism office, is one of the best arts-and-crafts stores in Martinique. Pass over the junk and focus on the more accomplished handmade items, including ceramics, painted fabrics, and patchwork quilts.

The French consider libations an art, and aficionados consider Martinican rum among the world's finest. **La Case à Rhum,** in the Galerie Marchande, 5 rue de la Liberté, stocks all the local brands and allows sample nips to help you decide which bottle to buy.

If you find yourself across the bay in Pointe du Bout, stop by **La Belle Matadore,** Immeuble Vermeil Marina (midway between the La Pagerie Hôtel and the Méridien Hôtel). This boutique takes the history and tradition of Creole jewelry seriously, and virtually every piece for sale replicates designs developed during slave days by *matadores* (prostitutes), midwives, and slaves.

BEACHES

Serious beach bunnies hop south of Fort-de-France to **Grand Anse des Salines,** widely regarded as Martinique's nicest strand. At the island's extreme southern tip, about an hour from the capital by car, it features coconut palms, views of Diamond Rock, and white sand that seems to go on for miles. During summer holidays and weekends, it's busy with families and children, but during the week, it's often quiet and uncrowded. Beachside stands offer refreshment.

Conveniently located across the bay from Fort-de-France, **Pointe du Bout** is Martinique's most lavish resort area. Aside from a marina and a variety of watersports, the area has some modest man-made white-sand beaches. The sandy, natural beaches at nearby **Anse Mitan** and **Anses d'Arlets** are popular with both swimmers and snorkelers.

Beaches north of Fort-de-France have mostly gray (they like to call it silver) volcanic sand. The best of the bunch is **Anse Turin,** just to the side of the main Caribbean coastal road, between St-Pierre and Le Carbet. Extremely popular with locals and shaded by palms, it's where Gauguin swam when he called the island home.

Martinique has no legal nudist beaches, but toplessness is as common here as anywhere in France. As a rule, public beaches lack changing cabins or showers, but hotel lockers and changing cabanas can be used by nonguests for a charge.

SPORTS

GOLF   When Robert Trent Jones, Sr., designed **Golf de la Martinique** (✆ **596/68-32-81**) in 1976, he chose a picturesque, historic site: the seaside hills neighboring La Pagerie, the birthplace of Empress Joséphine. Thirty-two kilometers (20 miles) from Fort-de-France, this good, tough, 18-hole, 6,640-yard, par-71 course features emerald hills, swaying palms, constant vistas of the turquoise sea, and, thankfully, year-round trade winds that help keep things cool. The par-5 12th, with a dogleg to the right, is the most difficult hole. The fairway here is narrow, the green is long, and the wind, especially between December and April, is tricky. The 15th and 16th require shots over sea inlets. Facilities include a pro shop, golf academy, bar, restaurant, and tennis courts. English-speaking pros are at your service. Greens fees and cart rental run about US$130 for 18 holes, US$75 for 9 holes. A set of clubs is another US$25.

SCUBA DIVING & SNORKELING   Favorite dives in the coastal waters off Martinique include the caves and walls of Diamond Rock and the dozen ships sunk by the 1902 volcanic eruption at St-Pierre (the most popular wreck, the metal-hulled *Roraima,* was made famous by Jacques Cousteau and rests on a slant in 45m/148 ft. of water).

For cruisers, the most convenient dive operators are across the bay from Fort-de-France in Pointe du Bout. **Espace Plongée,** at the Kalenda Resort (formerly the Hôtel Méridien; ✆ **596/66-01-79**), and **Planète Bleue,** at the Pointe du Bout marina (✆ **596/66-08-79**), are among the island's best operators. If you want to dive around St-Pierre, try **UCPA** (✆ **596/78-21-03**). Single-tank dives with all equipment run about US$40.

The waters of Pointe du Bout and nearby Anse Mitan and Anse Dufour are popular with snorkelers, as are the small bays of Ste-Anne and Anses d'Arlets on the southwest coast. Snorkeling equipment from on-site vendors runs about US$10.

GREAT LOCAL RESTAURANTS & BARS

Hey, it's France: Expect great food. More than any other island in the French West Indies, Martinique gives French and Creole cuisine equal billing. If you're on a mission to sample the booze of every port of call, Martinique's local beer is **Lorraine;** among the island's best rums are **Clement, Depaz,** and **Saint James.** Too early in the day for demon rum? Slake your thirst with **Didier,** the Caribbean's only naturally carbonated spring water.

IN FORT-DE-FRANCE   A small, elegant restaurant located in a beautiful 19th-century mansion in the hills above Fort-de-France, **La Belle Epoque,** route de Didier (✆ **596/64-41-19**), serves exquisite classic French cuisine. The fixed-price lunch special, which includes an appetizer, main course, and dessert, is a steal at about US$30. Enjoy the languid atmosphere and savor the seafood ravioli in wine-and-lobster sauce.

AT POINTE DU BOUT   Just minutes by car from the resorts of Pointe du Bout, **La Villa Créole,** Anse Mitan (✆ **596/66-05-53**), serves down-home Creole staples such as *accras de morue* (codfish beignets), *boudin Créole* (Creole blood sausage), and *féroces* (avocado, codfish, and manioc hush puppies). Don't leave your garden table without indulging in the chocolate fondant with bittersweet chocolate and pear sauce. The nearby **Au Poisson d'Or,** Anse Mitan (✆ **596/66-01-80**), a rustic roadside eatery, offers more Creole choices such as grilled conch in coconut milk and stewed shrimp, as well as lobster soup and shark in hot sauce. Lunch is US$18.

NEAR ST-PIERRE   Fifteen minutes north of St-Pierre, **Habitation Céron,** Anse Céron, Le Prêcheur (✆ **596/52-94-53**), a 17th-century sugar estate, offers Creole crayfish freshly harvested from the on-site farm. Fish, octopus, and vegetables straight from the garden are also served at the open-air, riverside tables. Lunch is about US$32.

23 Nevis

Off the beaten tourist track, south of St. Martin and north of Guadeloupe, Nevis is the junior partner in the combined Federation of St. Kitts and Nevis, which gained self-government from Britain in 1967 and became a totally independent nation in 1983. Nevis's 1998 referendum for separation from its larger partner failed by the slimmest of margins, and while there is still a movement toward independence—which would make Nevis the smallest country in the world (and probably won't be happening anytime soon)—the dual-island nation, for the most part, lives in peaceful coexistence.

Though smaller than St. Kitts and lacking a major historic site like Brimstone Hill Fortress, Nevis is nevertheless the more appealing and upbeat of the two islands. When viewed from its sister island, about 3.2km (2 miles) away, Nevis appears to be a perfect cone, rising gradually to a height of 970m (3,182 ft.). Columbus first sighted the island in 1493, naming it Nuestra Señora de las Nieves, Spanish for "our lady of the snows," because its peak reminded him of the Pyrenees. Settled by the British in 1628, Nevis became a prosperous sugar-growing island as well as the most popular spa island of the 18th century, when people flocked in from other West Indian islands to visit its hot mineral springs.

Nevis's two most famous residents were **Admiral Horatio Nelson,** who married a local woman here in 1787, and **Alexander Hamilton,** who was born here and went on to find fame as a drafter of the American Federalist Papers, as George Washington's treasury secretary, and as Aaron Burr's unfortunate dueling partner. Today, the island's capital city, Charlestown, has a lovely mixture of port-town exuberance and small-town charm, and the popular Pinney's Beach is just a knockout.

COMING ASHORE   Only small ships call on Nevis, docking right in the center of **Charlestown** and/or dropping anchor off the coast of **Pinney's Beach.**

LANGUAGE   English is the language of both Nevis and St. Kitts.

CURRENCY   The local currency is the **Eastern Caribbean dollar** (EC$2.70 = US$1; EC$1 = US37¢). Many shops and restaurants quote prices in U.S. dollars. Always determine which currency the locals are talking about. We've used U.S.-dollar prices in this section.

INFORMATION   The **Nevis Tourism Authority** is in the historic Treasury Building, on Main Street near the docks (© **869/469-7550;** www.nevisisland.com). Hours are Monday through Friday from 8am to 4pm, Saturday from 8am to noon. For information before you go, call © **866/55-NEVIS.**

CALLING FROM THE U.S.   When calling St. Kitts or Nevis from the United States, you need dial only a "1" before the numbers listed here.

GETTING AROUND

BY TAXI   The entirety of Charlestown is accessible on foot, but if you want to visit Pinney's Beach or elsewhere on the island, you can hop a taxi in Charlestown. The cost to Pinney's is about US$5.50. Taxi drivers double as guides on Nevis, so if you want to take a general tour of the island, negotiate a price with your driver.

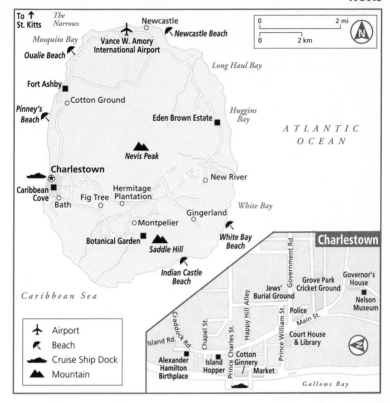

BY RENTAL CAR   Because driving is on the left side in Nevis and most of the worthwhile sites are within walking distance or easily reached by taxi, we don't recommend renting a car here.

BEST CRUISE LINE SHORE EXCURSIONS

Few organized excursions are offered on Nevis. Some of the small ship lines offer a day at **Pinney's Beach** as part of their regular visit, and might also offer hiking and snorkeling options, but the island is so small and easy to negotiate on your own that excursions aren't really necessary. If you want some local commentary, you can hire a taxi driver to give you an island tour. (See "Getting Around," above.)

ON YOUR OWN: WITHIN WALKING DISTANCE

If your ship docks in Charlestown, you're dead center in a perfect walking-tour opportunity. Charlestown is a lovely little place, laid-back in somewhat the same manner as St. John, but with some of the really rural character of sister island St. Kitts.

If you head left from the docks and walk a little ways (maybe .4km/¼-mile) along Main Street, you'll come to the **Alexander Hamilton Birthplace** (© 869/469-5786; www.nevis-nhcs.org/nevishistory.html), where the road curves just before the turnoff to Island Road. It's a rustic little two-level house set right on the coastline. On the first floor is the Museum of Nevis History and gift shop (admission is US$5 for adults,

Frommer's Favorite Nevis Experiences

Wandering around Charlestown: The capital city is a fine place to wander around on your own, visiting the birthplace of American statesman Alexander Hamilton, the small but appealing Nelson Museum, and the 17th-century Jewish cemetery; poking your head into some of the small shops; and greeting the goats and chickens that wander past, evidently taking their own walking tours. (See "On Your Own: Within Walking Distance," below.)

Taking Some Downtime on Pinney's Beach: Lounge back, have a beer, take a swim in the reef-protected waters, do a little snorkeling, or engage in some beachcombing. Talk about relaxation. (See "Beaches," below.)

US$2 for children under 12), but in all honesty, you'll do just as well to skip it and just appreciate the outside, taking a moment to read the historic plaque. Far be it from us to take a couple dollars out of the island's economy, though, so if you're feeling philanthropic, drop your $5 and then head on for the rest of your walk.

Backtracking along Main Street, you'll pass several serviceable, if unremarkable, shops (see "Shopping," below). Keep walking through the center of town, saying hello to the occasional mama goat and kids you'll pass, and then turn left onto Government Road. One block up on the left, you'll find the **Jews' Burial Ground,** with graves from 1684 to 1768. Stones left atop the graves attest to the visitors who have been there before you to pay their respects. When we were there, the dead were being entertained with reggae music coming from the doorway of a shop across the street, while a breeze stirred the few trees on the property. All in all, not a bad resting spot.

Backtrack to Main Street, turn left, and continue on past the Grove Park Cricket Ground, bearing left when the road forks. Head up the hill (where you'll see first an abandoned hotel and then several buildings standing alone on the hill to your right), and then turn at the first right, which will bring you back behind those buildings, the first of which is the inaccessible Government House and the second of which is the **Nelson Museum** (© 869/469-5786; www.nevis-nhcs.org/nelsonmuseum.html). A very small, very homemade kind of place, it's nonetheless an interesting spot, and well worth the US$5 admission (US$2 for children 12 and under). The museum traces the history of Admiral Horatio Nelson's career enforcing England's Navigation Acts in the Caribbean. It also houses artifacts from Nevis's Carib, Arawak, and Aceramic peoples; a small display on Nevis today; and a number of wonderful clay artworks, including a replica of the old "Coolie Man's Store," by local artist Gustage "Bush Tea" Williams. The timeline of Nelson's Caribbean career includes ship models, ceramic and bronze Nelson figures, paintings of his battles and other scenes, and an actual ticket to his funeral, with wax seal. Open Monday through Friday from 8am to 4pm, Saturday from 9am to noon.

Once back outside, amble slowly off in the same direction you were going (right from the gate). Keep bearing right and you'll eventually be back on Main Street, in plenty of time to do a little shopping or stop into one of the local bars or restaurants.

ON YOUR OWN: BEYOND THE PORT AREA

The 3.2-hectare (8-acre) **Botanical Garden of Nevis** (✆ **869/469-3509**) is located 4.8km (3 miles) south of Charlestown on the Montpelier Estate. Fountains, ponds, and re-creations of Mayan sculptures dot the grounds, which are open Monday through Friday from 9am to 4pm. Admission is US$9 for adults, US$6 for children. Also on-site are a restaurant and gift shop.

SHOPPING

Nevis is not a shopping hub on the order of St. Thomas or even the much more laid-back St. John. In fact, it's no kind of shopping hub at all. Still, there are a few shops worth poking your head into, all of them along Main Street, right in the port area.

Island Hopper, on Main Street, 1 block north of Prince Charles Street (✆ **869/ 469-0893**), is the best shop in town for visitors, stocking a huge selection of batik clothing. Across from Island Hopper is **Pemberton Gift Shop,** Main Street (✆ **869/ 469-5668**), which is also sparse but does carry a selection of T-shirts, gift items, and a shelf of CSR (Cane Spirit Rothschild), the local cane-sugar liquor. **Jerveren's Fashions,** in the Cotton Ginnery complex right at the pier (✆ **869/469-0062**), has a decent selection of T-shirts and gifts.

Collectors can browse the range of Nevis stamps at the **Nevis Philatelic Bureau at the Head Post Office,** on Market Street (✆ **869/469-5535**). It's next to the public market, 1 block south and 1 block east of the docks.

BEACHES

The name to know on Nevis is **Pinney's Beach,** located north of Charlestown. A lovely spot for swimming, snorkeling, beachcombing, or just sitting back and watching the pelicans divebomb into the surf, it's home to the Four Seasons Resort, reopened in late 2000 after being obliterated by 1999's Hurricane Lenny. As a counterpoint to conspicuous luxury, the rickety **Sunshine's Bar and Grill** (✆ **869/469-5817**), "Home of the Killer Bee," sits right on the beach, offering beer and other refreshments along with the aforementioned Bee, a "killer" drink.

24 Panama

The Panama Canal is an awesome feat of engineering and human effort. Construction began in 1880 and wasn't completed until 1914, at the expense of thousands of lives, and the vast majority of the original structure and equipment is still in use. Transiting the canal, which links the Atlantic Ocean with the Pacific, is a thrill for anyone even vaguely interested in engineering or history.

Passing through the canal takes about 8 hours from start to finish and is a fascinating procedure—the route is about 80km (50 miles) long and includes passage through three main locks, which, through gravity alone, raise ships over Central America and down again on the other side. Between the locks, ships pass through artificially created lakes such as the massive Gatun Lake, 26m (85 ft.) above sea level. It often costs ships about US$100,000 to pass through, with fees based on each ship's weight. Your ship will line up in the morning, mostly with cargo ships, to await its turn through the canal. While transiting, there will be a running narration of history and facts about the canal by an expert who's brought on board for the day.

Cruises that include a canal crossing are generally 10 to 14 nights long, with popular routes traveling between Florida and Acapulco. These generally visit a handful of

Caribbean and Mexican ports and a few ports in Central America along the way, including Panama's San Blas Islands, Costa Rica's Puerto Caldera, and Guatemala's Puerto Quetzal.

COLON

In compliance with a treaty signed between the United States and Panama in 1977, canal operations passed from American to Panamanian hands at the stroke of midnight on December 31, 1999. Not only did the transition go smoothly, but the canal changeover spurred government agencies and private developers in Panama to expand the canal zone's tourism infrastructure—not simply trying to attract as many ships as possible, but developing new attractions at the canal's Atlantic entrance to lure cruise passengers off their ships and into Panama's interior on shore excursions and for pre- and postcruise stays. Even ships not transiting the canal are being wooed, with a long-term goal of making the city of Colón a home port for cruise ships sailing to the southern Caribbean.

The linchpin project in the new canal-area developments is **Colón 2000,** a US$45-million private port development that opened in October 2000 in Colón, near the canal's Caribbean entrance, and that is capable of handling any size cruise vessel—even the 100,000-ton-plus ships that are too large to pass through the canal. Colón 2000's developer, Corporación de Costas Tropicales, has created a tour company, **Adventuras 2000** (www.colon2000.com), that offers a series of shore excursions highlighting Panama's history, culture, and diverse natural attractions (see "Best Cruise Line Shore Excursions," below). The project has opened many new jobs to locals, who are being trained as bilingual tour guides, drivers, and so on.

Colón 2000's glass-and-marble terminal building has a large lounge, an Internet cafe, a huge duty-free shopping mall (part of the Colón Free Zone, the second-largest tax-free zone in the world), restaurants, and crafts shops. Unfortunately, the town surrounding the splashy new development remains depressed, so there's no question that passengers calling here should book an organized tour.

Princess, Holland America, Celebrity, and Carnival were some of the first lines to include Colón 2000 as a port of call on some Panama Canal itineraries. It doesn't hurt that they're getting incentives by the Panamanian government: Panama has hedged its bets by establishing a 5-year program that pays cruise ships US$2.50 to US$12 per passenger for calls at any Panamanian port. The incentives grow as the passenger count rises, and additional incentives are offered to lines that register their ships in Panama.

Another new development in Colón, the **Cristobal Cruise Terminal** (Pier 6), offers piers for two ships of any size and has a duty-free shopping area, restaurants, and phones. A rail line here, connecting Colón and the capital of Panama City, is in the planning stages.

BEST CRUISE LINE SHORE EXCURSIONS

The following excursions represent a sampling of those offered from Colón:

Emberá Indian Village Tour (US$75, 3½ hr.): Today, Panama's Emberá Indians live much as they did in the early 16th century, when their first tourist—Vasco Nunez de Balboa, who "discovered" the Pacific Ocean—came through. You'll travel by dugout canoe up the Chagres River, visit the Emberá village, witness a performance of traditional dance, and (surprise, surprise) have an opportunity to purchase handicrafts.

Kayaking the Canal (US$132, 9hr.): You'll travel to Sol Melá Resort, where you'll spend about an hour kayaking amid the plant life, mammals, and birds. Then you'll

head by bus to the Gatun Locks for a look at the Canal's workings. A buffet lunch is served.

Panama City Tour (US$89, 5½–6 hr.): Visit the ruins of Old Panama, founded in 1519 by Pedro Arias Davila and destroyed in 1671 by the pirate Sir Henry Morgan; head to colonial Panama, built to replace the original capital; and then visit the Miraflores Locks for a look at the Canal.

Monkey Watch (US$84, 5½ hr.): After a 30-minute ride at high speed through the heart of the Panama Canal, the boat will slow down and enter the labyrinth of jungle-covered islands of Lake Gatun. Wildlife is plentiful in this protected area; you are likely to encounter capuchin monkeys, three-toed sloths, howler monkeys, toucans, turtles, butterflies, crocodiles, and more.

PORTS ALONG THE CANAL ROUTE

The **San Blas Islands** are a beautiful archipelago and home to the Kuna Indians, whose women are well known for their colorful, hand-embroidered stitching. If you get a chance to go ashore, the tiny women, dressed in their traditional *molas* (bright, intricately appliquéd blouses), sell all manner of this textile art in square blocks and strips, all of which are known as *molas* and make great pillow covers or wall hangings. They cost about US$5 to US$10 each, but don't try to bargain too much—the women will go only so low before standing firm. When your ship anchors offshore at the islands, be prepared for throngs of Kunas to emerge from the far-off distance, paddling (or, in a few cases, motoring) their dugout canoes up to the ship, where they will spend the entire day calling for money or anything else ship passengers toss overboard. The Kuna seem to enjoy diving overboard to retrieve coins thrown to them, but, of course, it's a sad sight, too, watching entire families so needy. Makes you feel damn guilty for rolling in on that fancy cruise ship of yours.

In Costa Rica, many ships call at **Puerto Caldera** on the Pacific side or **Puerto Limón** on the Atlantic side. While there's nothing to see from either cargo port, both are great jumping-off points for tours (offered by all visiting ships) of the country's lush, beautiful rainforests, which are alive with some 850 species of birds, 200 species of mammals, 9,000 species of flowering plants, and about 35,000 species of insects. After a scenic bus ride, the tour will take you on a nature walk through the jungle or a mild whitewater-rafting trip.

In Guatemala, most Panama Canal–bound ships call at **Puerto Quetzal,** on the Pacific coast; a few may call at **Santo Tomas** on the Caribbean side. Both are used as gateways to Guatemala's spectacular Mayan ruins at **Tikal.** They're the country's most famous attractions and are considered the most spectacular, with more than 3,000 temples, pyramids, and other buildings of the ancient civilization—some of them dating as far back as A.D. 300—nestled in a thick, surreal jungle setting. Excursions here are neither cheap nor easy—a 10-hour tour involves buses, walking, and a 1-hour flight, and costs about US$500—but the journey is well worth the effort. Tours to the less-spectacular Mayan sites in Honduras are also offered from Puerto Quetzal, as are several overland tours of Guatemala's interior.

25 Puerto Rico

San Juan, the capital of Puerto Rico, has the busiest ocean terminal in the West Indies and is one of the cruise trade's most important ports. While cruise groups, by their sheer size, can overwhelm many ports of call, San Juan absorbs cruise passengers with ease. The San Juan metropolitan area, home to about a third of Puerto Rico's four million people, is one of the largest and most sophisticated urban centers in the Caribbean, offering all the amenities of a modern major city: great shopping, interesting neighborhoods, beautiful people, excellent restaurants, glamorous bars and nightclubs, and fine

Frommer's Favorite San Juan Experiences

Strolling through Historic Old San Juan: Meander through block after block of narrow cobblestone streets lined with centuries-old Spanish colonial architecture. (See "Walking Tour: Old San Juan," below.)

Hiking in El Yunque National Forest: One of Puerto Rico's most popular attractions, El Yunque covers 11,331 hectares (27,988 acres) and receives up to 508cm (200 in.) of rain per year. There are 240 different tropical trees, more than 50 orchid species, 150 varieties of ferns, 68 types of birds, and millions of tiny coquí tree frogs. You can hike, picnic, and swim in mountain streams. (See "Best Cruise Line Shore Excursions," below.)

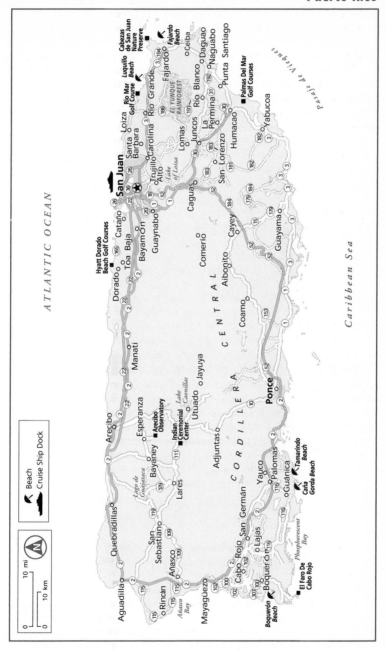

ATLANTIC OCEAN

Caribbean Sea

Pasaje de Vieques

Beach
Cruise Ship Dock

10 mi
10 km

Cabezas de San Juan Nature Preserve
Fajardo Beach
Ceiba
Daguao
Naguabo
Punta Santiago
Palmas Del Mar Golf Courses
Yabucoa
Luquillo Beach
Rio Mar Golf Course
Fajardo
Rio Grande
Rio Blanco
La Pernina
Humacao
EL YUNQUE RAINFOREST
Loiza
Santa Barbara
Carolina
Lomas
Juncos
San Lorenzo
San Juan
Trujillo Alto
Lake of Loiza
Caguas
Cayey
Guayama
Cataño
Toa Baja
Bayamón
Guaynabo
Comerío
Aibonito
Coamo
Hyatt Dorado Beach Golf Courses
Dorado
CENTRAL
Manatí
Jayuya
Lake Caonillas
Utuado
Ponce
Esperanza
Arecibo Observatory
Indian Ceremonial Center
Arecibo
Bayaney
Adjuntas
CORDILLERA
Tamarindo Beach
Palomas
Caña Gorda Beach
Guánica
Quebradillas
Lago de Guajataca
Lares
San Germán
Yauco
San Sebastián
Añasco
Mayagüez
Cabo Rojo
Lajas
Phosphorescent Bay
Aguadilla
Rincón
Añasco Bay
Boquerón
El Faro De Cabo Rojo
Boquerón Beach

San Juan as a Port of Embarkation

Puerto Rico is the number-one port of embarkation in the Caribbean, with more than 1.2 million visitors embarking on 700 cruises every year from here. Most cruise lines have packages that include hotel rooms on the island.

GETTING TO SAN JUAN & THE PORT   **Luis Muñoz Marín International Airport** (© 787/791-1014) is on the city's east side, about 12km (7½ miles) from the port. Taxi fares from the airport are fixed at US$8 to Isla Verde, US$12 to Condado and Ocean Park, and US$16 to Old San Juan and the cruise ships. The ride to the port takes at least 30 minutes—longer if traffic is heavy, and it often is.

ACCOMMODATIONS

In Old San Juan   The quietly elegant **Hotel El Convento,** 100 Calle del Cristo (© 800/468-2779 or 787/723-9020; www.elconvento.com; rates: US$345–US$410 winter; US$160–US$250 summer), is Puerto Rico's most famous lodging. A former Carmelite convent, it offers large rooms, many with views of the Old Town. The **Sheraton Old San Juan Hotel,** 100 Brumbaugh St. (© 800/325-3535 or 787/721-5100; www.sheratonoldsanjuan.com; rates: US$235–US$735), is on the waterfront across the street from the cruise ship docks. Rooms are comfortable, and Old San Juan is a step away. Set on Old San Juan's highest hill, with a sweeping view of the sea, **Gallery Inn at Galería San Juan,** 204 Calle Norzagaray (© 787/722-1808; www.thegalleryinn.com; rates: US$225–US$350), was the home of a Spanish aristocrat in the 1700s. Many of the rooms open onto patios, fountains, and gardens. Art is everywhere, contributing to the hotel's cultured, contemplative, bohemian ambience.

In Condado   The original high-rise, high-glamour section of modern San Juan, Condado boasts numerous hotels, restaurants, and clubs. Among its best hotels are the **El Condado Plaza Hotel & Casino,** 999 Ashford Ave. (© 800/468-8588 or 787/721-1000; www.luxuryresorts.com; rates: US$119–US$260), and the **San Juan Marriott Resort & Stellaris Casino,** 1309 Ashford Ave. (© 800/981-8546 or 787/721-7000; www.marriottpr.com; rates: US$230–US$390). **Aleli by the Sea,** 1125 Sea View St., a block off Ashford Avenue (© 787/725-5313; rates: US$66–US$103), is a small, charming option

museums. It also offers some of the drawbacks: traffic, crowded sidewalks, and, in some areas, crime (avoid the La Perla neighborhood, along the north-central edge of Old San Juan).

Founded in 1521 by Spanish conquistador **Juan Ponce de León,** the city is one of the oldest in the New World. The cobblestone streets of the hilly old section of the city—**Old San Juan,** the ancient walled city on San Juan Island—are lined with brightly painted colonial town houses, ancient churches, intimate parks, and sun-drenched plazas. Like the pyramids of Egypt and the Great Wall of China, Old San Juan's Spanish colonial forts and city walls are United Nations World Heritage Sites. Another attraction is the people: Puerto Ricans are warm, quick to laugh, and proud on the beach. Rooms are basic but clean; the big draws are the sound of the surf just outside your window and the low rates.

Motels in Condado include the **Holiday Inn Express,** 1 Mariano Ramirez Bages, off Ashford Avenue at Joffre Street (© **787/724-2460;** www.ichotels group.com/h/d/ex/1/en/home), and **San Juan Comfort Inn–Condado Lagoon Hotel,** 6 Clemenceau St. (© **787/721-0170;** www.choicehotels.com).

In Isla Verde Similar to Condado in atmosphere and abundance of hotels, but more recently developed, Isla Verde has a number of dazzlingly deluxe resort complexes, including the **El San Juan Hotel & Casino,** 6063 Isla Verde Ave. (© **800/468-2818** or 787/791-1000; www.luxuryresorts.com; rates: US$162–US$405), and the **Ritz-Carlton San Juan Hotel Casino & Spa,** Avenue of the Governors (© **800/241-3333** or 787/253-1700; www.ritzcarlton.com; rates: US$279–US$709). At the other end of the spectrum, motels include the **Howard Johnson Carolina,** 4820 Isla Verde Ave. (© **787/728-1300;** www. hojo.com).

SAN JUAN AFTER DARK

The San Juan club scene is hot. In general, people get pretty dressed up, so forget about T-shirts or shorts. **Brava,** in the El San Juan Hotel & Casino, 6063 Isla Verde Ave. (© **787/791-1000**), attracts a rich and beautiful crowd, as well as hundreds of wannabes. On weekends, you may have to wait a couple hours to get in. In the Old Town, head for **Club Lazer,** 251 Calle del Cruz (© **787/725-7581**), where you can dance the night away to the sounds of salsa and merengue. San Juan's exuberant gay scene is easily the Caribbean's best, and no club in town surpasses the energy of **Eros,** 1257 Av. Ponce de León, Santurce (© **787/722-1131**). Also in Santurce is the enduringly popular lesbian bar **Cups,** 1708 Calle San Mateo (© **787/268-3570**).

For a mellow and sophisticated atmosphere in Old San Juan, try **Carli Café Concierto,** on Plazoleta Rafael Carrión (© **787/725-4927**), a bistro offering live piano and jazz music. With its giant chandelier and intricate wood-paneled ceiling, the **Palm Court,** in the Wyndham El San Juan Hotel & Casino, 6063 Isla Verde Ave. (© **787/791-1000**), is probably the island's most glamorous meeting place.

of their multicultural heritage, a distinct blend of Amerindian, Spanish, African, and American influences that is present in the culture of the island, from salsa music to Puerto Rican cuisine.

San Juan's shopping ranks among the Caribbean's best, and the city's historic sights, beaches, gambling, and other diversions make it, overall, the number-one port of call in the region. You'll find some of the Caribbean's best restaurants here, as well as sprawling beaches with high-rise luxury hotels reminiscent of those in Miami.

Old San Juan is the prime tourist haunt, but there's much more to the metropolitan area. Other interesting neighborhoods include **Santurce,** linked with San Juan Island by a causeway; **Condado,** a strip of beachfront hotels, restaurants, casinos, and nightclubs on a peninsula stretching from San Juan Island to Santurce; **Hato Rey,** the business center; **Río Piedras,** site of the University of Puerto Rico; and **Bayamón,** an industrial and residential quarter. **Isla Verde,** another resort zone, is connected to the rest of San Juan by an isthmus. Rumor has it that a second cruise ship pier will be greatly expanded on the other side of the island, near the quaint city of **Ponce.** In addition to art, history, museums, and beaches, many of the interior-based natural attractions are equally accessible from San Juan and Ponce.

Puerto Rico has been inhabited since about 3000 B.C., when the earliest people arrived from Florida or Central America. In 1493, Christopher Columbus landed on the island, and within 50 years, the native population had been decimated by forced labor, malnutrition, Western diseases, and warfare with the Spanish.

The island remained part of Spain's empire for 4 centuries. Spanish rule ended in 1898, when Puerto Rico was ceded to the United States in the wake of the Spanish-American War. In 1917, Puerto Ricans became U.S. citizens, and in 1952, the island became a semiautonomous commonwealth of the United States. In the last referendum on statehood, in 1998, slightly more Puerto Ricans voted for maintaining the status quo than for joining the union; a small fraction favored independence.

COMING ASHORE   Cruise ships dock in historic Old San Juan, a short walk from the Plaza de la Darsena, Old San Juan's main bus station, and most of its historic treasures. During periods of heavy volume—such as Saturday and Sunday in midwinter, when as many as eight cruise ships dock on the same day—additional, less convenient piers are used. Many of Old San Juan's shops and attractions are within walking distance from these docks. For information about the port, contact the **Port of San Juan,** P.O. Box 362829, San Juan, PR 00936-2829 (© 787/723-2260).

LANGUAGE   Spanish is the native tongue, but most people on the island also speak English (both are the official languages here). The farther you venture from San Juan, the more likely it is you'll have to practice your Spanish.

CURRENCY   Puerto Rico is part of the United States, so the **U.S. dollar** is the coin of the realm. Canadian currency is accepted, albeit reluctantly, by some of San Juan's bigger hotels. Credit cards and traveler's checks are widely accepted.

INFORMATION   For advice and maps, drop by the **Tourist Information Center** at La Casita, near Pier 1 (© 787/722-1709). For info before you go, contact the **Puerto Rico Tourism Company** (© 800/223-6530 or 800/866-7827; www.prtourism.com or www.gotopuertorico.com).

CALLING FROM THE U.S.   Calling Puerto Rico from the continental United States is as simple as dialing between U.S. states: Just dial "1" before the numbers listed here.

GETTING AROUND

Driving in congested San Juan is frustrating, and parking in some areas is impossible. You're better off walking around Old San Juan. Take buses or taxis to Condado, Ocean Park, and Isla Verde.

BY TAXI   Taxis operated by the Tourist Transportation Division are metered in San Juan, but the fare structure between major tourism zones is standardized. The set rates from the cruise ship piers are US$6 to Old San Juan, US$10 to Condado, and US$16 to Isla Verde. You can also hire a taxi for US$30 per hour. If the meter's used, the initial charge is US$1, plus 10¢ for each additional ⅑th of a mile and 50¢ for each suitcase.

San Juan at a Glance

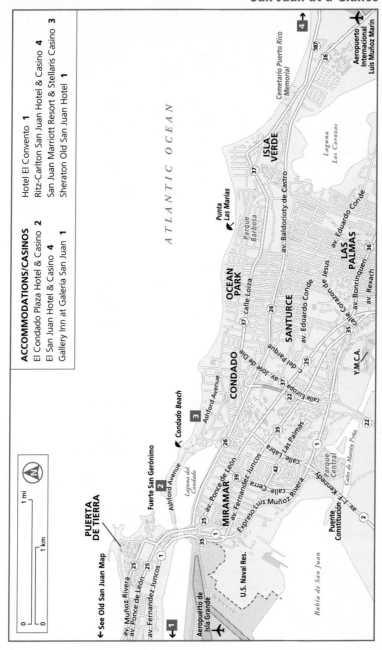

ACCOMMODATIONS/CASINOS

El Condado Plaza Hotel & Casino **2**
El San Juan Hotel & Casino **4**
Gallery Inn at Galería San Juan **1**

Hotel El Convento **1**
Ritz-Carlton San Juan Hotel & Casino **4**
San Juan Marriott Resort & Stellaris Casino **3**
Sheraton Old San Juan Hotel **1**

The minimum fare is US$3. After 10pm, there's a night surcharge of US$1 to the meter reading. To order a cab, call **Metro Taxi** (© **787/725-2878**) or **Taxi Association** (© **787/795-5286**).

BY TROLLEY   When you tire of walking around Old San Juan, board one of the free trolleys. They depart from Plaza de la Marina and piers 2 and 4, but you can hop on anywhere along the route.

BY BUS   The **Metropolitan Bus Authority** operates extensive bus service in the greater San Juan area. Bus stops are marked by signs that read PARADA, and terminals are in front of Pier 4. For route and schedule information, call © **787/250-6064.**

BY RENTAL CAR   Puerto Rico has expressways as well as thousands of miles of other paved roads, so travel by car is pretty effortless, except in metropolitan San Juan, where traffic can be heavy and nightmarish—the 500-year-old streets in Old San Juan just weren't built with cars in mind. Driving is on the right side of the road, and all other U.S. rules apply. Signs are in Spanish, though, and the metric system is used for distance markers (kilometers rather than miles) and at gas stations (liters instead of gallons); confusingly enough, speed limits are posted in miles per hour. **Avis, Budget, Dollar,** and **Hertz** all have offices here.

BEST CRUISE LINE SHORE EXCURSIONS

Unless you want a guide to offer historic perspective (US$37, 2½ hr.), don't bother with organized tours of Old San Juan—it's easy enough to get around on your own. On the other hand, if you explore somewhere farther afield, an organized tour is a good idea.

El Yunque Rainforest (US$32, 4–5 hr.): Get acquainted with one of Puerto Rico's premier natural wonders. After arriving at Baño Grande, a natural swimming hole, hike half an hour along the Camimitillo trail and see parrot nests, giant ferns, orchids, and palms. Listen for the song of Puerto Rico's national symbol, the tiny coquí tree frog. After a short stop at an interpretive station, proceed to the Yohaku observation tower and Coca waterfall.

Tropical Horseback Riding (US$89, 3½ hr.): Once you reach the ranch, you'll meet your horse, briefly learn the ropes, and then ride down a beautiful beach. Take a quick swim during the refreshment stop.

City Tour & Bacardi Rum Distillery (US$30, 4 hr.): After a tour of the old city, with a stop at the San Cristóbal fort, you'll travel to the Bacardi distillery to learn about the Puerto Rican sugar and rum industries, watch giant fermenting tanks transform sugar cane into rum, learn how to pronounce the product's name (baa-carrrr-*di!*), and then get a taste for yourself.

EXCURSIONS OFFERED BY LOCAL AGENCIES

If you're staying in a hotel before or after your cruise, book excursions at your hotel's tour desk. Otherwise, try **Rico Suntours,** 176 Calle San Jorge, San Juan (© **787/722-2080** or 787/727-2080), or **Castillo Tours & Travel Services,** 2413 Calle Laurel, Punta La Marias, Santurce (© **787/791-6195** or 787/726-5752; www.castillotours.com). For serious adventure, rock climbing, rappelling, cave exploring, or canyoneering, your best bets are **Aventuras Tierra Adentro,** 268-A Av. Piñero, Río Piedras (© **787/766-0470;** www.aventuraspr.com), or **Acampa,** 1211 Av. Piñero, San Juan (© **787/706-0695**). You can also check *Que Pasa* magazine for more detailed information.

WALKING TOUR | OLD SAN JUAN

Start:	Plaza de la Marina.
Finish:	Fort San Cristóbal.
Time:	Approximately 1½ to 2 hours at a leisurely pace; allow extra time for poking around gift shops or touring museums along the way.
Best Times:	Mornings, starting at 9 or 10am, while it's still cool; late afternoons, when the sun is less harsh (although be warned that most attractions close between 3–5pm).
Worst Times:	Midday, between 10am and 2pm, when it can get quite hot—bring extra water and sunscreen.

The streets are narrow and teeming with traffic, but strolling around Old San Juan is like walking through 5 centuries of history. More than 400 Spanish colonial buildings from the 16th and 17th centuries, many featuring intricate wrought-iron balconies with lush hanging plants, have been lovingly restored here. The streets' blue paving stones were used originally as ballast by ships crossing the ocean from Spain. Although Old San Juan is a National Historic Zone, it's as vibrant today as it ever has been. Block after block, you'll find shops, cafes, museums, plazas, people, and pigeons. The crowds thin out by late afternoon, so linger a while to experience Old San Juan's more sedate charms.

Begin your adventure near the post office, amid the taxis, buses, and urban hubbub of:

❶ Plaza de la Marina

The plaza is a small park that overlooks San Juan Bay, which was one of the New World's most important harbors for trading and for military protection. Walking west from the plaza, you'll come to San Juan's showcase promenade, Paseo de la Princesa. This renovated 19th-century walkway traces the ancient city walls past heroic statues, gurgling fountains, and landscaped gardens.

Proceed along the Paseo to:

❷ La Princesa

This gray-and-white building on the right served as one of the Caribbean's most notorious prisons for centuries. Today it houses contemporary Puerto Rican art exhibits and the offices of the Puerto Rico Tourism Company.

Continue walking westward to the fountain near the sea's edge. Turn right and follow the promenade as it skirts the base of the:

❸ City Wall (La Muralla)

The wall was completed in the 1700s and once formed part of the New World's most impregnable defense against enemy invaders and pirates. Marvel at the immensity, antiquity, and engineering genius of the wall, which on average is 12m (39 ft.) high and 6m (20 ft.) thick.

Follow the promenade until you reach the:

❹ San Juan Gate

The San Juan Gate stands at Calle San Juan and Calle Recinto del Oeste. Turn right through the portal. The gate was built in 1635 and served as the main entrance into San Juan. Today it's the only remaining passage through the wall into the city.

Turn right at the first street and walk uphill along Calle Recinto del Oeste to the wrought-iron gates of:

❺ La Fortaleza

Also known as Santa Catalina Palace, La Fortaleza is the residence of Puerto Rico's governor. Although it initially served military purposes, it's the oldest executive mansion in continuous use in the Western Hemisphere (built in 1540). Over the past 4 centuries, numerous additions and alterations have been made, resulting in the current amalgam of marble, mahogany, and stained glass. The architectural pastiche includes medieval, baroque, gothic, neoclassical, and Moorish elements. English-language tours are given Monday through Friday (except holidays) every hour on the hour (except noon) from 9am to 3pm.

Now retrace your steps along Calle Recinto del Oeste, downhill to Caleta de San Juan. The colonial house at no. 51, on the northeast corner, is the:

❻ Felisa Rincón de Gautier Museum

This is the former home of one of San Juan's most popular mayors. An organizer of the city's women and other dispossessed, Fela, as her many admirers called her, swept into power in 1946 and led the city for 22 years. The first woman in the Western Hemisphere to be the chief executive of a major city, she was the brains behind Head Start, the preschool program for low-income children. Watch the short English-language documentary of her life, tour the modest rooms of her home, and view some of the hundreds of pictures of Madame Mayor with the world's celebrities (© **787/723-1897**; free admission; open Mon–Fri, except holidays, from 9am–4pm).

Walking back to Calle Recinto del Oeste, turn right and proceed 1 block to Caleta de las Monjas. Fork left to a panoramic view and a modern statue marking the center of:

❼ Plazuela de la Rogativa

According to local legend, the British, while besieging San Juan in 1797, misidentified the flaming torches of a *rogativa,* or religious procession, as Spanish reinforcements. Frightened by the display, the would-be invaders hastily retreated. Statues in this plaza memorialize the event.

Continue westward, parallel to the city wall, passing through a pair of urn-topped gateposts. The road will fork. Bear to the right and continue climbing the steep cobblestone-covered ramp to its top. Walk westward across the field toward the neoclassical gateway leading to the:

❽ Castillo de San Felipe del Morro ("El Morro")

This castle, whose treasury and strategic position were for centuries the envy of both Europe and the Caribbean, was where Spanish Puerto Rico defended itself against the navies of Great Britain, France, and Holland, as well as hundreds of pirate ships. First built in 1539, and substantially enhanced in 1787, the fortress was part of a comprehensive defense network. The six-level complex rises 43m (141 ft.) above the sea on a rocky promontory. You can spend the better part of the morning exploring its labyrinth of dungeons, barracks, towers, ramps, and tunnels on your own. Check out the small, air-conditioned military museum and the gift shop. Both El Morro and San Cristóbal (see stop 19, below) are managed by the U.S. National Park Service, which provides continuous video presentations and scheduled guided tours in English (at western end of Calle Norzagaray; © **787/729-6960**; admission to El Morro and San Cristóbal is US$3 for adults, US$2 for seniors over 62, and US$1 for ages 13–17; daily 9am–5pm for El Morro and 9am–6pm for San Cristóbal).

Retrace your steps through the treeless field to Calle del Morro, then walk uphill to the small plaza at the top of the street. On the right is:

❾ Casa Blanca

Though it was his family home, Juan Ponce de León, the conquistador and Puerto Rico's first governor, never actually lived here: While the structure was being built, he was off looking for the Fountain of Youth, ironically dying (from battle wounds) along the way, in 1521. The city's oldest fort, Casa Blanca was San Juan's only defense against attacks until La Fortaleza was completed in 1533. Today it features a small museum illustrating Indian life and 16th- and 17th-century colonial family life. The garden and fountains in back are a tranquil respite from

Old San Juan Walking Tour

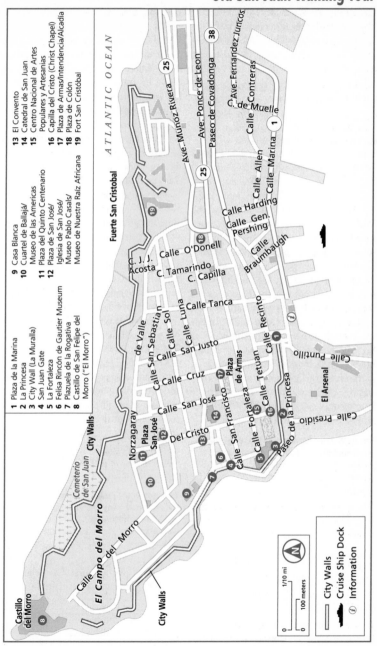

1 Plaza de la Marina
2 La Princesa
3 City Wall (La Muralla)
4 San Juan Gate
5 La Fortaleza
6 Felisa Rincón de Gautier Museum
7 Plazuela de la Rogativa
8 Castillo de San Felipe del Morro ("El Morro")

9 Casa Blanca
10 Cuartel de Ballajá/ Museo de las Americas
11 Plaza del Quinto Centenario
12 Plaza de San José/ Iglesia de San José/ Museo Pablo Casals/ Museo de Nuestra Raíz Africana

13 El Convento
14 Catedral de San Juan
15 Centro Nacional de Artes Populares y Artesanias
16 Capilla del Cristo (Christ Chapel)
17 Plaza de Armas/Intendencia/Alcadia
18 Plaza de Colón
19 Fort San Cristóbal

ATLANTIC OCEAN

Fuerte San Cristóbal

Castillo del Morro

El Campo del Morro

Cemeterio de San Juan

City Walls

- City Walls
- Cruise Ship Dock
- (i) Information

1/10 mi
100 meters

the streets (1 Calle de San Sebastián; © 787/725-1454; admission is US$3 for adults, US$2 for seniors, US$1 for children; Mon–Sat 9am–4pm, except for an hour at noon).

Exit through the front entrance and walk downhill, retracing your steps for a half-block; then head toward the massive tangerine-colored building on your right, the:

⑩ Cuartel de Ballajá

These former military barracks once housed 1,000 Spanish soldiers and their families. Built between 1854 and 1864, the complex is the last and largest military building erected by Spain in the Western Hemisphere. The three-story quadrangular structure, constructed in a sober neoclassical style, has long arcades that enclose a large patio once used as a parade ground. Today, the building's second floor is home to the Museo de las Americas, which showcases Caribbean as well as North, Central, and South American cultures. The popular exhibits focus on housing and furniture styles, handicrafts, tools, musical instruments, toys, clothing, and religious objects. The *santos* (carved wooden saints) are especially interesting (© 787/724-5052; free admission; Tues–Sun 10am–4pm).

Exit through the barracks' eastern door, where you'll immediately spot the dramatic and modern:

⑪ Plaza del Quinto Centenario (Quincentennial Plaza)

This plaza is dominated by a large totem pole–like column that commemorates the 500th anniversary of Columbus's arrival.

Now walk a short block southeast to the borders of:

⑫ Plaza de San José

This plaza features a statue of Juan Ponce de León cast from an English cannon captured during a 1797 naval battle. Three sites around this square are worth visiting. Built in 1532, the **Iglesia de San José** is where Ponce de León's descendants worshipped. Despite being looted over the years, the church, on the plaza's north side, still has several treasures, including a carved crucifix presented to Ponce de León, paintings by Puerto Rican 18th-century master José Campéche, and works by Francisco Oller, who painted in the late 1800s and early 1900s. A 15th-century Flemish work in the Chapel of Belém is venerated by many who believe it works miracles. The **Museo Pablo Casals** (© 787/723-9185; admission US$1 for adults, 50¢ for children under 12; Tues–Sat 9:30am–4:30pm) honors the Spanish-born cellist who adopted Puerto Rico as his home (his mother and wife were Puerto Rican). Original manuscripts of the musician's music, his cello, and his piano are displayed in the main hall. The video library upstairs archives many of his performances. Casals's legacy on the island includes the annual Casals Music Festival and the Puerto Rico Symphony Orchestra. The **Museo de Nuestra Raíz Africana,** or Museum of Our African Roots (© 787/724-4294; free admission; Tues–Sat 9:30am–5pm, Sun 11am–5pm), compactly and ingeniously chronicles the history of Africans in Puerto Rico. Various exhibits trace the slave experience and focus on African contributions to local music, dance, clothing, art, cuisine, religion, and language. Placards are in Spanish, but the exhibits are fascinating and often self-explanatory.

Exiting from the plaza's southwestern corner, walk downhill along one of the capital's oldest and best-known streets, Calle del Cristo. Two blocks down, on the north side of shady Plaza de las Monjas, look for:

⑬ El Convento

The New World's first Carmelite convent, El Convento opened in 1651 with 9m-thick (30-ft.) walls designed to withstand hurricanes and enemy attacks. The building remained a convent for 250 years but fell on hard times early in the 20th century and served as a dance hall and flophouse. Today, the beautifully restored building is the Hotel El Convento, possibly Puerto Rico's most elegant hotel.

Across the street from El Convento stands the island's most famous church, the:

⑭ Catedral de San Juan

The original thatch-roofed wooden cathedral, built in the early 1520s, was destroyed by a hurricane in 1529. Reconstruction in 1540 added a circular staircase and vaulted Gothic ceilings, but most of the current church was built in the 1800s. Look for the tomb of Ponce de León and the wax-encased mummy of St. Pio, a Roman martyr (153 Calle del Cristo; ℂ **787/722-0861;** free admission; daily 8am–5pm).

Now walk 2 blocks south along Calle del Cristo, through one of the Caribbean's most attractive shopping districts. After passing Calle Fortaleza, look on your left for the:

⑮ Centro Nacional de Artes Populares y Artesanias

Operated by the Institute of Puerto Rican Culture, this center displays a collection of the island's folk arts and crafts (253 Calle del Cristo; ℂ **787/722-0621;** free admission; Mon–Sat 9am–5pm).

Continue to the southernmost tip of Calle del Cristo (just a few steps away) to the wrought-iron gates that surround a chapel no bigger than a newspaper kiosk, the:

⑯ Capilla del Cristo (Christ Chapel)

Legend has it that in 1753, a young rider lost control of his horse in a race down Calle del Cristo during the feast of St. John the Baptist and plunged over the steep precipice at the street's end. A witness to the tragedy promised to build a chapel if the young man's life was saved. Records maintain that the horseman died, but lore contends otherwise. In another version of the story, the horseman, after himself praying to God while falling over the cliff, survived to build the chapel. The delicate silver altar here can be seen through glass doors (free admission; Mon, Wed, and Fri 10:30am–3:30pm).

Retrace your steps about a block north along the Calle del Cristo, then turn right on Calle Fortaleza. One block later, take a left onto Calle San José; then proceed another block to the capital's liveliest square, the:

⑰ Plaza de Armas

This broad, open plaza has lots of pigeons, several old men playing dominoes, office workers and shoppers basking in the sun, and a 19th-century statue representing the four seasons. Originally used for military drills, the plaza now hosts folk dances and concerts on weekends. The neoclassical **Intendencia** (which houses offices of the U.S. State Department) and the **Alcadía** (San Juan's City Hall) flank the square.

Walk eastward along the plaza's northern border, Calle San Francisco, for 4 blocks until you reach another square:

⑱ Plaza de Colón

This park is notable for its statue of Cristóbal Colón (Christopher Columbus). Bronze plaques at the monument's base commemorate episodes in the explorer's life.

Finally, walk to the plaza's northeast corner, where Calle San Francisco meets Boulevard del Valle. Turn left and follow the signs to:

⑲ Fort San Cristóbal

Built in 1634 (and expanded in the 1770s), this fortress rises more than 46m (151 ft.) above the sea. A complex maze of tunnels and moats connects the central fort with wave after wave of outlying posts. Don't miss the **Garita del Diablo** (Devil's Sentry Box), uphill from Plaza de Colón on Calle Norzagaray. This lonely post at the edge of the sea is where, legend has it, the devil himself snatched away solitary sentinels (ℂ **787/729-6960;** admission US$3 for adults, US$2 for seniors over 62, US$1 for ages 13–17; note that your ticket stub from El Morro is good for admission here; daily 9am–5pm).

SHOPPING

San Juan has some great bargains—prices are often even lower than those in St. Thomas—and U.S. citizens pay no duty on items bought in Puerto Rico. Every tourist zone offers ample shopping opportunities, but the streets of the **Old Town,** especially **Calle San Francisco** and **Calle del Cristo,** are the major venues. Generally, shopping hours are Monday through Thursday and Saturday from 8am to 6pm, Friday from 8am to 9pm. Some stores are open Sunday from 11am to 5pm, but most are closed. Local handicrafts can be good buys, including *santos* (hand-carved wooden religious figures), needlework, straw work, hammocks, guayabera (lightweight shirts worn untucked), papier-mâché masks, and paintings and sculptures by local artists.

El Alcazar, 103 Calle San José, has the largest collection of antique furniture, silver, and art objects in the Caribbean. You'll need help to wade through the massive inventory, though—it fills several buildings. Smaller but still impressive, **Olé,** 105 Calle Fortaleza, has antique *santos,* coins, and silver. It's also the place to get a custom-fitted Panama hat.

Puerto Rican Arts & Crafts, 204 Calle Fortaleza, has authentic handicrafts, including papier-mâché carnival masks from the town of Ponce. **José E. Alegria & Associates,** 152–154 Calle del Cristo, is half antiques shop and half gift arcade, while **Galería Botello,** 208 Calle del Cristo, once the home of late Puerto Rican artist Angel Botello, sells his paintings and sculptures, as well as antique *santos.*

Old San Juan's best book and music store, **Cronopios,** is at 255 Calle San José. Most titles are in Spanish, but there are plenty in English, too. Looking for Puerto Rican novels? Try *The House on the Lagoon,* by Rosario Ferré, or *The Renunciation,* by Edgardo Rodríguez Julia. And pick up some salsa CDs while you're browsing.

Designer outlet shops include **London Fog,** 156 Calle del Cristo; **Polo Ralph Lauren,** 201 Calle del Cristo; **Coach,** 158 Calle del Cristo; and **Tommy Hilfiger,** 206 Calle del Cristo.

BEACHES

Puerto Rico is ringed by hundreds of miles of sandy beaches, and you won't have to leave San Juan to play in the surf. Perhaps the most famous beach in the Caribbean, **Condado Beach,** at the western end of Ashford Avenue, is the backyard playground of Condado's resort hotels. A favorite of families, it can get pretty crowded in winter. The beaches of **Isla Verde,** behind the hotels and condominiums along Isla Verde Avenue, are less rocky and are excellent for people-watching. If you're looking for a more picturesque, sedate scene, head to **Ocean Park,** north of McLeary Street. The waters here are sometimes choppy, but they're still swimmable. Popular with college students on weekends, the beach is also very gay-friendly. Condado Beach, Isla Verde, and Ocean Park all have white sand, palm trees, ocean breezes, beautiful bodies, and ample eating and drinking options. Snorkeling gear and other watersports equipment are available to rent.

If you're anxious to get out of the city, **Luquillo Beach,** about 48km (30 miles) east of San Juan, near the town of Luquillo, stretches along a vast coconut grove. Coral reefs protect the clear lagoon from the fierce Atlantic, and a "Sea Without Barriers" facility caters to people with physical disabilities. Be aware, however, that some sections of the beach aren't as well maintained as they once were.

All *balnearios*—government-run beaches with dressing rooms, showers, lifeguards, snack bars, and parking—are open to the public. They're closed on Monday; however, if Monday is a holiday, the beaches will be open that day but closed the next. Hours are

9am to 5pm in winter, 9am to 6pm during the off season. If you find a secluded spot, be vigilant about your surroundings: Solitude is nice, but there's safety in numbers.

SPORTS

DEEP-SEA FISHING Many say that Capt. Mike Benitez, who's chartered boats out of San Juan for more than 40 years, sets the standard by which other deep-sea-fishing captains are judged. Contact him at **Mike Benitez Marine Services,** P.O. Box 9066541, Puerto de Tierra, San Juan, PR 00906-6541 (*© 787/723-2292;* www.mikebenitezfishing.com). **Capt. Bill Burleson,** P.O. Box 8270, Humacao, PR 00792 (*© 787/850-7442*), operates charters off the southeast coast. For both companies, expect to pay US$680 for a half-day excursion for up to six anglers.

GOLF Puerto Rico is a golfer's dream, but you'll need to sign up for a ship excursion or rent a car to reach the major courses from San Juan. With 72 holes, **Hyatt Dorado Beach Resort & Country Club** (*© 787/796-8916;* www.hyatt.com), about 48km (30 miles) west of San Juan, offers the greatest concentration of golf in the Caribbean. Greens fees, including cart, are US$195 for play before 1pm and US$105 after 1:30pm. Club rentals are US$55.

All four 18-hole courses at the **Hyatt Regency Cerromar** and **Dorado Beach** properties here were designed by Robert Trent Jones, Sr. Jack Nicklaus ranks the 4th hole at the Dorado Beach East course as 1 of the 10 best-designed holes in the world. Greens fees are US$145 for 18 holes.

The **Doral Resort at Palmas del Mar** (*© 787/285-2256;* www.palmascountry club.com), 72km (45 miles) east of San Juan, has two courses: the par-71 Palm course designed by Gary Player, and the newer 18-hole Flamboyan course designed by Rees Jones. Greens fees for 18 holes are US$150 at the Palm, US$170 at the Flamboyan course, including cart.

The **Westin Rio Mar Country Club** (*© 787/888-7060;* www.westinriomar.com), 32km (20 miles) from San Juan in Rio Grande, also has two 18-hole courses, one designed by Tom and George Fazio, the other by Greg Norman. Greens fees, including cart, are US$190 (or US$130 for play after noon).

SCUBA DIVING & SNORKELING Puerto Rico offers excellent diving and snorkeling, but the best sites aren't within easy reach of San Juan. **Caribe Aquatic Adventures,** 1062 Calle 19, Villa Nevarez, San Juan (*© 787/281-8858;* www.caribeaquatic adventure.com), will take you to good diving and snorkeling sites around the capital or near Fajardo on the northeast coast. Caribe operates out of the Park Plaza Normandie (Avenida Muñoz-Rivera, at the corner of Calle Los Rasales in Puerta de Tierra). A local reef dive is US$50. Much more interesting trips to Fajardo (which include a picnic) require a minimum of four passengers; the cost is US$135 per person for certified divers, US$115 for divers who have completed a resort course, and US$85 for snorkelers. The Fajardo excursion must be booked a week in advance, the local reef dives a day in advance.

WINDSURFING, KITEBOARDING & JET-SKIING The most popular windsurfing beach in the San Juan area is **Puntas las Marías,** between Isla Verde and Ocean Park. You can rent equipment and take lessons from nearby **Velauno,** 2430 Calle Loiza (*© 866/778-3521* or 787/728-8716; www.velauno.com). Boards and a complete rig are US$75 per day; 4-hour beginner lessons are US$150. Velauno also offers kiteboarding (windsurfing powered by a large kite rather than sails); lessons are US$75 an hour, including equipment. Another popular place for windsurfing is along the beachfront of the **Hyatt Dorado Beach Resort & Country Club,** about 48km (30 miles) west of San Juan. **Blue Dolphin Watersports** (© 787/796-1234, ext. 3768), rents windsurfing equipment, jet skis, kayaks, and sailboats.

GAMBLING

Casinos are one of San Juan's biggest draws, and most large hotels have one. They're generally open daily from noon (slots from 10am) to 4am, and many never close. Dress, usually informal during the day (though no bathing suits, flip flops, or tank tops), becomes impressive in the evenings. The **Casino at the Ritz-Carlton,** Avenue of the Governors, Isla Verde (© 787/253-1700), is the largest in Puerto Rico. Combining elegant 1940s decor with tropical fabrics and patterns, it's one of the plushest entertainment complexes in the Caribbean. The **Inter-Continental San Juan,** 5961 Isla Verde Ave. (© 800/443-2009 or 787/791-6100), is another elegant place to rendezvous. One of its Murano glass chandeliers is "longer than a bowling alley." Most convenient for cruise ship passengers is the **Sheraton Old San Juan Hotel & Casino,** 100 Brumbaugh St. (© 787/721-5100), directly across from Pier 3 and often bustling.

GREAT LOCAL RESTAURANTS & BARS

San Juan has some of the best restaurants in the Caribbean and a variety of cuisines that only a major city can offer. A favorite local beer is **Medalla.** The most famous local rum is **Bacardi,** in all of its varieties; **Don Q** is also popular.

In Old San Juan, **Amadeus,** 106 Calle San Sebastián (© 787/722-8635), offers nouvelle Caribbean dishes and features an intimate courtyard in back. Lunch is about US$22. **El Patio de Sam,** practically next door at 102 Calle San Sebastián (© 787/723-1149), is a popular gathering spot for expatriates, journalists, and shopkeepers. Lunch is around US$13.

The unpretentious **La Bombonera,** 259 Calle San Francisco (© 787/722-0658), famous for its homemade Puerto Rican meals and 1940s diner atmosphere, has attracted the island's literati and Old San Juan families for decades. San Juan's trailblazing nuevo Latino bistro, **Parrot Club,** 363 Calle Fortaleza (© 787/725-7370), blends Spanish, Taíno, and African cuisines. Lunch is about US$30.

In Condado, **Miró Marisquería Catalana,** 76 Condado Ave. (© 787/723-9593), serves seafood and traditional Catalonian dishes. Lunch is around US$20. Not far away, **Ajili Mójili,** 1006 Ashford Ave. (© 787/725-9195), serves some of the island's best upmarket Puerto Rican cuisine. Lunch is about US$20.

For stylish but relaxed beachfront dining and sublime Caribbean delicacies, no place beats **Pamela's,** 1 Calle Santa Ana, in Ocean Park (© 787/726-5010). You'll savor every bite. Lunch is about US$30.

26 St. Barts

Chic, sophisticated St. Barts (or, technically, St. Barthélemy, a name nobody ever uses) is internationally renowned as one of the ritziest refuges in the Caribbean, rivaled only by Mustique as the preferred island retreat of the rich and famous. From early fans Nureyev, Baryshnikov, and Buffett to later enthusiasts Mick Jagger, Princess Di, Calvin Klein, Madonna, and Naomi Campbell, the glitterati who've played here form a veritable who's who of fabulousness. Despite its transformation over the past couple of decades into a celebrity hot spot, St. Barts retains its charm, serenity, natural beauty, and Gallic flavor. Just 24km (15 miles) from St. Martin and politically part of Guadeloupe, the island's 21 sq. km (8 sq. miles) of dramatic hills and pristine white-sand

beaches are decidedly French, like a peaceful slice of the Côte d'Azur transplanted in the Caribbean. A combination of things—including the roller-coaster terrain, strict zoning and construction laws, and a local consensus that stratospheric pricing is the surest way to maintain exclusivity—protects the island from massive development that would certainly change its character.

First inhabited about 3,000 years ago by Ciboney Indians, then later by Arawaks (A.D. 200) and Caribs (A.D. 1000), St. Barts was first spotted by Europeans in 1496, when Christopher Columbus named the island after his baby brother, Bartolemeo. The French took possession of the island in the mid–17th century, and then in 1784, traded it to the Swedes, who built forts, houses, and roads and declared St. Barts a free port. Sweden transferred it back to France in 1878 after its colony began to falter. It wasn't until the 1980s that St. Barts began to impress jet-setting tourists. Later, tax breaks for French nationals fueled investment in tourism.

In sharp contrast to most Caribbean islands, where descendants of African slaves form the majority, the 7,000 year-round residents of St. Barts are primarily of French ancestry, mostly from Brittany and Normandy. Many affluent Americans and Europeans have villas on the island—some living in the Caribbean year-round, others making seasonal visits.

COMING ASHORE   Cruise ships anchor off **Gustavia,** the main town, and ferry passengers to the dollhouse-size harbor and town via tenders. Phones and ATMs are in the immediate vicinity of the harbor. The post office (or PTT), which also serves as a telecommunications center, is located at the back corner of the harbor opposite the dock.

You can check your e-mail at the second-floor offices of **Centre @lizes,** on rue de la République (© **590/29-89-89**), a few blocks to the right of the dock. Internet access is about US$6 per 30 minutes. Be sure to ask for an American keyboard: The position of letters on French keyboards is not significantly different, but it's just enough to cause frustration. Open Monday through Saturday from 8:30am to 8:30pm, Sunday from 3 to 8:30pm. From May through November, it's closed for lunch. Another option is **Terrazza** (© **590/27-70-67**), a cheery Internet cafe, lounge, and Italian restaurant on the side of a steep cobblestone hill in St. Jean (across from **Hotel Le Village St. Jean**). Open November through May Thursday through Tuesday from 7:30am to 11pm, and June through October daily from 7:30am to 6pm.

LANGUAGE   French is the official language, but virtually everyone speaks English as well.

CURRENCY   St. Barts is part of the French overseas region of Guadeloupe, so the **euro** (€) is now the official currency (exchange rate at press time: .82€ = US$1; 1€ = US$1.22). Each euro is divisible by 100 cents. You'll have no trouble using Visa, Mastercard, and traveler's checks. Unless otherwise noted, prices mentioned in this section are in U.S. dollars.

INFORMATION   The **Office Municipal du Tourisme,** adjacent to the dock on quai Général de Gaulle (© **590/27-87-27**), is open Monday through Friday from 8:30am to 12:30pm and 2 to 5:30pm (Fri until 5pm). For information before you go, get on the horn to the U.S. office of **Maison de la France** (© **212/838-7800;** www. st-barths.com).

CALLING FROM THE U.S.   When calling St. Barts from the United States, dial the international access code (011) and 590 before the numbers listed here, which also begin with 590. That's right: If you want to make a connection, you have to dial 590 twice. It's just one of those oddities that makes the world go 'round.

GETTING AROUND
BY TAXI   Taxis meet cruise ships at Gustavia's harbor. Because the island is so small, no destination is too distant. Consequently, fares seem reasonable. Dial © **590/27-66-31** for service if you don't spot a cab. The fare ranges from approximately US$10 to US$22, depending on your destination.

BY SHUTTLE   A new option for day-trippers is the **St. Barts Shuttle** (© **590/29-44-19**), which runs every 15 minutes nonstop from 9am to 1am. It can be picked up at various hotels and restaurants around the island. Most restaurants and stores in Gustavia sell tickets, which cost about US$12 round-trip.

BY MOTOR SCOOTER   Terrified by the winding roads and speeding drivers, mothers on St. Barts are loath to let their kids ride scooters. Few bikes have the power to make it up the steep hills anyway. If you have a death wish, go ahead and rent a motorbike or scooter from **Tropic'all Rent,** rue du Roi Oscar II, Gustavia (© **590/27-64-76**). Expect to pay about US$36 for the day, mandatory helmet included. A US$200 deposit or credit card imprint is required.

Frommer's Favorite St. Barts Experiences

Making the Scene at Le Select: For more than 50 years, this garden cafe has been the most popular gathering spot in Gustavia and the best place to get a taste of local life. (See "Great Local Restaurants & Bars," below.)

Bronzing on the Beach: St. Barts has several gorgeous beaches, some social, some private. (See "Beaches," below.)

Zipping Around the Island in a Suzuki Samurai: Few experiences are as exhilarating as zooming along the island's roller-coaster roads in an open-air vehicle. (See "Getting Around," above.)

BY RENTAL CAR   If you love adventure, rent a Suzuki Samurai: Zipping up and down the island's jagged, picturesque hills is more thrilling than riding most amusement-park rides. Local drivers are alert and competent, but they tend to drive aggressively and the roads aren't exactly in top condition. Automatic transmissions are in short supply, so reserve in advance: If you're not already adept at using a stick shift, St. Barts is not the place to learn. **Avis, Budget, Hertz,** and **National** have offices here, as do local firms **Turbé Car Rental** (© **590/27-71-42**) and **Europcar** (© **590/27-74-34**). The island has only two gas stations: one near the airport, the other in Lorient. Both are closed on Sunday, but the airport station has a pump that accepts credit cards any time of day, any day of the week.

BEST CRUISE LINE SHORE EXCURSIONS

Jet-Set Boat & Beach Excursion (US$200, 4 hr.): Circumnavigate St. Barts in a 12m (39-ft.) cruiser, then tender ashore at St. Jean Beach for a swim, a snorkel, or drinks from the open bar.

St. Barts on Horseback (US$55, 1½ hr.): Travel to northern St. Barts for a relaxed guided ride through the island's outback.

ON YOUR OWN: WITHIN WALKING DISTANCE

Aside from shopping, eating, and hanging out in sidewalk cafes, cruisers sticking close to port can visit Gustavia's modest points of interest. **St. Bartholomew's Church,** rue Samuel Fahlberg, dates from the 1850s and features limestone and volcanic-stone walls, as well as imported pitch-pine pews. Its tiny Anglican, English-speaking congregation is an anomaly on this overwhelmingly French Catholic island.

Evidence of St. Barts's faint but lingering Swedish presence, the **Wall House,** rue Duquesne, is a staid stone building near the harbor's mouth, across from the dock. Once a Swedish home, the structure was rebuilt after fire devastated it (and much of Gustavia) in 1852. Since 1989, it has housed the **Municipal Museum** (© **590/29-71-55**), an unfocused but respectable introduction to the history, sociology, ethnology, economy, and ecology of the island. The most interesting items include Amerindian artifacts, rustic farm furnishings, clothing used by early French settlers, and photos documenting hurricane devastation. Admission is US$2 for those over 12. The exhibits are open Monday, Tuesday, Thursday, and Friday from 8:30am to 12:30pm and 2:30 to 6pm; Wednesday from 8:30am to 12:30pm; and Saturday from 9 to 9:30am.

ON YOUR OWN: BEYOND THE PORT AREA

Visiting the tiny fishing village of **Corossol** is a vibrant way to experience the St. Barts of the past. About 10 minutes by taxi from the dock, this quaint, totally un-chic hamlet is home to traditional folk who still live off the sea. It's your best bet for spotting women in traditional 17th-century bonnets and for watching roadside vendors weave items from palm fronds. On the town's waterfront, about 30m (98 ft.) to the left of the road from Gustavia, the **Inter Oceans Museum** (© 590/27-62-97) catalogs thousands of shells, corals, sand dollars, sea horses, sea urchins, and fish from around the world. One (now very old) man's obsession, the museum's homemade, thorough displays are completely endearing and sure to enthrall the child in everyone. Don't miss the collection of sand from beaches around the world: A cocktail umbrella is planted in each specimen. Admission is US$3. Doors to this extension of the owner's home are open Tuesday through Saturday from 9am to 12:30pm and 3 to 6pm. Afterward, stop by **Le Regal** (© 590/27-85-26) and have a beer or a bite with the locals.

SHOPPING

A duty-free port, St. Barts is a good place to buy liquor, perfume, and other French luxury items. Good deals on apparel, crystal, porcelain, and watches can also be found, especially during April, the biggest sale month. Moisturizer mavens can stock up on the island's own cosmetic line, **Ligne St. Barth.** Shops are concentrated in Gustavia and St. Jean, where the quality-to-schlock ratio is as high as anywhere in the Caribbean. Most shops and offices close for a long lunch, usually from noon to 2pm.

If you're looking for big-name brands, you'll find them all in Gustavia, from **Burberry** and **Cartier** to **Hermès** and **Roberto Cavalli.** But there are also plenty of sophisticated local boutiques worth exploring.

In Gustavia, **Carat,** rue de la République; **Fabienne Miot,** rue de la République; and **Diamond Genesis,** rue du Général de Gaulle, offer an array of fine jewelry, some handcrafted on the premises. **St. Barth Style,** rue Lafayette, near rue du Port, stocks fashionable beachwear, while **Sabina Zest,** cours Vendôme, carries cotton voile, silk, linen, and lace clothes and accessories, all made in St Barts. High-style women's fashion is also available at **Stéphane & Bernard,** rue de la République, behind Carat.

Men in search of a stylish new shirt or tie should try **Café Coton,** rue du Bord de Mer. Both men's and women's shoes can be found at **Human Steps,** rue de la France. **Privilège,** rue du Roi Oscar II, and **Ana Taïna,** rue Schoelcher, are your best bets for perfumes and cosmetics.

Le Comptoir du Cigare, rue du Général de Gaulle, sells cigars from Cuba and the Dominican Republic along with connoisseur-quality rums, while **Pipiri Art Gallery,** rue du Général de Gaulle, features the work of local artists—and is also a boutique and restaurant with a delightful garden.

In St. Jean, **Kiwi Saint Tropez** and **Pain de Sucre** stock chic beachwear, **Bleu Marine** has French and Italian women's fashions, **Elysees Caraïbes** sells high-style handbags and luggage, and **Boutique Iléna** offers gorgeous lingerie.

BEACHES

The 22 beaches of St. Barts are first-rate. Few are ever crowded, even during the peak season, and all are public, free, and easily accessible by taxi from the cruise pier (make arrangements with your driver to be picked up at a specific time). As St. Barts is a French island, toplessness is common at all beaches. Full nudism is officially prohibited, but bathers at several sites—Saline and Gouverneur, to name a couple (see below)—willfully flout the rules. Defying a common stereotype, most nude bathers on the island actually have attractive bodies.

Shell Beach, just a short walk from the harbor in Gustavia, is the most convenient place to soak up the sun if your time is limited. The water is calm and **Do Brazil** (_C_ 590/29-06-66), a lively fusion restaurant right on the beach, is an ideal spot for lunch or for watching the sunset. You can also grab a sandwich to go at **Zen Beach Bar** (_C_ 590/27-19-39), a snack bar below.

St. Jean, the busiest and most social beach on the island, is protected by a coral reef; its calm waters attract families and watersports enthusiasts, including windsurfers and, when the winds gather greater force, the occasional surfer. Near the end of the airport's incredibly short runway, St. Jean also provides numerous eating, drinking, shopping, and people-watching opportunities.

Gouverneur, on the south-central coast, is quiet and relatively remote. Its idyllic setting and unspoiled beauty make it number one with locals and discerning visitors who want privacy and serenity. (The steep and winding drive to the beach is an experience in itself.)

Farther east, in a wild and rustic area that was once the site of salt ponds, **Saline** is reached by a 3-minute walk over a sand dune. It's most famous for its adult environment and nude bathers. Plan on eating lunch at one of the many nearby dining spots (see "Great Local Restaurants & Bars," below).

For a more serious hike, start at the end of the beach at Flamands and trek about 20 minutes to **Colombier.** This beach is magnificent—and you'll enjoy the views of the rugged coast along the way.

If you'd rather skip the trek, just stay at **Flamands,** which boasts great bodysurfing waves. If you long to feel a part of the St Barts scene, park yourself on a lounge chair on the sand in front of the **Isle de France** hotel and splurge on a salad or sandwich at the restaurant, **La Case de L'Ile** (_C_ 590/27-61-81). A light lunch will cost you about US$38. (Don't say we didn't warn you.)

SPORTS

SAILING, SCUBA DIVING & SNORKELING   **Marine Service,** quai du Yacht Club (_C_ 590/27-70-34), operates from the marina across the harbor from the busier side of Gustavia. Most dive sites served by this five-star PADI operator are a 10- to 20-minute boat ride from the harbor; depths vary from 3 to 30m (10–98 ft.). Reef dives are the rule, although one wreck dive for more experienced divers is a possibility. One-tank dives are about US$66; two-tank dives are about US$120, including beverages and all equipment. The operation also offers half-day snorkeling cruises (about US$78, including snorkeling gear, a French snack buffet, and an open bar) and catamaran or sloop charters (starting at US$540 for half a day in the off season and US$650 in winter, including cheese, fruit, beverages, and music). The cost is for a maximum of eight people and includes a crew. Call for Christmas and New Year's rates.

Vendors at both St. Jean and Grand Cul de Sac rent snorkel gear and other watersports equipment—jet skis, Sunfish sailboats, and so on.

WINDSURFING   Try **Waterplay,** near the Tom Beach Hotel at St. Jean (_C_ 590/27-32-62), or **Windwave Power,** at Grand Cul de Sac (_C_ 590/27-82-57). Expect to pay about US$32 an hour for a full rig.

GREAT LOCAL RESTAURANTS & BARS

Mix lots of rich, discerning diners with the French tradition of culinary expertise, and it's no wonder that so many of the island's restaurants consistently receive high accolades. It's a pity that some of the best open only for dinner, well after your ship has gone out to sea. Luckily, enough serve lunch to assure you one of the best meals of your cruise.

IN GUSTAVIA If you're interested in seeing and being seen, make a beeline for **Le Select,** rue de la France at rue du Général de Gaulle (✆ **590/27-86-87**), the epicenter of Gustavia's social life for more than 50 years. This cafe's tables rest in a tree-shaded garden a block from the harbor. A full bar is available to complement the burgers, salads, and other simple fare. Salty locals, celebrities, and chic tourists are among the clientele. The classic, funky ambience supposedly inspired Jimmy Buffet's "Cheeseburger in Paradise." Lunch costs around US$15.

At the foot of the Gustavia harbor, **La Route des Boucaniers** (✆ **590/27-73-00**) looks like any seaside restaurant around Chesapeake Bay or on the Jersey Shore, but its traditional and nouvelle Creole cuisine is anything but run-of-the-mill. Try the octopus gratin served in a potato shell, or the braised scallops with passion fruit. Lunch is about US$30.

AT ST. JEAN **Eden Rock** (✆ **590/29-79-99**) has three restaurants at St. Jean beach: one on the rock promontory that bisects the strand, one next to the ocean, and one in the sand, aptly dubbed the Sand Bar, which serves lunch at a cost of about US$42. Traditional French cuisine, seafood, and tropical drinks are the trio's strong suits. For great pizza and friendly ambience, try the **Hideaway** (✆ **590/27-63-62**), where lunch will be around US$25. You can relax on the open-air terrace or get your order to go. If you're more in the mood for a sandwich and want to get back to the sun, head to **KiKi-e Mo** (✆ **590/27-90-65**), an Italian gourmet shop that whips up tasty, relatively inexpensive light fare to go. Lunch is about US$12.

AT LORIENT For a *très* French experience, have a café au lait and a pain au choco-lat at the sunny **La Petite Colombe** (✆ **590/29-74-30**), which will cost you about US$8.

AT SALINE A handful of restaurants are within walking distance of the Saline beach. **PaCri** (✆ **590/29-35-63**) is a pretty little indoor/outdoor Italian spot serving pizza and sandwiches. Lunch is about US$25. More upscale but still relaxing, **Le Tamarin** (✆ **590/27-72-12**) specializes in beef, salmon, and tuna carpaccios; fresh grilled lobster; and inventive Creole dishes. Lunch is around US$55.

AT PUBLIC If you're lucky enough to be on a ship that stays in port past sunset, get yourself to **Maya's** (✆ **590/27-75-73**) for sunset cocktails or dinner (opens at 4pm; closed Sun). Feast your eyes on an unbeatable view of the sea and the glamorous clientele while enjoying flavorfully prepared fresh seafood. Dinner is about US$65. If, alas, your ship leaves port earlier, you can at least enjoy the food at **Maya's to Go** (✆ **590/29-83-70**), located across from the airport in St. Jean. It's open Monday through Saturday from 7am to 7pm and offers pastries, sandwiches, quiche, and salads.

27 St. Kitts

Somewhat off the beaten tourist track, south of St. Martin and north of Guadeloupe, St. Kitts forms the larger half of the combined Federation of St. Kitts and Nevis, which gained self-government from Britain in 1967 and became a totally independent nation in 1983. The two islands are separated by only about 3.2km (2 miles) of

St. Kitts map — Legend: Airport, Beach, Cruise Ship Dock, Ferry Route, Mountain. Locations: Dieppe Bay Town, Dieppe Bay, St. Paul's, Sandy Bay, Sadlers, Newton Ground, Mt. Liamuiga, Hermitage Bay, Ottley's, ATLANTIC OCEAN, Sandy Point Town, Brimstone Hill Fortress, Cayon, Keys, Half-Way Tree, Romney Gardens/Carib Rock Drawings, Middle Island, Old Road Town, St. Peter's, Conaree Beach, Challengers, Carib Brewery, North Frigate Bay, Basseterre, North Friar's Bay, Frigate Bay, Royal St. Kitts Golf Club, South Friar's Bay, Turtle Beach, Sand Bank Bay, Great Salt Pond, Caribbean Sea, White House Bay, St. Anthony's Peak, Cockleshell Bay, Banana Bay, Nag's Head, to Nevis. Scale: 5 mi / 5 km.

ocean, and while the citizens of Nevis have, in the past, expressed a strong urge for independence from St. Kitts, in recent years, this movement has died down and the dual-island nation, for the most part, lives in peaceful coexistence.

St. Kitts—or St. Christopher, a name hardly anyone uses—is by far the more populous of the two islands, with some 36,000 people. It was the first English settlement in the Western Hemisphere, and during the plantation age, its 176 sq. km (69 sq. miles) enjoyed one of the richest sugar cane economies in the Caribbean—until 2005, when it ceased the production of sugar cane for export. Cane fields still climb the slopes of a volcanic mountain range, and you'll see ruins of old mills and plantation houses as you drive around the island.

St. Kitts is lush and fertile, dotted with rainforests and waterfalls, and boasting some lovely beaches along its southeast coastline. After being hit by several successive hurricanes in the late 1990s, a push to improve the amenities and infrastructure of the country, among other efforts at wooing tourists to bring in badly needed cash, has proved fruitful. The bulk of the island's revenue now comes from tourism, followed by agriculture.

The island is crowned by the 1,156m (3,792-ft.) **Mt. Liamuiga,** a crater that, thankfully, remains dormant. The island's most impressive landmark is the **Brimstone Hill Fortress,** one of the Caribbean's most impressive forts. The capital, **Basseterre,** is rife with old-time Caribbean architecture and has a few worthwhile landmarks, but overall the city offers little to hold the interest of visitors.

COMING ASHORE **Port Zante** has undergone a rebuilding and expansion, including a second cruise pier that, at press time, is scheduled to be completed in 2006. The new port, which stretches from the center of town into the deep offshore waters, will offer about 64,100 sq. m (689,966 sq. ft.) of shopping and office space, restaurants, a hotel/casino, and a welcome center.

LANGUAGE English is the language of both St. Kitts and Nevis.

CURRENCY The local currency is the **Eastern Caribbean dollar** (EC$2.70 = US$1; EC$1 = US73¢). Many shops and restaurants quote prices in U.S. dollars. Always determine which currency locals are talking about. We've used U.S.-dollar prices in this section.

INFORMATION You can get local information at the **St. Kitts Tourism Authority,** Pelican Mall, Bay Road, in Basseterre (© **869/465-4040**), open Monday through Friday from 8:30am to 5pm. For info before you go, call © **800/582-6208** or go to www.stkitts-tourism.com.

CALLING FROM THE U.S. When calling St. Kitts or Nevis from the United States, you just need to dial a "1" before the numbers listed here.

GETTING AROUND

BY TAXI Taxis wait at the docks in Basseterre and in the Circus, a public square near the docks at the intersection of Bank and Fort streets. Since most drivers are also guides, this is the best means of getting around the island. Taxis aren't metered, so you must agree on the price before heading out. Always ask if the rates quoted are in U.S. dollars or Eastern Caribbean dollars.

BY RENTAL CAR **Avis** and **Thrifty** have offices on the island, as do local rental agencies **Cool Profile** (© 869/465-4448) and **Williams Car Rental** (© 869/663-6119). Road conditions are good, but keep in mind that driving is on the left side.

BEST CRUISE LINE SHORE EXCURSIONS

Brimstone Hill Fortress (US$39, 3 hr.): Among the largest and best preserved of all the forts in the Caribbean, Brimstone Hill (www.brimstonehillfortress.org) dates from 1690, when the British fortified the hill to help recapture Fort Charles, located below, from the French. In 1782, an invading force of 8,000 French troops bombarded the fortress for a month before its small British garrison, supplemented by local militia, surrendered. When the British took the island back the next year, they proceeded to enlarge the fort into the "Gibraltar of the West Indies." In all, the structure took 104 years to complete. Today, it's the centerpiece of a national park crisscrossed by nature trails, with a population of green vervet monkeys to keep things lively. Perched on the upper slopes of a tall, steep hill, it's a photographer's paradise, with views of mountains, fields, and the Caribbean Sea—on a clear day, you can see six neighboring islands. From below, the fort presents a dramatic picture, poised among diabolical-looking spires and outcroppings of lava rock. Its name comes from the odor of sulfur released by nearby undersea vents. Tours typically include a visit to the beautiful **Romney Gardens,** located amid the ruins of a sugar estate between Basseterre and the fort. You can check out the lush hillside gardens (featuring giant ferns, orchids, poinsettias, and "The Tree," a 350-year-old Saman tree), say hi to the cows that graze just across

Frommer's Favorite St. Kitts Experiences

Visiting Brimstone Hill Fortress: This is one of the most impressive forts in the Caribbean, with battlement after battlement leading up to a spectacular view of the sea. (See "Best Cruise Line Shore Excursions," below.)

Hiking Mt. Liamuiga: The hike up this dormant volcano will take you through a rainforest and along deep ravines up to the rim of the crater at a cool 788m (2,585 ft.). (See "Best Cruise Line Shore Excursions," below.)

Taking a Rainforest Adventure Hike: Departing from Romney Gardens, about 8km (5 miles) from Basseterre, you'll hike along a loop trail through rainforest, which lets you get a feel for the island's lush interior.

the hill, or shop at **Caribelle Batik** (© 869/465-6253), one of the island's most popular boutiques, where you'll find rack after rack of Indonesian-style, hand-printed, brightly colored clothes. (If you're coming here on your own, look for signs indicating a turnoff along the coast road, about 8km/5 miles north of Basseterre in the town of Old Road.)

Mt. Liamuiga Volcano Hike (US$109, 7 hr.): The name of this dormant volcano, in the northwest area of the island, means "fertile land" in the Carib Indian language. It sputtered its last gasp around 1692, and today its summit is a major goal for hikers. On this excursion, you'll hike about 1,156m (3,792 ft.) to the summit, traveling along narrow trails and through the island's rainforest. It takes about 3 hours to reach the top. Two lookout points offer views of the crater and the crater lake below. Refreshments are offered before the hike back down. This is a great trip, if you're in shape.

Mountain Biking & Beach Tour (US$78, 4 hr.): From the pier, you'll ride through Basseterre and then out through sugar cane fields and up 450m (1,476-ft.) Olivees Mountain for views and refreshments. After the ride down, you'll stop at Friar's Bay for a swim and snack. It's a nice way to see this lush island.

St. Kitts Scenic Railway (US$99, 3½ hr.): Take a scenic ride on the "Sugar Train," a deluxe, double-decker train that follows the same tracks built in 1912 to haul cane from the fields to the sugar mills. Learn about the island's culture, people, and history while you view abandoned windmills and chimneys from old sugar estates, along with a canopy of rainforest vegetation along the slopes of Mt. Liamuiga.

EXCURSIONS OFFERED BY LOCAL AGENCIES

Rainforest Tours: For a great rainforest walk in the thickets around Romney Gardens, contact Addy of **Addy's Rainforest Safaris** (© 869/465-8069). He knows the flora and fauna of St. Kitts like the back of his hand and delivers a satisfying, personal rainforest experience, ending his tour by sharing a plate of his wife's tasty homemade banana bread and some fresh guava and passion-fruit juices.

Hikes: Call **Greg's Safaris** (© 869/465-4121; www.gregssafaris.com) to arrange full-day hikes to Mt. Liamuiga (US$85 per person) or assorted half-day hikes around the island (US$50). The owner, Greg Pereira, is a local folklore and botanical expert.

Taxi Tours: You'll find a fleet of taxis waiting at the dock as you disembark from your ship. Taxi drivers will take you on a 3-hour tour of the island for about US$60. Lunch can be arranged at one of the local inns. Good inn choices are **Golden Lemon,** at Dieppe Bay (© 869/465-7260), and **Rawlins Plantation,** in Mount Pleasant (© 869/465-6221).

ON YOUR OWN: WITHIN WALKING DISTANCE

The capital city of Basseterre, where the docks are located, has typical British colonial architecture and some quaint buildings, a few shops, and a market where locals display fruits and flowers—but even this description might be giving you the wrong idea about the place. The truth is, it's a very poor town, with few attractions aimed at visitors. When we were last here, there were chickens walking around in front of the government buildings. **St. George's Anglican Church,** on Cayon Street (walk straight up Church St. or Fort St. from the dock), is the oldest church in town, and is worth a look. **Independence Square,** a stone's throw from the docks along Bank Street, is pretty, with its central fountain and old church, but there's no good reason to linger unless it's to sit in the shade and toss back a bottle of Ting, the local grapefruit-based soda.

ON YOUR OWN: BEYOND THE PORT AREA

All of the good out-of-town sites here are covered under "Best Cruise Line Shore Excursions," above.

SHOPPING

Basseterre is not a shopping town, despite handout maps that show a listing of shops that would put St. Thomas to shame. Look closer and you'll see entries such as "R. Gumbs Electrical," "TDC/Finco Finance Co.," and "Horsford Furniture Store." Turns out the list just includes every business on every street in town, no matter whether it's of interest to visitors or not. Strength in numbers, we suppose. Still, the port complex offers a number of shopping options.

At Romney Gardens, you'll find **Caribelle Batik** (© 869/465-6253), one of the island's most popular boutiques for Indonesian-style, hand-printed, brightly colored clothes. The Brimstone Hill excursion and the rainforest hike typically include a stop here. If you're coming on your own, look for signs indicating a turnoff along the coast road, about 8km (5 miles) north of Basseterre in the town of Old Road.

BEACHES

The narrow peninsula in the southeast contains the island's salt ponds and also boasts the best white-sand beaches (approach via the winding, hilly road for a dramatic and gorgeous view). All beaches, even those that border hotels, are free and open to the public. However, you must usually pay a fee to use a hotel's beach facilities.

You'll find the best swimming at **Conaree Beach,** 4.8km (3 miles) from Basseterre; **Frigate Bay,** with its talcum-powder-fine sand; and the twin beaches of **Banana Bay** and **Cockleshell Bay,** at the southeast corner of the island. The most popular choice is **Turtle Beach,** where you might just be greeted by the resident pig, Wilbur. If you're lucky, the green vervet monkeys may come down from the hillside behind the beach to say hello as well. Food and drink are available. (*Beware:* The monkeys have been known to steal drinks from unsuspecting tourists.)

SPORTS

GOLF   The **Royal St. Kitts Golf Club** (© 869/466-2700; www.royalstkittsgolf club.com) is less than a 10-minute drive from the cruise port. Greens fees at the recently remodeled championship golf course are US$170 for 18 holes and US$120 for 9 holes during high season; rates are cheaper from May through October (cart rental included). A cab from the cruise terminal will cost you about US$10 for up to four people.

SCUBA DIVING & SNORKELING Practically unknown as a dive destination, the waters surrounding St. Kitts boast plentiful and virtually untouched coral reefs, shoals, hot water vents, shallows, sloping canyons, walls, and swim-through caverns that are all home to colorful marine life at depths 12 to 60m (40–200 ft.). One recently discovered and excavated dive site is located at **White House Bay,** where the wreck of a 1740s English troopship rests.

One of the best diving spots is **Nag's Head,** at the southern tip of St. Kitts. This is an excellent shallow-water dive for certified divers, starting at 3m (9¾ ft.) and extending to 21m (69 ft.). You'll see a variety of tropical fish, eagle rays, and lobster here. Another good site is **Booby Shoals,** between Cow 'n' Calf Rocks and Booby Island. Booby Shoals has abundant sea life, including nurse sharks, lobster, and stingrays. Dives here are up to 9m (30 ft.) in depth and are good for both certified and beginning divers.

Local dive operators include **Dive St. Kitts,** at Bird Rock Beach Hotel in Basseterre (✆ 869/465-1189; www.divestkitts.com), and **Pro Divers,** at Fisherman's Wharf (✆ 869/466-DIVE; www.prodiversstkitts.com). Single- or two-tank dives depart from the Port Zante dock at 9am and return by 1pm. Two-tank dives with equipment run about US$95.

GREAT LOCAL RESTAURANTS & BARS

The favorite local beer is **Carib,** brewed right on the northern edge of Basseterre. There's a local cane-sugar drink called **CSR (Cane Spirit Rothschild)** that tastes a bit like Brazilian *cachaça* (clear rum), but with a slight licorice flavor, and is usually mixed with the Jamaican grapefruit soda **Ting** or with the locally produced **Brinley Gold Vanilla Rum** (also available in coffee and mango flavors; look for the Brinley Rum shop at the port).

For some of the best baby back ribs in town, head to **Ballahoo Restaurant** (✆ 869/ 465-4197), located at Basseterre's most picturesque intersection (the Circus, right by the cruise dock). Seafood platters, such as garlic shrimp, curried conch, or fresh lobster, are served with salad and rice. Lunch is US$25.

There are also a number of pastry shops nearby, or you can try the roti and other local favorites at **Excelsior Restaurant,** on New Street (✆ 869/465-6693). Lunch will cost about US$15.

28 St. Lucia

With a turbulent history shared by many of its Caribbean neighbors, St. Lucia (pronounced *Loo*-sha), second largest of the Windward Islands at about 622 sq. km (243 sq. miles), changed hands often during the colonial period—it was British seven times and French seven times. Today, though, it's an independent state that's become one of the most popular destinations in the Caribbean, with some of the finest resorts. The heaviest development is concentrated in the northwest, between the capital of Castries and the northern end of the island, where there's a string of white-sand beaches. The interior boasts relatively unspoiled green-mantled mountains and gentle valleys, as well as the volcanic **Soufrière.** Two dramatic peaks, the **Pitons,** rise along the southwest coast.

Castries, the capital, is a large harbor surrounded by hills. Because of fires that devastated many of its older structures, the town today has touches of modernity, with glass-and-concrete buildings, although there's still an old-fashioned Saturday-morning market on Jeremie Street. The country women dress in traditional cotton headdress to sell their luscious fruits and vegetables, while weather-beaten men sit close by playing warrie (a fast game played with pebbles on a carved board) or fleet games of dominoes using tiles the color of cherries.

COMING ASHORE Most cruise ships arrive at a fairly new pier at **Pointe Seraphine,** within walking distance of the center of Castries. Unlike piers on other islands, this one boasts St. Lucia's best shopping. You'll also find a visitor information bureau. Phone cards are sold for use at specially labeled phones.

If Pointe Seraphine is too crowded (not too likely, as two megaships can pull alongside at once), your ship might dock at **Port Castries,** on the other side of the colorful harbor. There's a shopping terminal here called La Place Carenage, with duty-free stores and telephones. At press time, the port was in the process of adding a center depicting St. Lucia's history. If you still want to shop in Pointe Seraphine, a water taxi (US$1) runs between the two locations all day. A land taxi will cost you around US$4, or you can walk between the two areas.

Some smaller vessels, such as Star Clippers', Seabourn's, and Clipper's, anchor off **Rodney Bay** to the north or **Soufrière** to the south and carry you ashore by tender.

LANGUAGE English is the official language.

CURRENCY The official monetary unit is the **Eastern Caribbean dollar** (exchange rate: EC$2.70 = US$1; EC$1 = US73¢). Prices quoted in this section are in U.S. dollars, which are accepted by nearly all hotels, restaurants, and shops.

INFORMATION The **St. Lucia Tourist Board** is at Vide Bouteille, outside Castries (© 758/452-4094). The board runs a visitor information bureau at Pointe Seraphine, which is open Monday through Friday from 9am to 5pm. For info before you go, call the U.S. office at © 800/456-3984 or 212/867-2950, or check out www. stlucia.org.

CALLING FROM THE U.S. When calling St. Lucia from the United States, you need only dial a "1" before the numbers listed here.

GETTING AROUND

BY TAXI Most taxi drivers have been trained to serve as guides. Their cars are unmetered, but the government fixes tariffs for all standard trips. Be sure to determine whether the driver is quoting a rate in U.S. or EC dollars. There is an official taxi association servicing both Pointe Seraphine and La Place Carenage; this association will have standard fares posted. You can also hire a taxi to go to Soufrière on your own: A 3- to 4-hour tour for four passengers will cost about US$120, including a beach stop, photo ops, shopping, and sightseeing.

BY RENTAL CAR Driving is on the left, and roads are decent (but not great). The roads are narrow and not always clearly marked. We wouldn't recommend renting a car, but if you're set on it, **Avis, Budget,** and **Hertz** all have offices here, as does **Courtesy Rent-A-Car** (© 758/452-8140).

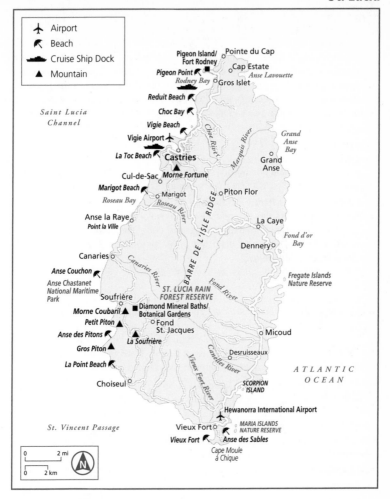

St. Lucia

Map legend:
- ✈ Airport
- ⚑ Beach
- 🚢 Cruise Ship Dock
- ▲ Mountain

Saint Lucia Channel

Pigeon Island/ Fort Rodney ○ Pointe du Cap
Pigeon Point ⚑ ▪ ○ Cap Estate
Rodney Bay ○ Anse Lavouette
Gros Islet

Reduit Beach ⚑

Choc Bay ⚑

Vigie Beach ⚑

Vigie Airport ✈

Choc River

Marquis River

Grand Anse Bay

La Toc Beach ⚑ **Castries**
▲ Morne Fortune
Grand Anse

Cul-de-Sac ○
Marigot Beach ⚑
Roseau Bay ○ Marigot
Roseau River
Piton Flor ○

BARRE DE L'ISLE RIDGE

Anse la Raye ○
Point la Ville
La Caye ○
Fond d'or Bay
Dennery ○

Canaries ○
Canaries River
Fond River

Anse Couchon ⚑
Anse Chastanet National Maritime Park
Fregate Islands Nature Reserve

Soufrière ○
ST. LUCIA RAIN FOREST RESERVE

Morne Coubaril ▲ ▪ Diamond Mineral Baths/ Botanical Gardens
Petit Piton ▲ ○ Fond
Anse des Pitons ⚑ St. Jacques
Gros Piton ▲ ▲ La Soufrière
Micoud ○

La Point Beach ⚑
Desruisseaux

Vieux Fort River

Canelles River

ATLANTIC OCEAN

Choiseul ○
SCORPION ISLAND

Hewanorra International Airport ✈
MARIA ISLANDS NATURE RESERVE

St. Vincent Passage
Vieux Fort ○ ✈
Vieux Fort ⚑ Anse des Sables
Cape Moule à Chique

0 — 2 mi
0 — 2 km
Ⓝ

BEST CRUISE LINE SHORE EXCURSIONS

Because of the difficult terrain, shore excursions are the best way to see this beautiful island in a day or less. In addition to the sampling below, most ships typically offer bus tours (many visiting the island's banana plantations) and snorkeling cruises.

Pigeon Island Sea Kayaking (US$69, 3 hr.): After transferring to Rodney Bay, you'll make the approximately 30-minute paddle out to the island, where you'll have time to swim, kayak some more, or make the steep climb up to Fort Rodney. From the summit of the fort, you'll have great views of the Pitons, and sometimes you'll even be able to see Martinique. (See below for more info.)

Rainforest Bicycle Tour (US$49, 4½ hr.): After being dropped off by bus in the middle of the forest, you'll ride past banana plantations and the Errard Falls waterfall,

Frommer's Favorite St. Lucia Experiences

Taking a Coastal Cruise: The best way to really see the lush coast of St. Lucia and the mighty Pitons is from the water. This tour allows you to explore the coast via catamaran or boat, with a chance for a quick swim in the crystal-clear waters of Anse Couchon. Afterward, via minibus, you'll visit the Sulphur Springs, where you can head right into a volcanic crater to see pools of bubbling mud, and then drive through the Roseau banana plantations and the fishing villages of Anse la Raye and Canaries. (This tour is also offered in reverse.)

Exploring a Banana Plantation: See how St. Lucia's leading export is grown and harvested. (See "On Your Own: Beyond the Port Area," below.)

Hiking up to Fort Rodney in Rodney Bay: The beautiful Pigeon Island on Rodney Bay offers the chance to hike up to Fort Rodney, an 18th-century English base that was used as an American signal station during World War II. From the top, you can catch sight of Martinique. (See "Best Cruise Line Shore Excursions," below.)

stopping to sample various fruits that grow along the roadside. Some time for swimming is usually included at the falls. A different tour called **Jungle Biking** (US$104, 4½ hr.) takes you by boat to the Jungle Biking facility, located on an 18th-century sugar plantation within the Anse Chastenet Resort. Here you can explore 19km (12 miles) of trails at your own pace. Beach time is included at the end.

Soody Nature Hike & Mineral Waterfall (US$55, 7 hr.): Drive along the west coast through fishing villages, banana plantations, and the edge of the rainforest before arriving at Soufrière, location of the Pitons and the Diamond Botanical Gardens. A guided hour-long hike through the volcanic forest introduces you to the island's flora and fauna; it ends up at a therapeutic sulfuric waterfall where you can take a dip to cure what ails ya. Lunch at a Creole restaurant is included.

Beach Snorkel (US$64, 3½ hr.): Snorkeling is spectacular around St. Lucia. This trip departs the Castries harbor by boat, traveling an hour en route to the island's marine reserve, which has an area set aside especially for snorkeling. There's also a supersize 7-hour (US$93) version of this trip that includes a buffet lunch.

EXCURSIONS OFFERED BY LOCAL AGENCIES

Horseback Treks: North of Castries, **Trim's National Riding Stables** offers picnic trips to the Atlantic side of the island, with a barbecue lunch and drinks included. Departure is at 10am. The fee is US$70 for a 2-hour ride. Nonriders can also join the excursion; they are transported to the site in a van and pay half-price. To make arrangements, contact René Trim at ✆ **758/450-8273.**

ON YOUR OWN: WITHIN WALKING DISTANCE

First, a tip: The last time we were at the duty-free marketplaces right at Castries' dock, a guy was doling out 5-minute massages for US$5. If he's still there, this could save you a bundle on those expensive Steiner massages aboard the ship!

Castries has a very colorful **Central Market,** right near the dock, which is worth a visit. The airplane-hangar-size emporium sells local food, trinkets, and produce. Buy some banana ketchup or local cinnamon sticks to take home.

The principal streets of Castries are William Peter Boulevard and Bridge Street. Don't miss a walk through town: People are very friendly, and **Jeremie Street** is chocka-block with variety stores of the most authentic local kind, selling everything from spices to housewares.

A Roman Catholic cathedral stands on **Columbus Square,** which has a few restored buildings. Take a gander at the enormous 400-year-old "rain" tree, also called a "no-name" tree, which grows in the Derek Walcott Square, named after the St. Lucian Nobel Prize winner for literature. The nearby Government House is a late Victorian structure.

Beyond Government House lies **Morne Fortune,** which means "Hill of Good Luck." Actually, no one's had much luck here, certainly not the French and British soldiers who battled for Fort Charlotte. The fort switched nationalities (from French to English, and vice versa) many times. You can visit the 18th-century barracks, complete with a military cemetery, a small museum, the Old Powder Magazine, and the Four Apostles Battery—four grim muzzle-loading cannons. The view of the harbor of Castries is panoramic from this point. You can also see north to Pigeon Island or south to the Pitons. To reach Morne Fortune, head east on Bridge Street.

ON YOUR OWN: BEYOND THE PORT AREA

Bananas are St. Lucia's leading export, so if you're being taken around the island by a taxi driver, ask him to stop at one of the huge plantations. (Most island tours include a drive through one of the plantations as a matter of course.) We suggest a look at one of the three biggest: the **Cul-de-Sac,** just north of Marigot Bay; **La Caye,** on the east coast in Dennery; or the **Roseau Estate,** south of Marigot Bay.

An ideal spot for picnics and nature walks is St. Lucia's first national park, **Pigeon Island National Landmark** (© 758/450-0603). It was originally an island but is now joined to the northwest shore of the mainland by a very environmentally unfriendly causeway that has disrupted offshore currents, thereby upsetting the local fishing industry. The 18-hectare (44-acre) island got its name from the red-neck pigeon, or ramier, which once made this island home. Interestingly, Pigeon Island is covered with lemongrass, which spread from original plantings made by British light-opera singer Josset, who leased the island for 30 years and grew the grass to provide thatch for her cottage's roof. Every few years the grass, which is full of volatile oils, catches fire and immolates much of the island before it can be put out. The best way to get to Pigeon Island National Landmark is to take a taxi and arrange to be picked up in time to return to your ship (the trip is 30 min., at most, back to the docks). Some small ships anchor here and bring passengers ashore by tender. Hours are daily from 8:30am to 5pm; admission is US$5 for adults, US$1 for children 6 to 12.

The island's **Interpretation Centre** contains artifacts and a multimedia display of local history, covering everything from the Amerindian settlers of A.D. 1000 to 1782's Battle of Saints, when Admiral Rodney's fleet set out from Pigeon Island and defeated the French admiral De Grasse. Right below the interpretation center is a cozy pub called the **Captain's Cellar** (© 758/450-0918), located in what was formerly a soldier's mess. From the tables outside, you get wonderful views of the crashing surf on the Atlantic coast, just a few steps away.

From the center, you can walk up the winding and moderately steep path to a look-out from which you can see Martinique. In 1780, Admiral Rodney said of this spot, "This is the post the Governor of Martinique has set his eye on and if possessed by the enemy would deprive us of the best anchorage place in these islands, from which Martinique is always attackable." Remember that when planning your own assault. You get a wonderful view from the pinnacle, and the cannons that ring the space are a nice place to pose for "I was there" pictures.

Pigeon Island's west coast has two white-sand beaches. There's also a restaurant, **Jambe de Bois** ("Leg of Wood"; ℂ **758/452-0321**), named after a peg-legged pirate who once used the island as a hideout.

Soufrière, a fishing port and St. Lucia's second-largest settlement, is dominated by the dramatic Pitons, Petit Piton and Gros Piton. These two pointed peaks rise right from the sea to 738m and 786m (2,421 ft. and 2,578 ft.), respectively. Formed by lava and once actively volcanic, these mountains are now cloaked in green vegetation, with waves crashing around their bases. Their sheer rise from the water makes them such visible landmarks that they've become the very symbol of St. Lucia.

Near the town of Soufrière lies the famous "drive-in" volcano, **La Soufrière,** a rocky lunar landscape of bubbling mud and craters seething with fuming sulfur. You can literally drive into an old crater and walk between the sulfur springs and pools of hissing steam. The fumes are said to have medicinal properties. A local guide is usually waiting nearby; if you do hire a guide, agree—then doubly agree—on what the fee will be.

Nearby are the **Diamond Mineral Baths** (ℂ **758/459-7115** or 758/452-4759), surrounded by a tropical arboretum. They were constructed in 1784 by order of Louis XVI, whose doctors told him that these waters were similar in mineral content to the waters at Aix-les-Bains. The baths were built to help French soldiers who had been fighting in the West Indies recuperate from wounds and disease. Later destroyed, they were rebuilt after World War II. The water's average temperature is 106°F (41°C). You'll also find another fine attraction here: a waterfall that changes colors (from yellow to black to green to gray) several times a day. For about US$4, you can bathe and benefit from the recuperative effects of the baths yourself. Open daily from 10am to 5pm.

SHOPPING

Many stores sell duty-free goods and will deliver tobacco products and liquor to the cruise dock. Keep in mind that you are allowed to purchase only one bottle of liquor here (in St. Thomas, you can buy five). You'll find some good, but not remarkable, buys in bone china, jewelry, perfume, watches, liquor, and crystal. Souvenir items include designer bags and mats, local pottery, and straw hats—again, nothing remarkable. *Tip:* If your cruise is also calling in St. Thomas, let the local vendors know; it may make them more amenable to bargaining.

Built for cruise ship passengers, **Pointe Seraphine** has the best collection of shops on the island. You must present your cruise pass when making purchases here. Liquor and tobacco will be delivered to the ship.

Gablewoods Mall, on Gros Islet Highway, 3.2km (2 miles) north of Castries, has three restaurants and one of the densest concentrations of stores on St. Lucia. Since this mall is near some lovely beaches (and near the Sandals St. Lucia Resort), it's possible to plan a day that combines shopping and sunbathing.

At **Caribelle Batik,** Howelton House, Old Victoria Road, the Morne (ℂ **758/452-3785**), just a 5-minute taxi ride from Castries, you can watch St. Lucian artists creating intricate patterns and colors through the ancient art of batik, which involves application of removable wax before dyes are applied so that the waxed area repels the dye.

Eudovic Art Studio, Goodlands, Morne Fortune (② 758/452-2747), sells wood-carvings by St. Lucia native Vincent Joseph Eudovic and some of his pupils. Take a taxi from the cruise pier.

Southwest of Soufrière, just past the small village of Choiseul, **Choiseul Craft Centre,** La Fargue (② 758/459-3226), is a government-funded retail outlet and training school that perpetuates the tradition of handmade Amerindian pottery and basketware. Some of the best basket weaving on the island is done here, using techniques practiced only in St. Lucia, St. Vincent, and Dominica. Look for place mats, handbags, woodcarvings (including bas-reliefs crafted from screw pine), and pottery. Open Monday through Friday from 8:30am to 4:30pm.

BEACHES

If you don't take a shore excursion, you might want to spend your time on one of St. Lucia's famous beaches, all of which are open to the public, even those at hotel properties (but you must pay to use a hotel's beach equipment). Taxis can take you to any of the island's beaches, but we recommend that you stick to the calmer shores along the western coast, since the rough surf on the windward Atlantic side makes swimming potentially dangerous.

Leading beaches include **Pigeon Island,** off the northern shore, with white sand and picnic facilities; **Vigie Beach,** north of Castries, with fine sand; **Marigot Beach,** south of Castries, framed on three sides by steep emerald hills and skirted by palm trees; and **Reduit Beach,** between Choc Bay and Pigeon Point, with fine brown sand. Just north of Soufrière is a beach connoisseur's delight, **Anse Chastanet** (② 758/459-7000), boasting an expanse of white sand at the foothills of lush green mountains. This is a fantastic spot for snorkeling.

SPORTS

SCUBA DIVING   In Soufrière, **Scuba St. Lucia** (② 758/459-7755; www.scuba stlucia.com), located in the **Anse Chastanet Resort** (② 758/459-7000), is a five-star PADI dive center offering great diving and comprehensive facilities. The resort is at the southern end of Anse Chastanet's .4km (¼-mile) secluded beach. Some of St. Lucia's most spectacular coral reefs—many only 3 to 6m (9¾–20 ft.) below the surface—provide shelter for sea creatures just a short distance offshore.

WATERSPORTS   **Joy Tide Watersports,** on Reduit Beach at the Royal St. Lucian Rex Resort (② 758/458-0085), is the best place to rent watersports equipment and arrange water-skiing.

GREAT LOCAL RESTAURANTS & BARS

A really, really great local beer is **Piton**—very refreshing on a hot day, like Corona but better. A favorite local rum is **Bounty.**

IN CASTRIES   At the **Green Parrot,** Red Tape Lane, Morne Fortune, about 2.4km (1½ miles) east of the town center (② 758/452-3399), there's an emphasis on St. Lucian specialties and homegrown produce (the restaurant has trained cruise ship chefs in the use of local products). Try the *christophine au gratin* (a Caribbean squash with cheese) or the Creole soup made with callaloo (a leafy green) and pumpkin. Lunch is about US$15.

AT MARIGOT BAY Doolittle's, at the Marigot Beach Club (© **758/451-4974**), showcases Caribbean and international dishes. To reach the place, you'll have to take a ferryboat across Marigot Bay. The ferry runs to and from the Moorings Marigot Bay Resort about every 10 minutes throughout the day and evening. Lunch is about US$25.

Rainforest Hideaway (© **758/286-0511**), tucked amid the mangroves at the **Discovery at Marigot Bay Resort, Spa & Marina Village** (© **758/458-5300**), offers Caribbean and international fusion cuisine in a casual atmosphere overlooking the bay. It's open only for lunch on Sunday, when it costs about US$28. Like Doolittle's (above), it is accessible only by ferry.

IN THE SOUFRIÈRE AREA Chez Camilla Guest House & Restaurant, 7 Bridge St., 1 block inland from the waterfront (© **758/459-5379**), is the only really good place to eat in the village of Soufrière itself. It serves sandwiches, salads, omelets, and burgers at lunch. A meal costs about US$9.

Dasheene Restaurant & Bar, in the Ladera Resort (© **758/459-7323**), serves the most refined and certainly the most creative cuisine in St. Lucia. The chef is particularly adept in the creation of seafood pasta and marinated sirloin steak. Your best bet is the catch of the day, likely to be kingfish or red snapper, grilled to perfection. Other standouts are the dumpling-and-callaloo soup, the fresh pumpkin risotto with red-pepper coulis, and the banana-stuffed pork with ginger-and-coconut sauce. The restaurant is perched atop a 300m (984-ft.) ridge and is framed by the rising twin peaks of the Pitons. Everything is locally produced, including the furniture. Lunch is about US$20.

AT RODNEY BAY The Lime, north of Reduit Beach (© **758/452-0761**), is a casual local place specializing in stuffed crab backs and Creole-seasoned fish steaks. It also serves shrimp, steaks, lamb, pork chops, and rotis (Caribbean burritos). Lunch will be around US$14.

The **Edge Restaurant,** in the Harmony Marina Suites, Rodney Bay Lagoon (© **758/450-3343**), is a new sushi bar and restaurant owned and operated by celebrated chef Bobo Bergstrom. In addition to an intriguing fusion of European and Caribbean cuisine, with a touch of Asian flavor, the Edge offers indoor/outdoor dining with a view of the boats moored at the nearby marina.

29 St. Martin/Sint Maarten

Who can resist a two-for-one sale? On the island of St. Martin, you get two cultures, two nationalities, and two different experiences for the price of one. Occupying the bend where the Lesser and Greater Antilles meet, about 242km (150 miles) southeast of Puerto Rico, this is the smallest territory in the world that is shared by two sovereign states: France, with 52 sq. km (20 sq. miles), and the Netherlands, with 44 sq. km (17 sq. miles). (At press time, the French side has appealed to the government of France for independence; a decision is expected to be reached by the end of 2006.) The two nations have shared the island in a spirit of neighborly cooperation and mutual friendship for more than 350 years. Although the border between the two sides is virtually imperceptible—a monument along the road marks the change in administration—each side retains elements of its own heritage. The French side, with some of the best beaches and restaurants in the Caribbean, emphasizes quiet elegance. French fashions and luxury items fill the shops, and the fragrance of croissants mixes with the spicy aromas of West Indian cooking. The Dutch side, officially known as

St. Martin/Sint Maarten

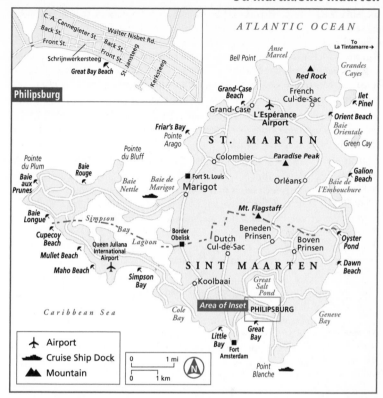

Sint Maarten, reflects Holland's anything-goes philosophy: Development is much more widespread, flashy casinos pepper the landscape, and strip malls make the larger towns look as much like Anaheim as Amsterdam. The 100% duty-free shopping has turned both sides of the island into a bargain-hunter's paradise.

St. Martin's first inhabitants, the Stone Age hunter-gatherer Ciboneys, arrived as early as 1800 B.C. The first Dutch and French colonists arrived in the early 17th century, and exchanged some martial rumblings before deciding, in 1648, to just get along, splitting the island roughly in two. Coffee, sugar, rum, and salt brought relative prosperity to the island, but not to the slaves brought over from Africa. Tourism supplanted agriculture as the major industry in the last half of the 20th century.

Today, the Dutch side holds a slight population edge: 41,000 people to the French side's 36,000. Most locals are descendants of African slaves, but residents born in France, Holland, and the U.S. occupy many of the villas and condominiums around the island.

COMING ASHORE Most cruise ships dock on the Dutch side, at **A. C. Wathey Pier,** about 1.6km (1 mile) southeast of Philipsburg. Many passengers take water taxis (which cost about US$5 round-trip) to the smaller **Captain Hodge Pier,** at the center of town, but others choose to take regular taxis or walk the distance on a newly renovated boardwalk. The Wathey Pier has credit card phones, cafes and bars, and a shopping area. For its part, Hodge Pier offers access to phones, tourist information, and taxis.

Smaller vessels sometimes dock on the French side of the island, at **Marina Port la Royale,** adjacent to the heart of Marigot. The waterfront here features restaurants, shopping arcades, and a tourist office. The pier accommodates only one ship at a time, so passengers on subsequently arriving vessels are tendered ashore.

LANGUAGE   Surprise, surprise: The official language on the Dutch side is Dutch, and the official language on the French side is French. Most people on both sides also speak English. Among locals on the street, patois is often spoken: Papiamento on the Dutch side, Creole on the French.

CURRENCY   The legal tender in Dutch Sint Maarten is the **Netherlands Antilles florin,** also called the **guilder** (1.75 NAF = US$1; 1 NAF = US56¢), while the official currency on the French side is the **euro** (exchange rate at press time: .82€ = US$1; 1€ = US$1.22). U.S. dollars are widely accepted on both sides, though, so there's no need to change money. Most prices are quoted in U.S. dollars, too, so you're spared the work of calculating exchange rates. Credit cards and traveler's checks are also readily accepted. ATMs abound in both Philipsburg and Marigot. Unless otherwise noted, prices in this chapter are given in U.S. dollars.

INFORMATION   On the Dutch side, the **St. Maarten Tourist Bureau,** in the Vineyard Office Park, 23 W. G. Buncamper Rd., Philipsburg (© **599/542-2337**), is open Monday through Friday from 8am to 5pm. There's a smaller but more conveniently located satellite office at the town pier. For information before you go, call © **800/786-2278** or go to www.st-maarten.com.

On the French side, the **St. Martin Tourist Office,** adjacent to the pier at Marina Royale in Marigot (© **590/87-57-21**), is open Monday through Friday from 8:30am to 1pm and 2:30 to 5:30pm. For advance info, call © **212/475-8970** or go to www. st-martin.org.

CALLING FROM THE U.S.   When calling Dutch Sint Maarten from the United States, simply dial the international access number (011) before the numbers listed here. Calling French St. Martin requires more of an effort: Dial 011, then 590 before the numbers listed. Yes, 590 appears in our listed numbers, but those three digits must be dialed twice to make a connection.

GETTING AROUND

BY TAXI   Taxis on both sides of the island are unmetered. Agree on a rate and currency before getting in. Dutch law requires that drivers list government-regulated fares, which assume two passengers (each additional passenger is another US$4). Shorter rides, including the route between Marigot and Philipsburg, average around US$15; longer trips can climb to US$20-plus. Drivers, who greet cruisers in both Philipsburg and Marigot, expect at least a US$1 tip for short runs, more for extended 2-hour sightseeing trips around the island. To call a taxi on the Dutch side, dial © **599/545-4317.** On the French side, dial © **590/87-56-54.**

BY MINIVAN   Privately owned and operated minivans are a reasonable way to get around, if you don't mind frequent stops, potential overcrowding, and the local zouk and soca music that's usually playing (a plus or a minus, depending on your tastes). These jitneys run daily from 7am to midnight and serve much of the island. The most popular run, between Philipsburg and Marigot, has almost constant service. Fares

Frommer's Favorite St. Martin/Sint Maarten Experiences

Sizzling in the Sun: On the French side, colorful, open-air restaurants and bars line Orient Beach, a social, very European strand humming with motorized water toys. (See "Beaches," below.)

Competing for the America's Cup: Race on and against 12m (39-ft.) yachts that once competed in the famed America's Cup race. (See "Best Cruise Line Shore Excursions," below.)

Snorkel on the Uninhabited Island of Pinel: A 5-minute ferry ride from Cul-de-Sac will take you to the best snorkeling area on the island. The beach is sheltered, the water shallow and clear. Lunch, beach chairs, and umbrellas are available on the beach. Go for a hike or just relax while sipping homemade banana rum at the Caribuni Restaurant. (See "Best Cruise Line Shore Excursions," below.)

Trekking up to the Ramparts of Fort St. Louis: A 10- or 15-minute walk from the heart of Marigot will take you to the top of the fort, where you're treated to panoramic views of Marigot and beyond. (See "On Your Own: Within Walking Distance," below.)

range from about US$1 to US$5. The vans, which have signs to indicate their destination, can be hailed anywhere on the street.

BY RENTAL CAR   Rental cars are a great way to make the most of your day and see both sides of the island. Driving is on the right side, roads are generally in decent shape, and signage is in either international symbols or English. Parking can be a headache in both Philipsburg and Marigot, and road construction and drawbridges sometimes exacerbate congestion. Away from the two main towns, however, zipping along is a breeze. **Avis, Budget,** and **Hertz** all have offices here.

BEST CRUISE LINE SHORE EXCURSIONS

America's Cup Sailing Regatta (US$89, 3 hr.): Get a taste of nautical exhilaration by competing in a race aboard an America's Cup–winning sailboat. This hands-on, extremely popular excursion lets you grind winches, trim sails, and duck under booms—after professionals have trained you, of course. Alternatively, sit back and watch others do all the work.

Ilet Pinel Snorkeling Tour (US$37, 3½ hr.): After a scenic bus ride to the French town of Cul-de-Sac, along the northeast coast, hop on a tender to the small offshore island of Ilet Pinel for some of St. Martin's best snorkeling.

Hidden Forest Hike (US$85, 4 hr.): You'll take a 45-minute drive to Loterie Farm, where you'll do a 2-hour hike through the tropical forest, eventually emerging at Pic Paradise, the island's highest point. Along the way, your guide will point out a secret freshwater spring and the island's famous guavaberry trees. Return to Loterie for a complimentary rum or fruit punch and a typical Caribbean farmhouse lunch.

Butterfly Farm & Marigot (US$39, 3½ hr.): After a scenic drive through both the French and Dutch sides of the island, walk through a surrealistic enclosed garden that features pools, waterfalls, and hundreds of exquisitely beautiful and exotic butterflies from around the world. Amusing guides identify species, describe courtship and mating rituals, and give tips on attracting butterflies to your garden at home. Afterward, absorb the Creole charm and French atmosphere of Marigot.

EXCURSIONS OFFERED BY LOCAL AGENCIES

Horseback Treks: The **Bayside Riding Club,** Coconut Grove, next to the Butterfly Farm (© **590/87-36-64**), offers 2-hour riding expeditions through the Nature Marine Reserve that conclude on an isolated beach, where horses and riders enjoy a cool post-ride romp in the water. The price of US$70 per person includes a complimentary drink at a bar on the beach. Half-hour pony rides with a handler, for the little ones, are US$25. Riders of all experience levels are welcome.

Mountain-Biking Tours: On the Dutch side, **TriSport,** in Simpson Bay (© **599/ 545-4384**), offers 2½- to 3-hour tours of varying difficulty (US$49 per person). It also arranges kayaking, hiking, and snorkeling trips.

Scuba Diving: Of the island's 40 dive sites, the 1801 British man-of-war HMS *Proselyte,* which sank to a watery grave on a reef 1.6km (1 mile) off the coast, is the most popular. Other favorites include Ilet Pinel, for shallow diving; the Green Key barrier reef; and Flat Island, for its sheltered coves and geologic faults. On the Dutch side, **Pelican Watersports,** Simpson Bay (© **599/544-2640**), employs some the most knowledgeable guides on the island. Dives are US$45 to US$90.

ON YOUR OWN: WITHIN WALKING DISTANCE

Shopping, sunbathing, and gambling are the pastimes that interest most cruisers who hit this island, but folks with a taste for culture and history can make a day of it here as well.

ON THE DUTCH SIDE   Directly in front of the Philipsburg town pier, on Wathey Square, the **Courthouse** combines northern European sobriety with Caribbean brightness. Originally built in 1793 of freestone and wood, this venerable old building has suffered numerous hurricanes but has been restored after each tempest and continues to house government offices. East of the Courthouse, down a little shopping alley, the tiny **Sint Maarten Museum,** 7 Front St. (© **599/542-4917**), features modest, cluttered exhibits that focus on the island's history and geology. There's no admission fee, but donations are appreciated. Open Monday through Friday from 10am to 4pm, Saturday from 10am to 2pm. The street-level gift shop stocks handicrafts, postcards, and books.

Historically, **Fort Amsterdam** is the Dutch side's most important colonial site. Since 1631, the fort has looked out over Great Bay from the hill west of Philipsburg. The fort was the Netherlands' first military outpost in the Caribbean. The Spanish captured it 2 years later, making it their most significant bastion east of Puerto Rico. Peter Stuyvesant, who later became governor of New Amsterdam (now New York), lost his leg to a cannonball while trying to reclaim the fort for Holland. The site provides grand views of the bay, but ruins of the walls and a couple of rusty cannons are all that remain of the original fort.

ON THE FRENCH SIDE   **Fort St. Louis** is Marigot's answer to Fort Amsterdam. Built in 1767 to protect the waterfront warehouses that stored the French colony's agricultural riches, this bastion frequently fired its cannons on hostile British raiders from Anguilla. After restorations and modification in the 19th century, the fort was

Day-Tripping to Anguilla & St. Barts

One of the best things about St. Martin is that once you're here, it's easy to visit the more serene and unspoiled neighboring islands of Anguilla or St. Barts. To get to **Anguilla,** simply take the *Voyager* ferry, which leaves every 30 minutes from Marigot Bay and arrives on Anguilla just 10 minutes later. You do not need a reservation. The cost is about US$26 round-trip.

Intrepid travelers in search of natural beauty, quiet, and understated glitz may find a trip to **St. Barts** worth the time, money, and potentially queasy stomach. The *Voyager* to St. Barts departs from one of two locations on the French side of St. Martin; it takes between 40 minutes and 1½ hours, depending on your departure point, and can be extremely choppy. The round-trip fare is about US$62 for adults, US$$30 for children. Reservations are recommended and can be made at www.voyager-st-barths.com. *Note:* The only trip back to St. Martin leaves St. Barts at 4:30pm most days (5:30pm on Sun), so be sure you have ample time to make it back to your ship before it leaves port!

Another boat option to St. Barts is the **Rapid Explorer** (© 599/544-2640), which leaves from Chesterfield Marina at Point Blanche on the Dutch side. It takes about half the time and costs US$106 round-trip for adults, US$54 for children. Call for reservations and information.

eventually abandoned. You'll find cannons, crumbling walls, and a French flag flapping in the breeze. The short climb up the hill flanking Marigot Bay's north end affords splendid vistas. As a respite from the sun, duck into **Marigot's Museum of Saint Martin** (© 590/29-22-84), next to the Tourist Office and adjacent to the marina. Much more thorough and scholarly than its Philipsburg counterpart, this institution boasts a first-rate collection of Ciboney, Arawak, and Carib artifacts excavated from the island's Amerindian sites, plus a reproduction of a 1,500-year-old burial mound. Another display details the history of the plantation and slavery era, and early-20th-century photographs trace the island's modern development. Open Monday through Friday from 9am to 4pm, Saturday from 9am to 1pm. Admission is US$5 for adults, US$2 for children.

SHOPPING

This island is a true free port—no duties are paid on any item coming in or going out—and neither side has a sales tax.

ON THE DUTCH SIDE Shops in the much busier Dutch side are concentrated in **Philipsburg,** along Front Street and, to a lesser extent, Back Street and the numerous alleys radiating from them. The district is largely nondescript, but you'll find all the usual suspects—the omnipresent jewelry and luxury-item shop **Little Switzerland** and a host of other jewelry/gift/luxury-item shops—as well as some quirky local boutiques. In general, prices in the major stores are nonnegotiable, but at small, family-run shops, you can try your luck with a little polite bargaining. The T-shirt and souvenir epicenter is in the open-air market behind the Courthouse, in front of the town pier.

Guavaberry Emporium, 8–10 Front St., sells Guavaberry "island folk liqueur," an aged rum with a distinctive fruity, woody, almost bittersweet flavor; it's available only on St. Martin. Parrotheads in search of all things Jimmy Buffett should cross the street to **Last Mango in Paradise,** 17 Front St., for CDs, T-shirts, and more—you name it, they got it.

Walking west, Old Street, off Front Street, features a couple dozen boutiques, including **Colombian Emeralds** and the **Belgian Chocolate Shop.** For cigars, **La Casa del Habano,** 24 Front St., has Cohibas, Montecristos, and the like; while **Lipstick,** 31 Front St., is your best bet for perfumes and cosmetics. Next door, **Dutch Delft Blue,** 29 Front St., stocks the distinctive blue-and-white porcelain.

ON THE FRENCH SIDE   Marigot features a much calmer, more charming, and sophisticated ambience, with waterfront cafes where you can rest your weary feet. Many shops here close their doors for a 2-hour lunch break starting at noon.

The wide selection of European merchandise is skewed toward an upscale audience, but French crystal, perfume, liqueur, jewelry, and fashion can be up to 50% less expensive than in the States.

At Marina Port la Royale, **Havane** offers casual and high-fashion French clothing for men, while **L'Epicerie** stocks caviar, foie gras, and a host of French wines. For chic women's clothing, especially Italian styles, start your search at **Act III,** rue de la République. **Oro de Sol Jewelers,** rue de la République, is one of many purveyors of bracelets, necklaces, and watches, while **Beauty & Scents,** rue du Général de Gaulle, has your favorite perfumes and cosmetics.

An inviting open-air crafts market sprawls along the waterfront next to boulevard de France every day, while on Wednesday and Saturday, another open-air market stretches from the base of Fort St. Louis to the wharves below, offering a colorful array of homegrown produce, tropical fruits and spices, and fresh fish. On market days, look for **Fifi's Rum Store,** which offers 20 flavors of rum (and lets you sample them).

BEACHES

Beach lovers, rejoice: The island has more than 30 beautiful white-sand beaches, some social, some serene. The busier ones boast bars, restaurants, watersports, and hotels, where changing facilities are usually available for a small fee. Toplessness is ubiquitous; nudism is common on the French side, and increasingly found on the Dutch side as well.

ON THE DUTCH SIDE   **Great Bay Beach** is your best bet if you want to stay in Philipsburg. This 1.6km-long (1-mile) stretch is convenient, but because it borders the busy capital, it lacks the tranquillity and cleanliness of the more remote beaches. The water is calm, though, and all the amenities of Philipsburg are a step away.

Just west of the airport, on the west side of the island, **Maho Beach** boasts a casino, shade palms, and a popular beachside bar and grill. Its biggest attraction, however, seems to be its views of takeoffs and landings (keep your belongings outside the flight path; jumbo jets sometimes blow items into the surf).

Farther west, **Mullet Beach** borders the island's golf course. Shaded by palm trees and crowded on weekends, it's popular with swimmers and snorkelers. On-site vendors rent an array of watersports equipment.

Just around the corner to the west (just below the Dutch-French border), but miles away mentally, lies perfectly serene **Cupecoy Beach.** Set against a stunningly beautiful backdrop of mysterious caves and sandstone cliffs that provide morning shade, this beach has no facilities, but a vendor at the parking lot rents beach chairs and umbrellas. The clientele is adult: primarily in the buff, quiet, and, not infrequently, gay. The surf can be strong, and aficionados claim that the sun here is more intense than anywhere else on the island.

ON THE FRENCH SIDE   Far and away the island's most visited strand, **Orient Beach,** on the northeast coast, fancies itself the "Saint Tropez of the Caribbean." Hedonism is the name of the game here: plenty of food, drink, music, and flesh (a naturist resort occupies the beach's southern tip, but nudism isn't confined to any one area). Watersports abound.

South of Orient Beach, the waveless waters of **Coconut Grove** or **Galion Beach** are shallow 30m (98 ft.) out. Protected by a coral reef, this area is number one with kids and popular with windsurfers.

On the island's west coast, just north of the Dutch border, **Baie Longue** (Long Bay) is the island's longest beach and another refuge for adults seeking peace and quiet. There are no facilities, but this wild beach bordering some of the island's grandest mansions is popular with the rich and (sometimes) famous. The water and sand here are silky.

Friar's Bay Beach, outside of Marigot, is a quiet sheltered cove at the end of a bumpy road, offering gorgeous views of the neighboring island Anguilla on clear days. Beach chairs, umbrellas, and food are available on the beach.

SPORTS

GOLF   The **Mullet Bay Resort** (✆ 599/545-2850), on the Dutch side, has an 18-hole course designed by Joseph Lee that's considered one of the more challenging in the Caribbean, especially the back 9. Though the resort on which this course sits has been closed for years and the buildings surrounding it are in disrepair, minimal maintenance keeps the course itself in decent enough shape. Greens fees and cart rental are US$120 for 18 holes; club rental is an additional US$26. The course opens daily at 7am.

SNORKELING   Tiny coves and calm offshore waters make St. Martin a snorkeler's paradise. **Dawn Beach,** on the Dutch east coast, is one of the best snorkeling sites on the island (rent equipment from **Busby's Beach Bar,** which is right on the beach). Also worthy are the Dutch side's **Maho Beach** and the French side's **Baie Rouge** and **Ilet Pinel,** the latter of which can be reached by ferry from Cul-de-Sac (about US$5 per person, round-trip). Most hotels and restaurants at these sites rent equipment for about US$10.

WATERSPORTS   Most of the large hotels on Orient Beach offer an array of watersports adventures, often from makeshift kiosks on the beach. Two independent operators function from side-by-side positions near the Esmeralda Hotel: **Kon Tiki Watersports** (✆ 590/87-46-89) and **Bikini Watersports** (✆ 590/87-43-25). Jet skis and WaveRunners go for about US$45 for 30 minutes, US$80 for an hour; parasailing is US$50 to US$80.

GAMBLING

Slot machines and game tables can be found in the Dutch side's dozen casinos. Most of the heavy betting takes place after dark, but a handful of casinos open before noon. In the heart of Philipsburg on Front Street, **Coliseum Casino** (✆ 599/543-2101), **Diamond Casino** (✆ 599/543-2565), and **Rouge et Noir** (✆ 599/542-2952) all open at 11am, early enough to snag cruisers. West of Philipsburg, **Hollywood Casino,** at the Pelican Resort, Simpson Bay (✆ 599/544-2503), features a panoramic view of the water and offers craps, roulette, blackjack, stud poker, and slots after 1pm.

Farther west, **Casino Royale,** Maho Bay (© **599/545-2590**), has roulette, Caribbean stud poker, craps, blackjack, baccarat, minibaccarat, and slots, also after 1pm, while **Atlantis World Casino,** Cupecoy Bay (© **599/545-4601**), has baccarat, blackjack, craps, poker, roulette, and Texas Hold 'em.

GREAT LOCAL RESTAURANTS & BARS

The indigenous rum liqueur is the fruity and slightly bitter **Guavaberry.**

ON THE DUTCH SIDE   As might be expected, food is usually better on the French side, but Dutch Sint Maarten has a number of appealing restaurants, too. You can even enjoy a *très* French dining experience right in Philipsburg at **L'Escargot,** 96 Front St. (© **599/542-2483**), a bright-yellow house with snails painted all over it, in case you don't know French. Try the crispy duck in a pineapple and banana sauce, the Dover sole, or rack of lamb. Lunch is about US$35.

On the pier, **Taloula Mango's Carib Café** offers tapas, burgers, pizza, pasta, salad, and island favorites such as blackened mahimahi and Felix Ortega–style chicken curry. Lunch is about US$20.

Over in Simpson Bay, feast on crispy coconut shrimp on the water at **Turtle Pier** (© **599/545-2562**). Lunch is about US$12.

ON THE FRENCH SIDE   On the Marigot waterfront, Madame Claude runs the show at **Mini Club,** rue des Pêcheurs (© **590/87-50-69**), one of the oldest restaurants in town. Savor the rich flavors of spicy conch stew, Creole-style fresh fish, or other West Indian and French dishes on the bright-yellow upstairs terrace.

For light salads, sandwiches, and ice-cream concoctions, claim a harborside table at **La Vie en Rose,** at rue de la République and boulevard de France (© **590/87-54-42**). Lunch is US$15.

In Grande-Case, a stroll down "restaurant row," boulevard de Grand-Case, will lead you to seemingly endless dining options. Unfortunately, many of the finest are open only for dinner, after your ship has left the port. But you won't be sorry you made the 10- to 15-minute taxi ride to Grand-Case when you're feasting on swordfish and shrimp kebab, Greek salad, or chicken sate with your feet in the sand at **Calmos Café** (© **590/29-01-85**), where tables are right on the beach with views across the bay to Anguilla. Beach toys are available for children, and the piña coladas are out of this world. Lunch is about US$20.

30 Trinidad & Tobago

The southernmost islands in the Caribbean chain, Trinidad and tiny Tobago (which together form a single nation), manage to encompass nearly every facet of Caribbean life. Located less than 16km (10 miles) east of Venezuela's coast, Trinidad is large (the biggest and most heavily populated Caribbean island) and diverse, with an industrial, cosmopolitan capital city, Port of Spain, and an outgoing, vibrant culture that combines African, East Indian, European, Chinese, and Syrian influences. Little sister Tobago is the more natural of the two, with rainforested mountains and spectacular secluded beaches.

Trinidad and Tobago won independence from Britain in 1962 and became a republic in 1976, but some British influences, including the residents' love of cricket, remain. Trinidad grew rich from oil, and the islands are still the Western Hemisphere's largest oil exporters.

The music of Trinidad is another local treasure. The calypso, steel-pan, and soca styles that originated here have influenced musical trends worldwide. These rhythmic, soulful sounds are a main feature of Carnaval, the Caribbean-wide bacchanalian celebration held each year on the Monday and Tuesday before Lent. Among all the Carnaval celebrations in the Caribbean, Trinidad's is king.

The local people are charming and friendly, and love to talk. With a literacy rate of 97%, the populace is full of well-informed conversationalists. You'll find Trinis (as residents call themselves) happy to socialize with visitors and discuss just about anything.

LANGUAGE   The official language is English, but like many of their Caribbean neighbors, Trinis speak it with a distinct patois. Hindi, Creole, and Spanish are also spoken among various ethnic groups.

CURRENCY   The unit of currency is the **Trinidad and Tobago dollar,** sometimes designated by the same symbol as the U.S. dollar ($) and sometimes just by "TT." The exchange rate is TT$6.32 = US$1; TT$1 = US16¢. Vacationers can pay in U.S. dollars, but be sure you know what currency prices are being quoted in, and try to get change in U.S. dollars. Local ATMs mainly dispense TT notes. Unless otherwise specified, prices in this section are given in U.S. dollars.

CALLING FROM THE U.S.   When calling Trinidad and Tobago from the United States, you need only dial "1" before the numbers listed here.

TRINIDAD

Trinidad is one of the most industrialized countries in the Caribbean, and it shows—if you're looking for a sleepy, quiet Caribbean retreat, go to Tobago instead. Trinidad's capital and commercial center, **Port of Spain,** is an energetic, bustling metropolis of 300,000. There are few distinct attractions—Port of Spain isn't necessarily a tourist city—but the central shopping area at the south end of Frederick Street is a colorfully crowded mix of outdoor arcades and air-conditioned mini-malls. **Independence Square,** in the heart of Port of Spain, is the place to get a taxi, find a bank, and get good, cheap food. There are mosques, shrines, and temples here, and locals gather at **Woodford Square** to hear public speakers or attend outdoor meetings.

Note: While Port of Spain is interesting and not threatening by day, it's unsafe at night, and strolling around is not recommended if your ship happens to be in port late.

COMING ASHORE   Cruise ships visiting Trinidad dock at Port of Spain's 1.6-hectare (4-acre) cruise terminal, built in the early 1990s to accommodate the island's growing cruise traffic. The complex, which includes a shopping mall and car-rental agencies, is within easy walking distance of the center of town. Steel-pan musicians and colorfully dressed dancers usually greet arriving passengers. Outside the terminal, there's a crafts market with T-shirts, straw items, and other souvenirs.

INFORMATION   The **Tourism Development Corporation of Trinidad and Tobago (TIDCO),** 10–14 Phillips St., at the Port of Spain terminal (© **800/816-7541** or 868/675-7034), is open Monday through Friday from 8am to 4:30pm. For info before you go, call © **212/682-7272** or go to www.visittnt.com.

GETTING AROUND

BY TAXI   Taxis are available at the cruise terminal. The registered taxi association here is the **Trinidad and Tobago Tourist Transport Association.** These drivers are trained tour guides, identifiable by their dark pants and shirts with printed taxi association monograms. Their car license plates begin with the letter H (for "hiring car"). The taxis are unmetered, but the Port Authority posts fares on a board by the main entrance. Always establish a fare before loading into the taxi and shoving off. Private cabs can be relatively expensive.

BY VAN   Maxitaxis (minivans operating regular routes within specific zones) have a yellow stripe and are lower priced than taxis. There are also route taxis, which are shared cabs that travel along a prescribed route and charge about US$1 to US$1.50 to drop you at any spot along the way.

BY RENTAL CAR   Driving is on the left. Trinidad has a fairly wide network of roads, and streets in town are generally well marked, but traffic is frequently heavy. None of the major rental companies has an office here.

BEST CRUISE LINE SHORE EXCURSIONS

Caroni Bird Sanctuary (US$54, 3 hr.): This sanctuary—a pristine network of lush mangroves, quiet canals, and shallow lagoons—is considered a world-class bird-watching preserve. Following a 30-minute drive from the cruise pier, passengers embark for the tour in flat-bottomed boats, which glide through calm canals and lagoons. Guides will point out unique flora and fauna during the ride. Heron, osprey, and scarlet ibis are among the bird species native to this area.

Frommer's Favorite Trinidad Experiences

Visiting the Asa Wright Nature Center: This 80-hectare (198-acre) preserve, located in Trinidad's rainforest in the northern hills, features intertwined hiking trails, a bird sanctuary, and a conservation center. (See "Best Cruise Line Shore Excursions," below.)

Touring the Caroni Bird Sanctuary: This ecological wonder features dense mangroves, remote canals, and shallow lagoons that are the breeding grounds for spectacular scarlet ibis. Visitors tour the sanctuary in guided boats and are advised to bring plenty of insect repellent. (See "Best Cruise Line Shore Excursions," below.)

Trying a Drink with Angostura Bitters: This local specialty contains citrus-tree bark and is made from a secret recipe. Just a few drops are enough to add zing to any drink. My Trini brother-in-law loved it in lemonade as a kid.

Maracas Waterfall Hike (US$59, 4 hr.): Work up a sweat as you hike to the magnificent Maracas Waterfall, in the Maracas Valley. Afterward, chill out in the mountain pool at the fall's base.

Asa Wright Nature Center (US$84, 6 hr.): Set within 80 hectares (198 acres) about 360m (1,181 ft.) up into Trinidad's rainforested mountains, the center is known to bird-watchers throughout the world. You can see hummingbirds, toucans, bellbirds, manakins, several varieties of tanagers, and the rare oilbird. Hiking trails line the grounds. A Creole-style buffet lunch is served at the center's Old Plantation House.

ON YOUR OWN: WITHIN WALKING DISTANCE

Among Port of Spain's chief centers of activity, **Independence Square,** a stone's throw from the cruise complex, isn't really a square at all, but parallel streets running east and west and connected at one end by a pedestrian mall. The scene here resembles a Middle Eastern bazaar, with a dense thicket of pushcarts, honking cabs, produce hawkers, and inquisitive shoppers moving to the irresistible beat of soca, reggae, and calypso music blaring from nearby stores and sidewalk stands. Some parts of the square have become run-down, and some locals consider the area less than safe. Visitors should keep an eye out for pickpockets and petty thieves.

Woodford Square, laid out by Ralph Woodford, Trinidad's early-19th-century British governor, is among the most attractive areas in town, full of large, leafy trees surrounding a rich lawn with landscaped walkways. This area has traditionally served as a center for political debates, discussions, and rallies. The **Cathedral of the Holy Trinity,** built in 1818 by Woodford, lies on the square's south side. The church's carved roof was designed as a replica of Westminster Hall in London. Inside the church is a memorial statue of Woodford himself. To reach the square, take Independence Square North and then go left on Abercromby Street, or Wrightson Road to Sackville Street.

On the square's western border is **Red House,** an imposing (and, yes, red) Renaissance-style edifice built in 1906. Today, it houses Trinidad's parliament. The building was badly damaged in 1990, when militants took the prime minister and parliament members hostage.

A little farther north of the city center is **Queen's Park Savannah,** originally part of an 80-hectare (198-acre) sugar plantation, and now a public park with 32 hectares (79 acres) of open land and walkways, with great shade trees. A depression at the park's northwest section, known as the Hollows, has flower beds, rock gardens, and small ponds—it has become a popular picnic spot. Most streets heading north from the cruise complex end at the park.

There are a number of notable sights along the park's outer, western edge, including the **Magnificent Seven,** a row of seven colonial buildings constructed in the late 19th and early 20th centuries. The buildings include Queen's Royal College, White Hall (the prime minister's office), and Stollmeyer's Castle, which was designed to resemble a Scottish castle—complete with turrets.

Beyond the northern edge of Queen's Park Savannah lies the **Emperor Valley Zoo** (© 868/622-3530), featuring local animals such as tropical toucans and macaws, porcupines, monkeys, and various snakes. The zoo emphasizes colorful tropical plants, which are in evidence all over the grounds. Open daily from 9:30am to 5:30pm; admission is US$4 adults, US$2 for children.

The 28-hectare (69-acre) **Royal Botanical Gardens** are east of the zoo. Laid out in 1820, the gardens are landscaped with attractive walkways and great flowering trees, among them the wild poinsettia, whose bright red blossom is the national flower. The **President's House,** built in 1875 as the governor's residence, is adjacent to the gardens and is open daily from 6am to 6pm.

ON YOUR OWN: BEYOND THE PORT AREA

All out-of-town attractions are covered in "Best Cruise Line Shore Excursions," above.

SHOPPING

Shopping in the Port of Spain area means crafts, fabrics, and fashions made by local artists, a range of spices, and colorful artwork. Most of the shopping opportunities lie in the area around Independence Square, particularly near Frederick and Queen streets.

Art lovers will find a handful of galleries and studios featuring the work of local and regional artists. **Art Creators,** at Seventh Street and St. Ann's Road, in the Aldegonda Park section (© 868/624-4369), is a serious gallery offering year-round exhibits of both emerging and established artists. **Aquarela Galleries,** 1A Dere St., exhibits the work of recognized and up-and-coming Trini artists, and also publishes high-end art books.

Art Potters Ltd., at the cruise terminal, is a pottery specialist. For crafts outside of the terminal area, try the **Trinidad and Tobago Blind Welfare Association,** 118 Duke St., with accessories and gifts of rattan and other natural materials, all made by blind craftsmen.

For distinctive gifts and apparel, hire a cab to take you to the **Hotel Normandie,** 10 Nook Ave., in the St. Ann's section (© 868/624-1181), where the **Village Market** shops feature clothing and jewelry by some of the country's top designers.

Music is one of Trinidad's signature products, and the latest soca and reggae can be purchased at **Crosby Music Center,** 54 Western Main Rd., in the St. James area (© 868/622-7622).

BEACHES

Unlike its tiny sister Tobago, Trinidad is not blessed with many beautiful beaches. The most popular of the beaches is **Maracas Bay,** a scenic 40-minute journey from Port of Spain. The drive takes you over mountains and through a lush rainforest. As you near the beach, the coastal road descends from a cliffside. The beach itself is wide and sandy, with a small fishing village on one side and the richly dense mountains in the background. There are lifeguards, changing rooms and showers, and areas for picnics. You'll also see many stands selling "shark and bake" sandwiches (a local favorite made with fresh slabs of shark and fried bread).

SPORTS

GOLF The oldest and best-known golf course on the island is the 18-hole, par-72 **St. Andrews Golf Club,** in the suburb of Maraval (*C* **868/629-2314**). Also known as Moka Golf Course, it was established in the late 19th century. Greens fees are US$66. A caddy will cost US$10 more; club rentals are US$18.

GREAT LOCAL RESTAURANTS & BARS

Trinidad is home to some of the most diverse culinary styles in the Caribbean, a result of its African, Chinese, English, French, Indian, Portuguese, Spanish, and Syrian influences. A favorite local beer is **Stag,** and a favorite local rum is **Vat 19 Old Oak.**

Set in an old rum house with brick walls and hand-finished ceilings, **Rafters,** 6A Warner St. (*C* **868/628-9258**), offers sandwiches, chili, and chicken in its bar. There's also an elegant dining room for more formal meals. Lunch is about US$9. **Plantation House,** 38 Ariapita Ave. (*C* **868/628-5551**), is a quality restaurant located in a charming colonial house. Lunch is around US$14.

Near the Hotel Normandie is **Solimar,** 6 Nook Ave. (*C* **868/624-6267**), which features a changing menu of international dishes engineered by owner Joe Brown, a peripatetic Englishman who was once a chef for the Hilton hotel chain. Lunch is about US$30.

Cricket Wicket, 149 Tragarete Rd., is a pub with various bands performing on weekends.

TOBAGO

Tobago is the antithesis of its larger cousin, as peaceful, calm, and easygoing as Trinidad is loud, crowded, and frenetic. The island is filled with magical white-sand beaches, languid palm trees, and clear blue waters, and you'll find lots of spots for diving and snorkeling. There are also magnificent rainforests and hundreds of tiny streams and waterways carved into a steep crest of mountains that rise 600m (1,968 ft.) and snake down the island's center. The bird life and nature trails here are impressive.

COMING ASHORE Most cruise passengers arrive at a small but orderly cruise terminal in central **Scarborough,** the island's main town. There's usually a fleet of taxis ready to go just outside the terminal, and detailed cab rates are posted inside the terminal at the main entrance. Larger ships must anchor offshore and transfer passengers to the terminal via tenders. There are a number of phones inside the terminal.

INFORMATION The small information booth at the terminal in Scarborough is open Monday through Friday from 9am to 3pm. For info before you go, call *C* **212/682-7272** or go to www.visittnt.com.

GETTING AROUND

BY TAXI Taxi is the preferred mode of transportation for visitors here; the island is small enough that any location worth visiting can be reached this way. Distances can be deceptive, though, because some of the roads are in very bad shape and others wind along the coast and twist through the mountains. There is no road that completely circles the island. As in Trinidad, visitors should use registered drivers who are part of the

Trinidad and Tobago Tourist Transport Association; see the Trinidad taxi section for more information.

BY RENTAL CAR   There's really no need for a cruise passenger to rent a car on Tobago.

BEST CRUISE LINE SHORE EXCURSIONS

Pigeon Point Beach Trip (US$49, 5½ hr., including lunch): By taxi, you'll head toward Tobago's most popular beach, where you'll find a restaurant, a bar, restrooms, and small cabanas lining the beach. You have your pick of watersports, including snorkeling and banana-boat rides (for a fee, of course).

Argyle Waterfalls (US$57, 4 hr.): Drive along Tobago's windward coast to Roxborough, then hike 20 minutes though a forest preserve to the three-tiered waterfall for a swim.

Buccoo Reef Snorkeling (US$45, 3 hr.): From Pigeon Point, board a glass-bottom boat for the ride out to Buccoo Reef for your snorkeling dip. From there, you'll head off to the Nylon Pool, a sand bank named for its crystal-clear water.

ON YOUR OWN: WITHIN WALKING DISTANCE

The well-restored, British-built **Fort King George,** dating from 1777, overlooks Scarborough's east side. There's no admission charge to enter the grounds. The fort offers a great view of Tobago's Atlantic coast. Other historic buildings here include **St. Andrew's Church** (built in 1819) and the **Courthouse** (built in 1825). The small **Tobago Museum** (© **868/639-3970**) is located in the fort's old barracks guardhouse; it charges US$1 admission and is open Monday through Friday from 9am to 4:30pm.

Scarborough's **botanical gardens** are situated between the main highway and the town center, less than .4km (¼ mile) from the cruise dock, but they are not much more than a glorified public park with a few marked trees.

Other than this, there aren't many attractions within walking distance of the cruise terminal, and even the terminal shops are small and limited.

SHOPPING

There simply isn't much here beyond the shops inside the cruise terminal and the sporadic crafts merchants at the popular beaches at Fort King George. It's best to put aside the shopping excursions for another port and simply enjoy Tobago's relaxed atmosphere and fine beaches.

Frommer's Favorite Tobago Experiences

Visiting Pigeon Point Beach: One of the most beautiful and distinctive spots in the Caribbean, Pigeon Point is an oasis of white sand, aqua water, and tall palm trees. (See "Best Cruise Line Shore Excursions," above.)

Snorkeling at Buccoo Reef: The spot is a must-visit for its exotic fish and impressive underwater coral, which can also be observed by glass-bottom boat. (See "Best Cruise Line Shore Excursions," above.)

Checking Out Nylon Pool: Named for its crystal-clear water, this small lagoon is located near Buccoo Reef and is filled with tropical fish. It's great for wading and swimming. (See "Best Cruise Line Shore Excursions," above.)

Tobago

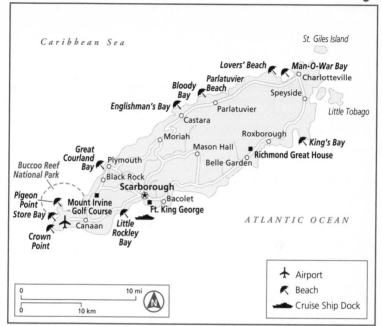

BEACHES

Pigeon Point, near the southern tip of Tobago on the Caribbean side, is the best beach on an island filled with great beaches. **Store Bay,** south of Pigeon Point, has white sands and good year-round swimming (there's a lifeguard, too). Vendors hawk local wares here, and glass-bottom-boat tours depart for Buccoo Reef. Despite their names, **Parlatuvier Beach** and **Bloody Bay,** on Tobago's Caribbean coast, are tranquil, secluded, and beautiful.

SPORTS

GOLF   About 8km (5 miles) from Pigeon Point, the championship 18-hole, par-72 course at the **Mount Irvine Bay Hotel & Golf Club** (✆ 868/639-8871) is among the most scenic in the Caribbean, overlooking the sea from gently rolling hills. The clubhouse sits on a promontory and offers great views. Greens fees are US$55, club rentals are US$18, and cart rentals are US$42.

SCUBA DIVING   Tobago is virtually surrounded by shallow-water reefs filled with colorful marine life, easily visible through the clear water. All kinds of diving experiences, from beginner-level dives at Buccoo Reef to drift diving for experienced divers at Grouper Ground, are available. **Frontier Dive,** at Pigeon Point (✆ 868/631-8138; www.frontierdiverstt.com), offers rentals and resort courses, catering to both beginners and experienced divers.

GREAT LOCAL RESTAURANTS & BARS

There are several moderately priced restaurants in Tobago, including the **Old Donkey Cart House,** on Bacolet Street, Scarborough (✆ 868/639-3551), which occupies a restored colonial home that once served as Tobago's first guesthouse. Today, it's a bistro serving French wines, light snacks, salads, and soups. Lunch is about US$8.

The beach at Store Bay is lined with a row of cheap food stands offering rotis (chicken or beef wrapped in Indian turnovers and flavored with curry), shark-and-bake, crab with dumplings, and fish lunches.

31 U.S. Virgin Islands: St. Thomas, St. John & St. Croix

Ever since Columbus discovered the Virgin Islands during his second voyage to the New World in 1493, they have proven irresistible to foreign powers seeking territory, at one time or another being governed by Denmark, Spain, France, England, Holland, and, since 1917, the United States.

Vacationers discovered **St. Thomas,** the largest of the islands, right after World War II and have been flocking here in increasing numbers ever since to enjoy its fine dining, elegant resorts, and, in recent years, shopping. Tourism and U.S. government programs have raised the standard of living to one of the highest in the Caribbean, and today, the island is one of the busiest and most developed cruise ports in the Caribbean, often hosting more than six ships a day during the peak winter season. **Charlotte Amalie** (pronounced Ah-*mahl*-yah), named in 1691 in honor of the wife of Denmark's King Christian V, is the island's capital and has become the Caribbean's major shopping center.

By far the most tranquil and unspoiled of the islands is **St. John,** the smallest of the lot, more than half of which is preserved as the gorgeous Virgin Islands National Park. A rocky coastline, forming crescent-shaped bays and white-sand beaches, rings the whole island, whose miles of serpentine hiking trails lead past the ruins of 18th-century Danish plantations and let onto panoramic ocean views.

St. Croix, the largest of the USVIs, gets nowhere near as many visitors as St. Thomas, making for a more tranquil port experience. The island's major attraction is Buck Island Reef National Monument, an offshore park full of gorgeous coral reefs.

The largest number of cruise ships dock in St. Thomas's Charlotte Amalie, but a few anchor directly off St. John or tie up at the Anne Abramson Pier in Fredericksburg, St. Croix. Those that dock in St. Thomas usually offer excursions to St. John, but if yours doesn't, it's quite easy to get there on your own via water taxi or ferry.

LANGUAGE   English is spoken on all three islands.

CURRENCY   The **U.S. dollar** is the local currency.

INFORMATION   For information before you go, contact the **U.S. Virgin Islands Department of Tourism** (© **800/372-USVI;** www.usvitourism.vi).

CALLING FROM THE U.S.   When calling the Virgin Islands from the States, you just need to dial a "1" before the numbers listed in this section.

ST. THOMAS

With a population of about 50,000 and a large number of American expatriates and temporary sun-seekers in residence, tiny St. Thomas isn't exactly a tranquil tropical retreat. You won't have any beaches to yourself. Shops, bars, and restaurants (including a lot of fast-food joints) abound here, and most of the locals make their living off the tourist trade. Most native Virgin Islanders are the descendants of slaves brought from Africa. In fact, Charlotte Amalie was one of the major slave-trading centers in the Caribbean.

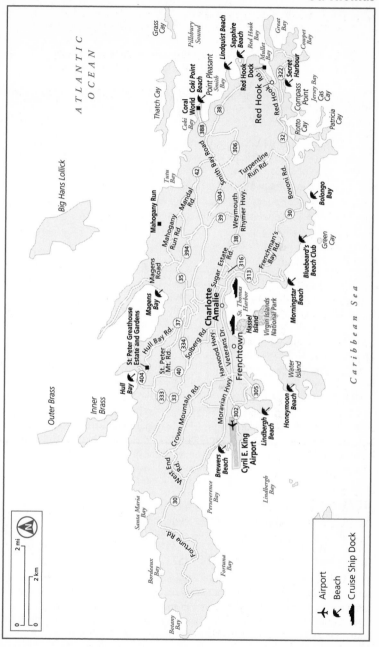

St. Thomas

Frommer's Favorite St. Thomas Experiences

Biking Around the Island: You'll get great views and a great workout, too. Biking on Water Island is a great experience, too. (See "Best Cruise Line Shore Excursions," below.)

Kayaking Among the Island's Mangroves: You'll learn about the local lagoon ecosystem and get some exercise, to boot. (See "Best Cruise Line Shore Excursions," below.)

Visiting the Colorful Village of Frenchtown: Have lunch in a village settled by French-speaking citizenry who were uprooted after the Swedes invaded the island of St. Barts. (See "On Your Own: Beyond the Port Area," below.)

Taking a Nature Walk: The lush St. Peter Greathouse Estate and Gardens has 200 varieties of plants and trees, plus a rainforest, an orchid jungle, and more. (See "On Your Own: Beyond the Port Area," below.)

COMING ASHORE   Most cruise ships anchor at **Havensight Mall,** at the southern end of Charlotte Amalie Harbor, 2.4km (1½ miles) from the town center. The mall has a tourist information office, restaurants, a bookstore, a bank, a U.S. post office, phones that accept long-distance credit cards, and a generous number of duty-free shops. Many people make the long, hot walk to the center of Charlotte Amalie, but it's not a scenic route in any way—you may want to opt for one of the open-air taxis for about US$4 per person.

If Havensight Mall is clogged with cruise ships, your ship will dock at the **Crown Bay Marina,** to the west of Charlotte Amalie. A taxi is your best bet—the 30-minute walk into Charlotte Amalie feels longer on a hot day and isn't terribly picturesque. A taxi ride into town from here costs about US$4.

INFORMATION   The **U.S. Virgin Islands Department of Tourism** has offices at the pier in Charlotte Amalie (© 340/774-8784), open Monday through Friday from 8am to 5pm, Saturday from 9am to 3pm, and Sunday from 9am to 1pm. Stop by and pick up *St. Thomas This Week,* which includes maps of St. Thomas and St. John. There's also an office at the Havensight Mall.

GETTING AROUND
BY TAXI   Taxis are the chief means of transport here. They're unmetered, but a guide of point-to-point fares around the island is included in most of the tourist magazines. The official fare for sightseeing is about US$50 for two passengers for 1½ hours. For radio-dispatch service, call © 340/774-7457.

BY BUS   Comfortable and often air-conditioned, the government-run **Vitran** buses serve Charlotte Amalie and the countryside as far away as Red Hook, a jumping-off point for St. John. You rarely have to wait more than 30 minutes during the day. A one-way ride costs about 75¢ within Charlotte Amalie, US$1 to outer neighborhoods, and US$3 for rides as far as Red Hook. For routes, stops, and schedules, call © 340/774-5678.

BY TAXI VAN   Less structured and more erratic are "taxi vans," privately owned vans, minibuses, and open-sided trucks operated by local entrepreneurs. They make unscheduled stops along major traffic arteries and charge the same fares as the Vitran buses. If you look like you want to go somewhere, one will likely stop for you. They may or may not have their final destinations written on a cardboard sign displayed on the windshield.

BY FERRY   Ferries run every 2 hours from Charlotte Amalie to St. John until 5:30pm and all day hourly from Red Hook to St. John. The ride from Charlotte Amalie takes about 45 minutes and costs US$8 one-way; the ride from Red Hook takes 20 minutes and costs US$4. For information, call © **340/776-6282.**

BY RENTAL CAR   No need to rent a car here.

BEST CRUISE LINE SHORE EXCURSIONS

In addition to the excursions below, a bajillion booze cruises, island tours, and beach/snorkeling tours are offered here. The waters off these islands are rated among the most beautiful in the world.

Coral World & Island Tour (US$39, 3 hr.): Coral World Marine Park & Undersea Observatory is St. Thomas's number-one attraction. The 1.4-hectare (3½-acre) complex features a three-story underwater observation tower 30m (98 ft.) offshore, plunging into the depths to provide views of tropical fish, coral formations, sharks, and other sea beasts. In the Marine Gardens Aquarium, saltwater tanks display everything from sea horses to sea urchins, and a touch pool lets you fondle some of them. Another tank is devoted to sea predators, including circling sharks. From here, the tour zips around the island for a brief tour, visiting Cassie Hill for great views of St. John and the British Virgin Islands.

Kayaking Tour of the Marine Sanctuary (US$72, 3½ hr.): Kayak from the mouth of the marine sanctuary at Holmberg's Marina and spend nearly an hour paddling among the mangroves while a naturalist explains the mangrove and lagoon ecosystem. This trip includes 30 minutes to snorkel or walk along the coral beach at Bovoni Point.

St. John Eco-Hike (US$54, 4½ hr.): Take the ferry to St. John for a walkabout through the Virgin Islands National Park. The Lind Point Trail ascends about 76m (249 ft.) to the Lind Point Overlook for views of St. John, St. Thomas, and the surrounding islands. An expert guide discusses the park's ecosystem and St. John's cultural history while you walk to Honeymoon Beach for a little swimming.

Atlantis Submarine Odyssey (US$92, 2 hr.): Descend about 30m (98 ft.) into the ocean in this air-conditioned submarine for views of exotic fish and sea life.

Water Island Bike Trip (US$74, 3½ hr.): After a ferry ride to Water Island, a 5-minute bus ride brings you to the island's highest point, from which you get a nice downhill ride. Your guide will point out various historic sights and wildlife en route to Honeymoon Beach, where you can swim and enjoy a drink.

EXCURSIONS OFFERED BY LOCAL AGENCIES

St. John Yachting/Snorkeling Excursion: Many yachts and catamarans are available for snorkel and scuba excursions and champagne sails. You can join a full- or half-day sail aboard Top Tours' 49-passenger catamaran *Dancing Dolphin* (© **340/775-7245** or 340/998-6789; www.thedancingdolphin.com), visiting local beaches, coves, wrecks, and reefs. The owner, Capt. Tim Trilling, makes special accommodations for handicapped passengers and runs special sails for children as well. A half-day cruise will run US$69, while a full-day trip, including lunch, is US$99.

For a more personal experience, the six-passenger *Fantasy* (© 340/775-5652; www.daysailfantasy.com) departs from the American Yacht Harbor at Red Hook (on the west coast of St. Thomas) at 9:30am daily, sailing to St. John and nearby islands for swimming, snorkeling, beachcombing, or trolling. The normal full-day trip departs at 9:30am and returns at 3:30pm, but shorter sailings can be arranged. The cost is US$125 per person, including continental breakfast, an open bar, a hot lunch served on board, a guided tour, and snorkel gear. Call to book in advance.

ON YOUR OWN: WITHIN WALKING DISTANCE

Depending on your level of energy, you can either walk from the port into **Charlotte Amalie** (about 2.4km/1½ miles) or take a taxi. In days of yore, seafarers from all over the globe flocked to this old-world Danish town, including pirates and, during the Civil War, Confederate sailors. The old warehouses that once held pirates' loot still stand and, for the most part, house shops. The main streets (called Gades here, in honor of their Danish heritage) are a veritable shopping mall, usually packed with visitors. Sandwiched among the shops are a few historic buildings, most of which can be covered on foot in about 2 hours.

Before starting your tour, stop off at the so-called **Grand Hotel,** near Emancipation Park. No longer a hotel, it contains a restaurant, a bar, shops, and a visitor center. There are views of the harbor below from the wood-paneled pub/restaurant at **Hotel 1829** (© 340/776-1829), one street farther up Government Hill.

Stray behind the seafront shopping strip (Main St.), and you'll find pockets of 19th-century houses and the truly charming, cozy, brick-and-stone **St. Thomas Synagogue** (© 340/774-4312), built in 1833 by Sephardic Jews. There's a great view from here as well. It's located high on the steep-sloping Crystal Gade.

Dating from 1672, **Fort Christian,** 32 Raadets Gade, rises from the harbor to dominate the center of town. Named after the Danish king Christian V, the structure has been everything from a governor's residence to a jail. Many pirates were hanged in its courtyard. Some of the cells have been turned into the rather minor **American-Caribbean Historical Museum,** displaying Indian artifacts of only the most passing interest. The fort is open Monday through Friday from 8am to 3pm. Admission is US$8 for adults and US$4 for children.

Seven Arches Museum, Government Hill (© 340/774-9295), is a 2-century-old Danish house completely restored to its original condition and furnished with antiques. You can walk through the yellow ballast arches and visit the great room with its view of the busy harbor.

The **Paradise Point Tramway** (© 340/774-9809; www.paradisepointtramway.com) affords visitors a dramatic view of Charlotte Amalie's harbor at a peak height of 212m (695 ft.). The tram travels from the Havensight area to Paradise Point in just 15 minutes, where riders disembark to visit shops and a popular restaurant and bar. A day pass is US$18 for adults, US$9 for children 6 to 9.

ON YOUR OWN: BEYOND THE PORT AREA

Twenty minutes from downtown Charlotte Amalie is **Coral World Marine Park & Undersea Observatory,** 6450 Coki Point, off Route 38 (© 340/775-1555; www.coralworldvi.com), the number-one attraction in St. Thomas. The 1.4-hectare (3½-acre) complex features a three-story underwater observation tower 30m (98 ft.)

Charlotte Amalie

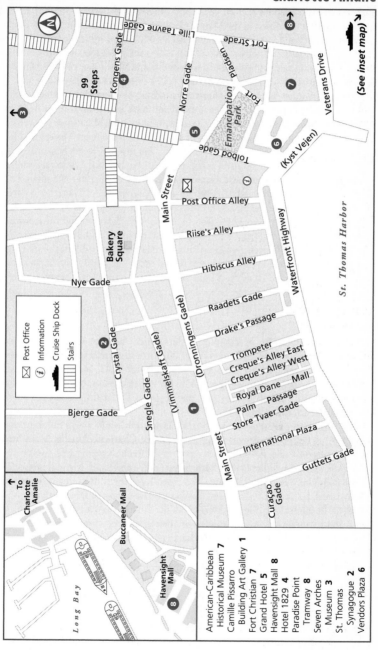

Map labels:

99 Steps
Lille Taavne Gade
Kongens Gade
Norre Gade
Fort Strade
Pladsen
Emancipation Park
Fort
Veterans Drive
(See inset map)
Tolbod Gade
(Kyst Vejen)
Main Street
Post Office Alley
Riise's Alley
Hibiscus Alley
Bakery Square
Nye Gade
Raadets Gade
Drake's Passage
Waterfront Highway
St. Thomas Harbor
Crystal Gade
(Dronningens Gade)
Trompeter
Creque's Alley East
Creque's Alley West
Royal Dane Mall
Palm Passage
Store Tvaer Gade
(Vimmelskaft Gade)
Snegle Gade
Bjerge Gade
International Plaza
Main Street
Guttets Gade
Curaçao Gade

Legend:
Post Office
Information
Cruise Ship Dock
Stairs

To Charlotte Amalie
Buccaneer Mall
Havensight Mall
Long Bay

Index:

American-Caribbean
Historical Museum **7**
Camille Pissarro
Building Art Gallery **1**
Fort Christian **7**
Grand Hotel **5**
Havensight Mall **8**
Hotel 1829 **4**
Paradise Point
Tramway **8**
Seven Arches
Museum **3**
St. Thomas
Synagogue **2**
Vendors Plaza **6**

offshore—you'll see sponges, fish, coral, and other underwater life in their natural state through the windows. In the Marine Gardens Aquarium, saltwater tanks display everything from sea horses to sea urchins. An 80,000-gallon reef tank features exotic Caribbean marine life. Another tank is devoted to sea predators, including circling sharks. The entrance is hidden behind a waterfall. Coral World is open daily from 9am to 5pm. Admission is US$18 for adults and US$9 children 3 to 12.

West of Charlotte Amalie, **Frenchtown** was settled by a French-speaking citizenry who were uprooted when the Swedes invaded and took over their home of St. Barts. These settlers were known for wearing cha-chas, or straw hats. Many of the people who live here today are the direct descendants of those long-ago residents. The colorful fishing village contains several interesting restaurants and taverns. To get here, take a taxi down Veterans Drive (Rte. 30) west and turn left at the sign to the Admirals Inn.

The lush **St. Peter Greathouse Estate and Gardens,** at St. Peter Mountain Road (Rte. 40) and Barrett Hill Road (© **340/774-4999**), ornaments 4.5 hectares (11 acres) on the volcanic peaks of the island's northern rim. It's the creation of Howard Lawson DeWolfe, a Mayflower descendant who, with his wife, Sylvie, bought the estate in 1987 and set about transforming it into a tropical paradise. It's filled with some 200 varieties of plants and trees, including an umbrella plant from Madagascar. There's also a rainforest, an orchid jungle, waterfalls, and reflecting ponds. From a panoramic deck, you can see some 20 of the Virgin Islands. The house itself is worth a visit, its interior filled with local art. The estate and gardens are open daily from 9am to 5pm. Admission is US$10 for adults, US$5 for children.

SHOPPING

St. Thomas is famous for its shopping opportunities. As in St. Croix and St. John, American shoppers can bring home US$1,600 worth of merchandise without paying duty—twice the amount of other Caribbean islands. You'll sometimes find well-known brand names at savings of up to 40% off stateside prices, but you'll often have to plow through a lot of junk to find the bargains. The main goodies are jewelry, watches, cameras, china, and leather.

Many cruise ship passengers shop at the **Havensight Mall,** where the ships dock, but the major shopping goes on along the harbor of **Charlotte Amalie. Main Street** (or Dronningens Gade, its old Danish name) is the main shopping area. Just north of Main Street is merchandise-loaded **Back Street,** or Vimmelskaft. Many shops are also spread along the Waterfront Highway (also called Kyst Vejen). Running between these major streets is a series of side streets, walkways, and alleys, all filled with shops. All the usual Caribbean megatourist shops sell all the usual jewelry, watches, perfume, gift items, and so on; but there are a number of other interesting, more unique shops. Just do a little comparison shopping from place to place and be a little cautious of people trying to lure you into their shop and offering you a special rate if you bring in others from your group.

The **Camille Pissarro Building Art Gallery,** upstairs at 14 Dronningens Gade, is in the house where the impressionist painter Pissarro was born on July 10, 1830. In three high-ceilinged and airy rooms, you'll see all the available Pissarro paintings relating to the islands. Many prints and cards by local artists are available, too, as well as original batiks.

Huddled under oversize parasols, hundreds of street vendors ply their trades in a designated area called **Vendors Plaza,** at Veterans Drive and Tolbod Gade. It's open

Monday through Saturday from 7:30am to 5:30pm, plus Sunday if a cruise ship is expected. Food vendors set up on sidewalks outside.

BEACHES

St. Thomas has some good beaches, all of which are easily reached by taxi. Arrange for your driver to return and pick you up at a designated time. All the beaches in the U.S. Virgin Islands are public, but some still charge a fee. If you're going to St. John, you may want to do your beaching there, as they are somewhat nicer.

ON THE NORTH SIDE   Located across the mountains, 4.8km (3 miles) north of the capital, **Magens Bay** was once hailed as one of the world's 10 most beautiful beaches, but its reputation has faded. Though still beautiful, it isn't as well maintained as it should be and is often overcrowded, especially when many cruise ships are in port. It's less than a mile long and lies between two mountains. Admission is US$3 for adults and 25¢ for children under 12. Changing facilities, bathrooms, a snack bar, picnic tables, snorkel gear, and float rentals are available. There's no public transportation here, so take a taxi. The gates are open daily from 6am to 6pm (you'll need insect repellent after 4pm).

Located in the northeast near Coral World, **Coki Point Beach** is good, but it, too, becomes overcrowded when cruise ships are in port. Snorkelers come here often, as do pickpockets—protect your valuables. Lockers can be rented at Coral World, next door. An East End bus runs to Smith Bay and lets you off at the gate to Coral World and Coki.

ON THE SOUTH SIDE   On the south side, **Morningstar Beach** lies about 3.2km (2 miles) east of Charlotte Amalie at the Marriott Frenchman's Reef & Morningstar Beach Resort. You can wear your most daring swimwear here, and you can also rent sailboats, snorkeling equipment, and lounge chairs. The beach can be easily reached via a cliff-front elevator at the Marriott.

Also on the south coast, **Bluebeard's Beach Club** (formerly known as Limetree Beach) offers a secluded setting and is a quick ride from the cruise ship pier.

Bolongo Bay lures those who love a serene spread of sand. You can feed hibiscus blossoms to iguanas, rent snorkeling gear and lounge chairs, or try a variety of watersports, including parasailing. There's no public transportation, but it's a US$10 taxi ride from Charlotte Amalie. Unlike Magens Bay (see above), where there's only a snack bar, Iggy's Restaurant is right on Bolongo's beach.

Brewers Beach, one of the island's most popular, lies in the southwest near the University of the Virgin Islands, also along the Fortuna bus route.

ON THE EAST END   Small and special, **Secret Harbour** sits near a collection of condos. With its white sand and coconut palms, it's a veritable cliché of Caribbean charm. No public transportation stops here, but it's an easy taxi ride east of Charlotte Amalie heading toward Red Hook.

Sapphire Beach is one of the finest on St. Thomas, set against the backdrop of the Doubletree Sapphire Beach Resort & Marina, where you can lunch or order drinks. Windsurfers like this beach a lot. You can rent snorkeling gear and lounge chairs here. A large reef lies close to the shore, and there are great views of offshore cays and St. John. To get here, take the East End bus from Charlotte Amalie, going via Red Hook. Ask to be let off at the entrance to Sapphire Bay; it's a short walk to the water.

SPORTS

GOLF   Designed by Tom and George Fazio, **Mahogany Run,** Mahogany Run Road, on the north shore (© **800/253-7103** or 340/777-6006), is one of the most beautiful courses in the West Indies. This 18-hole, par-70 course rises and drops like a roller coaster on its journey to the sea. Cliffs and crashing sea waves are the ultimate hazards at the 13th and 14th holes. The golf course is an US$8 to US$10 taxi ride from the cruise dock. Greens fees are US$145, including cart.

SCUBA DIVING & SNORKELING   The waters off the U.S. Virgin Islands are rated one of the "most beautiful areas in the world" by *Skin Diver* magazine. Thirty spectacular reefs lie just off St. Thomas alone. **Dive In!,** at the Doubletree Sapphire Beach Resort & Marina, Smith Bay Road, Route 36 (© **866/434-8346;** www.divein usvi.com), offers professional instruction, beach and boat dives, custom packages, underwater photography and videotapes, and snorkeling trips.

GREAT LOCAL RESTAURANTS & BARS

IN CHARLOTTE AMALIE   In downtown Charlotte Amalie, **Beni Iguana's Sushi Bar,** in the Grand Hotel Court, just behind Emancipation Park (© 340/777-8744), was the first sushi bar on St. Thomas. Lunch is around US$20. **Lillian's Caribbean Grill,** 43–46 Norre Gade, in the Grand Galleria Courtyard directly across from Emancipation Park (© **340/774-7900**), serves authentic Caribbean dishes. Conveniently located near the Vendors Plaza shopping area, it makes for a nice lunch stop. Lunch is about US$10.

Greenhouse, Veterans Drive (© 340/774-7998), attracts cruise ship passengers with daily specials, including American fare and some Jamaican-inspired dishes. Lunch is about US$13. **Virgilio's,** 18 Dronningens Gade (© **340/776-4920**), is a good northern Italian restaurant that serves excellent lobster ravioli. Lunch is about US$18. The entrance is on a narrow alleyway running between Main and Back streets.

IN FRENCHTOWN   West of town, **Bella Blue,** rue de St. Barthélemy (© **340/ 774-4349**), puts a heavy emphasis on seafood—the menu even includes conch schnitzel on occasion. Other dishes include a mouthwatering Wiener schnitzel. Lunch is about US$18. **Craig & Sally's,** 22 Honduras (© **340/777-9949**), serves dishes that, according to the owner, are not "for the faint of heart, but for the adventurous soul"—roast pork with clams, filet mignon with macadamia-nut sauce, and grilled swordfish with a sauce of fresh herbs and tomatoes. Lunch is about US$15.

ST. JOHN

A tiny gem of an island, lush St. John lies about 4.8km (3 miles) east of St. Thomas across Pillsbury Sound. It's the smallest and least populated of the U.S. Virgins, only about 11km (6¾ miles) long and 4.8km (3 miles) wide, with a total land area of some 49 sq. km (19 sq. miles). The island was slated for big development under Danish control, but a slave rebellion and the decline of the sugar cane plantations ended that idea.

Since 1956, more than half of St. John's landmass, as well as its shoreline waters, have been set aside as the **Virgin Islands National Park** (© 340/776-6201; www. virgin.islands.national-park.com), and today the island leads the Caribbean in eco- (or "sustainable") tourism. Miles of winding hiking trails lead to panoramic views and the ruins of 18th-century Danish plantations. Mysterious geometric petroglyphs incised into boulders and cliffs can be seen all over the island (ask a guide to point them out if you can't find them). These figures, of unknown age and origin, have never been

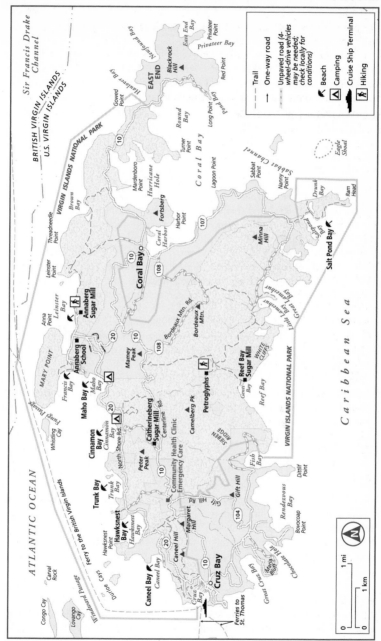

Legend:
- - - - - Trail
- One-way road
- Unpaved road (4-wheel-drive vehicles may be needed; check locally for conditions)
- ⚓ Beach
- △ Camping
- Cruise Ship Terminal
- 🥾 Hiking

ATLANTIC OCEAN

Sir Francis Drake Channel

BRITISH VIRGIN ISLANDS
U.S. VIRGIN ISLANDS

VIRGIN ISLANDS NATIONAL PARK

Congo Cay
Lovango Cay
Carval Rock
Durloe Cays
Whistling Cay
Ferry to the British Virgin Islands
Windward Passage
Fungi Passage
Waterlemon Cay

MARY POINT
Anna Point
Leinster Point
Threadneedle Point
Brown Bay
Leinster Bay
Annaberg Sugar Mill
Annaberg School
Francis Bay
Maho Bay
Maho Bay
Cinnamon Bay
Cinnamon Bay
Trunk Bay
Trunk Bay
Hawksnest Bay
Hawksnest Bay
Hawksnest Point
Caneel Bay
Caneel Bay
Caneel Hill
Margaret Hill
Peter Peak
Mamey Peak
North Shore Rd.
Centerline Rd.
Catherineberg Sugar Mill
Community Health Clinic Emergency Care
Cruz Bay
Ferries to St. Thomas

Gowed Point
EAST END
Blackrock Hill
Newfound Bay
Haulover Bay
Privateer Bay
Privateer Point
East End Bay
Red Point
Long Point Bay
Round Bay
Turner Point
Coral Bay
Mardenboro Point
Hurricane Hole
Fortsberg
Coral Harbor
Harbor Point
Lagoon Point
Sabbat Point
Nanny Point
Sabbat Channel
Eagle Shoal

Bordeaux Mtn. Rd.
Bordeaux Mtn.
Camelberg Pk
Petroglyphs
Reef Bay Sugar Mill
WHITE CLIFFS
Reef Bay
Genti Bay
Great Lameshur Bay
Little Lameshur Bay
Salt Pond Bay
Drunk Bay
Ram Head
Sabbat Bay
Minna Hill

Camelberg Pk
SIEBEN RIDGE
Gift Hill
Fish Bay
Dittlif Point
Rendezvous Bay
Boccoccap Point
Chocolate Hole
Great Cruz Bay
Maria Bluff
Bovoni Rock

VIRGIN ISLANDS NATIONAL PARK

Caribbean Sea

10
20
104
107
108
10
20

N

0 — 1 mi
0 — 1 km

293

Frommer's Favorite St. John Experiences

Touring the Island in an Open-Air Safari Bus: The views are spectacular from the island's coastal road, and you'll visit the ruins of a plantation and one of St. John's excellent beaches. (See "Best Cruise Line Shore Excursions," below.)

Beaching Yourself in Trunk Bay: Although it can get somewhat crowded, it's a gorgeous beach with some decent snorkeling, too. (See "Beaches," below.)

deciphered. Since St. John is easy to reach from St. Thomas and the beaches are spectacular, many cruise ship passengers spend their entire day here.

COMING ASHORE   Cruise ships cannot dock at either of the piers in St. John. Instead, they moor off the coast at **Cruz Bay,** sending in tenders to the National Park Service Dock, the larger of the two piers. Most cruise ships docking at St. Thomas offer shore excursions to St. John's pristine interior and beaches.

If your ship docks on St. Thomas and you don't take an organized shore excursion to St. John, you can get here from Charlotte Amalie by ferry. Ferries leave the Charlotte Amalie waterfront for Cruz Bay at 1- to 2-hour intervals, from 9am until around 5:30pm. The last boat leaves Cruz Bay for Charlotte Amalie at 3:45pm. The ride takes about 45 minutes and costs US$8 each way (US$3.50 for children 2–11). Another ferry leaves from the Red Hook pier on St. Thomas's eastern tip more or less every hour, on the hour, starting at 6am and ending at midnight. It's a 30-minute drive from Charlotte Amalie's port to the pier at Red Hook; the ferry trip takes another 20 minutes each way. The one-way fare is US$4 for adults, US$1.50 for children. Schedules can change without notice, so call ℂ **340/776-6282** for more information on either ferry. You can take a Vitran bus from a point near Market Square (located near the west end of Main St. in Charlotte Amalie) directly to Red Hook for US$1 per person, or negotiate a price with a taxi driver.

GETTING AROUND

BY TAXI   The most popular way to get around is by surrey-style taxi. Typical fares from Cruz Bay are US$5.50 to Trunk Bay, US$7 to Cinnamon Bay, and US$11 to Maho Bay. Taxis wait at the pier. In the very unlikely event you don't see one, you can call **St. John Taxi Service** (ℂ **340/693-7530**). Almost any taxi at Cruz Bay can take you on a 2-hour tour of the island; it will cost around US$25 per person for three or more riders, but fares are negotiable.

BY RENTAL CAR   The extensive Virgin Islands National Park has kept the island's roads undeveloped and uncluttered, opening onto some of the most panoramic vistas anywhere. Renting a vehicle is the best way to see these views, especially if you like to linger at particularly beautiful spots. Open-sided jeeplike vehicles are the most fun of the limited rentals here. There's sometimes a shortage of cars during the busy midwinter season, so try to reserve early. **Avis** and **Hertz** both have offices here. Remember to drive on the left (even though steering wheels are on the left, too—go figure). Your car is likely to come with just enough fuel to get you to one of the island's two gas stations, so fill 'er up: Due to the distance between stations, it's never a good idea to drive around St. John with less than half a tank of gas.

BEST CRUISE LINE SHORE EXCURSIONS

Island Tour (US$39, 4–5 hr.): Since most ships tie up in St. Thomas, tours of St. John first require a ferry or tender ride to Cruz Bay in St. John. Then you board open-air safari buses for a tour that includes a stop at the ruins of a working plantation (the Annaberg Ruins), as well as a pause at Trunk Bay or one of the other beaches. The island and sea views from the coastal road are spectacular.

ON YOUR OWN: WITHIN WALKING DISTANCE

Most cruise ship passengers dart through **Cruz Bay,** a cute little West Indian village with interesting bars, restaurants, boutiques, and pastel-painted houses. **Wharfside Village,** near the dock, is a complex of courtyards, alleys, and shady patios with a mishmash of boutiques, restaurants, fast-food joints, and bars. Down the road from the dock is **Mongoose Junction** (see "Shopping," below).

Located at the public library, the **Elaine Ione Sprauve Museum** (✆ 340/776-6359) isn't big, but it does have some local artifacts, and it will teach you about some of the history of the island. It's open Monday through Friday from 9am to 5pm. Admission is free.

ON YOUR OWN: BEYOND THE PORT AREA

In November 1954, the wealthy Rockefeller family began acquiring large tracts of land on St. John. They then donated more than 2,023 hectares (4,997 acres) to the Department of the Interior for the creation of the **Virgin Islands National Park,** which Congress voted into existence on August 2, l956. Over the years, the size of the park has grown steadily; it now totals 5,109 hectares (12,619 acres), including over two-thirds of St. John's landmass, plus submerged land and water adjacent to the island. Stop off first at the **visitor center,** right on the dock at St. Cruz (✆ 340/776-6201), where you'll find some exhibits and learn more about what you can see and do here. You can explore the park on the more than 32km (20 miles) of biking trails; rent your own car, jeep, or mini-moke; or hike. If you decide to hike, stop at the visitor center first to pick up maps and instructions. The starting points of some trails are within walking distance, while others can be reached by taxi for about US$5 to US$20. Trails can also be reached by Vitran bus service for US$1. All trails are well marked and entrance is free.

Within the park, try to see the **Annaberg Ruins,** Leinster Bay Road, where the Danes founded thriving plantations and a sugar mill in 1718. You'll find tidal pools, forest, hilltops, wild scenery, and the ruins of several Danish plantations. It's located off North Shore Road, east of Trunk Bay on the north shore. On certain days of the week (dates vary), guided walks of the area are given by park rangers. Check at the visitor center.

SHOPPING

Compared to St. Thomas, St. John is a minor shopping destination, but the boutiques and shops at **Cruz Bay** are generally more interesting than those on St. Thomas. Most of them are clustered at **Mongoose Junction** (www.usvi.net/shopping/mongoose), in a woodsy area beside the roadway, about a 5-minute walk from the ferry dock. **Bamboula** (✆ 340/693-8699), for example, has an unusual and appealing collection of gifts from the Caribbean, Haiti, India, Indonesia, and Central Africa.

BEACHES

For a true beach lover, missing the great white sweep of **Trunk Bay** would be like touring Europe and skipping Paris. Trouble is, the word is a little more than out. This gorgeous beach is usually overcrowded, and there are sometimes pickpockets lurking about. The beach has lifeguards and rents snorkeling gear to those wanting to explore the underwater trail near the shore. Both taxis and "safari buses" to Trunk Bay meet the ferry as it docks at Cruz Bay.

Caneel Bay, the stamping ground of the rich and famous, has seven perfect beaches on its 69 hectares (170 acres), but only one—**Honeymoon Beach**—that's open to the public. Since it's the closest beach to Cruz Bay (and is very beautiful, if a bit narrow and windy), it's often overcrowded. Safari buses and taxis from Cruz Bay will take you along North Shore Road.

The campgrounds of **Cinnamon Bay** and **Maho Bay** have their own beaches. Snorkelers find good reefs here, and it's a great place to spot turtles and schools of parrotfish. Changing rooms and showers are available. There's also **Hawksnest Bay,** on the island's north shore. It's known as the beach locals frequent during peak tourist season.

SPORTS

HIKING The network of trails in Virgin Islands National Park is the big thing here. The visitor center at Cruz Bay hands out free trail maps of the park. Since you don't have time to get lost—you don't want the ship to leave without you—it's best to set out with someone who knows his or her way around. Both **Maho Bay Camps** (© 340/776-6226) and **Cinnamon Bay Campground** (© 340/776-6330) conduct nature walks.

KAYAKING & WINDSURFING The **Cinnamon Bay Watersports Center,** on Cinnamon Bay Beach (© 340/776-6330), rents kayaks and Hobie monohull sailboats. The windsurfing here is some of the best anywhere, for both beginners and experts.

SCUBA DIVING & SNORKELING **Low Key Watersports,** Wharfside Village (© 800/835-7718 or 340/693-8999; www.divelowkey.com), offers two-tank, two-location wreck dives on its own custom-built dive boats. It also arranges day-sailing charters, kayaking tours, deep-sea sportfishing, and snorkel tours, plus rents watersports gear, including masks, fins, snorkels, and dive skins. **Cruz Bay Watersports,** at the Westin and in Cruz Bay (© 340/776-6234; www.divestjohn.com), is a PADI and NAUI five-star diving center. Snorkel tours are available daily.

GREAT LOCAL RESTAURANTS & BARS

In Wharfside Village at Cruz Bay, the upscale **Cafe Wahoo** (© 340/776-6600) offers a lovely view of the harbor. Lunch is about US$11. For a more casual meal and drinks, try the **Beach Bar,** downstairs (© 340/777-4220), with the same view to go with your burgers and bar food.

ST. CROIX

More tranquil and less congested than St. Thomas, St. Croix is rocky and arid on its eastern end (which, incidentally, is the easternmost possession of the U.S.) but more lush in the west, with a rainforest of mango and mahogany, tree ferns, and dangling lianas. Rolling hills and upland pastures make up much of the area between the two extremes, and the vivid African tulips are just one of the many tropical flowers that add a splash of color to the landscape, which is dotted with the ruins of sugar cane plantations. The major St. Croix attractions are the coral reefs of **Buck Island Reef National Monument,** located offshore. There are some fine beaches here as well, including Sandy Point, Sprat Hall, and Rainbow Beach.

Although large cruise ships moor at Frederiksted, most of the action is really in **Christiansted,** located on a coral-bound bay about midway along the north shore and featuring more sights and better restaurants and shopping. Showing 2½ centuries of Danish influence in its architecture, the town is being handsomely restored and the entire harborfront area is a National Historic Site. St. Croix's population is descended from both Africa and Europe, and some families have been here for 10 generations, with roots dating back to colonial times.

COMING ASHORE   Only cruise ships no longer than 107m (351 ft.) can land directly at the dock at **Christiansted.** Others moor at newly renovated **Anne Abramson Pier** at **Frederiksted,** a sleepy town that springs to life only when the ships arrive. There's space for two megaships, and both piers have information centers and phones.

We suggest you spend as little time as possible in Frederiksted and head immediately for Christiansted, some 27km (17 miles) away. It's easy to explore either town on foot (it's the only way, really). You might want to consider one of the shore excursions outlined below to see more of the island, especially its underwater treasures.

Although St. Croix is relatively safe, it's wise to stay on the beaten path and watch your belongings on the beaches (as you should on any island); in late 2001, four incidences of muggings and robberies were reported involving Carnival Cruise Lines passengers and crew.

GETTING AROUND

BY TAXI   The **St. Croix Taxicab Association** (© 340/778-1088) offers door-to-door service. Taxis are unmetered, and rates are set from point to point. It costs US$25 to US$30 to go from Christiansted to Frederiksted. Taxi tours are a great way to explore the island; the cost is US$100 for one to four people for 3 hours.

BY BUS   Air-conditioned buses run between Christiansted and Frederiksted about every half-hour between 5:30am and 9pm weekdays, till 7:30pm weekends. The main stop in Christiansted is on Hospital Street, near the National Park office; the main stop in Frederiksted is on Budhoe Park, near Fort Frederick and King Street. The fare is US$1 for adults, 75¢ for children, and 55¢ for seniors. For more information, call © **340/778-0898.**

BY SEAPLANE   Daily seaplane shuttles between St. Croix and St. Thomas are available for US$168 round-trip. Booking in advance is strongly recommended. Flights depart every 15 to 45 minutes in both directions; flight time is a mere 18 minutes, but figure 30 minutes from dock to dock. For more information, contact **Seaborne Airlines,** 34 Strand St., Christiansted (© **340/773-6442;** www.seaborneairlines.com).

BY RENTAL CAR   We don't recommend renting a car here.

BEST CRUISE LINE SHORE EXCURSIONS

Buck Island Tour/Snorkeling (US$80; 6½ hr.): The most popular tour in St. Croix takes you to a tropical underwater wonderland of blue water, a dazzling rainbow of sea life, and colorful coral reefs, sailing aboard either a glass-bottom catamaran or a speedboat. An experienced guide provides snorkel lessons. A shorter version of this tour is available for US$60 (4½ hr.).

Salt River Kayak Tour (US$53, 4 hr.): The Salt River Bay National Historic Park and Ecological Preserve, on the island's northern shore, is the only site that Columbus is known to have landed on in what is now U.S. territory. The park today is in a natural state, with the largest mangrove forest in the Virgin Islands, sheltering many

Frommer's Favorite St. Croix Experiences

Visiting Buck Island Reef National Monument: Within this 324-hectare (800-acre) preserve (the only underwater national monument in the U.S.), you can snorkel over a series of unique, marked underwater trails and experience some of the best-preserved coral reefs in the Caribbean. A snorkeling instructor guides the excursion. (See "Best Cruise Line Shore Excursions," below.)

Strolling through Christiansted: Because of its well-preserved 18th- and 19th-century Danish architecture (particularly evident at Fort Christiansvaern), Christiansted has been designated a National Historic Site. In the late 1700s, it was a crown colony of Denmark and one of the Caribbean's major ports. Today many street signs are still in Danish.

endangered animals and plants. You'll kayak for about 2 hours through secluded estuaries, birding areas, and mangroves, including a visit to the site of the original Carib village explored by Columbus and his men.

St. Croix Heritage Tour (US$55, 6 hr.): Visit St. George Village Botanical Garden, the Cruzan Rum Factory; the Estate Whim Plantation Museum, and a patch of rainforest in the company of a local guide, stopping for lunch along the way.

EXCURSIONS OFFERED BY LOCAL AGENCIES

Horseback Tour: On this 1½-hour tour, run by **Paul and Jill's Equestrian Stables,** Sprat Hall Plantation, Route 58 (© **340/772-2880;** www.paulandjills.com), you'll climb the hills of St. Croix's western end and pass ruins of abandoned 18th-century plantations and sugar mills. The stables are set on the sprawling grounds of the island's oldest plantation, and are known throughout the Caribbean for the quality of the horses and the exceptionally scenic forest trails. The grounds also boast an exquisite tropical fruit orchard. Both beginner and experienced riders are welcome. Make reservations in advance.

ON YOUR OWN: WITHIN WALKING DISTANCE

IN FREDERIKSTED   Frederiksted is nothing great, but if you decide to hang around, you should begin your tour at russet-colored **Fort Frederik** (© **340/772-2021**), next to the cruise ship pier. Some historians claim it was the first fort to sound a foreign salute to the U.S. flag, in 1776. The structure, at the northern end of Frederiksted, has been restored to its 1840 look. You can explore the courtyard and stables, visit the police museum, peruse exhibits of antique cannons and clothing, and see photographs of life on St. Croix in the days of yore. Admission is US$3 for adults, free for children under 16. The fort is open Monday through Friday from 8am to 5pm.

IN CHRISTIANSTED   Start off at the **visitor bureau** (© **340/773-0495;** www.usvitourism.vi), a yellow building with a cedar roof near the harbor. It was built as the Old Scalehouse in 1856 to replace a similar, older structure that burned down. In its heyday, all taxable goods leaving and entering the harbor were weighed here. The scales could once accurately weigh barrels of sugar and molasses weighing up to 1,600 pounds.

St. Croix

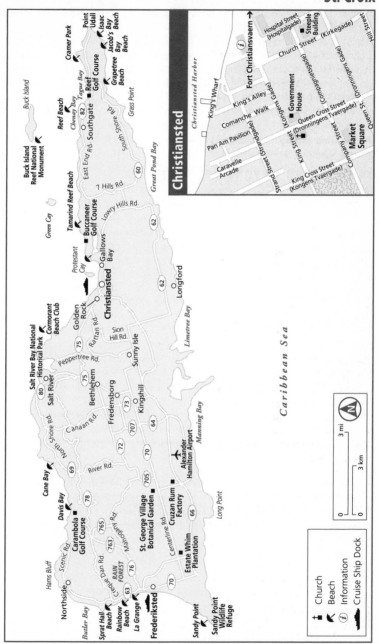

Christiansted

Hospital Street (Hospitalgade)
Steeple Building
Fort Christiansvaern
Church Street (Kirkegade)
Christiansted Harbor
King's Wharf
King's Alley
Comanche Walk
Kongens Gade
Government House
Queen Cross Street (Dronningens Tvaergade)
Pan Am Pavilion
King Street (Dronningens Gade)
King Street (Kongens Gade)
Queen St.
Market Square
Caravelle Arcade
Company Street (Kompagniets Gade)
Hill Street
King Cross Street (Kongens Tvaergade)
Strand Street (Strandgade)

Point Udall
Isaac Bay Beach
Jacob's Bay Beach
Cramer Park
Grapetree Beach
Grass Point
Reef Golf Course
Tague Bay
Southgate
82
Chenay Bay
Reef Beach
East End Rd.
South Shore Rd.
Buck Island
Buck Island Reef National Monument
Tamarind Reef Beach
1 Hills Rd.
Great Pond Bay
60
Green Cay
Buccaneer Golf Course
Lowry Hills Rd.
Gallows Bay
62
Protestant Cay
Christiansted
Golden Rock
62
Longford
Cormorant Beach Club
Salt River Bay National Historical Park
Salt River
80
North Shore Rd.
75
Peppertree Rd.
Sion Hill Rd.
Sunny Isle
Limetree Bay
Caribbean Sea
75
Bethlehem
Fredensborg
73
Kingshill
Canaan Rd.
707
64
Manning Bay
72
70
Alexander Hamilton Airport
69
River Rd.
705
Cane Bay
Davis Bay
78
Carambola Golf Course
765
Cruzan Rum Factory
66
Long Point
763
St. George Village Botanical Garden
Mahogany Rd.
Scenic Rd.
Centerline Rd.
76
RAIN FOREST
Creque Dan Rd.
63
Estate Whim Plantation
70
Hams Bluff
Northside
Butler Bay
Sprat Hall Beach
Rainbow Beach
La Grange
Frederiksted
Sandy Point
Sandy Point Wildlife Refuge

N

3 mi
0
3 km
0

Church
Beach
Information
Cruise Ship Dock

299

Follow Hospital Street to the **Steeple Building,** or Church of Lord God of Sabaoth (© **340/773-1460**), which was completed in 1753 as St. Croix's first Lutheran church. It contains an exhibit on island heritage in general and the church in particular, with photos and artifacts. The building was deconsecrated in 1831 and has served at various times as a bakery, a hospital, and a school. Admission is US$3 for adults, free for children under 16, and also includes entry to **Fort Christiansvaern** (© **340/773-1460**), the best-preserved colonial fortification in the Virgin Islands. The National Park Service maintains the fort as a historic monument, overlooking the harbor. Its original star-shaped design was at the vanguard of the most advanced military planning of its era. Hours are Monday through Friday from 8am to 5pm, Saturday and Sunday from 9am to 4:45pm.

ON YOUR OWN: BEYOND THE PORT AREA

Salt River, on the island's northern shore, is the only site that Columbus is known to have landed on in what is now U.S. territory. To mark the 500th anniversary of the arrival of Columbus, former President George H. W. Bush signed a bill creating the 369-hectare (911-acre) **Salt River Bay National Historic Park and Ecological Preserve.** The landmass includes the site of the original Carib village explored by Columbus and his men, along with the only Taíno ceremonial ball court (used for ceremonial sporting events) ever discovered in the Lesser Antilles.

The park today is in a natural state. It has the largest mangrove forest in the Virgin Islands, sheltering many endangered animals and plants, plus an underwater canyon attracting scuba divers from around the world. The **St. Croix Environmental Association,** 3 Arawak Building, Gallows Bay (© **340/773-1989;** www.stxenvironmental.org), conducts tours of the area. Hours are Monday through Friday from 9am to 5pm.

The **Cruzan Rum Factory,** West Airport Road, Route 64 (© **340/692-2280**), distills the famous Virgin Islands rum. Guided tours depart from the visitor pavilion Monday through Friday from 9am to 11:30am and 1pm to 4pm; the cost is US$4 for adults and US$1 for children under 12.

Restored by the St. Croix Landmarks Society, the **Estate Whim Plantation Museum,** Centerline Road, about 3.2km (2 miles) east of Frederiksted (© **340/772-0598**), is composed of only three rooms and is unique among the many old sugar plantations dotting the island, with 1m-thick (3¼-ft.) walls made of stone, coral, and molasses. Also on the museum's premises are a woodworking shop, the estate's original kitchen, a museum store, servants' quarters, and tools from the 18th century. The ruins include remains of the plantation's sugar-processing plant, complete with a restored windmill.

The **St. George Village Botanical Garden of St. Croix** (© **340/692-2874;** www. sgvbg.org) is a much-loved, popular Eden of tropical trees, shrubs, vines, and flowers, located 6.4km (4 miles) east of Frederiksted off Queen Mary Highway. Hours are daily from 9am to 5pm. Admission is US$6 for adults and US$1 for children under 12.

SHOPPING

Americans get a break here, since they can bring home US$1,600 worth of merchandise from the U.S. Virgin Islands without paying duty—double the amount allowed from most other Caribbean ports. And liquor here is duty-free, too.

The **King's Alley Complex,** a pink-sided compound created right on the Christiansted waterfront following the hurricanes of 1995, is filled with the densest concentration of shopping options on St. Croix. There are a number of worthwhile specialty shops in Christiansted as well.

Skirt Tails, in the Pan Am Pavilion, Strand Street, is one of the most colorful and popular boutiques on the island, specializing in hand-painted batiks for both men and women. **Many Hands,** also in the Pan Am Pavilion, sells Virgin Islands handicrafts, spices and teas, handmade jewelry, and more.

White House/Black Market, King's Alley Walk, stocks women's clothing, ranging from dressy to casual and breezy—with all apparel in black and white. **Elegant Illusions Copy Jewelry,** 55 King St., sells credible copies of the baroque and antique jewelry your great-grandmother might have worn, priced from US$10 to US$1,000. **Larimar,** on the Boardwalk/King's Walk, specializes in its namesake, a pale-blue pectolyte stone prized for its sky-blue color, in various gold settings.

Sonya Ltd., 1 Company St., focuses on traditional Caribbean hook bracelets, while **Folk Art Traders,** 1B Queen Cross St., deals in Caribbean art and folk-art treasures, such as carnival masks, pottery, ceramics, original paintings, and hand-wrought jewelry.

BEACHES

Beaches are the biggest attraction on St. Croix. The drawback is that getting to them from Christiansted or Frederiksted isn't always easy. Taxis will take you, but they can be expensive. From Christiansted, you can also take a ferry to the **Hotel on the Cay,** a palm-shaded island in the harbor.

NEAR FREDERIKSTED Most convenient for passengers arriving at Frederiksted is **Sandy Point,** the largest beach in all of the U.S. Virgin Islands. Its waters are shallow and calm, perfect for swimming. You may remember this beach from the last scene of the movie *The Shawshank Redemption.* Sandy Point is also the nesting ground for endangered leatherback, hawksbill, and green sea turtles, who lay their eggs every year between early April and early June. Parts of the beach are roped off during this time, but you can watch these fascinating creatures from outside of the protected areas.

On Route 63, a short ride north of Frederiksted, is the inviting **Rainbow Beach,** with white sand and ideal snorkeling conditions. **Sprat Hall Beach** is another good beach in the vicinity, also on Route 63, about 5 minutes north of Frederiksted. You can rent lounge chairs here, and there's a bar nearby.

We highly recommend **Cane Bay** and **Davis Bay.** They're both the type of beaches you'd expect to find on a Caribbean island—palms, white sand, and good swimming and snorkeling. Cane Bay attracts snorkelers and divers with its rolling waves, coral gardens, and drop-off wall. It's near Route 80 on the north shore. Bodysurfers are drawn to nearby **Davis Beach,** also off Route 80, in the vicinity of the Carambola Beach Resort. There are no changing facilities here.

NEAR CHRISTIANSTED At the **Cormorant Beach Club,** about 8km (5 miles) west of Christiansted, palm trees shade some 366m (1,200 ft.) of white sand. A living reef lies just offshore, making snorkeling ideal.

SPORTS

GOLF St. Croix has the best golfing in the U.S. Virgin Islands, hands down. In fact, guests staying on St. John and St. Thomas often fly over to St. Croix for a day, just to play. On the northeast side of the island is the 18-hole, par-72 **Carambola Golf Course** (© 340/778-5638), designed by Robert Trent Jones, Sr., who called it "the loveliest course I ever designed." Golfing authorities consider its collection of par-3 holes to be the best in the tropics. Greens fees are US$95, including cart.

The 18-hole, par-70 **Buccaneer,** 3.2km (2 miles) east of Christiansted (© **340/ 773-2100,** ext. 738), is a challenging 5,685-yard course with panoramic vistas.

Players can knock the ball over rolling hills right to the edge of the ocean. Greens fees are US$75; cart rentals are an extra US$20.

The 3,100-yard, 9-hole, par-35 **Reef Golf Course,** at Teague Bay (✆ **340/773-8844**), is over on the east end of the island. Greens fees are US$20 (yes, that's correct), plus US$10 for those wishing to rent a cart.

SCUBA DIVING   Divers love St. Croix's sponge life, beautiful black-coral trees, and steep drop-offs near the shoreline. This island is home to the largest living reef in the Caribbean. Its fabled north-shore wall begins in 7.6 to 9.1m (25–30 ft.) of water and drops—sometimes almost straight down—to 4,023m (13,195 ft.). There are 22 moored diving sites. Favorites include **Salt River Canyon,** the coral gardens of **Scotch Banks,** and **Eagle Ray,** filled with cruising eagle rays. **Pavilions** is another good dive site, boasting a pristine coral reef. The best site of all, however, is **Buck Island,** an underwater wonderland with a visibility of more than 30m (98 ft.) and an underwater nature trail. All minor and major agencies offer scuba and snorkeling tours to Buck Island.

Divers who really cares about the reef should head to **Dive Experience** (✆ **340/773-3307;** www.divexp.com), an outfitter with a friendly style that welcomes both beginner and experienced divers. Owner Michelle Pugh, who is in the Women's Diver Hall of Fame, opened this dive shop 23 years ago on the premise that the reef deserves protection. She founded a program called Anchors Away, which sets up moorings so boats won't damage the reef with anchors, and she continues to fund-raise to maintain these moorings, now used by all dive boats on the island.

GAMBLING

St. Croix's first casino opened in 2000 on the east side of the island, at the new **Divi Carina Bay Resort,** 25 Estate Turner Hole (✆ **340/773-9700;** www.divicarina.com). By taxi, it takes approximately 45 minutes and costs about US$30 per person to get here from Frederiksted. The casino opens at noon.

GREAT LOCAL RESTAURANTS & BARS

Favorite local beers include **Carib** and **Blackbeard's** (made on St. Thomas); the preferred local rum is **Cruzan.**

IN FREDERIKSTED   **Le St. Tropez,** Limetree Court, 67 King St. (✆ **340/772-3000**), is the most popular bistro in Frederiksted, offering crepes, quiches, soups, and salads in its sunlit courtyard. Lunch is about US$15. **Pier 69,** 69 King St. (✆ **340/772-0069**), is a cozy hangout for Frederiksted's counterculture as well as a top spot for sandwiches and salads. Lunch is about US$10.

IN CHRISTIANSTED   **Harvey's,** 11B Company St. (✆ **340/773-3433**), features the thoroughly zesty cooking of island matriarch Sarah Harvey. The main dishes are the type of food Sarah was raised on: barbecue chicken, barbecue spareribs (barbecue is big here), broiled snapper, and lobster when she can get it. Lunch is about US$9.

Across from Government House, **Paradise Cafe,** 53B Company St., at Queen Cross Street (✆ **340/773-2985**), serves burgers and New York deli–style sandwiches throughout the day—everything from a Reuben to a tuna melt. Lunch is about US$8.

Fort Christian Brew Pub, King's Alley Walk (✆ **340/713-9820**), has one of the best harbor views in Christiansted. As the only restaurant/microbrewery in the Virgin Islands, it serves beer, plus burgers, sandwiches, and Cajun cuisine. Lunch is around US$9.

Index

THE NEW TRAVELOCITY GUARANTEE

EVERYTHING YOU BOOK WILL BE RIGHT, OR WE'LL WORK WITH OUR TRAVEL PARTNERS TO MAKE IT RIGHT, RIGHT AWAY.

*To drive home the point,
we're going to use the word "right" in every single sentence.*

Let's get right to it. Right to the meat! Only Travelocity guarantees everything about your booking will be right, or we'll work with our travel partners to make it right, right away. Right on!

Here's a picture taken smack dab right in the middle of Antigua, where the guarantee also covers you.

The guarantee covers all but one of the items pictured to the right.

For example, what if the ocean view you booked actually looks out at a downright ugly parking lot? You'd be right to call – we're there for you. And no one in their right mind would be pleased to learn the rental car place has closed and left them stranded. Call Travelocity and we'll help get you back on the right track.

Now, you may be thinking, "Yeah, right, I'm so sure." That's OK; you have the right to remain skeptical. That is until we mention help is always right around the corner. Call us right off the bat, knowing that our customer service reps are there for you 24/7. Righting wrongs. Left and right.

Now if you're guessing there are some things we can't control, like the weather, well you're right. But we can help you with most things – to get all the details in righting,* visit **travelocity.com/guarantee**.

*Sorry, spelling things right is one of the few things not covered under the guarantee.

I'd give my right arm for a guarantee like this, although I'm glad I don't have to.

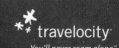

travelocity
You'll never roam alone.